MW00422748

THE POWER OF CULTURE

EDITED BY
KATHARINE BIRBALSINGH

First Published 2020

by John Catt Educational Ltd,
15 Riduna Park, Station Road,
Melton, Woodbridge IP12 1QT

Tel: +44 (0) 1394 389850
Email: enquiries@johncatt.com
Website: www.johncatt.com

© **Michaela Community School 2020**

All rights reserved.

No part of this publication may be reproduced, stored
in a retrieval system, transmitted in any form or by
any means, electronic, mechanical, photocopying,
recording, or otherwise, without the prior permission
of the publishers.

Opinions expressed in this publication are those
of the contributors and are not necessarily those
of the publishers or the editors. We cannot accept
responsibility for any errors or omissions.

ISBN: 978 1 912906 21 5

Set and designed by John Catt Educational Limited

Contents

Chapter Summaries

Culture

Michaela – a School of Freedom, Jonathan Porter

The prevailing view in the modern West is that freedom means the absence of constraint. This idea has profoundly influenced British education, which tends to see limits and forms of authority as intrinsically oppressive. However, this chapter argues that modern educationalists should look back to ancient insights to see that true liberty is as much about 'freedom to' and 'freedom for' as it is about 'freedom from'. Michaela adopts this more positive view of freedom by directing its pupils in their character and in their curriculum. Michaela pupils are not just born free; they become free.

Schools Should Teach Dead White Men, Katie Ashford

We teach literature so that children can understand what makes us human. But many believe that children must be able to see themselves in the books they read. If this is the case, then why should we teach a curriculum rich in "dead white men"? This chapter argues that prioritising writers such as Dickens and Shakespeare is vital for inner-city children .

National Identity, Michael Taylor

In this chapter, I will explain why I think it is important for schools to encourage their pupils to feel a sense of pride in their country. Schools exist to impart knowledge and skills to pupils, but critically, they must also impart the social and cultural knowledge that will enable them to navigate the society in which they reside and will be expected to play a greater part in. A crucial aspect of a school's role is to ensure that pupils feel a strong connection to the country they live in. In this chapter, I will explain why we believe it is right that pupils feel a sense of pride in their country, so that they see Britain and England as their home. We believe that if pupils do not see themselves as part of this country, they will never be truly happy and successful.

We Believe in Authority, Becky Staw

We all love the idea of children being allowed to follow their instincts while the strict teacher evokes Trunchbull-esque images of a cold and unfeeling authoritarian figure. Why then would we argue for more, not less, teacher authority in our schools? At Michaela we believe that teacher authority is essential if children are to grow up safe, happy and able to flourish.

I Was Wrong About Michaela, Charlie Burkitt

This chapter is a reflection on how my views on education have become more progressive since joining Michaela. At the end of my Teach First placement I had come to believe that teachers should not focus on building great relationships with pupils, as this undermined other members of staff. My time at Michaela has made me realise that relationships are essential to the success of the school, but only because they are built on a foundation of adult authority.

A Vindication of Our Values, Jozef Butterfield

This brief chapter discusses our first ever GCSE results day - which defied even our own expectations. Reflecting on the countless obstacles the school has overcome, the chapter celebrates the great success our Y11 pupils achieved, and how their lives are now fundamentally different for having been Michaela pupils.

Being 'Michaela': Our Ethos, James Sibley

The values pupils have shape the decisions they make and who they become as people. As teachers, we have a duty to pass on a set of values that will help our pupils become good people who will serve their families and communities. We believe in: a duty to the community before the self; gratitude and humility over entitlement; personal responsibility over excuses. I tell this story from the point of view of Head of Year 8.

The Culture of Gratitude, Iona Thompson

This chapter is all about the culture of gratitude at Michaela. It answers two questions: why do we teach our kids the importance of gratitude and how do we do this?

The Transformative Power of Values, Pritesh Raichura

To succeed in life, taking personal responsibility is paramount. The happiest and most grateful people in life understand the importance of doing their duty. Running a school with these values requires teachers to embrace their authority. In this chapter, I explore how the three values of personal responsibility, duty and authority permeate every decision we make at Michaela. They help our pupils (and staff) to become both successful and happy.

Is Climate Activism the True Purpose of Education? Nathanael Smith

The recent school strikes for the climate, led by Greta Thunberg, have galvanised pro-activist sentiments among many educators. Is it right that children should forego their education to protest? Why are educators so willing for pupils to become activists? What does all this say about the state of education today? Is there an alternative?

Why I am Still Talking to White People About Race, Natalie Jones

Inner-city kids face unique challenges when it comes to their childhood and education. From music to knife crime this chapter explores some of those challenges; with particular reference to the part that race plays in it all. Is violent rap music OK because it is part of "black culture"? Should we be making lessons relevant to inner-city kids because they just can't relate to Shakespeare? Is Oxbridge racist because ethnic minorities are underrepresented? The short answer is no, and this chapter will help explain why.

Curriculum

History at Michaela, Michael Taylor

In this chapter I discuss why we prioritise substantive knowledge and chronological understanding in history and how this helps pupils to think like historians. School history has to be much wider than just preparing pupils for further study, and so I will explain why we think it is vital that English and British history provides the backbone to any history curriculum in an English school.

Geography at Michaela, Grace Steggall

This chapter argues for the importance of teaching geography with an emphasis on place (both global and national). This provides a hinterland of knowledge and understanding for pupils to understand key concepts and processes in the curriculum. The way to make sure pupils are geographically literate is to widen the curriculum at KS3 to ensure pupils are confident in the foundations of the discipline. This can then be deepened at GCSE level using case studies and larger examples. Not only will this make pupils more confident in their national and global understanding of place, but it will give them a sense of belonging and connection to England and The United Kingdom.

Religious Education at Michaela, Sarah James

Teachers in Britain strongly disagree about what good religious education looks like and whether it should be taught at all. This chapter argues that understanding the rich tapestry of beliefs and practices that underpin civilisations is a vital part of any knowledge-rich education. However, it also argues that RE teachers in Britain have a particular responsibility to teach their pupils about the Christian tradition and the ideas that underpin western assumptions. The chapter explains both what we teach in religion at Michaela and also how our teaching of the subject differs from other schools.

Why Stormzy Could Never Replace Mozart, Pritesh Raichura

Being a form tutor at Michaela was where I first truly encountered classical music. In this chapter, I use the journey of my relationship with classical music to explore the importance of a curriculum that takes pupils beyond their everyday experiences. A curriculum that allows pupil choice denies those pupils their right to the most enduring legacies of civilisation and only exposes children to that with which they are already familiar. In contrast, an excellent curriculum curates the best that human civilisation has thought and said about each discipline and takes pupils on a guided tour of these achievements.

Michaela Misconceptions, Tom Kendall

This chapter addresses some common misconceptions about Michaela. Do we only teach facts? Are lessons thoughtlessly pulled from text books? Is Assessment for Learning just a progressive fad? Are our lessons totally joyless? In this chapter, I argue that these misconceptions are not only incorrect, but represent a complete misunderstanding of what our school is all about.

Leadership

Servant Leadership, Katharine Birbalsingh

We expect our children to do their duty and we expect the same of our leaders. We are here to serve an idea that is bigger than ourselves. It is the same for me as it is for anyone else. The ideas of personal responsibility and duty are part of everything we do at Michaela.

Michaela6th – What's Stopping You? Jessica Lund

Michaela opened its Sixth Form in September 2019. Almost half of our Year 11s achieved the required average of a GCSE grade 7 to attend, and the vast majority of those chose to study at Michaela6th. Our stated aim is to prepare students for entry to, and success at, the best universities in the UK and abroad: our shorthand for that is "Oxbridge and Russell Group". This is an account of the challenges, both expected and unexpected, that we have so far faced in preparing our inner-city cohort to achieve that goal.

Being Head of Year for Our First Year 11, Hin-Tai Ting

Michaela's first cohort are through their GCSEs and the results are in. They tell an amazing story. But, as amazing as those results are, they don't tell the full story of what we do at this school. As Head of Year of this first cohort, I had the privilege of getting to know them beyond the classroom. I'd love to introduce you to some of these fuller, richer stories.

My Year 11 Nurture Group, Cassandra Cheng

This chapter explores what it is like to be a Michaela form tutor to a small year 11 nurture group. What happens in tutor time? How do tutors support their form class? How are meaningful relationships between tutors and tutees developed? How does the Michaela culture support form tutors?

Getting the Culture Right in Year 7, Alexandra Gazi

Written from the perspective of a form tutor, this chapter is all about the importance of having a powerful school culture right from the start of Year 7. Through the stories of three children, it illustrates how this culture can be transformative for our most disadvantaged pupils.

Systems and Structures

Being PA to Katharine Birbalsingh, Gita Khatri

This chapter is about my experiences being Katharine's PA. Yes, she is just a little bit mad.

The School Office, Victoria Squire

This chapter is about how the office is central to the success of a school and at Michaela. The office staff live and breathe the school's values and goals as much as the teachers.

Cutting the Crap, Alice Cresswell

Hours of marking that will be ignored by the pupils? Exhausting build up to a termly observation, the feedback on which is vague and unhelpful? Hours of resourcing for one lesson, when you should have spent the time focusing on questioning? Here at Michaela we've cut the nonsense. This chapter is about how Michaela teachers work hard to ensure that everything the teachers does has a higher value for the children than the output from the teacher. Teachers burn out because they're worked to the bone. We work hard at Michaela, but it seems easier because everything we do makes sense.

Behaviour at Michaela is Misunderstood, Amelia Andrews

Perhaps it is unsurprising that a school with a public profile as high as Michaela's should attract its fair share of misunderstandings. This chapter will address three of the most commonly held misconceptions regarding behaviour from the perspective of a teacher in their first year at Michaela.

Being New at Michaela, Charlotte Perry

I'm sure any teacher would testify that starting a new school can be challenging: nerves about making a good impression, not knowing where to go when you arrive or even just wearing the right tie. The lack of information can make starting at a new place very stressful. Having started at Michaela in September 2019, I wrote this chapter to reflect on the main differences between starting at other schools and being brought on board at Michaela.

Silent Corridors, Jane Brierly

This chapter is all about the controversial silent corridors at Michaela. Why do the corridors have to be silent? Why does that make us feel uncomfortable? Why do the pupils actually prefer it? I discuss the practical and the important pastoral reasons for keeping the corridors silent. At Michaela, the teachers are in charge of the corridors rather than the louder pupils, or even the bullies.

Tough Love, Jozef Butterfield

This chapter discusses whether there is a contradiction between our no-excuses behaviour policy and the relationships we build with pupils. It considers misconceptions about the school and how we actually interact with pupils. It looks at "strictness" and "warmth" as two sides of the same coin - with great teachers requiring mastery of both. I also contrast my difficulties with building relationships at a previous school with those I am able to build now.

Digital Detox, Sam Hurst

As a Head of Year at Michaela, 90% of the pastoral problems I deal with start on smartphones. 21st century technology is extremely addictive and bad for our pupils' working memory. Whilst the tech entrepreneurs make their nannies in California sign agreements that stop them using their phones, our kids in inner London are competing in a race to the bottom of who has the newest iPhone. It is vitally important that all schools are aware of the damage technology can do to our pupils' brains, grades and lives. At Michaela we have used a number of strategies to help families appreciate the dangers of technology, but it has not been an easy battle.

Michaela Family Lunch, Michael Taylor

Family Lunch is the beating heart of Michaela. Every day, all of our pupils eat lunch, together with their teachers and guests. Pupils serve one another, discuss the topic of the day and learn the vital skill of engaging in polite conversation. After lunch, pupils give appreciations to the people in their lives who they are grateful to. This chapter will outline what Family Lunch is, and why we think it is so important for our pupils.

Teaching

Thinking Hard and Asking Questions: AFL at Michaela, Dani Quinn

This chapter is about AFL (assessment for learning) at Michaela, and the approaches we take to ensure that children aren't just behaving, but are behaving for learning. This ranges from techniques to help them focus on the key ideas to creating a culture of accountability for thinking hard and asking questions.

The Culture of Feedback, Abi Smith

Our open-door culture has completely transformed not only my teaching, but also my mind-set on giving and receiving feedback. In this chapter, I will discuss exactly how teachers give feedback to one another at Michaela and how, ultimately, our shared values are the key to making these feedback methods successful.

Knowledge Organisers: Proceed with Caution, Katie Ashford

Knowledge organisers are everywhere. Schools across the country have integrated the condensed, one page summary of curriculum units into their teaching, using them to support pupil memorisation. In 2014, we began using knowledge organisers, combining them with daily 'self-quizzing' homework. But has this efficient memorisation tool gone too far? In this chapter, I will explain how knowledge organisers are not the panacea many believe them to be.

Art at Michaela, Elizabeth Stiles

This chapter is about how we teach art at Michaela.

I remember when there were no pupils, no parents, no results, no buildings, no teachers – nothing, except an idea, a team and vehement opposition. Fast forward 9 years and many milestones later, and I am extremely proud to be Chair of Governors of this inspirational school.

The chapters within this compendium are the distilled ideas from nearly 30 members of staff at Michaela, including teachers and support staff. Michaela is not just an outstanding school (Ofsted), it is a unique and extraordinary beacon of hope for all its pupils who are taught knowledge and equipped for life as an adult. As you read, you will understand that the "magic" at Michaela is the result of very carefully crafted ideas and strategies bound together by consistency and dedication.

The Governing Body of Michaela is grateful to the staff at Michaela for writing this book.

We are different. We are unique. We are Michaela!

Dr Chidi Amadi (representing the Michaela Governing Body)
Chair of Governors

'To love the little platoon...is the first principle of public affections. It is the first link in the series by which we proceed towards a love to our country, and to mankind.'
— Edmund Burke

Introduction

Katharine Birbalsingh
@Miss_Snuffy

Michaela Community School is one of the most successful and controversial state schools in England. In this book, we want to take you inside the school, show you how we work, dispel a few myths about what we do, demonstrate the power of culture, and hopefully inspire you with an alternative view of education.

To understand how Michaela Community School began and why what we do is so different and controversial, you have to go back to 2010. Back in 2010, the education system was a very different place.

Education in 2010

Back in 2010, there was a dominant set of assumptions about how education worked and it was unacceptable to question them. The behaviour systems that were praised by Ofsted (the English schools inspectorate) and implemented by senior teams were very different to what the Establishment generally admires now. Back then, there were few concrete and persuasive arguments made against the excuses culture which routinely ignored children's bad behaviour. In fact, 'Ignoring poor behaviour' was a popular strategy in the classroom. Restorative Justice, where one doesn't follow up bad behaviour with a punishment and instead aims to 'restore justice', was the norm in schools. It was common for teachers to be blamed for poor behaviour in their classrooms because they had not done enough 'to engage the child'.

The few new academy schools like Mossbourne, set up in 2004, that went against the grain with no-excuses discipline were taking a risk. Old-school teachers like Michaela, after whom our school is named, would quietly resist in their own classrooms, but they did so at the risk of being seen as 'dinosaurs' who lacked charisma and dynamism.

But it wasn't just behaviour. The teaching methods approved by the Establishment and senior teams were very different to what is admired now. In 2010, the Establishment believed that good teaching required group work, where the desks were not in rows but were turned to face each other, where children would lead their own learning and the teacher would roam amongst the desks, keeping them on task. A task might have been to stick post-its on each other's foreheads and then move about the room trying to find your other half.

The traditional alternative of desks in rows facing the teacher where the teacher imparts knowledge and leads class discussions was considered by many in the Establishment to be bad teaching. It was normal to advise teachers to never catch yourself standing and talking to a class for more than a few minutes. I should know. As assistant head, I used to advise teachers to 'keep moving' if an Ofsted inspector was in the room, in order to secure the much-prized 'outstanding' grade.

Before 2010, it really was the case that the traditional teaching methods of didactic teaching with explicit instruction were something to be ashamed of and few teachers would have wanted to admit to doing it, even though many did this behind closed doors.

Before 2010, it was also the case that teachers didn't generally talk to each other across the country, let alone the world. It isn't that anything special happened in education in 2010 that sparked the explosion of educational bloggers. It is just a coincidence that over time social media has developed as a phenomenon and a world of 'Edu-twitter' has emerged. In 2010, countless teachers like Michaela would never have found common ground with like-minded teachers 200 miles away on Twitter. I remember in 2006/7 when I used to blog about education, educational blogs were extremely rare. Andrew Smith was one teacher in the blogging world who I happened to stumble across by accident. He wrote a blog called *Scenes from the Battleground* and went by the name of Old Andrew. My blog was called *To Miss with Love* and I went by the name of Miss Snuffy, which in fact is the name that I call myself on Twitter to this day. I was actually Miss Snuffleupagus, the big mammoth/elephant from Sesame Street, who was friends with Big Bird and who no one could see (the elephant in the room).

Andrew and I would visit each other's blogs and leave comments as people used to do in those days. Discussions were had in the comment sections of blogs. There was nothing to draw people in or tie people together outside of the blog post itself as Twitter does today. Twitter was so obscure that MySpace was far better known.

What Andrew and I said on our blogs was highly controversial. We both had to blog anonymously and we never revealed who the other one was to each other. It was simply too dangerous. Tom Bennett also had a blog in 2009 and no doubt there might have been a few blogs I never knew about precisely because there was no established way of connecting people. Any teacher who dared to reject the orthodoxy in those days was, in psychological and practical terms, entirely alone.

I tried to speak out against the orthodoxy at the Conservative Party Conference in October 2010. But when I did so, there was no net to catch me, no cohesive group of people who thought like me amongst whom I might have found my footing. It was scary. I became ill. I was even sent racist abuse via email. I was told by educational head hunters that I might never work in the state sector again but that if I gave it a couple of years, I might be able to live it down and perhaps get back in. I had not only attacked the education system for being broken, but I had done so at the Conservative Party Conference.

But I couldn't wait years for a possible way back in. I had bills to pay. I also had a career that I loved and at which I was good. So in late 2010, I decided to set up a free school. I found a group of people who shared my vision and we set to it.

Setting up Michaela

It took three years of fighting to get the school open. Our detractors were local councillors or politicians, members of the then NUT (now NEU), the Anti-Academies Alliance or various groups opposed to free schools. There's a reason one of the mantras we have at Michaela is 'when you fall down, you pick yourself up and you keep on going'. I had to, time and time again.

We went from Lambeth to Wandsworth to finally settling in Brent. We were always searching for a building in an area of deprivation, always wanting to help those less fortunate. Our detractors would protest outside parent information evenings, infiltrate and shout over us so parents could not hear what we were saying. They would even shout abuse at me when I was in mid-flow in order to stop me from speaking. At one event, we were so frightened of possible violence, we hired a bouncer to keep the governors, staff and potential parents and pupils safe. That these people presumably thought they were doing good, never ceases to amaze me.

Eventually we managed to open Michaela in September 2014 with 120 Year 7s. But even once open, our detractors protested outside, handing out leaflets to our 11-year-old children, telling them their lives were in danger in the school building. They even broke onto the site. We've had hundreds of emails threatening violence, demanding my resignation, complaints to governors about what I think and how I am unfit to be a head because of my views. (These complaints continue to this day.) We have even had death threats. One of our office staff had a break down because of all the criticism being sent our way and in the end she left the school because she couldn't take it anymore. For some time, I used to look over my shoulder going to and from school, always a little worried about what someone might do to me.

Education currently

There has been a significant nationwide change in the way we approach education and Michaela has been part of that. So many teachers and senior leaders have changed their minds about what can work in a school. What is respected by the Establishment has shifted. What Ofsted, senior teams around the country, educational writers and even the media consider to be 'best practice' in 2020 is nothing like what was favoured in 2010.

There has been massive exam reform where we have eradicated coursework, stopped modular exams and given more attention to tougher subjects instead of equivalencies. ResearchED events explore the ideas inspired by cognitive science and research, and they have grown so much that they happen across the world. In 2020, there is now a huge team of self-confessed 'knowledge advocates' across schools everywhere who enjoy educational debates on Twitter. The change is simply extraordinary.

In 2010, there was no debate. There was only one way to think about education. These changes have made it easier for us at Michaela. Nowadays when we interview for new staff, there is a good chance they will have heard about the importance of long-term memory and the problems of working memory overload. Everyone in education knows that there is a debate about knowledge or skills. Some people support the ideas that 'Michaela type schools' implement and others find themselves firmly on the other side. But the point is that not only does the debate exist now, but many are very familiar with it.

When you read Jozef Butterfield's chapter on 'Tough Love' or what Amelia Andrews says on behaviour, these chapters might read now as if they are simply going over old established ground. Five years ago, when we and others said this, it was ground-breaking. So much has happened. We are so proud to have played a part not only in changing our children's stars, but in inspiring others to do things differently.

How is Michaela different?

Am I a Conservative? No. Am I a conservative? Yes. Some might say I am not even that because conservatives believe in conserving whereas I, on the other hand, seem to enjoy turning everything on its head, often challenging the status quo. Still, I think I am a social conservative and 'small c conservative' seems the best way to describe those values that I hold most dear.

The thing I am most proud of is filling a school with small 'c' conservative staff, from the caretakers, to the office staff to the kitchen staff, to the teachers. They all vote for different political parties of course, but at heart, they believe in tradition and are old-school. As was Michaela, my colleague originally from St Lucia, who always used to say to me, 'Katharine! They are the children, and we are the adults.' She believed there was an order to things. I was head of department and she was my second in charge. She was older than me and in the early days when I would suggest doing things I would consider silly and time-wasting now, she would raise her eyebrow as if to say, no Katharine, don't go there. You know who I am. I believe in children learning. That's what I'm here for.

Michaela would be so proud of what we have created in her name. She died of cancer in 2011.

We get over 600 visitors at Michaela every year. Most of these visitors are teachers, not just from the UK, but from across the world. Visitors come because they have heard through social media and word of mouth of the delight previous visitors have felt upon visiting the school. They hear of how many people have changed their minds about Michaela's methods and have also changed their practice as a result.

Visitors eat lunch with the children and have a tour. Everyone and anyone is welcome. You just need to book in on the website. It isn't easy opening our doors to everyone but we do it because we know how many people have valued their visits, taking ideas back to their own schools. Visitors are always struck by how polite and motivated our children are, how dedicated and enthusiastic the teachers are, and they often ask me what they need to do to make their school more like Michaela.

Visitors don't come because of the official stamps. But the official stamps don't hurt. In 2017, Ofsted gave us an Outstanding report which confirmed we weren't just a maverick school rejecting the norm simply to make a splash and be different. The alternative way that we offer has a genuine, lasting positive impact on children's lives.

Michaela Now

In 2019 we had our first set of GCSE results and we came 5th in the country in our Progress 8 (Progress 8 is how schools are judged) without alternative subjects that are considered to be equivalencies. Our Maths Progress 8 was top in the country, our Humanities 4th and our Science 3rd. Languages came 12th but we entered 83% of our cohort and all of the children learned French from scratch upon joining Michaela. None of them spoke French at home.

We did well by our children, who, let's face it, come from typical inner-city homes. Our school is in Brent, one of the poorest London boroughs. To give the reader an understanding of our school context: joining gangs, carrying knives, fear of getting stabbed on the way home, masked boys on bikes waiting outside the gates for our kids to come out... These are all standard issues that affect the children we serve. You will read a little more about our children's lives in Natalie Jones' chapter, 'Why I am still talking to white people about race' and Hin-Tai Ting's chapter, 'Being Head of Year 11'.

But results are only part of our story. Our curriculum also stands out as being different. Michael Taylor's chapter about how we teach history might make you raise an eyebrow. Grace Steggall's chapter on how we believe geography could be improved is a breath of fresh air. Sarah James' chapter on how one might teach religion will give you serious pause to think. Then there is Katie Ashford's chapter on why schools should teach dead white men. You might want to sit down before reading that one.

What is also exciting and interesting about Michaela is the character we instill in our children – the types of adults they will grow up to be. That isn't to say that other schools don't instill character in children, but at Michaela our values and ethos are unique. Indeed, that is what this book is about.

We believe our role as teachers is to help develop our children into adults we can admire and respect and that a particular school ethos is required for that to happen for all of the children in our care. Chapters like Iona Thompson's one on gratitude, or James Sibley's chapter on the importance of school ethos, or again Pritesh Raichura's chapter on our values explore these ideas in more depth.

So why is there a need for this book, *The Power of Culture?*

Because there is more to improving education than improving behaviour and teaching methods as mentioned above. A big theme in the world of education that has not had much airtime in the national debate over the last 10 years is school culture.

The reason you should read *The Power of Culture* is because this book explains in detail the importance of school culture and how different the Michaela school culture is to what is considered normal in 2020. Values in schools understandably tend to reflect the progressive values of the 21st century. At Michaela, we do things differently. Our culture isn't what you would expect. Charlie Burkitt explains this in his chapter where he describes how he was wrong about Michaela, as does Tom Kendall when he explores the misconceptions about Michaela that are out there. Simon Virgo's chapter explains what is so powerful about the Michaela culture and why staff love to work here. This chapter is worth reading before all the others if you wish to understand why we named the book 'The Power of Culture'.

If you are coming to this book from within education, you might be aware of all the debates over the past decade and I hope this book will give you some more concrete and specific examples of what these debates mean for us in practice. If you are not from within education, I hope you will learn a bit more about these debates and, again, how they're implemented in the classroom. We had an idea about what a great school would look like, but we didn't just talk about the idea: we put it into practice. And when you put things into practice, you learn. Things that sound great as ideas don't always work out. We have changed our minds on lots of things from when we first started. In fact, this book is quite different from the first book we wrote back in 2016.

Our first book, published in autumn 2016, *The Battle Hymn of the Tiger Teachers*, the title based on Amy Chua's book, *Battle Hymn of the Tiger Mother*, was well received within the education community despite it presenting some new and controversial ideas. It was also written by staff at Michaela. It explained the teaching and behaviour systems at the school and why we run the school as we do.

However what our first book missed out was our ethos and culture. At the heart of Michaela are 'small c conservative' values. We didn't mention them in the last book because I was always worried that people would dislike us even more if we did. That's how hard it is to be a conservative in 2020 in the world of education. When people would visit the school and ask me how to make their schools more like Michaela, I would shy away from talking about what makes us who we are. Instead conversations were often about ideas like silent corridors, homework or how to organise lunch. I didn't want to put teachers off our more practical ideas by talking about the beating heart within.

People often think conservatives must be really stern and boring. But I hope I'm not like that. When people meet me, they often express surprise at the fact that I am actually quite laidback and trusting. It doesn't really fit with the image of the stern 'Dragon Lady' who breathes fire, that some visitors picture in their heads. But that's part of being a teacher, isn't it? Putting on an act. It's not really who I am inside.

In fact, I actually feel quite shy talking about our ethos, because, for all the success the school has enjoyed, I'm just a teacher. I'm always astonished at the interest and attention the school receives from around the world. I was a teacher in the classroom for many years, then head of department, then assistant head, then deputy... Nothing unusual there. I have mainly worked in inner London in challenging schools so it is what I know best and it is what mainly informs my decisions and analysis of what is wrong with education. I lived in Brixton, rode my bike to school every day, and had a plan that one day, I would be a Head.

When I gave that speech in 2010, a lot of people said I wanted a job in politics. But for the life of me, I don't understand why anyone would want to be a politician. I gave that speech because I was naïve and I believed that what I was saying was true. Again, I pursued the idea of setting up Michaela because I had a naïve vision of building something wonderful. I found other people who had the same ambition and together we built Michaela. I love kids. I love schools. As I always say to the kids, your plan should be to find a job you love. That way, you'll never work a day in your life. That's how it is for me. I live and breathe education and I can't stop thinking about it. Of course, I make mistakes all the time. I would say that much of my earlier career was riddled with some fundamental mistaken thinking in terms of the values I held. I wouldn't have called myself a small c conservative then. Instead, I used to blame poverty and government for everything that was difficult in the lives of the children at school. It isn't that I no longer think these things have impact. They do. But the decades in the classroom, the innumerable days I've spent marking, planning lessons, chatting with children and meeting with parents have inspired me to develop my thinking on a great number of things over the years.

I now think that victimhood culture, lack of family support, inappropriate music choice and friend choice, refusal to take personal responsibility, inability to embrace one's duty, inability to be grateful for what one has (however little it is), and peer pressure to conform to the ways 'of the street' over academic pursuit are devastating obstacles in children's lives. Sadly, and perhaps most significantly for those of us in education, we also have a school system that doesn't always address these issues and I think that's wrong. So at Michaela, we address these issues head on. You will hear these themes time and time again in the various chapters. Poverty remains an obstacle of course. But we cannot do anything about that obstacle. What we can do is change mindsets on how to overcome that poverty. Instead of wallowing in victimhood, we can take charge of our lives and climb out of the quicksand that battles so hard and so tenaciously to pull us down.

My parents come from the Caribbean. My mother is Jamaican and my father is Indian Guyanese. My father came from real poverty in a developing country but he was the one the family chose to get to a good school, go on to a better life. My father made of his life as I hope our children will make of theirs. He refused to see himself as a victim, got himself half way across the world, then moved again to another part of the world, always looking and working hard to give his children a better life, so that I, in turn, could work hard to give other children a chance to change their stars. Like most ethnic minority families, my family all vote on the Left. But my parents are very 'small c conservative' in their habits. No doubt my upbringing in such a household formed who I was to become later, to reject the more fashionable way of thinking in the early 21st century. I gradually became someone whose values didn't quite fit with what I saw around me in the world of education.

Over the years, I would often get into heated discussions with other teachers in the staff room, and it was always clear to everyone that I was a bit of a square peg. I think that's how this book might feel at first: a little squarish. But my advice is to perhaps read it and then leave it for a bit. Come back to it six months later, and give it another try. Unless one remains open to new ideas, then in many ways, life becomes so very predictable and restrictive.

For that reason, I'm always interested in new thinking. Not only do I visit other schools, looking for new ideas, but even visitors have made suggestions that have altered the systems at Michaela. Things have changed so much at Michaela that our first book, *Battle Hymn of the Tiger Teachers*, is not entirely accurate anymore. Some of what happens at Michaela is now very different to what was said in that book in 2016. You'll see some of that in Katie Ashford's chapter on knowledge organisers. That's because we have developed as we have discovered better ideas, better ways of working, or in some cases, we just made outright mistakes. I have a framed quote by C.S. Lewis in my office, given to me by one of the teachers at Michaela.

'We all want progress. But progress means getting nearer to the place where you want to be. And if you have taken a wrong turning then to go forward does not get you any nearer. If you are on the wrong road progress means doing an about-turn and walking back to the right road and in that case the man who turns back soonest is the most progressive man.'

In that sense then, much to the amusement of our ardent supporters, I would say Michaela is the most progressive school in the country. Why? Because we're headed in the right direction – to the place where we want to be.

One of the things I have learned in the last few years, in trying to explain new thinking, is that I can say X, but sometimes people hear Y or even Z. And sometimes I think I've said X, but my staff tell me that I haven't said it very clearly. So unless I am very specific in my explanations, sometimes people can get the wrong ideas, even within our building. The same thing goes for Michaela's teachers and what they say to people outside our building. And that's our fault for not having been clear enough in the first place.

Too often I hear from guests or when I visit other schools that they have tried a Michaela idea and it didn't work in their context. Whenever I dig down into the detail, I discover the implementation of the idea wasn't quite right, or perhaps they underestimated the need for sustained consistency across staff, or perhaps they simply misunderstood the fundamental idea. An example of this is a chapter from *Battle Hymn of the Tiger Teachers*, entitled 'Just tell 'em'. That little word 'just' and how you interpret it makes all the difference. We meant it as, 'Come on guys... tell them!' ie – Sometimes teachers think telling kids the information is somehow cheating, when actually, it is simply teaching. So don't feel bad... JUST tell them! But what we hadn't considered, was the fact that some people might read the word 'just' and understand 'ONLY tell them'. Meaning that class discussions, talk to your partner activities and the like were not an important part of their learning, and that all you need to do as a teacher is stand at the front and speak. The horror of it! Yet, some people took us to be saying just that. We meant nothing of the sort.

Communication is hard, especially when trying to present new thinking. So I'm pretty nervous about this book. We say some things that teachers aren't meant to think, let alone say. I hope that we've expressed ourselves clearly and that you can forgive us if and when we haven't.

There is a list of chapter summaries at the start of the book so that you can dip in and pick and choose what is of interest to you. Teachers wrote about whatever they wanted. So you'll find a vast array of topics: from smartphones by Samuel Hurst to national identity by Michael Taylor to Assessment for Learning by Dani Quinn. Still, despite all the variety, I hope you'll find that thread of 'Michaela culture' pumping through them all. That is, for me, the most challenging and invigorating part of leading an organisation. You want to strengthen your school with consistency both in terms of thought and delivery, but you also want to keep enough variety to allow for innovation and creativity.

That is also the essence of teaching. A teacher provides the child with structure and scaffolding to strengthen him so that he can fly. Children may be born with wings, but they need teachers to show them how to fly.

The Power of Culture is arguing for the importance of culture in any organisation. Culture doesn't just eat strategy for breakfast. It is everything. 'Singing from the same hymn sheet' means the team sings in unison about a specific set of shared goals. *The Power of Culture* tries to capture Michaela's heart. That is why this book is so much more revealing than the last. It explains what makes Michaela, Michaela.

I always say to new staff that joining Michaela is like going on a journey. This book is one such journey, and I hope it gives you the courage to fly.

Something Worth Fighting For

Simon Virgo
@SimonVirgo

'You're doing what?' It was a look of incredulity I'd seen many times in the few weeks since I'd made the decision to join Michaela.

'But Wembley's miles away! Your commute will be murder!' I smiled back, thinking of the disastrous journey from my recent interview, which had taken nearly two hours. 'Let me get this straight,' he went on. 'You live a four minute walk from our school. Your kids go to school next door. Your wife teaches next door. You hold your little girl's hand on the way to school; she can even wave at you through your classroom window. You love this school and you've got a great set up here. And you're going to give all this up for a commute to *Wembley?*'

I'd had this sort of response so many times that I was fairly well practised in my reply by now.

'I know! But it's a pretty incredible school...', and I'd go on to explain what I'd been reading and hearing about Michaela, and all the various ways I'd been impressed and excited, even inspired as I'd discovered more. It wasn't the only response of course; congratulations came from those who already knew about Michaela, who'd perhaps read our book *The Battle Hymn of the Tiger Teachers*, but for those who were less familiar it usually took a while to explain what otherwise looked like a pretty crazy decision.

Of course I'm far from being the only one to make some significant adjustments to become part of the Michaela story. Ask around among the staff and you'll find people who've moved from far and wide to join the school, often having left far more comfortable situations behind to be rewarded with smaller, more expensive accommodation in inner-city London. But there's a sense among the staff that what you gain in being part of Michaela is well worth the sacrifice.

It's not necessarily unusual to find a company of people caught up together because of a common passion. But the level of commitment and the sheer absence of cynicism at Michaela makes for what feels like a unique dynamic. I've certainly never seen anything quite like it in a school before; teachers giving their absolute heart and soul each day with such devotion. There's a genuine sense that the teachers feel privileged to be part of it. We recognise the rare jewel we've stumbled upon and consider ourselves lucky to play a role in something so deserving of our very best. What's more, all this was already the case before the school achieved its official stamp of approval from Ofsted, and indeed long before its record-breaking GCSE results started making headlines. These events simply served to confirm to the outside world what everyone inside Michaela already knew: *there's something very special going on here.*

As Katharine Birbalsingh often says, you need to come and see it to believe it. A group of teachers who truly feel they're of one mind, one heart, one cause, and can't quite believe they get to do something so much fun together.

How does this happen? How can visits to a secondary school end up being life-changingly inspiring? There are some staff rooms where you'll often find battle-weary souls, bravely enduring their lot, the atmosphere heavy with frustration at the various struggles that burden a teacher's life. To find an atmosphere of optimism and excitement isn't necessarily normal. I was in my first year of teaching when I was told that less than a quarter of new teachers make it past their first five years, and I could see why. Teaching is tough. It's a battle, and sadly in so many places it feels like momentum is against teachers, and heads are down.

I still remember looking in the mirror after one of my first experiences in a classroom in my teacher training year. To this day, it was the worst experience I've ever had in a classroom. As a clueless new teacher, I'd innocently stumbled into a lesson with 9S, without the faintest notion as to what made for effective behaviour management, equipped only with a naïve sense that they were bound to respond to my confident delivery. On encountering the fresh-faced, smiling Mr Virgo, the class instantly smelled blood. Within moments my hopes of striking up a positive, respectful rapport with these no doubt lovable characters began to collapse, and by the end of the lesson any sense of control had almost entirely dissolved. Pupils were calling across the room to one another, things were being thrown, and my voice was just one among the din, all but lost in the chaotic waves. At one point a pupil poked my backside.

I remember staggering into the staff toilets afterwards and locking the door behind me, feeling utterly hollow, humiliated, horrified at what had just occurred. I'll never forget the face that stared back at me from the mirror. It looked like it had just aged about twenty years. Mercifully the lessons all this taught me meant that it never happened again, but one thing stood out from the experience: teaching is about far more than pedagogy. It's a test of spirit, a test of heart, a test of resolve. And if you don't fight, you won't last long.

The question is, how can we fuel the fighting spirit that sustains a teacher's heart? What can be done to establish a deep well of resolve that endures, and even thrives amidst the pressure? What I've observed at Michaela is a measure of courage and wholeheartedness among the teachers which would strengthen schools up and down the country if it could be bottled. But where does it find its root?

A Deeper Desire

Perhaps one of the most important things a leader does is help his or her people find courage. One extraordinary story of a leader doing that in a single moment of genius can be found in an incident that occurred during the French Revolution, in the critical Battle of Toulon. Toulon was a vitally important naval city which the French couldn't afford to lose, but it had recently fallen to the allied forces determined to quash the Revolution. The revolutionaries were stretched thin, lacking experience and short of leadership. Their hopes of regaining the crucial city were looking slim, and the success of the whole Revolution was hanging in the balance.

Just when defeat looked unavoidable, a twenty-four year old artillery officer named Napoleon Bonaparte arrived on the scene. He could see that the only hope of regaining the port lay in establishing a point from which they could effectively bombard the allied ships. In order to do this, one particularly effective but dangerously exposed gun battery needed to be constantly manned. The problem, however, was that the battery's exposed position meant that those who manned the post were all but certain to die doing so, and eventually it reached the stage where men were simply refusing to take the post, recognising it as the suicide mission that it was.

Napoleon knew that the battle had reached a decisive moment, and everything temporarily hung on this crucial point. He walked through the camp, considering what to do, when an idea struck him. He made a sign with a few words on it. He then attached it to the lethal battery position. After this, it never lacked a man, day or night; indeed, men were fighting over the chance to hold the post. The battle was won, and Napoleon's name was established. The words he'd written stated simply, 'The battery for men without fear.'

Something greater than the possibility of an immediate victory had been placed before the men. Something more than the threat of a sanction for cowardice, or an immediate reward for compliance. Something deeper had been appealed to and awoken; the prospect of engaging in something requiring wholehearted, full-blooded courage. The men were ultimately thirsty for the opportunity to harness everything they had, and give it their all.

People today are still looking for that kind of invitation: an invitation to give everything you have to something worth fighting for.

Being part of Michaela feels a bit like that.

Michaela's secret isn't just about its methods, even though these are given so much thought and are implemented so consistently. It isn't in how intelligent the faculty are or how responsive the pupils are, and it certainly isn't to do with the facilities, finances or resources. The fact is that the teachers feel part of something bigger, and have become persuaded of something much deeper, something that cannot be seen but cannot go unnoticed, at least not for long.

It is possible to miss it at first, and to simply be taken in by the immediately striking features; the silence in the corridors, the energy in the classrooms, the rigour, the standards, the politeness of the pupils, the uniqueness of family lunch, and dozens of other things. It's possible to come in to Michaela, observe some of these aspects, and be fooled into thinking that the genius lies in the systems alone, and that if a few of these tools were applied elsewhere, transformation would inevitably occur. While it's doubtless true that some of the systems and approaches are transferable (indeed many were imported from other schools in the first place), the danger of only incorporating certain individual aspects could be analogous to having an otherwise healthy body and hoping for life while lacking the beating heart.

It's natural for people to want to locate a secret ingredient and effortlessly slip it into the mix, without the need for any fundamental re-wiring of principles or the examining of foundational assumptions. And since so many of the features of Michaela's approach are so unusual, it's a pretty straightforward process to identify and adopt specific, noticeable practices, which may indeed lead to a measure of improvement. But these various individual practices aren't ultimately what makes Michaela unique. On their own they don't explain its success, and they certainly aren't the reason the staff are so united and wholehearted. No-one leaps out of bed in the morning simply to walk down a silent corridor, or to deliver a Turn To Your Partner routine. Every detail is important, many are indispensable – but none fully represents the essence. They aren't the engine. They aren't the heart.

The heart is found *beneath* all that immediately impresses about Michaela, where a company of people are united in a fight for something bigger than delivering great lessons, managing behaviour effectively and producing excellent GCSE results. It's found in the convictions of a group of people who believe they're making a difference in a day when a difference is sorely needed.

The Battle for our Culture

In the closing moments of the second Lord of the Rings film, *The Two Towers*, the fate of all Middle Earth hangs on a knife edge. Battles surge on every front, as the forces for good and evil clash in an epic conflict. In the midst of all the chaos, everything depends on the fate of one character, a hobbit called Frodo Baggins. Frodo carries the Ring of Power – the mysterious embodiment of evil which must be destroyed for hope to prevail, only now hope has all but abandoned him. Desperate, despairing, and now captured, he and his loyal companion Samwise have nearly given up.

'I can't do this, Sam', he whispers, as he labours under the weight of the seeming inevitability of defeat.

'I know, it's all wrong', Sam replies. 'By rights we shouldn't even be here. But we are.'

Samwise stands and surveys the scene. Before him lies the desolate wreckage of a previously great city, now ravaged by war, a few noble ruins left standing among the rubble.

'It's like in the great stories, Mr Frodo. The ones that really mattered. Full of darkness and danger, they were. And sometimes you didn't want to know the end. Because how could the end be happy? How could the world go back to the way it was when so much bad had happened? Those were the stories that stayed with you; that meant something. Even if you were too small to understand why. But I think, Mr Frodo, I do understand. I know now. Folk in those stories had lots of chances of turning back ... Only they didn't. They kept going. Because they were holding on to something.'

Frodo, still sitting, disconsolate, dejected, quietly offers back, 'What are we holding on to, Sam?'

Sam reaches down and pulls Frodo up onto his feet, and looks him in the eye. 'That there's some good in this world, Mr Frodo. And it's worth fighting for.'

While standing in front of a classroom may not seem much like battling for the future of a civilisation, the truth is that a battle is indeed underway, and what happens in our classrooms has a much greater significance than we may immediately recognise. For, if the culture of our schools affects the character of our pupils, and the character of our pupils then eventually shapes the culture of our society, undoubtedly what we teach our pupils does make a genuine difference to the world around us.

And that's why it's worth being careful about the beliefs that shape the culture of our schools. It's also why some of the beliefs which are increasingly common in our schools and in our society should be causing us much more concern than they are, as many of them are based more on sentiment than substance, and so provide a very flimsy base to build from. In so many ways, at Michaela it's our convictions that have given us strength, and it's the recognition that beliefs matter that makes us more suspicious of some of the beliefs which have gained broad approval in education. We're actually finding that some of the old beliefs, which many have come to dismiss, are providing us with a far better bedrock to build from.

A classic example is to consider the influence of the French philosopher Jean-Jacques Rousseau, whose ideas still permeate many of the assumptions undergirding modern education. Rousseau espoused the notion that children are inherently good, and essentially just need space and freedom, not instruction and authority, in order to flourish and develop into their full, naturally good selves. What many fail to realise is that Rousseau had his own children (some of whom he never even bothered naming) sent to an orphanage where their chances of survival were shockingly low. Had he put more of an effort into being a responsible father, he may have noticed that his notions of children's innate goodness were rather optimistic and didn't necessarily stack up with the evidence. Any parent will testify that children don't need to be taught to misbehave; it seems to come quite naturally. To help curb this tendency requires intervention, not abdication, and so reverting to maintaining order, structure and clear boundaries – ideas tried and tested for thousands of years – actually proves to make much more sense.

The Heart of Michaela

Perhaps the most profound way in which Michaela provides a contrast with much of the broader scene is echoed in our slogan, 'Knowledge is power'. It seems almost bizarre that anyone involved in education could downplay the value of knowledge, and yet this is the battle the team at Michaela has had to fight since its inception. Critics of Michaela's methods and approach have opposed this emphasis from the outset, preferring the acquisition of skills and the fostering of supposed creativity, both of which we have found are cultivated more fruitfully once basic knowledge is in place.

But ultimately it's not only knowledge that gives power; it's true convictions. That's why what makes Michaela so unique is about more than methodology; its originality finds its root in something deeper. It's who we are, not just what we do. It's the 'why' underneath all the attractive 'hows'. It's the foundation of key beliefs that gives our practices something solid to stand on. That may stand out in a day when it's not fashionable to hold to such convictions. But that's who we dare to be. We are people not only united in what we're against, but what we're for.

So let me finish by stating simply some of the beliefs we're prepared to own. These are some of the convictions holding us together, and I pray they'll keep us steady, and prove a foundation for many years, not only for us but for many others. Maybe you.

We believe that beliefs are important.

We believe that truth exists.

We believe knowledge matters.

We believe that teachers should teach and pupils should learn.

We believe authority isn't a dirty word.

We believe in the value of discipline.

We believe pupils should respect their teachers.

We believe teachers should love their pupils.

We believe loving pupils involves holding them to high standards.

We believe in the family.

We believe in personal responsibility.

We believe in tough love.

We believe in gratitude rather than entitlement.

We believe it's good for children to love their country.

We believe being a good teacher takes courage.

We believe education profoundly affects society.

We believe in the possibility of change.

We believe in hope.

And we believe it's worth fighting for.

CULTURE

Michaela – A School of Freedom

Jonathan Porter
@JHC_Porter

© Edward Monkton

The Butterfly of Freedom

Edward Monkton's popular cartoon shows you how we tend to think of freedom. We love the image because it appeals to the romantic instinct in all of us: we all yearn for emancipation rather than prescription, a loosening rather than a tightening of the fence. We imagine ourselves to be that butterfly – unshackled from the chains that history or tradition place on us. Like the adventurous butterfly, we all just want to be free.

Freedom means liberty

This view of freedom pervades the modern West. Monkton's cartoon is appealing because we instinctively baulk at the notion that family, custom, or community should curtail the life we want for ourselves. 'To thine own self be true', as the Old Man puts it to Peer Gynt, the eponymous anti-hero in the play by Henrik Ibsen who sets out from home for a life of self-definition and self-discovery. Monkton's 'Butterfly of Freedom' is popular because a little bit of Peer Gynt has soaked into all of us: we are steeped in a culture that encourages us to break free from the constraints that others put on us.

The origins of liberty

The origins of this philosophy lie with Enlightenment thinkers such as John Locke, whose social contract theory, conceived in the 17th century, understood human beings as free and independent and in their natural state ungoverned and unconstrained. In contrast to ancient theory – which understood true freedom to mean virtuous self-government – for Locke freedom meant each person's liberty to pursue their sovereign self, unencumbered by arbitrary external control.

Since Locke, the history of the Western world has been the story of this liberalising project, as we in the West have celebrated our freedom from stifling social and political authority: the Chartists of the 19th century, the Suffragists of the 20th century and, more recently, those who fought to decriminalise homosexuality. When Isaiah Berlin wrote his famous essay 'Two Concepts of Liberty' in 1958, he did so in the aftermath of one form of totalitarianism and still in the brutalising shadow of another. If social and political oppression down the ages were not sufficient, left and right-wing authoritarianism in the 20th century provide ample evidence for those who seek it of the dangers of abusive external authority.

Nor was this isolated to the political realm. In the economic sphere, this liberalising project challenged excessive state regulation, which its advocates argued stymied economic growth. Free-market liberals persuaded governments of the left and the right that lower taxes, and the removal of traditional restrictions on capital and labour, would enrich society as higher wages were spent on cheaper goods.

Since then, the project of political and economic freedom has been supercharged by the internet, which has ushered in unfettered and previously unimaginable freedom for both people and markets. Now, two family members can have a live video conversation from distant corners of the globe while using the Amazon app on their phone to order a birthday present that will arrive the same day.

This has been the overriding story of the modern West: constraints are obstacles on the path to freedom.

Abuse and education

A similar story can be told of education, where external constraint has often been abused by sadistic schoolmasters and terrible teachers. My own father well remembers being beaten at school simply for his poor handwriting. The historian Jonathan Rose notes that, in the late nineteenth and early twentieth centuries, 'a large minority of pupils suffered abuses of school discipline'. Rose estimates that around 31% of the working class suffered some form of abuse of school discipline with an even higher figure likely for the more affluent.[1]

At times, too, the quality of teaching was dire, with many schools resembling something not dissimilar to Dickens' satire in 'Hard Times'. The educational historian, H. C. Dent, who himself attended three public elementary schools between 1900-1904 remembers the classroom as 'a place of hatred':

> 'Teachers and taught were sworn enemies. The latter resisted by any means known to them (and some of these means were extremely unpleasant) the desiccated diet of facts the former insisted in pressing upon them; teachers retaliated with incessant applications of corporal punishment, impartially inflicted for crime, misdemeanour or mistake'.[2]

The effects on education

It should come as no surprise, then, that the movement that sought to liberate individuals from abusive authority would come to influence education.

---

1   Jonathan Rose, *The Intellectual Life of the British Working Classes (Yale: Yale University Press, 2010) p.172*
2   Ibid., p.149

Writing in the 18th century, Jean-Jacques Rousseau rejected the 'civilising' influence of adults when it came to the education of children. His book, *Émile*, articulated a philosophy of education that aimed to remove externally imposed constraints and the boundaries that stymied children's authentic or 'natural' flourishing. Rousseau believed that children should work things out for themselves rather than have adults tell them what to do.

His philosophy had already made its way to Britain at the beginning of the 20th century as state education became widespread. But this critique of adult authority and 'civilisation' took on a new resonance after the destruction of the First World War and the widespread disillusionment that followed. "Then suddenly, like a chasm in a smooth road, the war came" as Virginia Woolf would describe the way in which the war came to define a whole generation of modernist writers, whose literature railed against the authority-figures, and the traditional values, that had sent so many men to needless deaths.

Consequently, in the wake of the First World War, the 1931 Hadow report, 'Primary Education' suggested that a good school 'is not a place of compulsory instruction, but a community of old and young, engaged in learning by cooperative experiment'. It went on to note that 'the curriculum of the primary school is to be thought of in terms of activity and experience rather than knowledge to be acquired and facts to be stored'.[3]

This liberalising trajectory continued apace with the Plowden Report of 1967. Produced by British educationalists after the Second World War, it urged teachers 'to allow [pupils] to be themselves'.[4] A renewed spirit of progress sought to tear down the shibboleths of traditional education: the clear delineations in authority between 'teacher' and 'pupil' and a curriculum focussed explicitly on knowledge of the time-honoured canon.

The influence of Plowden's Report cannot be overstated: it was widely read and gave so-called 'progressive' education the government's seal of approval. It sold 68,000 copies in its first year, and 117,000 copies after three. Two years after its publication, Plowden wrote in the *TES*: 'The effect of the Report has been to accelerate the pace of change – to endorse the revolution in primary education which has been taking place since the war.'[5]

---

3   http://www.educationengland.org.uk/documents/hadow1931/hadow1931.html

4   Volume I, Part 5, Chapter 15, Paragraph 505.

5   Robert Peal, *Progressively Worse (London: Civitas, 2014) p.31*

This ascendant view of freedom wanted to liberate pupils – or 'learners' as they then became – from forms of authority and tradition that many believed had stifled children's innate creativity and which many educationalists believed were unfit for modern Britain. The philosophy that came to permeate our political and economic spheres came to dominate our educational arena, too. It says that only through the removal of barriers and the loosening of external constraints can we liberate our children.

It says that our young butterflies need to break out of the box if they are to be free.

Freedom and society

But what does this 'freedom' look like? Have we managed to construct an education system that avoids the vexed question of authority, a world where our learners are free from the corrupting influence of adult 'civilisation', growing into their authentic selves as Rousseau intended?

Not quite.

In reality, the space that was once totally occupied by traditional forms of authority – the teachers and parents who once had total control over what children would watch and read and at what time – is increasingly colonised by a new authority, the encroaching influence of which many parents are barely even aware: the internet.

Anyone working on the frontline in a pastoral role in a school, as I do, knows this. As they ask weary-looking pupils slumped over desks how many hours were spent yesterday evening on their smartphones, they know that many of them won't have gone to sleep until well after midnight, pretending to their parents that they're asleep so that they can stare at Instagram, Snapchat or Netflix. The 'Screentime' feature on smartphones is depressingly informative in this regard: one of our pupils clocked up eight hours on her phone on just one school day last year. Another pupil managed 18 hours one Sunday when her mum was at work.

'Our biggest competitor is sleep' as the CEO of Netflix recently admitted. Teachers and parents are increasingly circumvented by the modern-day nabobs – the Big Tech barons who design deliberately addictive apps for the sake of unscrupulous profits. The founders know this only too well, which is why they curtail their own children's access while profiting from other parents' naivety.

It is true that abuses existed in the past and it is true that there were teachers who acted appallingly towards the children in their care. But we should be careful about overstating this. As Jonathan Rose himself notes in his conclusion of attitudes to schooling in the late 19th and early 20th century, most people in Britain were satisfied with the education they received.[6]

And where once we had teachers and parents who were motivated to act in the best interests of the child, we now have new forms of authority motivated by the best interests of the market. Partly these new authorities are Big Tech and the social media giants whose influence now seeps into almost every corner of childhood. But it's also the advertising industry, the celebrity 'influencers' on YouTube and can even be seen in spaces where adult authority is practically, if not physically, absent, such as those classrooms where domineering and disruptive pupils are allowed to prevent more timid children from speaking up in front of their peers.

All of which underlines a point that is worth restating: like energy, we cannot remove authority; we can only move it elsewhere. The attempts by Rousseau and his ideological successors to remove or lessen the influence of parents and teachers in the hope that children would grow up more 'authentically' was, at best, desperately naïve. It simply gave way to other new and untested authorities, the influence of which is only now starting to come in to view.

Freedom and schools

The more subtle problem with the removal of constraints in education is that it radically misunderstands what it means to be free.

In the modern world, we are used to thinking that liberty means the absence of external constraint. When Monkton's butterfly breaks out from the box that surrounds him, he says, 'You may be safe, but I am *free!*' That butterfly, much like the rest of us, is conditioned into thinking that freedom is a state into which we are naturally born. 'Freedom', then, is the freedom *from* an

---

6   Jonathan Rose, *The Intellectual Life of the British Working Classes* (Yale: Yale University Press, 2010) p.186

external authority – a box if you're Monkton's butterfly, a murderous tyrant in the case of many 20th century dissidents.

This is the 'negative freedom' described and favoured by Isaiah Berlin in his famous essay, 'Two Concepts of Liberty', where 'positive freedom' – our freedom *to* or freedom *for* a particular end – is eschewed because of concerns as to whom it is that decides that end and whether doing so would impinge on the freedom of each of us to decide for ourselves. That Berlin first published his essay in 1958 is important in this regard: he had direct experience of the way in which 'positive liberty' had been, at times, 'no better than a specious disguise for brutal tyranny'.[7]

However, as Charles Taylor argued in response to Berlin's famous distinction, we cannot erase the view of positive freedom entirely, not least because our ability to *exercise* any freedom we might have hinges on certain ends.[8] For example, we would all say that someone who can decide the truth for *themselves* is more capable – 'freer' even – than someone who cannot. If we accept that to be the case, which group of young people do we try to nurture? Those who can decide the truth for themselves, or those that cannot?

For most of human history, true freedom was understood to be predicated on exactly this kind of self-mastery. As Patrick Deneen puts it:

> *'liberty is not a condition into which we are naturally born but one we achieve through habituation, training, and education – particularly the discipline of self-command. It is the result of a long process of learning. Liberty is the learned capacity to govern oneself using the higher faculties of reason and spirit through the cultivation of virtue. The condition of doing as one wants is defined in this premodern view as one of slavery, in which we are driven by our basest appetites to act against our better nature'.*[9]

The Plowden Report called on teachers to 'allow [pupils] to be themselves' because its authors, inspired by Rousseau, understood freedom to be something that a child will naturally arrive at without the overbearing influence of adult authority.

---

7   Isaiah Berlin, *Two Concepts of Liberty in Ed. David Miller The Liberty Reader* (Edinburgh: Paradigm, 2006) p.43

8   Charles Taylor, *What's Wrong with Negative Liberty in Ed. David Miller The Liberty Reader* (Edinburgh: Paradigm, 2006) p.141

9   Patrick J. Deneen, *Why Liberalism Failed* (Yale: Yale University Press, 2019) p.113

But a teacher that failed to shape, mould or direct a child's character would be just as damaging as the teacher who beat my father for his poor handwriting. They would be condemning that child to a life where they could not act as they believed they should or determine the truth as they saw it.

Freedom, properly understood, is not just about the negative freedom that protects us from arbitrary or abusive political authority. It is also about the positive freedom that shapes us to the best that we can be.

Michaela and freedom

Our teaching at Michaela reflects a more positive view of freedom: where some constraint and some direction frees our young people to be the best that they can be.

In this way, we continue an older tradition of education founded in ancient Greece and which was championed by those who sought to provide Athenian citizens with the knowledge and skills required for political independence in their new democracy. Over time, the education cherished by the Greco-Roman world was adapted for Christendom, later introduced to Britain by Anglo-Saxons such as Alcuin and Alfred. For over a thousand years, it has been the beating heart of education in Britain and the West, seeking to create citizens who are capable of persuading others of the truth by virtue of their self-mastery, reason and knowledge of, as Matthew Arnold famously put it, 'the best that has been thought and said'.

But it is a tradition that now feels counter cultural because it is explicitly concerned with the moulding or shaping of a pupil towards a human ideal.

O'Hear and Sidwell describe such aims well in their anthology of Western education:

> 'That ideal is characterised by personal freedom, guaranteed self-mastery and the capacity for rational thought together with an educated sensibility in matters of value and the aesthetic. Liberal education is not vocational; it sees training and education as separate endeavours. Nevertheless, liberal education is concerned to produce individuals able to engage with the world politically, seeking to persuade others to the causes dictated by their reason... Liberal education is, therefore, from

the very start an education in active political independence – not by compulsion, but in trust that reason will call its pupils to action.[10]

Michaela teachers are thus forced to embrace a paradox that jars with many contemporary assumptions about freedom. Where many are uncomfortable about the role that a teacher must play in guiding a pupil's character and their learning – a reluctance that largely explains the current fad for teachers (or 'facilitators') to be 'guides on the side' – Michaela teachers see such direction as a duty.

A Michaela pupil is free because, although healthy emotional response is an intrinsic part of our being, we want our pupils to learn to control their emotions so that they can adequately deploy their reason. But reason must get to work on knowledge and a Michaela pupil should know, understand and be able to evaluate the most valuable knowledge, and the most enduring questions, of our community. This vision of both character and curriculum is, as O'Hear and Sidwell put it, 'an education in active political independence' directed towards a citizen who is truly free to persuade others in society as to what he or she believes to be true and good.

As we've seen already, there are two main ways in which we mould, shape and form our pupils towards this ideal: we direct them in their character, and we direct them in their curriculum.

Character

> *'It is written in the eternal constitution of things that men of intemperate natures can not be free. Their passions forge their fetters'* – Edmund Burke

> *'Only the disciplined ones are free in life. If you are not disciplined, you are a slave to your moods; you are a slave to your passions.'* – Eliud Kipchoge

What do an Anglo-Irish philosopher and a Kenyan marathon runner have in common? They both understand what it means to be free.

Edmund Burke explains this in one of his letters, saying that a man whose nature is 'intemperate' cannot truly be free. For Burke, his unfettered emotions function like chains that prevent him from rationality, self-reflection and

---

10 Ed. Anthony O'Hear and Marc Sidwell, *The School of Freedom*, (Exeter: Imprint Academic, 2009) p.6

from persuading and influencing others. Unregulated emotion is an obstacle on the path to true liberty because someone who cannot manage their emotions is not free to act as they think they should.

The record-breaking marathon runner, Eliud Kipchoge, makes a similar point in one of his motivational videos. Kipchoge understands instinctively how much his athletic success owes to his habits of self-discipline. 'Only the disciplined are free in life', as he put it shortly before becoming the first man to run a sub-two-hour marathon.

Burke and Kipchoge – hundreds of years and continents apart – understand a universal truth that was once accepted by everyone from Aristotle to Aquinas: true freedom only comes with virtuous self-government. In this way, self-discipline is an act of freedom.

The evidence

These ancient insights are increasingly supported by psychological research. In a *New York Times* article, the psychologist Steven Pinker writes about some of the unevidenced assumptions that have made their way into popular consciousness. In particular, he notes the dogma:

> 'that repressing emotions is bad and expressing them is good — a folk theory with roots in romanticism, Freudian psychoanalysis, and Hollywood, but which is contradicted by a large literature showing that people with greater self-control, particularly those who repress anger rather than "venting," lead healthier lives: they get better grades, have fewer eating disorders, drink less, have fewer psychosomatic aches and pains, are less depressed, anxious, phobic, and paranoid, have higher self-esteem, are more conscientious, have better relationships with their families, have more stable friendships, are less likely to have sex they regretted, are less likely to imagine themselves cheating in a monogamous relationship.'

Elsewhere, the psychologist Jonathan Haidt has spoken about the continued popularity of cognitive behavioural therapy (CBT). In his view, this is explained by CBT's strength in privileging objective evidence-based responses over subjective emotional ones – what he calls 'emotional reasoning':

> 'subjective feelings are not always trustworthy guides; unrestrained, they can cause people to lash out at others who have done nothing wrong. Therapy

often involves talking yourself down from the idea that each of your emotional responses represents something true or important.'

However much our romantic side wishes it to be true that expressing emotions is good and repressing them is bad, we cannot dream the world to our convenience. What philosophers have known for centuries, psychologists can now prove empirically: those who learn to manage their emotions will lead happier and more fulfilling lives.

Character at Michaela

One of the quotations we have up on the walls at Michaela comes from Aristotle's Nicomachean Ethics:

'Our actions become our habits, our habits become our character, our character is who we are.'

At Michaela, we know that the formation of character cannot be achieved overnight. It takes time, patient feedback and deliberate practice. In this way, learning to regulate an emotional response becomes a practised skill in the same way that playing the piano or swinging a golf club is a practised skill. What begins as a single, laborious and studied action becomes, in time, a habit. And as that habit becomes ingrained, it becomes who we are. It passes from something that we do tentatively and deliberately, to something that we do automatically and instinctively. This is what Aristotle meant when he said that 'the palace of wisdom is arrived at through the courtyard of habit'.

Consequently, teachers at Michaela try to develop pupils' habits of self-control. Sometimes this is about encouraging modesty when a pupil has scored full marks on a quiz or scored the winning goal in PE. We try to explain to pupils that modesty is a virtue and that they will be respected much better by their peers if they resist the temptation to boast about their successes.

However, much of the time, self-control is most difficult when things do not go your way. If pupils at Michaela are just one minute late to school, they will receive a 30-minute detention at the end of the day. We do make exceptions, although these really are exceptions. Most days a handful of detentions will be given to pupils who slept through their alarms, didn't pack their bags the night before or left home late and didn't run to catch the bus. The purpose is to emphasise to the pupils the importance of personal responsibility: in almost all cases, getting to school on time is something that is within their control and, although we are forgiving, a future employer may not be.

Monster Moments

Occasionally, pupils get frustrated about the detention they've been given and might be inclined to answer back to the teacher or storm off in a huff – 'That's so UNFAIR', they might say, 'I was only FIVE minutes late!'

Where we think a pupil will be tempted to answer back in this way or be defiant or get angry about a consequence that they think is unfair we will try to pre-empt a bad reaction by referring to the danger of a 'Monster Moment'.

In our school lexicon, a 'Monster Moment' is when we lose control and allow the monster inside of us to decide our reaction. This is a phrase that we introduce our pupils to in our 'Bootcamp Week' at the beginning of Year 7 and which we expect our staff to be able to refer to confidently and consistently. It's one of a number of 'Michaela Mantras' like 'Work hard, be kind' that we'd expect our staff to deploy when interacting with pupils.

Early on in Bootcamp Week, the incoming pupils are given an assembly on 'Monster Moments' by a member of the Senior Team, followed up by a lesson that morning on the topic from one of our teachers. The lesson is always delivered in a humorous way and the teachers are encouraged to share their own 'Monster Moments' to help the pupils understand that there is nothing strange about strong emotional reactions when things don't go our way. (My own example is always my irritation when fellow-Londoners board the train before allowing me off!)

But, underlying the fun, is a serious point: an important part of growing up is learning to regulate your emotions and learning to reflect on the consequences before lashing out. We don't expect our pupils to understand this instantly (as we tell the pupils, this is something that adults struggle to perfect from time-to-time), but we do tell them that their success at school, and their success and flourishing in life, will be partly about how well they can learn to control their 'Monster Moments'.

We tell the pupils that these Moments often take various and more subtle forms. In one activity, we ask the pupils to discuss with their partners which of the following Moments might ever have applied to them.

- Get up late

- Ignore your teacher

- React badly to being told off

- Work less hard than you could in a lesson

- Avoid putting your hand up – even if you know the answer

- Walk slowly and miserably down the corridor

- Watch YouTube/TV/ play video games for hours

- Stay up late

- Spend hours on your phone

- Act unkindly towards a sibling or friend

In this way, they begin to see that self-control isn't just about biting your tongue when you've been given a detention that you don't like, it's also a bigger aim of being the best that you can be. In doing so, they learn to train themselves to realise that the temporary pleasure of hitting snooze on the alarm clock (as tempting as we all know it is) has to be overcome by the reflection that, doing so, will have consequences.

Such self-control is far more difficult for pupils now than it's ever been. The rise in the use of smartphones now means that, outside of school hours, many of our pupils are constantly being distracted away from their parents, homework or regular exercise. As we've seen, it is not unusual for some of our pupils, who often have completely unrestricted access to a smartphone, to be on their phones constantly from the moment they leave the school at 3.15pm to midnight or beyond. The levels of self-control required to resist modern social media is, for many of our pupils, so great that their only means of escaping its addictive influence is to 'strap themselves to the mast' – to do as Odysseus did on his way to Ithaca – and create an environment where it is physically impossible, however much they might want it, for them to be drawn in by the Siren calls of Snapchat or Instagram.

In practice, this means asking the school for help, either by requesting us to keep their phones for a day, a week or even a term, or by asking their Head of Year to set 'screen time' limits on their phones, a technique which restricts their access to social media in the evenings and requires a password to disable. Sometimes these 'Odyssean Pacts' are all we can do to free ourselves to be the best that we can be. This is the reason for the success of 'Freedom' – a computer programme and app that, appreciating that limits can sometimes be good for us, blocks unwanted distractions, such as social media, while we attend to our work.

However, at Michaela, most of the time our focus is on helping our pupils to be able to learn self-control so that they can do it for themselves. This means a school culture where pupils are encouraged to reflect on those moments in their day where they need to show more self-control, such as where they've blurted out an answer in class or laughed at a classmate who's tripped on the stairs. It also means constant support from teachers who continually help pupils consider how to react when things might not have gone their way.

By teaching our pupils about 'Monster Moments' we help them to become truly free. This freedom is not only a negative freedom – the freedom *from* some external authority. This is a positive freedom – the freedom *to be* the best form of themselves, which can only come about by through a process of practised reflection and self-control.

Curriculum at Michaela

The other way in which we direct our pupils is through our curriculum. To help understand this, consider a past *Newsweek* front cover and the knowledge you need to make sense of it. The cover shows a young woman holding a suitcase. Written across the front, in big letters, is one word – 'Exodus' – with the strapline, 'Why Europe's Jews are fleeing once again'.

Recognising what you already know is always harder than you first imagine. Adult readers of educational books are likely to be university educated and often the sorts of people who take vast swathes of their background knowledge for granted. This is often described as 'expert induced blindness'. It's the way in which those who are highly knowledgeable often struggle to see their own expertise. It's one of the reasons why just being an expert in a field doesn't necessarily make you a good teacher: only if you know what you know – and how you came to know it – can you help to break it down in bitesize chunks for others.

Understanding the *Newsweek* cover requires a lot of background knowledge. On a basic level, it requires that we know about the continent of Europe and the Jews as both a religious and ethnic group. Additionally, we need to know that the Jewish people have had to flee this continent in the past, demanding, at the very least, a basic historical understanding of the rise of Nazism and its implications. This is to say nothing of other times in history when Jews have had to flee our continent: the reign of Edward I in England, in 15th century Portugal and Spain, or throughout the Russian pogroms. The fullest understanding of the cover page would also depend on familiarity with perhaps *the* founding story of the Jewish people – the Israelites' ancient escape from bondage in Egypt as told in the second book of the *Torah*, 'Exodus'.

Does knowing all or some of this make you more free? We would say it does. Not 'free' in the same way that someone might be 'free' from an oppressive government, but free in that positive sense – the freedom to take part in the generational questions and conversations of your community.

Such a curriculum is not interested in directing pupils towards a particular answer, but it is interested in directing them towards particular questions, questions that have animated human beings over generations, as well as directing them to a range of answers that have been put forward in response. Because this is the paradox: such direction leads to liberation. If we were not to direct them towards that which is most valued by our community, then there is no way in which we could say they were free.

An adult who knows nothing about the history of Jews in Europe will be seduced by falsehood at every turn. They are more likely to be persuaded by strong men with weak arguments than gentler men with strong ones. They are constrained in knowing only their own local experiences rather than a wealth of knowledge that will help them to persuade others. And they are ignorant of the best of our cultural treasures – what generations of Westerners have believed to be true and beautiful and good.

In Practice

Much of our curriculum is uncontroversial, particularly in the maths and sciences where debates about which knowledge is most valuable are most easily resolved. Few people would quibble with our emphasis on maths and the sciences, all of which provide the tools our pupils need to make sense of the world around them. The same could be said for the study of French, which, as well as being the language of our oldest and closest neighbour, also provides our pupils with the technical vocabulary in order to study foreign languages, and thus foreign cultures, in the future.

More unusual is our emphasis on English, British and European political history. Whilst we recognise the importance of exposing our pupils to the varied and diverse histories from beyond our shores, we believe that our first responsibility is to the history of the country in which we live. If we were to focus on designing our curriculum around our pupils' individual lives and circumstances, we would necessarily limit pupils from particular backgrounds to a history with which they were already familiar. Although it is essential that we ensure pupils understand how other cultures have been shaped, we believe our pupils should know about the history of England and Britain so that they are free to shape our country in the future. Genuine political freedom requires a deep knowledge of the history of your polis.

It also means a greater emphasis than most non-denominational schools on scripture. This is not in any confessional sense (we are not a faith school) but we do teach biblical literacy in a way that empowers our pupils to speak knowledgeably about, perhaps, the most influential book that was ever written. Such a view is increasingly rare in British schools, whose general squeamishness about scripture alienates pupils from a great sweep of culture – music, art and literature – as well as the compendium of ideas that has done more to incubate Western assumptions than any other. Many of our pupils leave us with no personal faith whatsoever, but they do so able to speak about religion, and religions, with a depth of knowledge that they need to be free to engage in some of the most fundamental conversations we can have.

We are unusual, too, in emphasising British and world place knowledge in our curriculum. As important as a knowledge of geographical process is – volcanoes, tectonics, and migration, for example – many teachers will have had the experience of referring to Edinburgh or Berlin or Athens only to realise that their pupils could not even begin to place such cities on a map, let alone tell you their significance to contemporary world affairs. Such broad comprehension of the physical world around us is consistently underestimated by those who can't imagine not knowing it. But a greater emphasis on such place knowledge – the positions of human and physical features on maps of Britain, Europe and the world – frees our pupils to appreciate the island, continent and planet on which they live.

Finally, of course, there is literature, where, by teaching the classics, we free our pupils to be able to converse in their culture. There can be disagreement as to what constitutes 'a classic', and such definitions do change over time, but to deny that there is such a thing is dishonest, not least because those who do are so often the same people who are most fluent in it. A British man or woman who knows nothing of Shakespeare cannot be as free as they could otherwise be: they have been shut out from one of the most important conversations of their community and culture, as well as some of the most perceptive, and universal, insights into the human condition. It was a Hindu inmate at Robben Island, Sonny Venkatrathnam, who, aware of its radical insights into the nature of power and justice, smuggled in the Complete Works of Shakespeare disguised with pictures of Hindu deities. One of his fellow inmates, Nelson Mandela, who would go on to cite Shakespeare liberally in the speeches he gave to post-Apartheid South Africa, signed his favourite passage:

'Cowards die many times before their deaths.

The valiant never taste of death but once.'

There is nothing liberating about alienation. And there is nothing liberating about ignorance of the cultural references made on the newsstand, in your local bookshop or at the theatre. Our curriculum recognises this by directing our pupils to a specific compendium of knowledge that we value the most and that we believe will make them more free. Not only does our curriculum free our pupils to converse in the culture of their country but, even more importantly, it gives them the skills and the knowledge needed for genuine political independence. It gives them the knowledge and skills needed for reflection and debate, and to persuade others of what they believe is true and good.

Social mobility

Some will say that such ideas are interesting but ethereal: that they represent nothing more than dreamy philosophising, a privileged pastime for someone who doesn't need to worry about the real difficulties facing pupils in deprived areas – the material challenges of poverty, social mobility or even just 'getting ahead'.

But this would be to vastly underestimate the material freedom that our philosophy of education provides. Last year, our results placed us amongst the top five schools in England for 'Progress 8' – the difference a school makes to a pupil's GCSE grades between the age of 11 and 16. In maths, where the importance of a good grade directly translates into opportunities in the work place, there is not a single school in the country whose pupils make more progress than ours.

Philosophers have long questioned how much real freedom you have when the choice you face is whether to sleep beneath a railway arch or in a doorway. We hope that this is never a decision that our pupils have to make, and we would certainly agree that this is no real choice at all. We have no real freedom when the available avenues to us are limited by economic deprivation and hardship.

A Michaela education, then, liberates on more than one level. It is because we believe in the importance of character and curriculum, and because we have a clear vision for how each of these should be formed, that we are able to deliver material opportunity for our pupils.

The results speak for themselves: our pupils have a greater chance of improving their life chances than almost any other pupils in the country. This isn't just idle philosophising; these ideas are changing lives.

Conclusion

When the American national anthem is sung at sporting events, the cheering from the crowd usually begins on the line 'o'er the land of the free'. The singer usually lingers at this point with a lengthy high note. "Even though the song goes on to talk about 'the brave', Tim Keller writes, "this is an afterthought. Both the melody line and our culture highlight freedom as the main theme and value in our society."[11]

The idea that we have the right to be whomever we want to be, and that freedom means to be liberated from whatever box is placed around us, as Monkton's butterfly is, has become the dominant view in contemporary Western education.

---

11   Timothy Keller, *Making Sense of God* (New York: Viking Penguin, 2016) p.97.

However, to only understand freedom as 'freedom from' is to have only a very superficial sense of what freedom really means. Freedom also needs to be understood positively – the 'freedom to' achieve certain ends. A true appreciation of freedom must therefore accept that there are better and worse ways of being.

Therefore, at Michaela, we accept the paradox that our pupils cannot truly be free unless they have been shaped towards certain ends. These ends are seen in the young people that leave us at 16 and 18 with informed and reflective personal autonomy, young people who are not, as a child is, blown this way and that by the fast tides and turbulences of their emotions like ships buffeted by waves in a storm. Burke is right to say that someone of an intemperate nature cannot be free. But we could go further. We could say that the public conversation that we rely on to negotiate our political and philosophical differences depends on the use of our reason, a faculty which can only be guaranteed through the regulation of our emotions and personal self-mastery. As Kipchoge says, only through such discipline can we be free.

But our reason must get to work on knowledge, and our schools must form young people who, even if their *answers* differ, share a knowledge of the questions our community has put to itself over generations. Through this, we help our pupils to feel a sense of belonging. Their knowledge of the curriculum binds them to a shared cultural conversation of which they are now firmly and justly a part. But, more than that, they are now free to fly out themselves and to influence and persuade others. Their familiarity with the Western canon leaves them free to form their own opinion of what *they* believe to be most true, most beautiful and most good.

The contemporary world conditions us into thinking that a good education means allowing pupils to break free from the constraints and boundaries that are imposed on them, like Monkton's butterfly who breaks free from the box that surrounds him. We disagree. We believe that some constraints and some boundaries can be liberating.

At Michaela, our butterflies don't just break free; they become free.

Schools Should Teach Dead White Men

Katie Ashford

@katie_s_ashford

Many contemporary academics and politicians argue that we have a responsibility to 'decolonise' the curriculum. In recent years, the global campaign to 'decolonise the curriculum', which began in South Africa with the 'Rhodes Must Fall' movement, has made its way to the UK. As the 'Decolonise SOAS' website contends, the aims of the movement are to 'interrogate and transform the institutional, structural and epistemological legacies of colonialism, specifically where these produce injustices within higher education and barriers to knowledge and understanding.'[1].

For some, colonialism lives on. For groups in favour of decolonisation, the impact of colonial rule still underpins many of the structures in modern society. Those from minority backgrounds are excluded and marginalised as a result. The intellectual authorities we so revere have only obtained their status as a result of colonial oppression and the silencing of other, more diverse voices. As Professor Kehinde Andrews[2] argues, our country and culture is built on dark foundations: without the horrors of slavery and the mistreatment of millions of people, the West would not have gained its global dominance.

According to this view, the make up of our society is entirely racist and fundamentally unequal. And nowhere is this clearer than in the decisions that politicians and teachers make when determining the school curriculum. That we opt to make Shakespeare and Charles Dickens compulsory over W E B Du Bois and Maya Angelou speaks of the deeply entrenched values that lie at the heart of our country and its history.

---

1   School of Oriental Studies (2018) *Decolonising SOAS Retrieved from URL: https://blogs.soas. ac.uk/decolonisingsoas/about/*

2   Andrews, K. (30.5.17) *It's a dangerous fiction that one exam will decolonise Oxford's history degrees*. Retrieved from URL: https://www.theguardian.com/commentisfree/2017/ may/30/oxford-decolonise-british-history-degrees-rhodes-must-fall

Those at 'Decolonise SOAS' and other similar groups such as 'Why is my curriculum white?'[3], argue that a curriculum prioritising dead white men not only excludes the perspectives of minority thinkers, but further entrenches the very structures that created the injustices we see within our society today. Many argue that such a curriculum has no place in modern Britain. If we aim to be truly inclusive, we ought to shelve such retrogressive policies and look to teach a more diverse history – a history that is not merely told from the perspective of its victors.

The school curriculum is therefore perceived as unsatisfactory to those who believe we have a responsibility to decolonise. In its current form, the English Literature curriculum ensures that all school pupils study British history and 19th century history. At GCSE level, schools choose one British writer from a specified list of 19th century writers that includes Charles Dickens, Robert Louis Stevenson and Jane Austen. It is a curriculum that includes many dead white men. Mary Bousted, Joint General Secretary of the National Education Union (NEU), has argued against the curriculum in its current form, suggesting that schools need to do more to diversify the writers children are exposed to. Angela Rayner, in her previous role as Shadow Education Secretary, promised to support the campaign, should Labour come to power.

These arguments are understandable. It is of course true that immigrants to this country have been oppressed. Colonialism and the British Empire caused huge suffering for many millions of people. It is indeed the case that non-white, non-male voices have been excluded throughout the centuries. As a direct result of oppression, the works of many dead white men have risen to the top whilst the other perspectives have been pushed out of our collective consciousness. It is therefore understandable that there is a call for these marginalised voices to be heard, and that the nebulous concept of 'the canon', should be rigorously critiqued.

We should acknowledge that some aspects of our understanding of the canon have been shaped by racial prejudice: that Terence is remembered as a white man, not a freed black slave shows the canon should not be blindly accepted. There are certainly some ideas in the canon that we should consign to history. Immanuel Kant's racist analysis of intelligence must be rejected entirely, and the flagrant xenophobia described in Joseph Conrad's much debated *Heart*

---

3   Hussain, M. (11.3.15) *Why is my curriculum white? Retrieved from URL:* https://www.nus.org.uk/en/news/why-is-my-curriculum-white/

of Darkness. Some argue that these ideas were simply 'of their time' – but we should not feel afraid to cast out overt racism when we see it.

Furthermore, we must ensure that the curriculum is honest, and does not 'whitewash' important thinkers away. We must ensure that we provide as well-rounded and truthful a view of the canon as is reasonable within the time we have available. This should not be limited to English and humanities curriculums. As science teacher Pran Patel passionately explains in a TEDx talk, most children learn that Darwin devised the theory of evolution, but are far less likely to learn, for example, that African American scientist Charles R. Drew developed the first blood banks.[4] In English literature lessons, pupils are more likely to read Blake than the works of Phillis Wheatley, an enslaved black female poet. It is perfectly reasonable to expect teachers to explain any thinkers who made important contributions to the world. To omit important scientists, mathematicians or historians from the curriculum without cause would be distorting.

The English curriculum in UK schools is undoubtedly shaped by dead white men, denying a voice to the marginalised. Should we therefore cut out dead white men completely, or at least, reduce their prominence?

Michaela's Answer

We have to take some practical considerations into account. Those who seek to decolonise the curriculum do have some good ideas. However, we feel they go too far in questioning the existence of the canon itself. Inevitably, we have to teach something. Equally inevitably, we cannot teach everything. We are limited by the constraints of the curriculum and time. If we include one author, we must choose to leave out another. If we do not make choices, the result is not that our pupils study a perfectly democratic, representative body of content. The result is that we leave gaps that will be filled by the mass media, by peer pressure, and by sheer chance. We do believe the canon should adapt and change over time, and our curriculum does include authors from different backgrounds and eras. It may not be perfect, it will continue to evolve, and it may not include one's favourite authors. But we believe that the best thing we can do for our disadvantaged children is to teach a traditional curriculum that necessarily includes dead white men.

---

4   Patel, P. (23.8.2019) *Decolonise the Curriculum – TEDxNorwich. Retrieved from URL:* https://www.youtube.com/watch?v=8JjRQTuzqTU&t=479s

We believe that the literature of these men has a hugely positive impact on all pupils, particularly those from minority backgrounds, for three reasons. First, we believe that a traditional curriculum helps pupils from diverse backgrounds to feel that they belong in Britain. Second, we believe that one of the core purposes of the curriculum is to expand our pupils' horizons, rather than to resort to relevance. Finally, we believe that texts should be chosen according to the ideas they espouse, rather than the identity of their writers.

Belonging and Britishness

Some are critical of the supreme confidence of the men and women who are educated in the private sector, arguing that the privately-educated are often entitled and arrogant, and certain they are more powerful than their state educated peers. There is some truth in this. Oft-cited statistics, such as the Sutton Trust's findings that 65% of senior court judges in the UK are drawn from the 7% educated in private schools[5], show that the privately-educated elite have an unfair advantage. Whilst wealth and privilege give such people a huge head start, the beliefs imbued within them set them further apart from inner-city children. The privately educated grow up believing they are powerful, and should lead. Since birth, they are surrounded by discussions about politics, references to history, literature, art and culture; they visit places of historical or cultural importance at the weekends, read many more books, and are exposed to richer vocabulary. A result of this upbringing is a deep knowledge of the culture and history of the country, and a sense of their place within it. Part of their confidence therefore comes from knowing our country inside out. When they read Shakespeare, he belongs to them and to their cultural heritage. This sense of belonging bolsters their belief that they are future leaders of our society. Why are so many of the people in leading positions across the country drawn from the small pool of the privately educated? Because they believe that they are entitled to such power.

Of course, some people born into working-class homes are also exposed to this important cultural knowledge. Many poorer families take cultural knowledge extremely seriously, and go out of their way to make sure their children are well-versed in it, to help them to become more successful in later

---

5   Sutton Trust (2019) *Elitist Britain 2019: The Educational Backgrounds of Britain's Leading People.* Accessed at URL: https://www.suttontrust.com/wp-content/uploads/2019/12/Elitist-Britain-2019.pdf

life. But crucially, if this knowledge is *not* learned at home, as is often the case, schools must fill this gap.

At Michaela, we believe that this sort of confidence should not be the preserve of the privileged. We want our children to believe that they, too, are entitled to success. They, too, own this heritage of inspiring writing. They too have the potential to become the future leaders and thinkers who change the world. A traditional education including dead white men is a crucial stepping-stone in achieving such aims. These thinkers bind our pupils to their country.

A curriculum including dead white men levels the playing field and enables our pupils to be a part of the broader cultural conversation, to be able to join in with all members of the national community. Knowing nothing puts young people at a great disadvantage. Many dead white men have shaped our language and culture, created words and phrases that we use every day without thinking. Their literary characters and stories have come to shape the way that we view the world today. Hamlet, Ebenezer Scrooge and Frankenstein's Monster are vivid parts of our shared cultural consciousness. Not knowing or understanding these references makes it harder to engage with society. In this example from a 2018 article in *The Guardian* the headline 'Has Zuckerberg, like Frankenstein, lost control of the monster he created?' reveals our dependence on canonical references.

As teachers, we believe that exposing our pupils to such cultural knowledge is fundamental to our roles. Teaching texts written by dead white men inducts our young people into British society, enabling them to engage meaningfully with our democracy. Those who advocate the removal of dead white men from the curriculum actively contribute towards a greater inequality between the privileged, where such references during childhood are common, and those born into backgrounds where nobody speaks of Shakespeare or Dickens.

Moreover, we mustn't underestimate how much cultural knowledge some young people lack. For instance, some pupils don't realise that the First World War happened long after the Jacobean era, often assuming that Shakespeare and Wilfred Owen were contemporaries. Many are shocked to learn that televisions and phones didn't exist during the Victorian era. We must not underestimate the value of growing up in a family where visits to museums are common, and knowledge of British culture is drip-fed throughout daily life. For our pupils, acquiring such understanding isn't something that can be taken for granted.

Failing to expose disadvantaged young people to important cultural knowledge sets them at a significant disadvantage when they enter the adult world. Knowing the details of our language, its origin, idiosyncrasies and how to manipulate it is a crucial part of engaging with the higher strata of society. At an Oxford college dinner, or at a drinks party for wealthy bankers, one could easily feel alienated without some basic knowledge of important cultural references. When someone quips that they're 'a bit of a Scrooge' or tells a story similar to 'Romeo and Juliet', it is helpful to know what on earth they are talking about. These ideas are so embedded within British culture that we rarely stop to remember they were first conceived by Dickens and Shakespeare. The ability to keep up with the allusions is impossible if these gaps aren't filled in at school.

Of course, this isn't only important at dinner parties. Newspaper headlines, TV adverts, internet memes: all are in some way underpinned by countless cultural references. For example, take *The Independent* headline, 'A lot of sound and fury on the dollar, signifying nothing' – this sounds like complete nonsense unless you know this famous line from Shakespeare's Macbeth. In 2016, during Prime Minister's Questions, David Cameron said the recent Labour party reshuffle had 'turned into something of a comedy of errors'. Again, this is only meaningful if you've heard of the play. In both of these examples, the people who have studied Shakespeare and are familiar with his most famous plays and poems have the political power.

We want our pupils to have the power to respond to a politician or journalist with insight and clarity. Deny this knowledge, or leave it to chance, and we stop our pupils ever having the chance of engaging in meaningful social and political discourse.

The way in which we communicate is shaped by the past – it's a game that's been going on for centuries, where everyone knows the rules. All must feel welcome to participate in this game, with the same rules, on the same terms, to give everyone an equal chance to succeed.

Handed down through the generations, the language and culture written by dead white men points to our shared identity. Shakespeare is someone we share as a country. Not only that, but we share this with the generations who came before us. Our grandparents know Shakespeare. We are bound together by this shared knowledge. Without these important cultural ties, the delicate tapestry of our society begins to unravel. It should be a source of common national pride that perhaps the world's greatest writer honed his craft on our shores. Our pupils, whatever their backgrounds, must be taught to feel that pride.

Those who do possess powerful cultural knowledge feel so confident applying to Oxbridge or standing for public office because they feel that this country is *theirs*. Knowing the literature of a country adds to that important feeling of belonging.

Human beings naturally congregate into groups according to shared interests and values. But belonging to something is more than simply a way to socialise: it's a deep human need. We all have a strong drive to feel connected to others in some way. If we fail to give our pupils somewhere to belong, they'll find somewhere else to go. In the inner city, they are surrounded by gangs, drugs and crime. The temptation of the street is enormous. Every day, as they leave school, our pupils face gangsters dealing drugs and wielding knives. In their world, belonging to a gang is 'cool'. For a young person not yet particularly self-assured, not yet knowing their place in the world, joining a gang is entirely, and bleakly, logical. Without their sense of belonging to their local or national communities, a gang gives them an identity and a place to belong. In contrast, advantaged children have parents who place a higher value on education. They might come from a family where a university degree is not at all unusual, but expected. They're rarely threatened right at the school gates and are far less likely to witness crimes as teenagers.

In gangland Brent, our pupils urgently need to be rescued from alienation. If we can't help them, they join the ranks of the disengaged and drift further away from our shared culture.

Michaela believes that our pupils have the same right to belong here as anyone else; the culture that has grown over thousands of years is part of their history, too. When they feel that they belong here, they feel a greater entitlement to success.

Expanding Horizons

One argument against teaching dead white men is that they have very little in common with black boys living in the inner city. Why teach 'A Christmas Carol', when you could teach a novel by Malorie Blackman? The former

65

might seem antiquated and irrelevant to inner-city London life, whereas the latter deals with a range of gritty, challenging moral issues such as teenage pregnancy, gang warfare and crime. The vital consideration is that literacy rates among inner-city children are low. We have the lowest teenage literacy rate in the OECD[6], and one in eight disadvantaged children say they do not own a single book[7]. Thus it's entirely reasonable and logical to prioritise the teaching of books most relevant to our pupils' lives: it might make them enjoy reading more, and thus markedly improve their literacy.

But at Michaela we believe that such a rush to make the curriculum more relevant is problematic. We believe that teaching books by dead white men opens our pupils' minds to worlds they may never otherwise explore, that they're unlikely to come across on their own. Cultural knowledge should never be left to chance, and nor should opportunities to empathise with those from worlds different to ours.

Many schools across the country make the relevance of a text to the child's life very high on the list of priorities when choosing texts to teach. However, while many outsiders presume that pupils spend the majority of their time studying entirely irrelevant dead white men, the reality is, in fact, very different. Commonly pupils might read just one or two Shakespeare plays during these first years of secondary school. Teachers generally already tend to fill the rest of the available time with modern, 'relevant' young adult fiction, drama and poetry. Popular texts include Louis Sachar's 'Holes', Stephan Kelman's 'Pigeon English' and Robert Swindell's 'Stone Cold'. Pupils tend to enjoy these books, but they do little to expand their horizons beyond things they already know.

'Pigeon English', a text commonly taught to 11-13 year olds, tells of the poverty, gang warfare and murder experienced by a black boy living on a London estate. 'The Edge' by Alan Gibbons, another popular choice, explores themes of child abuse, teenage pregnancy and racism. Teachers choose these texts because they believe that they speak to the issues facing the young pupils they teach. They are selected for their relevance.

---

6   https://www.weforum.org/agenda/2016/02/which-countries-have-the-best-literacy-and-numeracy-rates/

7   https://literacytrust.org.uk/research-services/research-reports/book-ownership-literacy-engagement-and-mental-wellbeing/

But prioritising relevance in the texts we teach is extremely limiting. Children on council estates are already well versed in the trials and tribulations of life there. Prioritising relevance limits their imagination and underestimates their capacity to empathise with people of different experiences, different eras, and different circumstances. And if we only ever teach books relevant to their environment, why do we even need schools at all? Our mission is to expand horizons, not limit them.

Rather than locking our young in a prison of their own horizons, we resolve to show them the great breadth of the human experience. At Michaela we challenge them to explore poverty in Victorian England; or the dangers of all-consuming ambition in a Tudor era of beheading and treason; and the fate of women in a world that only celebrates men. School may be the only opportunity many young people have to explore the biggest questions of our humanity. We must not miss this opportunity. To study literature is to become acquainted with the unfamiliar, the broader human condition. Our humanity is about so much more than the life on our doorstep: we must expose pupils to a broader range of ideas, and reject relevance entirely.

Some might agree with us to the extent of admitting that relevance is problematic, but it does not follow, they may suggest, that we should still teach dead white men. Black boys from the inner city should not be denied the opportunity to explore the horrors of racism or colonial oppression. Nor should they be forced to read texts written by the very men who (whether directly or indirectly) benefitted from British Imperialism.

Again, is it not limiting to suggest that black children ought only to study black writers? Black literature often (and rightly) focuses on man's inhumanity to man, but as a result of not having to deal with oppression throughout history, white men were intellectually freer to explore other topics. Man's inhumanity to man is important, but it's only part of the human condition. There are other powerful themes in literature: love, loss, suffering, hatred, or our relationship to God, that equally deserve exploration. If we tell a black boy that he shouldn't study these themes because they were explored in writing predominantly by oppressive dead white men, we deny him the further opportunity to expand his horizons. Introducing the full spectrum of human experience is the only way we can truly expand our pupils' intellectual horizons.

This is not to suggest that children should never read books relevant to their condition, or written by black authors. We encourage pupils to feel pride in both their British identities and their other cultural influences, and are always pleased to see pupils reading more about their own interests. Crucially, all of the 'relevant' books I mention above are in the Michaela library. We actively encourage pupils to read these excellent works, and enjoy them.

But with the little curriculum time available, we prioritise teaching the texts that children are less likely to pick up of their own accord.

Pupils need the guidance of their teachers in order to access these texts and engage with them effectively. Texts that we opt to study, such as *Sherlock Holmes* and *Macbeth*, have been chosen because they explore a world that exists far outside that of our pupils. And, without the gentle direction of a teacher, pupils would be lost with such texts and therefore far less likely to read them.

Some say that Shakespeare and Conan Doyle are boring and teenagers do not enjoy reading them, but as an English teacher, I know this is not the case. Our pupils thoroughly enjoy these texts. Every time I teach *Macbeth*, I am amazed at how much our pupils love it. For example, in one scene, Lady Macbeth deceives Duncan, acting pleasant and polite as she welcomes him to her castle, only moments after discussing his murder with her husband. Hands instantly shoot up whenever pupils reach this point. They always have strong opinions: 'Miss, she's such a snake!' 'She is the absolute worst!' They simply cannot believe that someone could be capable of such deception.

Ideas over Identity

We should look to the traditional canon because it underpins our society and embodies the collective wisdom of the past, but also because we think it best to prioritise ideas above identities. As explored above, if we choose writers and thinkers on the basis of the colour of their skin, their religious background, or their gender, we create more problems than we solve.

If we tell disadvantaged young people that they are victims of an oppressive, racist society that wants to see them fail – what, then, is their motivation to try to engage with the society where they live? If, as I argue above, we ought to help our pupils feel as though they belong in this country, we must not make them feel like victims of it. It suggests to children that identity is the sum of our value, or our defining feature. At Michaela we do not believe that cultural background tells us everything we need to know about a person. Our beliefs, hobbies, likes and dislikes are among the many other things that make us who we are. It is important that we empower our pupils to believe this, not just that their cultural, religious or racial identity defines them, or that it should hold them back.

To take this approach is not to deny that millions have suffered horrendously at the hands of racists. But to tell a young black girl that she cannot succeed in British society because she is black and female is to set her up for failure. By reducing her to her racial identity in this way, we disempower her, make her feel she's not entitled to a place at the table. Why apply for Oxford if you've been told time and time again that it is a racist institution? The narrative of victimhood makes young people defeated and powerless: they feel that there's nothing to be done except feel angry about the status quo. There are of course a minority of racists out there who want our young black pupils to fail, but we don't want our pupils to feel such people are a barrier to them.

We want them to feel that this is a society in which they are welcome. This does not mean that they have to love everything about Britain, or that they shouldn't be invited to critique its culture or its past. Britain's history is littered with bad decisions and ignoble actions. It is a mess, but it's our mess, and we want our pupils to feel that too. They may very well face the obstacles of racism or sexism in their future but, rather than allowing the narrative of victimhood to consume them with anger, we want them to feel it is our shared responsibility to make it better.

We empower our young people therefore by teaching them that ideas are sovereign, and must be prioritised above identity. As such, we inevitably end up including dead white men. Shakespeare and Dickens, for example, are staple writers in our curriculum, much too important to omit. Sometimes, however, the writers will not be dead, white or male. It would be remiss of any school, for instance, to teach rhetoric or public speaking without including Martin Luther King's *I have a dream* speech. As an oft cited, highly skilfully executed piece of rhetoric, it rightly holds a seminal position in Western culture, and is very important in understanding many cultural changes that occurred during the 20th century. Similarly, the contributions of Maya Angelou and Langston Hughes to poetry should not be overlooked.

Crucially, the decision to include any writer in our curriculum is made on the basis of his or her ideas, rather than their identity.

Michaela's English Curriculum

When attempting to reverse the horrors of colonial rule and oppression, many activists argue that we should decolonise the curriculum and give a voice to the marginalised. However, at Michaela we believe that this overlooks three important aspects of our role as English teachers: first, to help pupils feel that they belong to British society; second, to expand our pupils' horizons; and third, to prioritise ideas over identity.

When determining our curriculum, these are the factors we take into account. We'd love to be able to teach a broad range of texts in depth but, given our time constraints, we must prioritise. To put this into context, in most schools, children receive 3 to 5 hours of English lessons per week for five years. In a typical year, an 11 year old receives around 160 hours of English lessons. How can we make the most of this with so many competing priorities? An English teacher requires around 25-35 hours to teach a book in depth. At this rate, around 20% of a child's lesson time is allocated to one book. 160 hours is just about enough to teach one novel, one play, one collection of poetry, and perhaps one collection of non-fiction texts per year, alongside instruction in writing, spelling and grammar.

We could decide to teach a greater number of texts in less depth, but we believe that this creates further problems. Firstly, teaching a text in less depth might result in tokenism. We could try to teach one text from China, but would that really tell our pupils much about such a culturally rich nation? Representing many voices from many continents leaves little time to study anything in depth at all. We believe it's wrong to reduce an entire country's history and people to one poem, or one short story.

Furthermore, teaching a variety of texts superficially provides less challenge than teaching them in depth. Reading longer blocks of texts enables pupils to explore character development across a whole story, whilst grappling with ambitious vocabulary and thinking about challenging, original ideas — these are all parts of what it means to study literature. Teachers who opt to study more texts in less depth, might thus prevent their pupils from being sufficiently challenged.

There is always a trade-off, but at some point we have to make a decision. We prioritise the texts that will help our pupils to feel that they belong in Britain: Shakespeare and Dickens have earned their positions in the canon for their contribution to our collective consciousness. Shakespeare's plays have been retold countless times in varying ways because they speak to something deeper within us all. Dickens also holds an important position in our nation's literary history, not least for his entertaining plots and carefully crafted characters, but owing to the role he played in shaping so much of what we think about life in Victorian England. The typical layperson's understanding of life, poverty, crime and the impact of the Industrial Revolution in the 19th century owes an enormous debt to Dickens.

We take what Michael Young terms 'powerful knowledge'[8] into account: that there is some knowledge that is more useful and powerful than other knowledge because of the transformative insights it gives. We want our pupils to study a range of human experiences, the breadth of the human condition. When choosing a mystery, for example, we do not opt for the arguably more relevant 'Stone Cold', but choose 'Sherlock Holmes' instead. Learning about life in Victorian England and the birth of the forensic criminal investigation is not only exciting and thrilling for children, but can open up their minds to an immense, unrecognisable world.

As emphasised, it isn't possible to devote equal time to both William Blake and Phillis Wheatley. We must decide which knowledge best serves our pupils. Is it more important that our young people know more about the English Romantic movement, or life for an 18th century African slave in Boston? Whatever we decide, the idea is sovereign, not the identity of its source.

It is a great tragedy that so many men and women's voices have been oppressed, but we cannot change the past. We can, however, aim to change the future, and we hope that by empowering our pupils with a traditional curriculum, they will be able to go out into the world and make their own, important contributions. If they know little of the canon and the Western tradition, they can do little to change it, or be a part of its evolution.

Conclusion

As teachers, we are the custodians of our culture. It is our duty to ensure that it is passed on to the next generation. In order to do so, we should present the canon as a gift handed to us by our ancestors for us to nurture

---

8   Young, M. (2014a). Powerful knowledge as a curriculum principle. In M. Young, D. Lambert, C. Roberts & M. Roberts, Knowledge and the future school: curriculum and social justice (pp. 65–88). London: Bloomsbury Academic.

and help grow. Rather than telling our pupils that they are the 'other', we should invite them to feel that the thinkers who have stood the test of time belong to them.

There is no reason the children from inner London shouldn't be able to learn to feel the same confidence as the privately educated. But inner-city children depend on their schools to give them access. If misguided teachers, thinking they are liberating their children, deny them access to this cultural body of knowledge, then they undermine the confidence and resilience of a new generation.

Visitors to Michaela often do comment on the confidence and resilience our pupils show. This is in part due to our curriculum and the values it conveys. They are never taught to feel victims of oppression, but rather that they have a vital and equal value to those who've had the power in the past. All of English culture, its literature, art, music and theatre, belongs to them because they belong here: they are not outsiders. They are the future of this country, and by teaching them that they should not be limited by their identity, we give them the freedom to make their own choices.

Rather than being transfixed on the idea that Western culture is something we should submit to, we must show our pupils that it is a gift handed to us, and that it forms the fundamental blocks of the society where we live today.

Ultimately, as we have shown, we must choose our texts based on how well they help us to understand the human condition, based on the values and themes they explore. Rather than focusing on the colour of the writer's skin, we must emphasise that life is about so much more than an experience of 'otherness' and victimhood. What binds us is not differences; but our great, common life themes: our colossal sense of love, joy, sadness, loss, suffering, desperation, and the ever-present threat of death. First and foremost, these are the things that we need to teach: the things that make us human.

National Identity

Michael Taylor
@mike_taylor11

When I first joined Michaela, I remember just how much of a 'marmite' place it was. It has been very humbling to see how teachers around the world have been inspired by our vision of providing pupils from inner-city London with an exceptional education which will set them up for life.

However, one aspect of our ethos that many seem to struggle to get on board with is our focus on giving the pupils a real sense that they are part of this country. As a school, we think it is essential that our pupils associate themselves strongly with England and Britain. In this chapter, I will outline the main reasons why we think national identity is so important and I hope to convince you that it is something schools should be thinking about carefully.

Where we have gone wrong

Before I outline what we do at Michaela, I want to briefly summarise where I think we have taken a wrong turn when it comes to issues surrounding patriotism and national identity.

There is no doubt that there have been occasions in the past when an uncritical account of Britain's history and culture was the norm in schools. To be clear, we think it is essential that controversial aspects of Britain's past are explored through the discipline of history and that pupils are exposed to different interpretations of the past and how those interpretations have been constructed. It is also right that Britain's history includes as many perspectives as possible, and shines a light on those individuals and groups which were an integral part of our past, but whose voices have either been explicitly or implicitly side-lined because of ignorance, ideology or neglect.

Equally, it is absolutely right that we want our pupils to have a thorough understanding of the world's people, places and cultures. Through our geography curriculum we ensure that we convey the richness of the world's diversity, and in religion we spend time covering the Abrahamic faiths and world religions.

However, in some schools and organisations, there is an embarrassment about our country which would be rarely seen in other nations.

In our view, that does not make our country particularly forward-thinking. On the contrary, we see it as deeply problematic. As a result of this embarrassment, teachers can often feel uncomfortable teaching their pupils about English history, culture and geography. Pupils can grow up knowing very little about the country they live in, let alone being able to express some element of pride in it. Similarly, citizenship lessons often lean heavily on diversity and multiculturalism. In effect, the focus is on what divides, rather than what unites us.

It is common for schools to embrace this difference and I am certainly not arguing that pupils should not be encouraged to have multiple identities. Far from it: identity is complicated. What I am arguing for is that English and British national identity is not side-lined, but should form a central part of an English child's education in this country. The one thing all pupils in this country have in common is that they live in England and they live in Britain.

In diverse cities, it is totally understandable why this happens. Embracing diversity and side-lining national identity is a natural response to working in diverse communities. Many of the motivations behind this push are completely reasonable. One of the main aims of this sort of thinking is to make us more tolerant. It is to move away from the appalling world-views and racism that have led to so much misery for different groups and communities. All of this is admirable and we have come so far in this respect.

However, embracing diversity in this country is often associated with a rejection of Britishness and in particular, Englishness. We celebrate every identity under the sun, yet we constantly fret and worry about our own. Despite this, Britishness and Englishness are facts of life. People feel British and people feel English.[1] This feeling is rooted in a common culture and history which has given rise to particular values and traits which are recognisably British and English.[2] If pupils are not exposed to these, then we are stopping

---

1   A recent YouGov survey stated that 80% of residents in England identify strongly as English and 82% of residents in England strongly identify as British. https://www.bbc.co.uk/news/uk-44306737

2   There is clearly a debate about what constitutes Britishness and Englishness, which I touch upon later. However, the fact that people strongly identify with both identities means that schools have a duty to expose pupils to both.

them from feeling part of their own country. At Michaela, we believe it is absolutely right that pupils feel a strong emotional bond with their country, so that they can thrive in Britain.

What do we do at Michaela?

We believe it is our duty to teach our pupils important aspects of both English and British culture. At Michaela:

- We fly the Union Flag outside school at all times during the school day.

- We sing three of our most important national songs on a rotation each week during assembly: 'God Save the Queen', 'Jerusalem' and 'I Vow to Thee My Country'.[3]

- We prioritise English and British history, geography, music, art and literature as part of a broad and balanced curriculum that incorporates European and global perspectives.

- We take pupils to visit important sites from our country's history, including Westminster Abbey, the Palace of Westminster, St Paul's Cathedral and the battlefields of the First World War.

- We use the 'we' pronoun whenever we talk about England or Britain. We discourage pupils from saying 'your country' or 'this country'.

- In November, we encourage all pupils to remember those who died in the two world wars, but in particular, our own country's young men and women who paid the ultimate price. We all stand for the two minute silence on Armistice Day.

- We celebrate the Queen's official birthday in June, St George's Day in April and we cheer England on whenever they are playing in sports tournaments.

- We regularly talk about how fortunate we are to live in a free, democratic and tolerant nation.

---

3 'God Save the Queen' is our national anthem, 'Jerusalem' is England's unofficial national song and 'I Vow to Thee My Country' is often sung around the time of Armistice Day and reflects the values of patriotism, duty and sacrifice.

* We teach important aspects of our shared identity and encourage respect for British institutions and values.

Why do we believe it is important to give the pupils an English and British identity?

1) Cultural Literacy and Socialisation

Most people agree that one function of schools is to help socialise pupils into the society in which they are going to live. It is also a given that we need to prepare our pupils for life in modern Britain. Granted, singing all three verses of God Save the Queen isn't necessarily the most important thing they need to know for them to get a job or go to university, or even to live a functional life in this country. However, ensuring that our pupils feel part of this country certainly is and our national anthem is an important part of helping them to do that.

Our pupils are living their lives in this country and so it is important that they are taught enough of our habits, culture, customs and values for them to survive and thrive in modern Britain. This is even more important for our pupils at Michaela, who come from such diverse backgrounds. As a school, we focus on what unites us. If we design our curriculum, school culture and pastoral programme entirely around pupil interests and the personal feelings and identities of each individual, then schools will never feel comfortable in encouraging pupils from diverse backgrounds to feel proud of their country, and connected to it in a meaningful way.

Of course, we don't say that pupils must have one identity, far from it. We stress however that Britishness and Englishness is a part of their identity, by virtue of living here. Knowing your national history and culture enables you to better understand the country in which you live. History and culture is something we either consciously or sub-consciously carry around with us. We live, feel and breathe it. To feel the pulse of a country, city, or village and to draw upon a rich mental map of stories, images and controversies is what a good understanding of your national culture and history gives you. Even when our national culture or history may seem controversial, it is still the right of any pupil in our country to know about it and to be able to engage in those debates in a meaningful way.

For most of us, we are employed by the state to educate our young people and prepare them for life in Britain. Schools are partly instruments of socialisation and so teaching British and English history and culture has to be relatively more important than teaching the history of another part of the world. Similarly, focusing on British culture and customs is relatively more important than teaching about other cultures. I understand that some will infer that this is all a way of conveying a partisan narrative of history and that we believe that only British history is important. That is definitely not what we do. We believe in exposing pupils to beliefs, attitudes and cultures from around the world. Anchoring pupils to the country they live in and teaching about diverse attitudes and cultures are not in opposition to one another.

Many of our pupils live in Zones 2 and 3 of the Transport for London network and yet some of them have never properly visited Zone 1. Many of them would fail to recognise and appreciate landmarks which are intimately associated with the city and country in which they live. Many young people know very little about this country's history, despite the existence of a national curriculum. Many school pupils do not realise what the rest of the country even looks like. This, ultimately, narrows their horizons and impoverishes them.[4]

If you think, as I suspect most in our country do, that there is an injustice in school pupils not knowing their country's history and heritage[5], then you will understand what we are trying to do.

We want our pupils to be able to live, work and visit all corners of this country and feel comfortable enough to engage in a meaningful way with the country in which they are probably going to spend the rest of their lives. We want our pupils to see all parts of Britain as theirs. The more they engage with their country's history, culture and values the more successful they will be as a citizen of this country and of the world.

---

4   The genericism of subject disciplines that has come to dominate much of education is partly to blame for this. The fear of teaching knowledge, covered elsewhere in this book, has ensured pupils know very little about the history of their country.

5   The history education community will be aware of the distinction between history and heritage. National history includes the exposure to differences in interpretation and the selection of evidence to construct those interpretations. Heritage is distinct from history and is best understood as 'sites of memory', to use the phrase of the French historian, Pierre Nora.

2) Communitarian values

Many of the values that underpin our ethos are communitarian. Communitarians believe that humans find fulfilment when they see themselves as part of something bigger than themselves. This wider focus on the community, as opposed to just the individual, was common across the left and right of the political spectrum. In Britain, it is a set of loose principles that has been represented by those who subscribe to small 'c' conservative values, as well as by many in the old Labour Party of the post-war period.

Communitarians and small 'c' conservatives on both the left and the right of the political spectrum see society as a network of reciprocal relationships and trust, in return for duties and responsibilities. The family and local community are an integral part of this, but the most logical point of our loyalty, whilst leaving plenty of room for critical analysis, should be the nation. This does not mean that the nation is the only identity pupils have or should have, but we believe it is vital that we ensure that our pupils feel that this is their country and we hope that this will give them fulfilment later in life.

Society and the individual are both stronger when we see ourselves as part of a larger whole. In the same way that we think the family is vital in the development and education of the child, so too do we think that inculcating a sense of identity to the wider community of the 'nation' is important in ensuring that pupils know that they do not exist in a vacuum. As well as ensuring that pupils know that they have certain rights which are accorded to them by virtue of having a British passport, they also have a series of obligations and responsibilities to their fellow citizens. We constantly strive to make sure our pupils understand that they have a duty not only to themselves, but to their families, teachers, communities and their country to work hard and to give something back. The antithesis of duty is entitlement. Nobody would deny that the rights and liberties of the individual are vital in ensuring a free and prosperous society. However, we have gone too far in Britain in creating a culture where a significant number of people appear to believe that rights are not always mirrored by responsibilities.

We believe that society is not just a framework for the present, it is also a point in an unbroken line from those who made decisions and sacrifices for our betterment, and to those we want to create a better world for. If people were more considerate of what has gone before, and hopeful that what will come after will be preserved and improved upon, then society will be stronger. Edmund Burke, the 18th century political philosopher, spoke of society as a 'contract between the dead, the living and the yet to be born'. We believe it is our duty to respect those that have gone before and who have built the country that we live in today.

We make a real effort to ensure that pupils know that what they have today has not been won lightly, and that they have a duty to preserve it and improve upon it. This is why we care so much about honouring those who have fought to defend their country. Every November, we ensure that the school community is made aware of those generations who have gone before us, where many have sacrificed their lives for our national way of life.

3) Nations are not bad things

Humans create shared stories and narratives which allow them to co-operate with other humans, through a unifying culture. There are also practicalities that unite people from different backgrounds. Language, law, and custom are all concrete realities that link people from Caithness to Cornwall. To deny our national inheritance to the next generation would be in part to deny them citizenship.

We have also created a shared narrative and identity based on collective traditions, history, institutions, literature and culture. This allows the people of our country to see one another as 'one and the same'. One of the mottos of the United States of America is 'E Pluribus Unam' (out of many, one). I find this to be an inspiring way of distilling why nations are so vital. Nations allow people who hold disparate beliefs and have different identities and ethnicities to come together as 'one' and co-operate in a meaningful and fulfilling way. Just like America, Britain is made up of different cultures and races. In America however, there is a much stronger belief in a unifying American dream and an American way of life, which gives Americans from all backgrounds meaning and fulfilment in their lives.

4) Moral Psychology and Human Nature

Research in the field of moral psychology has found that humans have evolved as 'groupish' as well as 'selfish'. We all have an instinctive ability to feel part of something bigger than ourselves and we actively wish to see ourselves as more than just individuals. Jonathan Haidt, a moral psychologist, makes the point well when he talks about humans as 90% chimp and 10% bee.[6] The idea here is that bees are able to visualise themselves as part of a larger 'whole' and crucially, can co-operate selflessly when needed.

Just as the beehive provides a framework for that co-operation, so does the family, local community and nation provide it for humans. Group rituals generate powerful collective emotions and enable people to overcome selfishness and feel a sense of belonging as part of a family community. Congregating and singing national hymns and anthems together (and wearing national emblems like the poppy) build trust and bring uplifting unity.

In evolutionary psychology, our ancestors were selective team players: under the right conditions, they could enter an 'all for one and one for all' mindset. That's how we want pupils to feel at Michaela. We see Michaela as a family. Pupils belong to their form, and in turn their form is part of the wider family of their year group. The year group forms part of the Michaela family and our school is part of the wider family of the nation. When children feel part of something bigger than themselves, it gives their lives meaning and instils them with purpose and motivation to learn.

If more pupils saw themselves as intimately bound to the wider community, to their family and to their country, they would be less likely to fall into the traps of selfish individualism, of social media, and the paths of crime and violence that are all too readily awaiting them outside the school gates.

British Values or British Culture?

In no other country would a government need to explicitly articulate its own values. Our ignorance of what it means to be British or English has huge consequences for how schools socialise pupils.

I remember once, at a teaching conference, attending a seminar on 'British Values in the classroom'. It was 2014 and Michael Gove had made it mandatory for schools to teach these nebulous values. A teacher stood up, clearly incensed at the whole thing. He was furious at the idea that democracy, the rule of law, tolerance etc could ever be considered British; they were universal and applied to all of humanity. The workshop co-ordinator, I

---

6   Haidt. J in 'The Righteous Mind'.

suspect, sympathised with his plight. He had probably been sent there to make sure that the conference's offer ticked all the Ofsted boxes.

On the one hand, the idea that democracy, the rule of law and tolerance are uniquely British is quite an odd assertion. To say they are universal, however, is faintly ridiculous. Unless of course you would like to make the case that human rights, tolerance and the rule of law are values which are applied consistently around the world. In fact, in the UK, we are in the minority of countries where those values do apply and have consistently done so for some time. According to *The Economist*'s democracy index, the United Kingdom is one of only 22 countries on the planet which are officially classed as fully democratic.[7] In many countries, women have appalling educational and employment opportunities and in the worst offending nations, women are routinely the victims of violence and discrimination. According to the Women, Peace and Security Index, the United Kingdom is the 7th best country to live in for women, beating almost every other country in the world on a range of metrics, with some of the highest financial access and education in the world, to some of the lowest domestic and organised violence.[8] We are clearly not perfect, but we really should not be ashamed to say that life in Britain is relatively good for the vast majority of people.

If British values are too vague, or universal, then what is the solution? It would sound farcical for Irish schools to start talking about 'Irish values'. Equally, I cannot imagine a day when the Scottish Parliament compels all schools to start discussing the 'Five Fundamental Scottish Values'. Granted, there are some nations whose identity is founded on abstract values, such as France and the USA. However, most countries talk about culture and not values.

Culture counts. The reason I meet up with close friends is not because we share a belief in the 'the rule of law'. It is because we share a common bond, often forged because of similarities in background, social class, professional life or regional and national identity. All of these come under the umbrella of 'culture'. Of course, many of these bonds transcend national boundaries but to deny that people in England and Britain don't feel a common connection is a mistake.

---

7   https://www.eiu.com/topic/democracy-index

8   https://www.nationalgeographic.com/culture/2019/10/peril-progress-prosperity-womens-well-being-around-the-world-feature/

The government codifies our values because we do not know how to talk about our identity. This is partly because we are so wracked by guilt and awkwardness, but also because a whole generation of collective memory, culture and history is passing into obscurity.

Culture is everything, particularly within a school. At Michaela, we talk about British and English culture and 'being British' and 'being English'. We talk about gratitude, for being able to live in a country where we can live peacefully, and speak freely no matter what our race, colour or creed may be. We teach our pupils about English and British history and make sure that pupils have a strong chronological grasp of England's story, from the fall of Rome to the present day.

In Year 7, as part of the geography curriculum, pupils undertake a tour of the world's people and places, but not before they have spent a large portion of the year ensuring they know their own country and can locate the main nations, counties and cities of the UK on a map. As part of this, pupils are introduced to the different parts of the UK, along with the songs, flags and emblems associated with each of the four countries of the UK. When studying English geography, we introduce pupils to the culture of England as well as the quirks and differences that exist across the country. This is so that whenever they travel around England, they begin to feel its pulse and understand it better.

There is neither time nor space in this chapter to outline precisely what English culture is. Climate, landscape, music, cuisine, literature, dialect, history, heritage, traditions, character and sense of humour are all things that have intimately English variations and have shaped our history and national character. It is clear, however, that there is such a thing as 'English culture' and it is the right of every schoolchild to be introduced to it. If they choose to reject it later in life, then at least they have the genuine and informed choice to do so, unlike so many others who know little aside from a faint sense of embarrassment, or outright criticism and dislike of their own country.

Creating a civic and inclusive patriotism

We have a peculiar inability in this country to talk honestly and openly about citizenship, identity and nationhood. When I say 'our country', I am talking about the United Kingdom and British identity, but the problem is more acutely felt in England than in the other nations of the United Kingdom. This is not the space to argue why this is the case, but critically, the vacuum that this creates, means English pupils do not feel part of their country in the same way that pupils around the world do with theirs, and pupils from diverse backgrounds suffer the most from this debilitating collective ignorance.

Our pupils are also not helped by the currents of cultural and political battles that often rage around the ideas surrounding Britishness and Englishness. When our headmistress tweets videos of our pupils proudly singing the national anthem, or Jerusalem, I often read two types of reaction:

1. Those on the extreme left who see it as an act of oppression to teach pupils about English culture, because the pupils come from such diverse backgrounds.

2. Those on the extreme right who can't seem to stand pupils from different backgrounds all coming together as English and British children, because they don't think such pupils can ever be English or British.

There is of course a third reaction, which is that of the sensible observer, who sees children of different backgrounds, religions and races coming together as Britons. Those on the extreme left, who say children from diverse backgrounds cannot experience English culture, and those on the extreme right, who say those children simply cannot be British, are as bad as each other. They create huge obstacles for our children by preventing them from connecting with the country they live in. We aim to create a civic and inclusive patriotism that allows all children to share in England's culture and history and to partake in the fullness of British society.

Conclusion

There is one central reason why I think a strong sense of national identity is vital in schools:

Learning about our country's culture, history and geography enriches pupils and prepares them for life in modern Britain. It ensures pupils feel part of something bigger than themselves, giving pupils' lives meaning and fulfilment.

I do not know of a society in the modern western world that has disavowed so much of its culture, history and heritage as much as England has. When the citizens of a country lose the ties that bind them, trust crumbles. I believe it is the responsibility of teachers to embrace moderate patriotism, to allow pupils to feel part of a wider community. Failure to do so keeps pushing Englishness to the fringes of the eccentric and the extreme. Even if one cannot get on board with all of what I have written here, we must surely accept that, as state employed teachers, with a responsibility to the people of this country as well as our pupils, we must expose our pupils to as much of our country's culture as we can, so that they can succeed and thrive.

An inability to talk about our identity, or to shy away from it and feel embarrassed, is part of the reason we have such a dysfunctional relationship with civic institutions and is also a reason why our young people, who generally feel less connection with their cultural heritage, are therefore less invested in wanting to preserve it. In our brave new world, the education system has been geared towards individualism, rather than community. Our songs, stories and our history have been largely side-lined, forgotten or wilfully neglected. We are in real danger of losing our culture and replacing it with an 'identikit' England and an individualistic generation who will never know what it is like to contribute to a national story.

I am incredibly lucky to work at a school where our pupils are taught about the culture of their country in a meaningful way, giving them membership of the community and enabling them to feel a real sense of Englishness and Britishness. As a nation we need to actively promote symbols of unity as the surest way to allow new members of the community to gain access to our way of life quickly and to flourish. Flags, mottos and songs are not antiquated relics of a bygone era, but are very real and tangible symbols of membership, which allow society to bond by sharing common experiences and to perpetuate a collective memory.

Just like any family, our country is clearly not perfect, far from it. It is our home nonetheless and despite its flaws, it remains one of the best places to live on our planet. To deny our country's culture and history to our pupils, not only inhibits their ability to partake in the fullness of modern English and British life, but is an act of cultural vandalism which will be impossible to repair for future generations.

We Believe in Authority

Becky Staw

The image of the cruel authoritarian schoolmaster pervades popular consciousness, from Dickens' Gradgrind to Dahl's Trunchbull. There is good reason for this. School life in the past looked very different from how it does today; corporal punishment was common and as a society we are only now picking up the pieces from decades of appalling abuse of children by adults in positions of care. Certainly, the societal expectation was once that children should be unquestioningly obedient to adults. Often, when children did try to speak out against abuse, they were silenced or not believed.

The child fighting against the prevailing adult order also appeals to our instinctive desire to support the underdog; the heroic individual battling the unjust system. Our most captivating protagonists in children's literature, from Matilda to Harry Potter, defy authority in pursuit of a noble goal. We want children to grow up to think independently and this rightly means that they should be able to question and challenge authority where it is illegitimate. Why then would I argue for more, not less, adult authority in our schools?

When I speak about the concept of authority with friends and fellow teachers and listen to their misgivings, I find that their concerns include one or both of the following:

1. Authority is cruel.

2. Authority stifles children's creativity.

Of course, there is a balance to be struck. I would not advocate that anyone models their teaching practice on our fictional tyrants mentioned above. Teacher authority, if left unchecked, could tend towards the authoritarian and it is the school's duty to guard against this. But the absence of clear adult authority in our schools today has condemned thousands of children to chaos. Based on my experience as a teacher and Head of Year at Michaela, I would argue that adult authority, when coupled with high aspirations and respect for the children in one's care, is essential to allow children to flourish.

1. Is authority cruel?

Oscar joined Michaela halfway through Year 9 aged thirteen, hoping that he would not suffer the bullying he had fallen victim to at his previous school. There he was taunted and physically assaulted by other pupils, culminating in a group of Year 11 pupils beating him up and leaving him in a bin. Speaking about his previous school Oscar said, *"I was scared to go to school. The teachers didn't do anything about it".*

Oscar is not alone in his experience. A recent study suggested that as many as three in five young people have suffered bullying at school[1] and yet, heart-rending as their stories always are, they are not the most shocking examples of bad behaviour in our schools today. Between April 2015 and the beginning of 2017, 2,579 knives and weapons were found in schools.[2] Other reports tell of beatings and racist and sexual abuse, including 600 rapes over a three-year period.[3] The teaching community may congratulate itself on ceasing to cruelly and unfairly punish children but now a very different problem should preoccupy us, that of our failure to keep children safe from each other. How have we allowed this to happen?

The state of our schools

Since the second half of the twentieth century the Romantic vision of childhood has become increasingly popular. Most influentially, though not exclusively, set out in Jean-Jacques Rousseau's *Émile, ou de l'Éducation*, the Romantic view asserts the child to be naturally good; it is exposure to society that corrupts his or her innate virtue. While the resurgence of the Romantic ideal was an understandable reaction to authoritarian teaching, in some modern teaching practice it has taken hold as the view that *all* adults necessarily stifle children and interfere with their natural development. The corollary of this can be the eschewal of adult authority itself. In practice, this means that in many schools,

1   *Three in five children have been victims of bullying at school*, The Independent, viewed 27 July 2019 <https://www.independent.co.uk/news/education/education-news/three-in-five-children-have-been-bullied-at-school-survey-finds-a8995761.html>

2   *Hundreds of knives seized in 18 months at UK schools*, The Guardian, viewed 16 April 2019, <https://www.theguardian.com/uk-news/2017/may/12/hundreds-of-knives-seized-in-18-months-at-uk-schools-figures-reveal-show-police-england-wales-weapons>

3   *Are we ignoring an epidemic of sexual violence in schools?*, The Guardian, viewed 16 April 2019, <https://www.theguardian.com/lifeandstyle/2017/dec/12/are-we-ignoring-an-epidemic-of-sexual-violence-in-schools>

teachers are not supported in the assertion of their own judgement over the individual wishes of the child. This leaves teachers in an impossible situation as they seek to control the class in front of them because, paradoxically, they are still responsible for behaviour management. Teachers are drowning in the workload that this situation creates and classroom discipline breaks down when the teacher's authority is called into question in this way.

I understand the unease a new teacher feels trying to accept the ill-fitting mantle of authority. I felt it myself when I first joined the teaching profession at the age of twenty-four. Why should children listen to me? Why should my opinion carry more weight than theirs? Who am I to tell them the rules? Unfortunately, as I came to learn, if the teacher does not assume the responsibility of their own authority, then the most dominant children will fill the void. As Hannah Arendt argued, *"by being emancipated from the authority of the adults the child has not been freed but has been subjected to a much more terrifying and truly tyrannical authority, the tyranny of the majority"* (1961, p181).

Clearly this chaos leaves our children vulnerable and it is also fuelling the teacher recruitment and retention crisis across the country. As chronicled in *The Secret Teacher* (2017) and Charlie Carroll's *On the Edge* (2010), teachers are being shouted at, sworn at, insulted, abused, threatened and intimidated by aggressive pupils on a daily basis. According to a 2019 survey of 5,000 teachers by the NASUWT[4], one quarter of teachers experience physical violence from pupils once per week with nearly a third having been punched, kicked or hit and 7% spat at.[5] In 2018, the Education Support Partnership issued its Teacher Wellbeing Index, highlighting what it termed an epidemic of teachers suffering depression, stress and anxiety at work. One in three teachers quit within the first five years and 70% of teachers would not recommend the profession to others.[6] Because of the assumption that strong, charismatic teachers can control the room without sanctions, many teachers are reluctant to admit to the poor behaviour in their own classrooms. But we all know it to be the elephant in the room that is driving competent teachers away from the profession.

---

4   National Association of Schoolmasters/Union of Women Teachers

5   *Physical violence against teachers is a weekly occurrence*, The NASUWT 2019, viewed 17 April 2019, <https://www.nasuwt.org.uk/article-listing/violence-against-teachers-weekly-occurrence.html>

6   *Teacher Wellbeing Index 2018*, The Education Support Partnership, viewed 17 April 2019, <https://www.educationsupportpartnership.org.uk/sites/default/files/teacher_wellbeing_index_2018.pdf>

It is not only the wellbeing of our pupils and teachers that we should be concerned about. In its most recent report on low-level disruption, Ofsted found that pupils are losing up to an hour of learning each day in schools due to behaviour such as shouting out, chatting, not having the correct equipment or using mobile phones inappropriately.[7] That's potentially a fifth of learning time. How can we possibly expect children to make the desired levels of progress in such an environment? We may be tempted to see the absence of adult authority as liberating, but there's nothing noble or freeing about a child leaving school functionally illiterate, as an estimated 1 in 5 children do.[8]

Closer inspection of this last statistic illustrates what we know to be the case: the disorder in British schools impacts on pupils from disadvantaged backgrounds the most. Less affluent children may not have access to books at home, they are less likely to sit at the dinner table discussing history or politics and they might not have an adult who is able to help them with their homework. These children, above all, cannot afford to waste lesson time at school. This is the blind spot of current educational orthodoxy: to bemoan the attainment gap between the rich and the poor, while disempowering the teacher in the classroom, is to condemn our disadvantaged pupils to poorer life chances. At Michaela, many of our pupils come from disadvantaged backgrounds. The consistency of behavioural expectations and the order within the school give those children the best chance of catching up with their middle-class counterparts. The classroom needs the adult to be in charge, to enforce the rules of the room, in the same way that a football match needs a referee to enforce the rules of the game. Can you imagine a football match without her? Even if the ref sometimes makes mistakes, her word must be final or the game falls apart.

Protecting our pupils

Far from being the authoritarian nightmare we might imagine, teacher authority gives children clear rules on acceptable behaviour, both in terms of how they should behave in the classroom and how they should behave

---

7   *Below the radar: low-level disruption in the country's classrooms*, Ofsted 2014, viewed 18 April 2019, <https://assets.publishing.service.gov.uk/government/uploads/system/uploads/attachment_data/file/379249/Below_20the_20radar_20-_20low-level_20disruption_20in_20the_20country_E2_80_99s_20classrooms.pdf>

8   *17% Of School Leavers 'Functionally Illiterate'*, Teaching Times 2010, viewed 31 October 2019, <https://www.teachingtimes.com/articles/school-leavers-functionally-illiterate.htm>

towards each other. Children need these boundaries so that they feel safe and have a sense of belonging. I believe this culture accounts for the relatively very low level of bullying within Michaela. Comparing his time here to his previous school Oscar says, *"Here it feels a lot safer. I know that if I have a problem, I can talk to the teachers and they'll help me. The teachers are tough on you, but it's made me stronger"*.

Many teenagers wish to defy adult authority and, as I outlined in my introduction, we are naturally sympathetic to the teenage rebel. At Michaela, because we are strict about uniform, about silent corridors and because these rules are so consistently enforced, a child can rebel in a way that is not disruptive or at all dangerous. If the naughtiest children in my year group wish to express their dislike of adult authority then they might simply wear the wrong colour socks. Many will think it ridiculous that we sanction such things, but isn't it better that a child can rebel simply by bending uniform rules? They are then far less likely to pursue the 'big ticket' behaviour of swearing at a teacher or bringing a knife to school. These incidents are incredibly rare at Michaela because teachers hold the line on the seemingly trivial. Equally, for those pupils who simply want to get on and follow the rules, Michaela is a safe environment. Nobody bullies or teases those pupils who are well behaved because good behaviour is the norm.

If the culture of a school does not unapologetically enforce the authority of the teacher then sanctions are often inconsistent. When one teacher accepts something another will not tolerate, how can a child know what behaviour is reasonable? This inconsistency is immensely stressful for children. The most vulnerable children already come from chaotic homes and so at school they crave the safety of an ordered environment. But structure and consistency elude many children in British schools today. They don't do their homework and there's often no consequence. They shout at a teacher and on some days there might be a detention but on other days not. They have a fight with another pupil but both children are allowed to remain in lessons. Then they bring a knife to school and they're expelled. In too many schools there is a permissive environment where clear decisions are only made once misbehaviour has reached such a point as to be deemed dangerous. Do we really believe this is the Romantic realisation of the child living out their best, most authentic self?

Despite the chaos in our schools, some adults hold fast to the belief that it is inherently cruel to discipline a child or even to have clear expectations of how they should behave. In my more cynical moments, I think that perhaps adults who make these comments are trying to signal their own virtuous belief in the goodness of children, with no thought given to how an adult should react when a child invariably falls short of this ideal. Perhaps they wish to remain blind to the uglier and more difficult aspects of childhood and so seek to impose an enforced innocence on young people who are beginning to outgrow it. Perhaps we, as teachers, do not know the young adults who failed their GCSEs and so cannot find work. We are not personally confronted with the problems of a young person whose school failed them. It is police, social workers and families who are left to pick up the pieces while we have a new cohort of eleven-year-olds to concern ourselves with. Whatever the reason, we are ignoring the dire consequences of a school system where adult authority is absent.

There has been extensive press coverage of the problem of pupil exclusions, with pupils who have been excluded more likely to end up in gangs and consequently become victims or perpetrators of knife crime. Is it possible that these children, lacking the boundaries and sense of community that a safe school provides, are easy targets for gang groomers? Perhaps it is they who, desperate for a sense of order and purpose in their lives, are also most vulnerable to radicalisation. Earlier intervention, a more proactive approach and more consistent discipline from a younger age in school systems that take their actions seriously, might help protect our young people from more than bullying.

Believing a child can do better

Andre joined Michaela halfway through Year 8 and last summer he finished Year 11. When he arrived aged twelve, he had been expelled from two secondary schools and was in a pupil referral unit (PRU) before coming to Michaela. At the PRU he admits that he, *"got into fights with other kids and then the teacher would try to get involved so you would fight the teacher"*. There were no rules, no sanctions and lessons were only thirty minutes long, as it was thought that pupils like Andre could not be expected to concentrate for more than half an hour at a time. Andre says that at the PRU, *"I felt like I wasn't getting anywhere with my life; it was not a place you wanted to be"*. I would never have guessed that Andre had ever been so badly behaved when I started teaching at Michaela. He got detention for poor homework every now and again, but he was polite and generally hard-working in lessons. After Andre had been at Michaela for a year, he wrote his application to be a pupil guide:

I believe that I have turned my behaviour around since joining Michaela which has drastically impacted my life. I do believe that I have more work to do in terms of my behaviour and the way I present myself... At Michaela, I believe that I have become more trustworthy.

During my teaching career I have personally seen the way pupils who have behaved in violent, rude or very disruptive ways are allowed back into lessons without a sanction. Not only does this damage the chances that other pupils in the class will be able to learn, but it also sends two possible messages to the offending child:

1. What you did was fine and you shouldn't receive any punishment.

2. What you did wasn't fine, but it's what I expect of you and I don't believe you can do better.

This is a significant aspect of benevolent adult authority which is ignored by those who so vehemently oppose it. To put yourself in a position of authority and to tell a child that you are disappointed in them, that they have behaved poorly, is also to say *I believe you can do better than this.*

I'm not saying this is easy. In a system where you are not supported with effective behaviour management systems, trying to discipline a child can lead to a showdown. Sometimes this doesn't feel worth it if there is a chance they won't back down and thirty other pupils are going to see you be undermined. This is particularly challenging if you are a teacher with an agreeable temperament who avoids conflict and confrontation.[9] When disciplining a child, I know that I'm incredibly lucky to have the weight and support of the school behind me. If all teachers were empowered to be the authority, if respect for the teacher were the default, then it might be a first step towards whole schools adopting a more consistent approach that supports the teacher, rather than looking for excuses for the pupil's behaviour and then letting them off the hook.

Far from being oppressed, children are empowered by a system which believes in them as individuals who have a capacity to behave well and achieve. It also recognises that these children need boundaries at a time

---

9   Roald Dahl, a fierce critic of authoritarian teachers, gives us a wonderful example of such a teacher: Miss Honey

when their brains are still developing and they might otherwise pursue high-risk behaviours. Not only can Andre see that he has improved, but he has also set his sights higher on what he wants to achieve; the person he wants to be in the future. When Andre opened his GCSE results on the 22nd of August last year, the look on his face was one of delight and astonishment. I have no doubt that, in Year 8, Andre would never have believed he could come so far. There are dozens of children like Andre at Michaela, children whose behaviour and prospects have been transformed thanks to our structures and the high expectations we have of them.

To help them adjust to these expectations, teachers at Michaela constantly narrate the reasons why we give the sanctions and consequences that we do. We also shower pupils with praise when they do something worth praising. Recently I had to give a homework detention to one of my Year 7s. I told her why she had the detention explaining, *"Look Jade, you didn't do your homework and the thirty others in the class did. That means that they've now had all this extra practice that you haven't had! I don't want you to fall behind and not do as well as them so I'm going to give you a detention to remind you that I have really high standards for you and for what you can achieve in my class"*. When Jade did complete her homework to a good standard the following week, I was genuinely thrilled and able to praise her. This is another aspect of teacher authority that people ignore: the authority to praise meaningfully. If everything a child does is wonderful, if your standards for them are low, then not only will they simply meet your low expectations but they also cease to trust your judgement.

Authority at Michaela

Far from being cruel, authority at Michaela protects boys like Oscar, believes the best of boys like Andre and pushes girls like Jade to do their best. The Romantic ideal might encourage us to leave children to their own devices, but this also means that children will receive no guidance as to how to regulate their more disruptive impulses. People are naïve to believe that children, on leaving school, will suddenly be able to flick a switch and behave professionally in the world of university or work. Paraphrasing Aristotle, at Michaela we always say, *"your behaviour becomes your habits and your habits become your character"*. We believe that it is the duty of the teacher to help children form good habits, a duty we share with the child's parents. We want to teach children pro-social behaviour because it is this kind of behaviour – kindness, empathy and resilience – which will allow them to be successful now and later in life. If nobody teaches them, they may never learn.

Sometimes telling a child off is the most compassionate and caring thing you can do because you are helping them progress towards a better future.

2. Does authority stifle children's creativity?

> *"The fact is that given the challenges we face, education doesn't need to be reformed – it needs to be transformed. The key to this transformation is not to standardise education, but to personalise it, to build achievement on discovering the individual talents of each child, to put students in an environment where they want to learn and where they can naturally discover their true passions."* – Ken Robinson (2009, p238)

Ken Robinson's view epitomises the Romantic perspective on education, that each child is brimming with undiscovered talent, but the industrial school system squashes it out of them; creativity is burgeoning everywhere but everywhere it is in chains. Ken Robinson's TED talk is the most viewed and liked talk on the website and it is still a favourite of trainee teachers. The child, PGCE students are taught, should be left to educate themselves away from the interference of societal expectation or constraint.

The idea is wonderfully appealing: images of children playing joyfully in nature and following their instinctive curiosities and passions, away from the harsh gaze of the authoritarian adult. Children do undeniably learn through play and experience as infants and, to a certain extent, they discover the world for themselves. Play and immersion lead to what evolutionary psychologist David Geary has termed 'biologically primary' knowledge, which includes the ability to speak one's mother tongue. The ability to read and write, however, is 'biologically secondary'.[10] This knowledge is culturally extremely useful, but our brains are not hard-wired to acquire it in the same way. Many educationalists are keen to retain the playful world of the infant for as long as possible, wishing that all learning could be 'learning by doing' and 'learning through experience'. Unfortunately, as we now know, this ideological position is ineffective. In the 1980s and 1990s, it led to the disastrous adoption of the whole-word recognition approach to early years literacy, a method based on the notion that children could pick up the skill of reading in the same way that they seemingly effortlessly learn to speak. But the world of the child is limited; not everything can be learned or

---

10 David Didau, *Education isn't natural – that's why it's hard*, viewed 16 April 2018 <https://learningspy.co.uk/psychology/can-learn-evolutionary-psychology/>

discovered and, far from flourishing in the way Robinson describes, children's development is inhibited in this infantilised world.

A friend told me about a CPD[11] session at her school where some science teachers were sharing advice on introducing the topic of electricity. The advice was that before actually telling pupils what an ammeter was or what it measured you should pass the ammeter around the class and they could guess what it was. This may be well-intentioned, but as a species it took us hundreds of thousands of years to discover and use electricity. The effect of passing an unnamed object around the room and being asked to guess what it is simply results in a feeling of helpless ignorance on the part of the child, as it is impossible to work out the answer. This progressive approach disempowers children as it belies the fact that they are no longer operating solely in the world of the child and discovery but crave knowledge of the adult world around them.

The classroom authority

When Jason joined Michaela in Year 7 he couldn't read. Two terms at Michaela improved his literacy levels to the extent that he can now read at a level appropriate for his chronological age. How did he achieve something in six months that had eluded him for six years at primary school? His teachers simply sat him down and taught him, letter by letter, phoneme by phoneme. Aisha is in the same year as Jason. She couldn't do her times tables and didn't want to practise at home. Of course she didn't want to practise: practising something you're not good at is hard! So she got a detention. She didn't practise again. She got a detention again. Eventually, she decided that the detentions weren't worth it. Now, she can do her times tables. Aisha and Jason's future prospects now look so much brighter because their teachers do not leave their pupils to discover inaccessible knowledge for themselves and are not afraid to give them a consequence for their lack of effort. Better to get a detention now than to leave school without a maths or English GCSE in five years' time.

When I started my MFL[12] teacher training, I was advised to encourage my pupils to work out grammar and vocabulary for themselves. But children feel restless and stupid when they cannot progress, and how could any child work

11 Continued Professional Development

12 Modern Foreign Languages

out what the word *nid-de-poule* means? Yes, language acquisition happens seemingly effortlessly to infants when completely immersed in the world of their mother tongue, but not only are we unable to recreate those conditions in a school but we also know that our natural ability to acquire languages starts to decrease from as young as six years old. Furthermore, we may be able to speak and understand language without formal instruction but, as already mentioned, reading and writing will always need to be taught. We would never dream of letting our children learn by doing when it comes to cooking, driving or rewiring a plug. Yet somehow, in the classroom, we leave our common sense at the door. But those same rules must still apply. I *want* the pupils I teach to use French creatively, to be able to form their own sentences and express ideas in French. But they cannot get there unless I teach them fundamental vocabulary and structures. Ken Robinson might say that creativity is as important as literacy but, unfortunately, one must precede the other: *I can't write poetry if I don't know how to write.* Far from squashing creativity, the teacher's authority is vital to allow children to achieve it. (It means pothole, in case you were wondering.)

Michaela does not produce the rows of thoughtless automata that many would have you believe. Once, my colleague was playing his Year 8 form *The Planets Suite* by Holst in form time. Unusually, he got his pupils to guess which planet they were listening to. Because this class had been taught about the Roman gods, they were able to make meaningful guesses saying, *"is this Mars because Mars was the god of war and this sounds very war-like?"* or, *"is this Venus? Venus is the Roman god of love and it has a very romantic sound"*. Had those pupils never learned about these gods then this would have been a pointless guessing game, but because of their background knowledge they were able to feel very clever! The more knowledge you have been given, the more of these links you are able to draw, the more creative you are able to be.

E. D. Hirsch has written extensively about how domain-specific knowledge precedes skill and creativity. He has also shown how, again, it is the most disadvantaged children who suffer the most when the teacher's role moves to being one of a facilitator, rather than the authority on the subject matter. Disadvantaged children arrive at secondary school with smaller vocabularies and less general knowledge than their wealthier peers. If you insist that children work everything out for themselves then wealthy children will far outstrip their poorer counterparts, as they have more knowledge to build upon. Over time the effect is compounded. Disadvantaged children struggle in a system where it is not the prerogative of the teacher to explain and impart knowledge, thereby allowing all children to start on a level playing field. The irony is that we create a new authority when we simply ask children to work things out for themselves – Google.

As much as we would love it to be true, two-year-olds are not all budding Picassos, waiting for the moment the adult's back is turned to produce their own *Guernica*. The Romantic ideal of the child prodigy, much beloved in Western culture, fools us into thinking that ability is something you are born with. Certainly, there may be some element of nature at play, but achievement in any discipline requires an immense amount of training, practice and hard work. Furthermore, the fundamentals must be taught before a child is able to use that knowledge creatively. You have to fill the bucket *before* you can light the fire.[13]

What prevents a teacher at Michaela from becoming a Trunchbull tyrant or a Gradgrindian bore?

While I am advocating more adult authority in our schools, there is clearly a fine line that all teachers are trying to tread: to assert their authority, so as to benefit their pupils' long-term interests, without behaving in a disciplinarian manner that leaves a pupil feeling ignored, unheard or unimportant. Naturally, all teachers have failed to achieve this balance at one time or another, being either too soft on a pupil who required stricter boundaries, or too harsh on an occasion that demanded a more conciliatory approach.

Given the emphasis on adult authority at Michaela, I can see how people might be concerned that Michaela teachers are likely to be too harsh, rather than too permissive. Just as it could be easy for a Michaela teacher to tend towards the authoritarian when it comes to behaviour management, so too might it be tempting for a teacher's lessons at Michaela to become a lecture. But I don't recognise Michaela principles in the criticisms of traditional methods, be they those embodied by Thomas Gradgrind, illustrated in the video to Pink Floyd's 1979 hit *Another Brick in the Wall* or highlighted by our many active detractors on Twitter today. How do we manage this? I think there are three elements of the culture at Michaela that encourage us to achieve a balance between the two, equally undesirable, ends of the teaching spectrum.

---

13 The quotation *"education is not the filling of a pail but the lighting of a fire"*, often attributed to WB Yeats, is popular among teachers.

1. A culture of observations and feedback

At Michaela I am likely to be observed at least once a day. Colleagues give me feedback on my pedagogy, presence, or the way I deal with poor behaviour. If I am being too heavy-handed in the classroom, in the yard or even in the corridor, I can be sure to be given constructive ideas on how to improve. Equally, if my lesson is turning into a lecture, or there is not enough questioning in the lesson, I will receive that feedback.

2. A school-wide emphasis on the importance of relationships

We discuss the importance of relationships constantly and give each other tips and ideas on building positive relationships. Not only do these relationships add to the school's warmth but, contrary to what might be expected, it is also far easier to sanction a pupil with whom you generally have a positive relationship.

3. Narration of consequences

As my example with Jade illustrates, narration of consequences crucially allows pupils to see the purpose in the sanctions they receive and stops them from harbouring resentment when they get a demerit or detention. This is especially important in Year 7 as pupils adjust to the rules and expectations of their new school.

Conclusion: The role of the teacher

> "What she needed was just one person, one wise and sympathetic grown-up who could help her." – Matilda (1988, p164)

The young people in our schools are moving from the world of the child to the world of the adult and it is this tension that makes this time in their lives so exciting and full of possibility yet also so full of anxiety. It seems to me that the so-called progressive approach combines the worst from both worlds. We hold young people back artificially and keep them in the world of the child and discovery, thereby infantalising them. By not offering guidance we ironically make them more dependent on us than they need to be. Simultaneously, we are disappointed when they fail to live up to our adult expectations of their behaviour and do not offer them consequences that would give them the opportunity to improve, to show them that we believe they can do better.

The historical tacit acceptance of the abuse of authority by adults can never be justified and we must always guard against the possibility of an individual in a position of authority becoming a tyrant. But trusting yourself as a benevolent figure of authority is crucial to being successful as a teacher. At Michaela, we believe that it is our duty as adults to give children guidance and to help them grow into successful adults that other people will like and respect. This means teaching them to be kind, considerate and responsible for their actions. It also means teaching them as much as we can about the immensely complex world around them. Failure to assume this responsibility is a disaster for the child, for their peers and does nothing but aggravate a problem which is then left to other members of society and future generations to contend with.

Bibliography

Arendt, H. (1961). *Between Past and Future : Six Exercises in Political Thought.* Retrieved from http://self.gutenberg.org

Robinson, K. (2009). *The Element: How finding your passion changes everything.* New York: Viking Penguin.

Hirsch, E.D. (2016). *Why Knowledge Matters.* Cambridge, Massachusetts: Harvard University Press.

Anon (2017). *The Secret Teacher: Dispatches from the classroom.* London: Guardian Faber Publishing.

Carroll, C. (2010) *On the Edge.* [Kindle edition]. Monday Books. Retrieved from Amazon.com

Dahl, R. (1988) *Matilda.* 2007 edition. London: Puffin.

I Was Wrong About Michaela

Charlie Burkitt
@BurkittCR

By the end of my Teach First placement, there were certain words that made me feel ill when I heard them. 'Engagement', 'restorative', and even 'relationship' all ranked highly on that list. These concepts are often defended by what I had come to see as the damaging and evil educational philosophy of progressivism, which broadly speaking views the child as innately good and adult authority as bad. This was strongly contrasted in my mind with educational traditionalism, which values adult authority, and which I believed was the antidote to every problem I had encountered in my school. The central argument of this chapter is that I was wrong to hold such a strong dichotomy, so please bear with me if that distinction sounds like an unhelpful simplification.

In my defence, I had good reason for developing an allergy to progressive ideals as I had seen them executed so poorly. If a pupil misbehaved in my lesson I had to give them three warnings, all written on the board, before eventually sending them out on the fourth strike. As a behaviour policy this sounds sensible, except for the fact that extremely disruptive behaviour only earned one warning. Of course in a class of thirty this would potentially mean ninety pens being thrown across the room, or being rudely and loudly spoken over ninety times before I was actually able to do anything. For this persistent high level disruption, I was not allowed to set a detention, but instead had to set a five minute restorative conversation in a chaotic room after school in order to 'repair the relationship'.

However, like a popular restaurant, the naughtiest children were fully booked for weeks, so this conversation was rarely completed on the same day. When I eventually managed to get the pupil face to face, the conversation was predictably fruitless. Most children would claim not to know why shouting swear words across the classroom was undesirable, and would then nod earnestly when I explained it to them, before doing exactly the same next lesson. This was of course compounded by the fact that I was still new to teaching and making lots of mistakes that I now cringe to think about, but a quick stroll around the building to listen to the riotous noise emanating from most classrooms was testament to the fact that I was not alone in my experience.

In order to survive in such an environment it becomes necessary to develop friendly relationships with the most disruptive pupils so that they might spare you the worst of their arsenal of poor behaviour. If they see you as one of the 'safe' teachers, they just might sit in their seat for 90% of the lesson, assuming you don't press them to work too hard. A race to the bottom between teachers quickly develops over who can be closest mates with the worst behaved. Supply teachers and new teachers are left floundering in a world where the only currency is how many jokes you've shared with the cool kids. At every transition teachers who have worked at the school long enough to hold some relationship capital have to resort to cajoling and pleading with kids to stop them play fighting in corridors and shepherd them into their lessons.

The pervasive idea across the leadership at the school was that if only teachers would more carefully consider the needs of their learners, and work harder to make their lessons more engaging, then no pupil would ever misbehave again. The idea that children should respect adults and their peers, whether or not they were being sufficiently entertained, was not ever mentioned. The staff at the school were all good people working extremely hard to improve the pupils' lives, but their well-intentioned notions of kindness were having totally counter-productive results. I concluded that progressivism was a purely poisonous influence on education, and that a traditional school was the answer. So I applied to Michaela, where I was sure I would never hear the word 'relationship' again.

Imagine my shock then, when on the first day in September 2018 new staff were emphatically told 'the pupils will not work their hardest for you unless they love you'. My lesson feedback from one of the deputies was all about adding warmth to my face and body language, 'imagine you are on mute' being a very useful trick for this. Walking around the school observing established staff, it became clear that they were all delivering an intimidating mixture of strict old-fashioned teaching and moments of light-hearted banter. Ten minutes in any of our Head of Humanities' lessons is guaranteed to be brimming with quick-fire Dad jokes; 'quit Stalin and answer the question', 'Truman, the opposite of falseman', snuck into the rigorous academic discussions. Across the school pupils can occasionally be spotted wearing crowns, novelty sunglasses, or even marathon medals, perhaps with a big feathery bird pen sat on their desk, as teachers energetically deliver what can only be described as extremely engaging lessons.

Teachers are encouraged to visit our centralised detentions to have restorative conversations with pupils, and it is common to hear whispered explanations of the rules across the otherwise silent hall. Lunch duties are deliberately organised to allow staff to eat with members of their class, and bond over their discussion of the topic for that day. I've seen the impact on my own lessons of playing basketball, table tennis, table football, and (less gracefully) skipping, with various members of my classes. At Michaela, we ask a lot of pupils. They have to pay close attention to every word we say for six lessons, every day of the year. A big part of the reason they do this with such enthusiasm is because we make an effort to know them and show them how much we care.

The key difference is this: in the strong relationships teachers have with pupils at Michaela, authority came first, and everything else was built on that. From the first day in September, all pupils must greet all teachers in the corridor with the same respectful 'good morning miss/sir'. It doesn't matter if the pupil is entering their fifth year at the school, and it is the teacher's fifth hour there. If a rule is broken and a teacher enforces it, the weight of a highly consistently-enforced system will be behind them.

When interacting with adults, pupils know that any rudeness or defiance will result in immediate palpable consequences regardless of that adult's position in the school's hierarchy. Detentions provide an important disincentive when pupils are weighing up the risks and rewards of misbehaving, and it is crucial that staff have the option of using them if necessary. When authority comes first, teachers do not need to lean on their relationships with naughty pupils to ensure they behave sensibly, and so all teachers can ensure they behave sensibly.

With this basic level of respect established automatically, and the calm orderly atmosphere it creates, teachers are then left free to focus their energy on building genuinely strong bonds with pupils. When you are not worried about having your explanation of solving equations interrupted every five seconds by screaming children, it frees up cognitive capacity to deliver the content in a warmer and more expressive way. When you don't go to your break duty exhausted from a day of battling through lessons, it's easy to find the energy to share a joke with pupils and ask them about their weekend. Then when those pupils are at home in the evening and considering how much effort to put into your homework, they will make the right decision because they don't want to disappoint you.

I had previously considered restorative conversations to be a complete waste of time, but at Michaela they are a genuinely useful tool. Why the difference? For a start, our detention hall is peaceful and purposeful, as opposed to noisy and disrupted; it gives a great opportunity to sit down and have a quick chat with a pupil you gave a detention to that day. Next, the strong underlying respect that all pupils have for all adults at the school means that they do not rudely pretend not to understand their detention, as they often did in my experience at previous schools. Instead the time can be used to dig a little deeper into how the pupil can avoid the detention next time. Finally, from boot camp to the end of Year 11 pupils hear from us about the importance of personal responsibility, so they know that they have to own their mistakes to improve – the discussion moves from "it wasn't my fault" to "I can control this and I can do better". This means when the pupil heads home that night, their last interaction with you was a positive one as you warmly discussed how they could do better, thus massively reducing the chance for built up resentment.

Another crucial principle at Michaela that allows relationships to flourish is that civilised behaviour is not viewed only as necessary for an orderly classroom, but good for kids' development. Across education it is common to hear the phrase 'behaviour for learning' when discussing how children should act. This seems innocuous, until you consider that the point of showing pupils how to behave is not just 'for learning', although that is important. A lot of how children conduct themselves at school, both inside and outside the classroom, may not be linked directly to their learning. The phrase 'behaviour for learning' does not capture why pupils shouldn't throw litter on the floor and refuse to pick it up because 'that's the cleaner's job', it doesn't capture why they should speak to a new pupil in the playground if they see them looking lonely. This has the result that schools who see good behaviour as only a means to increased learning do not direct enough energy towards demanding high standards of pupils in all their interactions.

At Michaela we are explicit in our attempts to help children become polite, confident and sociable adults, who can look strangers in the eye and give them a firm handshake. I think of this as 'behaviour for character', as they are the soft skills that provide someone with the sort of character that would make a great first impression at a job interview or a dinner party. They are exactly the sort of skills that are taken for granted in middle-class households, and end up making all the difference in stifling social mobility if not taken seriously. Top notch grades are necessary but not sufficient for the most highly sought-after jobs in the country, and we do children a disservice if we don't prepare them for this fact. In demanding eye contact and smiles when pupils greet us in corridors, in making pupils repeat themselves if they are not loud enough for everyone to hear at family lunch, we are teaching the pupils how to have a positive relationship with others. A relationship has to go in both directions, and if we didn't explicitly show pupils how to interact with us then all our hard work getting to know them over table tennis would be for nothing.

What I got wrong about Michaela is that it is far more moderate than most people realise. There is a lot about progressive education that is bad, and its ideas are genuinely damaging the chances of children all over England. However, there is something in it worth saving that extreme traditionalists (as I was) would be wrong to throw out. Teachers should not be robotic and unemotional with children to the point of oppressive boredom. Strong relationships are a key ingredient in achieving the pupil buy-in that allows a school like Michaela to function so well. Lessons should be engaging, or they will not be able to hold the attention of thirty teenagers for an hour. Teachers should have restorative conversations after setting detentions, so that pupils do not build up resentment.

However, all of these things have to be built on a bedrock of authority or relationships will quickly become the only currency, and one that inflates rapidly to the point of holding no real value. Engagement should never be the aim, but a means to an end, and can be achieved without watering down the academic content. Restorative conversations are only useful if teachers can also set detentions to communicate to the pupil that they can and should do better, and that their actions have consequences. A foundation of authority actually allows teachers to more easily build relationships with all pupils as they don't have to focus all their energy on the ones stopping everyone else from learning. High standards of conduct must be demanded of all pupils in every tiny interaction so that they know how to maintain positive relationships, and not just so that they learn some algebra.

I am now in the unexpected position of being a more progressive teacher than I was when I joined Michaela. I hope not to forget this lesson that there are shades of grey in a debate I had previously thought of as being black and white.

A Vindication of Our Values

Jozef Butterfield
@JozefTeacher

Written on Results Day 2019

In the movies, people drop their drinks when they're caught in a moment of sheer, dumb surprise. It wasn't until today that I realised this could also happen in real life. Looking at the figures for our school's first GCSE results, my grip on my Americano loosened and fell away. Amid splatters of medium roast, waves of emotion flowed through me: pride, joy, relief.

But mostly shock. I knew we were going to do well, but this well? Tears welled up. It's hard not to become invested when you work at Michaela. The time we spend interacting with pupils and the relationships we build are second to none. We have a connection to pupils, some of whom we may never have taught, such that when they opened their results today and felt the pride of their labour, saw their own bright futures lighting up, we could not help but cry with them. This was the pupils' celebration, which we were lucky enough to share with them. But this was also Michaela's vindication.

I joined late. The story — and battles — of Michaela Community School began years ago, beyond the nearly six years we've been open, back to when Katharine Birbalsingh and the other founders struggled to find a local authority that would even allow such a school as ours to exist. In the old days, the naysayers protested outside, shouted at our pupils, some even attempted break-ins. In time, they retreated to Twitter, where the bitterness persisted. They hated our no-excuses behaviour policy, our knowledge-based curriculum, our insistence on didactic teaching. Today, for what seems the first time, silence has fallen in their camp. What can they now say? Here are some of the stand-out statistics from today's results:

(The GCSE grading system has changed in the past few years. 4 is considered a standard pass, 7 is roughly an A, 8 an A*, 9 above an A*.)

- 91% Maths 9-4, 90% English 9-4, 85% 9-4 in both

- 54% of all exams were grades 7-9, versus the national average of 20.8%

- 18% graded as 9, versus the national average of 4.5%

- Subject highlights: 99% 9-4 MFL (Modern Foreign Languages), 98% 9-4 RE (Religious Education), 93% 9-4 Double Science, 100% 8+ Triple Science, 86% EBacc (English Baccalaureate) Entry

- Estimated Progress 8 approximately 1.5

- Nearly 1 in 4 received a 9 in Maths

- Nearly 1 in 3 received a 9 in RE

And this from a non-selective school in tough, disadvantaged inner-city London! Let's break down exactly what these results mean for our pupils.

Some would argue that the most able – say, the top quartile – don't benefit as much from the Michaela system as others. And yet, even for these pupils, we have made an evident, valuable difference. They would certainly pass their GCSEs at other schools, but it is hard to argue they would reach the same heights we've seen here today. Equally, the sky-high standards for homework and revision from Year 7 onwards will pay greater dividends as they go forwards into their A-Levels. After today, their sights are now firmly set on Russell Group universities.

But it is right to say that this isn't where we have been the most transformational. 54% of exams were graded 7-9, meaning many median-ability pupils achieved grades on the high-end that they may have only dreamed of before. And our low-ability pupils went above and beyond predictions. These pupils might have left with just a slew of 1s and 2s had they not attended Michaela.

Others could argue, by moving the goal posts, that 'exams aren't everything'. I entirely agree. I look at pupils opening their results, pupils who were once terrors (and would still be so elsewhere), and the transformation could not be starker. Yes, they feel pride for what they have earned through years of work, but there is also humility, a genuine appreciation for the community that enabled them to achieve all of this: 'Miss, these can't be real!', 'Thank you Ms Birbalsingh. Thank you to all the teachers!' When a pupil realised she had got straight 9s (straight 9s!) across all subjects, others pupils immediately surrounded her with congratulations. No jealousy, just community.

No doubt there were difficult patches, hours of homework, constant high expectations, but looking back the necessity is obvious. These pupils will have opportunities available to them that simply were not there for their own parents – indeed, perhaps not there for their family and friends at other schools. These results represent social mobility at work. This is what changing lives looks like.

So many people today have honoured us with their congratulations for our pupils and our school, from parents, to teachers, to politicians. We hope our Results Day will contribute further evidence to the free schools debate. The Michaela Method works. We and our supporters have known this for some time. To everyone else, it is now indisputable.

Being 'Michaela': Our Ethos

James Sibley

"*You can hardly open a periodical without coming across the statement that what our civilisation needs is more 'drive', or dynamism, or self-sacrifice or creativity... [Yet] we remove the organ and demand the function. We make men without chests and expect of them virtue and enterprise. We laugh at honour and are shocked to find traitors in our midst.*" – C. S. Lewis

As Head of Year 8, I love my year group like I love my football team: they are flawed, frustrating, but mine. Much as I am highly aspirational for their academic futures, my proudest moments have been when people are impressed by their personalities: visitors who find their lunch table conversation refreshing, members of the public who notice our pupils on school trips reading quietly and offering their seats to older members of the public, guests who are impressed with the guide who gives them a tour of the school. I love this because I don't just want my year group to be clever, I want them to be kind.

But why do they behave this way? And why didn't pupils at my old school behave like this? The wonderful behaviour on display at Michaela does not happen by accident. It arises from our commitment to instilling our ethos in each of our pupils.

I therefore open with this quote from C. S. Lewis because there is a gap between our expectations of young people (that they will be self-sacrificial and noble) and our attitude towards actually teaching them about right and wrong (namely, that it isn't our place). If we want our pupils to be kind citizens, we cannot expect this to happen magically. It takes a concerted effort to mould pupils into the sorts of successful and kind young people we want them to be.

Of course, many readers (perhaps even myself at the beginning of my teaching career) might take issue with this. What right does a school have to tell young people to behave in a particular way, without giving them a choice?

As with so many things, experience has shifted my thinking on this question. The first time a pupil you know gets stabbed or beaten up, or a pupil you love drifts towards violence against others, you realise that values are not inevitable or irrelevant. The ideas that surround someone control the decisions they take. It is through our shared values that we learn about truth, morality and acceptable ways to behave.

To care about a community as a teacher is not simply to teach them so that they can improve their economic earning power, but to consider what values will set them up to do what is right for their family and community. This is what C. S. Lewis means when he says you cannot expect the function without the organ. You have to tell pupils about the virtues that are expected of them as a member of a community. For the sake of simplicity, I have broken this down to three core values Michaela takes especially seriously, and have explained how we communicate them to pupils.

Rule 1: Duty to the community, before the self

David is a pupil who is deeply troubled. When criticised he will swear, behave violently, leave the classroom and even storm out of the school – on one occasion to his own quite serious risk. David's explanation of his behaviour is that he felt angry and therefore the situation warranted aggression – this is justification enough for the actions he took. It goes against our instincts to tell David that his behaviour is self-destructive. On the contrary, he may well be told he is special and that he is not to blame for how he behaves. I understand why some teachers may respond in this way. They do not wish to be seen as uncaring to someone whose life may be harder than their own. They may also feel that David is entitled to his anger – what right do we have to police his emotions when we have not gone through what he has experienced? Ultimately, his situation is not his fault, so it seems unfair to punish him for disruptive behaviours – particularly when their source may lie far out of his locus of control.

Whilst it may seem kinder to allow David to continue along this path of destruction, we have to ask ourselves: what are the consequences his actions will inevitably have on him and his classmates in the longer term? When David arrived at Michaela in year 7, aggressive behaviour was the norm for him. He was not able to resolve his frustrations or complaints in any other way. Are we really showing David a kindness by allowing this?

Two problems arise from absolving David of responsibility. Firstly, being told that he is not in control of his actions has entrenched behaviours that will harm him in the long term. Whilst relieving him of any responsibility might be comforting for him in the moment, it pushes the problem further into his future. As an adult, a failure to accept responsibility and act to change one's future can be disastrous.

Secondly, David's behaviour has a broader, perhaps more negative impact on the rest of his class. David's class is filled with sweet kids, and for the most part, they behave beautifully. But David disrupts their lessons frequently. Not only are the majority of his classmates from similarly challenging backgrounds, at significant risk of innumeracy and illiteracy and therefore of having reduced life chances if they don't get the education they deserve, but soon David's behaviour will start to rub off on others. Soon, David will not be the only pupil disrupting their lessons. Tolerating his actions sends a clear message to other pupils: behaving in this way is acceptable. It provides a disincentive for good behaviour, too. Think about it from a child's perspective: what is the point in behaving well when I could do what David does and get away with it? This is how culture works: the goalposts for what is acceptable shift and then become norms. If David does not change, the rest of his class will.

To stop this, we need to handle David differently. Rather than pitying his circumstances, rather than turning a blind eye to his behaviour, we need to be honest. David needs to learn that his emotions are not more important than the rest of the room. An important part of maturing into adulthood is learning that you cannot always have things the way that you want them. At some point, we all have to learn that we are not the centre of the universe. If David is allowed to grow up thinking that his own sense of unfairness or his feeling that his rights have been impinged always comes before others, he will struggle to integrate properly into society. David needs to learn that he is more than an individual: there exists a broader community to which he is inextricably linked. As a member of a community – whether David likes it or not – he is bound to others. He has obligations to them, as they do to him.

Communities rise and fall as one. If one individuals falls, they take the rest of the community down with them. If David falls, the class will follow.

David needs to learn that he is not the centre of the universe, but that he is part of something much bigger than him.

How do you create a sense of community?

Now if I tell David he is letting down the 'team' without any previously developed understanding of the idea, he will simply say he does not care. The only way that he can feel the weight of community is if he has quite a clear idea of what it means.

The idea of community is therefore deeply embedded within the culture of the school. We talk all the time about how we expect high standards from all of our pupils. We tell them that, at Michaela, we are never disrespectful towards our teachers. At Michaela, we greet our teachers politely and we thank them for lessons. At Michaela, we never show off in lessons by refusing to work or behaving foolishly. At Michaela, we always strive to concentrate and stay focused in lessons because we know we are all capable of doing so. Michaela pupils would never fight at the bus stop or swear in public: bringing the school into disrepute is simply unthinkable.

As a Head of Year, I narrate what makes us 'Michaela' all the time. In every assembly, every break time, every lunch time, in every meeting, and in every interaction. It is on the walls of the corridors and in the poetry we learn. It has to be everywhere, because we want our pupils to feel that it is part of our shared community identity.

Because these values form the basis of our school culture, they permeate everything we do. Our values become the norm, nudging our pupils towards an aspirational culture where every pupil strives to be in the best possible habits, and to be completely 'Michaela'. It isn't easy to hold oneself to such high standards all the time but striving to be the very best person you can be is a mark of the highest respect for oneself and one's community. By 'being Michaela', I make myself better, and I also help to make my community better.

The idea of 'being Michaela' is an attempt to create a counter-community to other communities that might tempt them to become worse people. Our kids live in the inner city, surrounded by knife crime, drug dealers and gang warfare. If we do not show them that they belong to our community, they will find somewhere else to belong. Anyone suspicious of the emphasis we place upon community and belonging should look at how any great competitive team in the world operates: it binds its parts into a shared aspiration and has the belief it can be better than the rest. We are no different and what we are trying to offer is a culture and an identity that pupils can belong to, and which raises their aspirations.

Our pupils belong to the Michaela community, but as a Head of Year, I also believe in a community for my own year group. I tell all 120 of them at break, lunch and in weekly assemblies that as well as being in the best school in London, I also think we are going to be the best year group it has ever produced. I mean it too. This creates a sense of belonging and shared experience that is meaningful. We are different: we have our own idioms, our own anecdotes, our own star sports players, our own characters and in-jokes. When Year 8 have an excellent day I genuinely feel something pretty close to watching Scotland win at football (ecstasy and profound surprise).

Form groups should have their own traditions and inside jokes. Some class traditions are frankly ridiculous. If 8 Poseidon, for example, have had a particularly excellent week, we sometimes play a game called 'Africa': this is where pupils have to label an entire map of Africa in exactly four and a half minutes (to the tune of Toto's 1982 classic, *Africa* - which helpfully lasts exactly four and a half minutes). Granted, the pupils are falling about laughing during the impassioned chorus of that fine song (all while remaining brutally competitive about labelling all 54 countries in time) but they also understand that this silliness is part of the reward for working well all week and being part of a team. The consequence is that these pupils identify as a member of that tutor group as a distinct experience from the other tutor groups: they know that being in 8 Poseidon is different from being in any other class. They belong to a community that means something to them.

By building communities at the tutor group, year group and school level, pupils like David quickly learn that they are not islands. When I have to address his behaviour, I can appeal to an identity he understands, and I can help him to see the impact of his behaviour on others. Over time, the bond pupils build with their communities deter them from misbehaving. They don't want to 'let the team down' or be the missing link. They want to belong, and if the culture among the community is to behave, then he is the odd one out if he misbehaves.

Community matters. It is a force for profound good because it is a weight against the voice in all our heads that tells us, our feelings matter more. It is the foundation of feeling obligation.

Rule 2: Personal responsibility, not excuses

At this point I am now going to introduce Sonia. She is a free-school-meals pupil from a historically highly underperforming demographic group, from an extremely large family. She has moved very frequently but currently lives in one of the most deprived areas of London. She is constantly late, does not do homework and is a consistent behavioural concern for many of her teachers. Sonia has family members who have spent time in prison. For a lot of teachers, kids like Sonia are why they became a teacher.

There are many reasons why well-meaning teachers might choose to lower their standards for Sonia. Once a teacher knows Sonia well, they can see why her homework and behaviour is not of a high standard. Why punish her for what are essentially the symptoms of her poverty?

It is certainly true that Sonia is more likely to be late than many other pupils. Her parents do not wake her up. But letting Sonia off for her lateness creates several problems:

1. Sonia has always turned up late to things and always will unless someone changes it.

2. Sonia cannot afford to miss lessons, or even parts of lessons if she is going to compete. She is already behind.

3. As we saw with David, the impact of one child's behaviour on the culture of her class should not be underestimated. If Sonia is allowed to be late, others will soon follow suit.

The same principle applies to behaviour. Sonia does not know how to behave, and her last chance is that Michaela creates a culture, shaping her into something that is more employable and more respectful. If her behaviour does not change then she is headed for disaster. But it is worse than that. By letting Sonia behave a certain way, it is impossible to isolate this contagion and prevent other pupils imitating this conduct. Culture defines how rules and institutions are understood and immediately the idea that certain actions are unacceptable has been broken. Defiance will become gradually more permissible across the board.

Even if Sonia manages to get good grades, fast forward five years and this 'kindness' at lowering standards could destroy her life chances. The story that keeps me up at night is of a young black boy from a difficult area on an internship in the Civil Service. He was in the same office as a friend of mine, herself an ethnic minority graduate who feels deeply frustrated at how white independent school candidates make up such a large body of the Civil Service. She took him under her wing and tried her best to spend as much time with this boy as she could. He turned up late because the tube was delayed. He got his phone out in meetings in front of senior Civil Servants to check his Instagram page. He had his shirt untucked and chewed gum. He didn't even thank her for spending hours of her day to try and find him different tasks to do which could give him a chance to impress. He will not get a job there and discrimination has nothing to do with it. He never learned how to behave and now it is too late. The truth is that a failure to teach and enforce social norms prevents the poorest from taking personal responsibility and keeps them in poverty.

Personal responsibility: how is it encouraged?

Personal responsibility, in its simplest form, means that you should focus on what you are in control of and take responsibility for it. There will always be problems that you cannot control and it can be tempting to obsess over the existence of unfairness (race, class, family, religion, wealth – the list is long). Personal responsibility is hard because it involves saying that the only way to improve yourself is by taking control of the things you can influence. To encourage this, all teachers have the idea as a fundamental part of their vocabulary and thinking when they speak with pupils. Below are daily and mundane examples:

A. Personal responsibility narration over minor mistakes	
Pupil problem	Narration
Late to school because bus was delayed	"This is why you have to leave extra early, just in case there's a problem like this. That's what Charlie and James did, they live on your street too, and they were here right on the bell. Imagine if you had an interview for that dream job that could help you look after your family and you were late because you weren't in the habit of leaving early! You've got to take responsibility, you will sit a detention after school."

No pencil	"Here is me dreaming that you were going to be a top scientist one day, Sam, and you don't even have your pencil! How are you going to get a job at NASA if you turned up for interview without your pencil? No worries – learn your lesson, move on. You will sit a detention after school."
Homework not done because of busy schedule	"Woah, hold on Jonny, this isn't good enough. I spent hours planning your lessons on this topic last week and an hour making that homework so that you can be at the top of your game. Mike, Andy, Sarah – they've all done extra work because they are pushing themselves. They haven't made excuses, they have taken responsibility. It has to be better. You will sit a detention after school."

There will be many teachers who have noticed all three narrations on personal responsibility ended with a detention and think to themselves: why does this have to be the way that these values are encouraged? Can't you just persuade them?

Sometimes getting a detention is a good thing. As someone who received many in school, I should know. I will never forget Ms Holdsworth, fierce Ayrshire vowels ringing in my ears, telling me: "James, I like you but on a deep and fundamental level you need to get over yourself. This homework is you giving 50% effort and we both know it. I'm giving you a detention because I haven't yet given up on you." That woman was hard as hell on me and she was a saint. My mother still speaks of her reverentially as being partially responsible for the fact I don't live in her attic.

Kids are short-term in their thinking and that is not their fault. They do not have the developed sense of long-term gratification that is required to fully understand why organisation, timekeeping and professionalism are so important. It is our job to impart to them the simple rule: if you get yourself organised, things are generally fine, if you are not, the world will punish you for it. I return again to the Civil Service intern – it would have been an act of kindness if he had been given more detentions at school for unprofessionalism, because he could have had a great job opportunity had his teachers done so.

Giving out detentions isn't the full story, however. There are many things that we do that encourage personal responsibility. The bulk of it is through praise for when pupils do show personal responsibility. Below are a few examples of things that a visitor might hear one of our teachers say to reinforce 'personal responsibility' in their classroom:

B. Personal responsibility narration – praise	
"Right 8P, I enjoyed marking your homework last night and I'll give you feedback in a moment. Before I do, I wanted to talk about something. Myles failed his quiz last week and was sat in detention on Friday for it. You know why I'm happy today? He has gone away and worked at it and his homework this week was excellent. I knew he had it in him!"	Part of this narration is for Myles – he made a mistake last week, but he put it right this week. He needs to hear that this is a good start and he will be rewarded in school and life for this attitude. The other part of this narration is for everyone else. They need to see that taking responsibility for your mistakes is part of how redemption works in the school. It needs to become aspirational.
"Iain, I'm upset that we've found ourselves in this situation again where you have been talking in lessons. It's a silly detention for a boy as smart as you to get. You see why Miss was disappointed with you don't you? Good. 12 months ago, you would have lost your temper and I'm really proud of how far you have come since then."	This is narrating to Iain that even when he is in trouble, the fact he accepts wrong doing is noticed as a positive and is seen as a redeeming feature of his mistakes. He needs to always feel it is better to own up and keep calm than it is to lose his cool. This narration does not make sense for pupils who are already pretty well behaved – it is for someone who is improving but still making mistakes. For this reason it would not be done publicly, like the last one, because this could introduce the idea that Iain is worthy of praise just because he did not lose his temper.

"Morning year 8, I'm really happy that I'm getting so much good news about Simon this week from his teachers. Can I be honest? Last term I was livid that he was letting himself down with his behaviour. Credit where it is due, he promised he would bounce back and he has done this term – good man, keep it up."	This is part of the constant narration of 'bouncing back'. Pupils always need to have an option to change and be better otherwise they will reject the entire value system and just become resentful. This is why in the earlier narration on Myles I gave very clear instructions about what he needed to do to 'respond' the right way to his mistakes. If he does this, I can then tell him (and others) he is bouncing back and I am proud of him.

One of the best pieces of advice I have found in teaching is to catch them being good. My phone will have around 10 WhatsApp messages per day from teachers with positive small anecdotes to pass on to me (we even have a dedicated Year 8 group to share anecdotes so that all tutors can praise pupils in their forms appropriately). This is the bread and butter for whenever I speak to my year group, and for my tutors when they speak to their form. We need to show that we see them at their best, as well as their worst. Personal responsibility is about encouraging pupils to see where they have choices and showing them that working hard is the redemptive choice. We reward these actions because we recognise that personal responsibility is hard and most people struggle to genuinely face up to where they are responsible for something going wrong.

Very quickly the excuses stop. In my old school, I would regularly have conversations with pupils about how they did not do their homework because they have football practice and then had too many subjects to do. This is extremely rare at Michaela. This is because they get it very quickly. If they focus on the choices that they do have rather than those they do not, on a deep level they will be more socially mobile and fundamentally happier people. This is true in every sense. I want Sonia to wake up early for a job interview because that way she can be on time even if the tube is delayed. I want my super academic pupils to go to Oxford and, when they hear the insecurity-inducing expensive accents, not to simply conclude this place isn't for girls from Neasden. I want them to think that the only real question is: what can I do to get better? This is personal responsibility and it is the only way these kids can have freedom.

Rule 3: Gratitude and humility, not entitlement

Christopher is a Year 11 pupil and so has not yet entered the world of work. His parents are nice people and drive him to football practice every day. Before he and his friends get the bus home they spend considerable time outside school talking loudly about their aspirations. So far, so good.

The problem is that talking to Christopher and his friends reveals some large popular misconceptions about the job market. One of them, who is struggling to pass GCSE English, explains that he knows he doesn't need it because he is going to become a 'business man', not a librarian. Another knows that his upcoming exams are null and void anyway as he is training with a League Two Football Club. Two more of his friends know someone who was at school with Christopher's brother who now records drill music and has an enormous following in the local community. They are all extremely aspirational in the purely material sense and all of them are aware that a teacher's salary "is about 30K – it is nothing". They are fairly convinced that they are destined for greater things. After results day, I spoke to one pupil privately about my cousin being a paramedic and the possibility to do this kind of job with some resits and hard work, but the answer was still clear: 'No way, sir, I'm better than that kind of crap job. I'm going to be a YouTuber.'

Christopher was a pupil at my previous school, but there are definitely pupils at Michaela who could fit this description. The culture that produces Christopher is too large to be resisted entirely. It is everywhere. To take some key examples for Christopher:

- Footballers: they will generally be very rich, good looking and display a predictable sense of Me vs. The World, go-out-and-seize-your-dreams bravado. They will either have no reference to hard work in school or may refer to how their teachers at school 'just didn't get it'.

- Rappers: for all his well-meaning comments on encouraging aspiration in young black teenagers, even individuals like Stormzy reinforce a lot of negatives.
  a. He explicitly suggests there is a 'system' working against inner-city kids (which begs the question, why work hard in that system?)
  b. He is very clear about his attitude to violence in order to get respect. Despite the odd incongruous aside reference to his Christianity, most pupils mysteriously seem to have inferred non-Biblical conclusions

from the songs 'Shut up' and 'Too Big for Your Boots'. He is cool because he is tough, good looking and respected.

- Local gangs: when there are older boys from other schools, wearing designer track suits with their hoods up, whose power and influence comes from how intimidating they are, pupils invariably become drawn to that. The idea that you don't need to work hard, the system is rigged and there's a tougher and cooler way out is extremely seductive.

The reality is that in Christopher's life, very little is reinforcing the value of humility or gratitude and quite a lot is pushing him towards a form of alpha male entitlement: few of the films he watches on Netflix involve a lazy and not tremendously academic teenager who realised that GCSEs matter and then studied hard, did his homework, got a job and then took his nice mother on holiday. A lot involve a guy who 'makes it big' from rags to riches, usually without GCSE English Literature and after swinging a few punches at some point. Rather than learning the importance of humility and gratitude, Christopher learns that he is special, that the world owes him something, and that hard work is beneath him.

The consequences of this rejection of hard work are profound for kids like Christopher. The idea that certain things are beneath pupils is everywhere. Why take care of your school books when education is a waste of time? Why leave the cafeteria tidy after lunch, when it is someone else's job to clean it up for them? Why say thank you to teachers, parents, or anyone else who helps them, if their success is entirely down to their own unique talent, and in no way related to the contributions made by others?

Kids are not born grateful or humble. This is not their fault: they simply do not realise the impact of their actions on others. They never see the cleaner picking up their rubbish, nor do they realise that the cleaner's day has been made harder and longer as a result of these avoidable small acts of selfishness and entitlement. Pupils do not automatically empathise with others because, like our aspirational YouTuber, they believe they are better than that. Without humility, pupils gear their world around status, wealth and notions of relative superiority. If these are the things you value most, there is simply no reason to value the cleaner's efforts.

To counter this, pupils need to be taught how to be grateful. Gratitude is not something that develops automatically. I hope some of them do end up rich and famous – but I also hope that they learn to have the humility to see that even if they are particularly talented, they are extremely lucky. I hope they learn to be grateful to have had good parents, or good teachers or great colleagues or a brilliant manager. I hope they learn to be grateful for the opportunities that came their way, and the people who helped them on their road to success.

If they lack this humility, there is little incentive to give something back or to avoid looking down on others. Humility brings gratitude, which in turn fosters a greater respect for others, and a deeper satisfaction with one's lot. Teaching gratitude explicitly is about helping our kids feel happy in a world of pure materialism, a world that places value on having more than others. Constant striving for more is a deeply unsatisfying approach to life. By teaching our pupils to be grateful, we guide them to lead more gratifying lives. Humility and gratitude are essential components in living a happy, satisfying life.

How can a school encourage gratitude?

If someone does not feel gratitude, you cannot tell them to feel it. And if a school tells pupils to feel gratitude, there is a risk that pupils will learn to sound grateful in order to receive praise.

What we can teach them is to spot where someone else has done something for them. The best analogy I can think of is that you cannot make someone love music, but you can teach them the scales, show them different genres, explain to them different parts of different songs and unpack where you and many others have seen beauty in that music. Some people still might not love music but quite a lot will. In fact, once you start to enjoy music you feel yourself reaching for patterns even as you listen. I think learning to become more grateful works much the same way.

One of the weirdest (but wonderful) aspects of Michaela lunch-time is 'appreciations'. This is when, in the final four minutes of lunch, pupils will all raise their hands and any chosen will stand up and say an 'appreciation' (essentially a thank you) to someone they are grateful for:

> "I would like to give an appreciation to Mr Lomas for giving us a lesson on the Second Barons' War, where we learned about Simon de Montfort's defeat at the Battle of Evesham."

This is excellent for improving public speaking because every pupil will at some point speak in front of 180 others in a room and, because it happens every day, it becomes quite normal. Our final lunch before schools closed because of coronavirus will always stay with me: Year 11s who were leaving the school felt comfortable standing up in front of one hundred people and speaking from the heart about why they were grateful for the last five years. It was moving because it was sincere. However, more important is the preparation. For five minutes every single day the pupils will be preparing their own appreciations and so will talk about what they could be grateful for that day. This can actually produce some heartfelt reflections – appreciations for teachers who have made a deep impact on a pupil over a term, appreciations for parents who came to the country as immigrants so that their children could have better lives in Britain, appreciations for family members who have cared for a pupil over the years and are now ill. As soon as you enter into these topics, there is genuinely fertile ground for quite profound conversations of what humans should value.

Gratitude is also worked into the culture of the school through the writing of postcards. All teachers write at least one postcard for each class per week, choosing a pupil who has worked particularly well or shown real improvement. All pupils will also write postcards at least once a term, with time set aside on the final day for them to write to teachers. On this occasion, they are free to write to whichever teachers they want and about whatever they want. What postcards do is make that quite lovely moment far more regular and it helps remind you that often even the toughest classes do understand what their teachers do for them. As pupils become more and more used to the idea of showing gratitude, the things they feel grateful for also become more nuanced and meaningful. On a more granular level, understanding of gratitude is integrated throughout the language of daily routines.

A. Language of gratitude in daily school narrations	
Situation	Narration
Break or lunch (after pupils have had food)	"Right ladies and gents, before we line up for lessons I'm just taking a look at the floor. The food is delicious but there's crumbs all over that floor. Let's not be ungrateful, if we leave the floor like this the cleaners will have to stay later and so see their family half an hour later – that isn't right. When I say go, we have 2 minutes to make sure this is spotless... GO!"
Homework feedback	"Afternoon team, I'm going to give you your homework feedback. Now... I spent 3 hours marking your essays... And there's a lot we're getting right... But we know our aim isn't just to be decent, it is to compete with the best. So you need to respect that I am giving everything I have got to give you the advice to get you top grades. I need to feel you are taking down every piece of feedback or it's like you're throwing that back in my face."

I am slightly embarrassed to walk with my grandmother down littered streets with chewing gum polka-dots and beer cans strewn across the pavement. This is because they didn't used to be like this and we both know this. I want Michaela pupils to feel the same disgust she does and have the humility to spot that a thing like that shows a profound lack of gratitude and respect. I need them to see through the culture that makes that permissible.

Conclusion: but haven't you missed the point?

Many years ago I may have argued that surely much of this thinking on ethos misses the point, and perhaps a similar thought may have occurred to others: the cultural breakdown that keeps poor kids poor and ruins lives is because of poverty, plain and simple, and talking about ethos doesn't change a lack of bread on the table. Christopher is the way he is because of the poverty he has grown up in, Sonia is the way she is because her family has so much less than others, David is the way he is because he has not had the resources and support that more privileged individuals have had. Educational inequality comes from a combination of private wealth allowing the best to pull away while poverty anchors many of the rest to the bottom.

For this reason, I thought it might be helpful to close by addressing this point directly. Teachers who believe in the Michaela way of personal responsibility are not saying they do not think poverty is relevant, they are saying the opposite. It is *more important* for the poor pupil from Harlesden to take responsibility than it is for the pupil from Hampstead precisely because they start so much further behind. If they let excuses lower their standards they won't ever catch up. If you're not born with the advantages of a good neighbourhood and well-connected parents, real freedom isn't something that you can be given, it's something you have to earn. It may not be fair and I don't like that either, but it's the truth. The role of a teacher is to see that a pupil has started at a disadvantage and guide them towards the only way out of that. Our pupils have to hear that it is damn tough but they are going to be damn tough as well. They will do it because they are part of a team that takes responsibility, even when it is difficult, especially when it is difficult.

The Culture of Gratitude

Iona Thompson

Lunchtime appreciations are still, for me, one of the most striking parts of Michaela. If you are lucky enough to be sat in our lower-school lunch you will witness one of our bright-eyed and bushy-tailed Year 7s boom appreciations for their teachers, peers, parents or guests. You will often see other pupils' heads nodding in enthusiastic agreement. Guests often write to the school, after their visit, to tell us that it is an experience that will stay with them for life.

Why do our lunchtime appreciations strike such a chord with our guests? It could be because teenagers being so generously and sincerely appreciative of those around them is a pretty rare sight.

Society has become used to the image of the surly, self-centered teenager who believes the whole world is against them. Teachers have been particularly exposed to this and have simply come to accept it. Most teachers have experienced lessons, which they have spent hours planning, routinely derailed by the whims of a handful of pupils in the class. They will have had that feeling of frustration when, after explaining to a class that they have have spent hours marking their essays, they are met with the obnoxious reply 'But isn't that your job Miss?'. At the end of the lesson, thirty pupils pile out of the classroom with the majority not even giving the teacher a glance of acknowledgement.

But that doesn't happen at Michaela. Some teachers elsewhere try to take on the culture of ingratitude in their schools, but will often be left more frustrated as a result. Demanding that a particularly surly pupil say 'thank you' after a lesson would most likely be a recipe for disaster.

After joining Michaela, as a Humanities teacher, I realised that it did not have to be this way. Having entered a culture where ingratitude is not accepted, standards, for both myself and my pupils, have been raised.

Like all teachers at Michaela, I believe that pupils have a duty to be grateful to their teachers for the gift of their education. But, to make this statement into more than an idealistic fantasy, we have a battle on our hands. In this chapter I will explain, first, why we think it is a battle worth fighting and, second, the mechanisms we use to combat the culture of ingratitude.

Why should we expect gratitude from the pupils we teach?

1. At Michaela, we believe that being grateful is in itself the right mindset to have (whatever the instrumental benefits, which I'll explain later). However bad life gets, there is always something or someone to be grateful for. Despite how self-sufficient and independent we think we are, there will always be others we rely on: as John Donne says 'No man is an island'.

2. People who are more grateful tend to be happier. This is because they notice all the little things which make their life better. By doing this on a daily basis your view of the world changes. It is like putting on rose-tinted glasses. The world is no longer against you, and instead you realise that there is a community of people around you who you are incredibly lucky to have. On a daily basis at Michaela, our pupils are forced to step outside of their natural self-centered state to see and register their huge support network. Despite the difficulties they may be facing in their lives outside of school, we remind them that there is always something or someone to be grateful for. This, in turn, will make them happier people. The pupils' gratitude partly explains why guests often comment that they all seem so happy to be at school.

3. Gratitude is a hugely motivating force. If you recognise people you are grateful for, you feel a strong sense of duty to repay them. This creates a cycle of reciprocity in which people want to help others. So often at Michaela, people are willing to help each other at a drop of a hat. An email asking for someone to cover a detention duty on a Friday after school will be met with multiple, instantaneous offers of help from staff. Even the busiest members of staff will give up their time to talk through their feedback from a lesson observation. This is because we are all driven by the force of gratitude.

The same cycle of reciprocity takes place in the relationships between pupils and staff. The pupils feel grateful for their teachers so they want to work hard for them, to show their gratitude. After receiving an appreciation at lunchtime or having every pupil leave your class saying 'Thank you, Miss' you go on to the rest of your day with a real spring in your step. Teachers feel grateful to teach pupils who recognise their hard work. It makes us work harder and teach with more enthusiasm.

How do we teach gratitude?

Like everything at Michaela, narration is critical in developing the right culture. From their first day in Year 7, all Michaela pupils will be taught about the importance of gratitude. Every Michaela teacher becomes clever at slipping in small gratitude-related narrations into their daily interactions with the pupils. These narrations aim to imbue pupils with a sense that they are incredibly lucky to be at Michaela. Here are some examples of how we try to do this:

◆ We expect every pupil to say thank you to their teachers as they leave their lessons and after they leave detention. Gone are the days when pupils would rush out of my classroom without a glance, with only the particularly polite pupils saying thank you.

◆ Form tutors and Heads of Years will often remind pupils who receive behavior or homework detentions during the day that they are so lucky to be at a school which cares enough about them to hold them to such high standards. This narration can have an incredibly powerful effect. I am still amazed when pupils give genuine appreciations to teachers for giving them detentions so that they can learn from their mistakes.

◆ Teachers explicitly tell pupils how many hours they and other teachers have spent creating booklets, marking essays and planning lessons. I have to admit, at first, I felt slightly uncomfortable doing this, fearing, from previous experience, that I would be reminded that 'this was my job'. However, I quickly realised that unless you tell pupils how hard you and other teachers are working for them, they will take you, and your effort, for granted.

◆ We reprimand pupils for ingratitude. For example, if a pupil moans about getting homework or picks at their lunch, we will remind them of their good fortune. We tell pupils that is it bad to show ingratitude, whilst always reminding them of the many things for which they can be grateful, and all the benefits which gratitude brings.

◆ Pupils are reminded that there are lots of people who work incredibly hard behind the scenes to make the school run so well. We remind them about these 'unsung heroes' whose hard work can easily go unnoticed. Pupils are encouraged to say thank you to the office staff and caretaker when they see them around school and write postcards to them at the end of term. These acts are all part of making them aware that there is whole community of people supporting their education.

I can imagine some of you reading this and thinking, 'isn't this continual narration slightly excessive?' Is it *really* necessary to tell the pupils throughout the day what they should be grateful for? My reply to this would be a whole-hearted 'YES!' We take a very realistic view of teenagers. Lovable as they are, they are also self-centered. To get our pupils out of their bad habits of ingratitude is a mammoth task which inevitably *does* require constant narration.

Earlier this year, I was reminded of why it is imperative to narrate the importance of gratitude. A group of Michaela teachers took some pupils to a concert in the city on a Friday evening; at the end of the trip only a handful of pupils said thank you. Before the trip we had taken it for granted that all of the pupils would be appreciative as that is something they're in the habit of expressing at school. We therefore did not even think about reminding the pupils beforehand. It showed us that without the continual narration and reminders that they get at school, some of our pupils would quickly return to their old bad habits.

With any habit, one has to teach it over and over until children internalise it. Eventually, it just becomes who they are. We all say please and thank you as adults because someone once insisted on us saying it and continually reminded us to do it. That habit is genuine and long-lasting, and different children will take different amounts of time for it to become part of who they are.

When Michaela teachers receive heartfelt postcards like some of the ones below, we can feel pleased that our continual narration is having an impact. Michaela allows teenagers to get out of their self-centered rut, to truly flourish into grateful and, ultimately, happier people.

NAME: Ms. Thompson ***

TUTOR GROUP: 9D

Merry Xmas!

Thank you for everything, from ever since I stepped into Michaela. You know when I'm down or happy and when I do my best work. You always push me further and beyond so that I can do best at school.

NAME: Ms Cheng

TUTOR GROUP:

I just want to appreciate all the effort and time you unconditionally dedicate to 10Zeus and our future success. You've pushed us to try harder every time we trip up such as quiz jails, so that we can become better. Thank you for also being realistic with our options so that we know what we most do to get the best possible GCSE results.
Yours sincerely

NAME: Mr Kendall

TUTOR GROUP:

Thank you so much for always putting so much effort into helping me catch up in maths. Your hard work is definitely appreciated. You're honestly such an amazing teacher and the effort you put into our lessons and outside our lessons is unmatched.
Thank you!
Enjoy your well deserved break.

NAME: Miss Jones

TUTOR GROUP: 11 Zeus.

Thank you for the past 3 years. These long years spent with you as our form teacher and as our maths teacher I just wanted to say thank you. It's very difficult for me to sum up all of what you have done for us in the short amount of time I have to write this but, trust me your presence still remains within 11Z (even if more than half the class weren't here)

NAME: Ms Brierly

TUTOR GROUP: Legend

Thank you for trusting me with the merits and for continuously building trust with me. You are such an important adult in my life, miss. Keep doing what your doing, smosh french Evidemment! because your such an inspiration and somebody who has taught me to control my reactions, you're a legend. I hope I've made you smile whilst your reading this.

NAME: Ms Gazi

TUTOR GROUP: 10D's maths teacher.

Merry Christmas, Ms Gazi!

You always know what to say, Ms Gazi! you say one thing that makes us smile and laugh, one thing that break awkward silences, and one things that motivate us to become better mathematicians and people ☺ The faith that you have in us is what inspires us to become better and work harder; we want to make you proud ☺ Have an incredible Christmas and new year, Ms Gazi. ☺ Thank you for every everything you have done for us.

Here are some fruit and vegetables to enjoy!

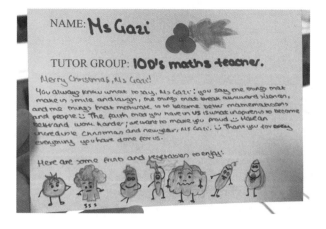

The Transformative Power of Values

Pritesh Raichura
@Mr_Raichura

School Culture

I grew up in the London Borough of Brent, just like most of our pupils at Michaela. Like any inner-city borough, Brent has its fair share of problems: gangs, drugs and crime. Underlying these issues is a poverty of aspiration and a lack of belonging. For pupils who live here, success comes from rejecting these negative influences and focusing on higher goals: becoming well-educated and aspiring to contribute to society. At Michaela, we believe that schools have a responsibility to create such strong positive influences on our pupils that they are able to overcome any obstacles that may come their way. The only way schools can achieve this is by focusing on the influence within their locus of control: cultivating an unshakeably powerful school culture.

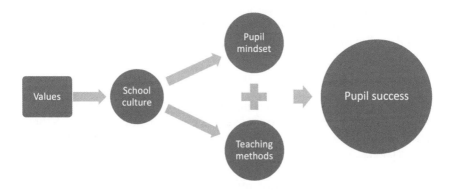

In this chapter, I explain the three values that underlie Michaela's powerful school culture: personal responsibility, duty, and a belief in authority. Every decision we make in the school can be traced back to one of these values. The outcomes of these decisions contribute to our culture in three ways. Pushing personal responsibility empowers our pupils to become *masters of their fates* and *captains of their souls*. The value of duty eradicates complacency and builds the discipline necessary to succeed. Finally, a belief in authority allows teachers to take charge and impart the knowledge of their subjects and the habits for success.

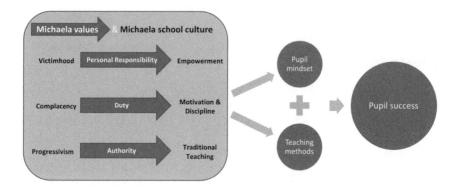

Personal Responsibility: Victimhood vs Empowerment

When Jacob didn't hand in his science homework, his teacher gave him a detention to sit after school. When the teacher asked him what had happened, he replied with a sullen look, 'But it wasn't my fault, sir. My cousins came over and I didn't get time to do it'.

In the scenario above Jacob blames his cousins. Here is the problem: Jacob has chosen to give away all of his power. Although he may not have chosen to invite his cousins over, he did choose to prioritise spending time with them *instead* of doing his homework first. It is important to recognise that Jacob made a choice.

In his excuse to his teacher Jacob refuses to take responsibility for failing to complete his homework. This is an entirely human and natural response. Taking responsibility is hard. It means recognising that you could have done something differently. It means accepting that the consequences you are now facing are linked to your past actions. It is far easier to blame someone or something else for these consequences because this makes your fate inevitable. It leaves no room for regret or reflection because there is no action to regret or reflect upon that could have influenced the outcome.

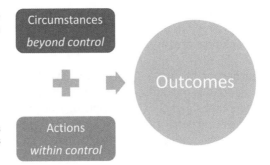

A belief that circumstances largely dictate outcomes encourages excuse making.

A belief that one's own actions largely dictate outcomes encourages taking personal responsibility.

If we can teach pupils to recognise and focus on the actions they can control to influence outcomes, rather than circumstances they cannot, we empower them. How do Michaela teachers teach personal responsibility? There are three main ways: our behaviour system; the support we offer to help pupils meet expectations; and stories about people succeeding despite facing difficult circumstances.

Firstly, we encourage pupils to reflect on their actions every time they fail to meet expected outcomes. We ask our pupils to seek out the excuses they make, and recognise that not doing homework, being late, or not bothering to put effort into lessons are all outcomes that can be traced back to a choice they had control over. For the pupil, the key question at the end is: how can you choose the path that results in better outcomes next time?

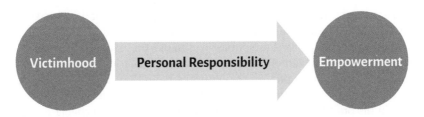

If we teach our pupils to recognise that the choices they make are within their sphere of control, we empower them to make better choices in the future: this is the power of personal responsibility. It transforms you from a helpless victim of your circumstances to a person with the agency to control the outcomes of your life. It is easy to be a victim: you get to complain about things, abdicate your responsibility, and avoid the feeling of regret that comes with knowing you could have altered the outcome had you made different choices. It is far harder to admit that you could have acted differently. The right choices are often the hardest ones to make.

Teachers at Michaela explicitly narrate this with every behaviour we praise or sanction, including: completing homework on time, bringing correct equipment to school every single day, revising for weekly subject knowledge quizzes, and behaviour in lessons. Our entire behaviour system is based on the premise that pupils control their actions. Consequently, when pupils make the right choices, the consequences are positive; wrong choices are sanctioned.

Secondly, we never thrust responsibility onto pupils without also offering the correct support — otherwise it would be unfair to sanction pupils. For example, our equipment shop is open every day before school to allow pupils to replace items they have lost or broken. We stream our pupils so that pupils of similar aptitudes have their lessons together, allowing teachers to set the pace of instruction and adjust the difficulty of homework to a suitable level. We regularly remind our pupils of the various school rules to ensure they are understood with clarity. The idea of personal responsibility is discussed at every possible opportunity.

Thirdly, our assemblies are filled with stories about people who have overcome barriers to succeed against the odds. The core of our message is always the same: hard work and taking responsibility for failure triumph over a mentality of 'it is out of my hands, and there is nothing I can do about it'.

Teachers might find these ideas hardest to apply to pupils with special educational needs or to pupils with a difficult home life. Unfortunately, it is too common for the adults in these pupils' lives to use these factors as excuses for the pupils' underachievement. This results in adults lowering their standards for these underachieving pupils, which only exacerbates the problem. For example, one of our pupils diagnosed with ADHD was regularly forgiven for losing focus in his primary school. He fell behind as a result. At Michaela however, teachers would never shy away from asking him questions and checking he was following explanations and instructions. He flourished at Michaela, making rapid progress as he was suddenly supported to fulfil his potential.

How liberating it must be, for a pupil who has lived with a label that led to adults expecting less of them, to suddenly be shown they have the opportunity to succeed! Teaching them about personal responsibility gives them the power to improve what they have been told is beyond their control to change. Of course, there are some difficulties that a change in mindset cannot overcome. In such cases, giving pupils specialised support is vital. But we have found that a significant number of pupils who lack the self-belief that their success can match other pupils' have transformed when we put the onus on them. These success stories illustrate the power of personal responsibility. That our pupils do not see themselves as victims, and take responsibility instead of making excuses, is an aspect of Michaela schooling that our exam results cannot measure.

Duty: Complacency vs Motivation & Discipline

Humans have evolved to take shortcuts. It is easier to watch a television show for an hour than do an hour of homework. It takes less effort to browse Instagram than it does to get stuck into a new novel, especially for a reluctant reader. How can we influence our pupils to build their motivation and develop their self-discipline so that they make better choices instead of easier ones? The idea of doing one's duty can provide answers. Duty is the sense of obligation one feels to do the right thing. It is acting not for personal gain, but for the benefit of others. It is best defined through the examples that follow.

We explicitly teach pupils about the idea of duty in order to help them become kinder. Why should pupils pick up litter that may not be theirs? Why should pupils be grateful to those who do kind things for them? Why should pupils make visitors and new pupils feel welcome? It is their *duty* to do so. This abstract idea can be made concrete to pupils by getting them to broaden their sense of 'self' to be more than just their own needs; to see themselves as *being* the school, and the community – the country even.

To achieve this, we give them lots of opportunities to belong to the country: we sing songs together like 'Jerusalem', 'God Save the Queen' and 'I Vow to Thee My Country'. We give them opportunities to belong to the school: we eat lunch together every day during 'family lunch' and have a strict uniform policy. We give them opportunities to belong to a year group: Heads of Year will say things such as, 'Come on Year 9, we need to show Michaela that we are the best year group!' We give them opportunities to belong to a form: form tutors say things like, 'We are 9Z – we are the best form in Year 9!'

By constantly reinforcing the pupils' different identities, we allow pupils to view themselves with these broadened perspectives. When you see yourself as a part of your community, it makes helping others in your community as normal as the left hand plastering a cut on the right hand. There is no sense of reluctance, hesitation or burden to help out. Help is given out of a sense of duty, with no expectation of a debt owed, and without ego.

Pupils also have a duty to work hard. This is because they not only owe it to themselves to fulfil their potential, but their hard work also allows pupils to make their parents and teachers proud. Failure to work hard might result in a pupil holding their entire class back since the teacher has to spend more class time ensuring they keep up. The more that pupils become explicitly aware of the effects of their actions on their peers, teachers and family, the more they appreciate their duty towards them.

Our school motto is, 'Work hard, be kind'. This sums up the sense of duty our pupils understand. The absence of these traits breeds complacency.

Michaela teachers eliminate complacency and build discipline by inculcating good habits in our pupils. This is our duty to our pupils. It is a testing task because it requires two things of teachers: first, teachers must view the impact of their actions in the long term rather than the short term, and second, teachers must work exceptionally hard to be consistent with each other.

Giving a pupil a detention because they lose focus twice in class is difficult for teachers at first, when it is not what they are used to doing. It is tempting and easy to make excuses for the pupil: 'They lapsed concentration only *briefly*'; 'It wasn't bad enough to warrant a *detention*'; 'My explanation might not have been *engaging* enough'. Nonetheless, teachers have to dig deep and follow through with a sanction. Teachers may sense that pupils dislike the sanction, which makes it even harder to follow through. In the short term, holding pupils to high standards is very difficult. But they must trust that holding the line will pay off in the long term.

A behaviour system is most powerful when expectations are consistently applied across the school. Being consistent is a duty all Michaela teachers have to their pupils. If expectations differ between teachers, the pupils essentially receive different feedback each time they misbehave in exactly the same way. How can pupils cultivate strong habits if they receive contradicting feedback? If pupils fail to cultivate good habits for learning because their teachers lack clarity or because teachers cannot act with consistency, then this amounts to a gross failure on the part of the teachers and leaders of the school to uphold their respective duties. Achieving consistency takes hours of training and feedback. It means, in the moment, all teachers need to hold the line by putting aside any instincts to let pupils off. All teachers must ensure they follow through with agreed sanctions.

The fruits of these difficult but consistent decisions are realised in the long term. For example, every single year, a few weeks after joining Michaela, the number of detentions given to Year 7s for lack of focus dips dramatically. Why? Because teachers perform their duty and teach pupils effective listening habits. The consistent feedback that pupils receive allows their attention spans to grow dramatically, and with it, their capacity to learn gets larger. Over the course of the following five years this amounts to staggering gains in the amount pupils learn during lessons. Pupils and teachers experience short-term discomfort, but the long-term pay-off is a skill for life: the ability to pay attention to something difficult for an extended period of time.

As teachers in a position of authority, we also have a duty to ensure our pupils are safe at all times. It is true that authority can be abused: what mechanisms do we have in place to prevent this? Our senior leadership team have developed very clear systems of accountability – they ensure high visibility of all staff and there are strong communication networks between teams in the school. For example, the senior team, which contains a teacher from every major subject department in the school, meets daily. All of our classrooms have an open-door policy; we have an exceptionally strong lesson observation culture. This allows any potential concerns to be picked up and acted upon with great speed. More widely, because lessons are free of disruption, pupils who are upset or behaving uncharacteristically are more noticeable, allowing teachers to pick up on any issues that the pupils might be having more easily.

Finally, every teacher has a duty to develop themselves. Unfortunately, ego – the false and perfect representations we have of ourselves in our minds – is the enemy of self-improvement because it makes us less receptive to feedback. An understanding of *duty* is essential for working on destroying our egos, which in turn makes it easier to receive (and give) feedback that will ultimately lead to improvement.

Every middle and senior leader in the country wants their staff to 'own' their own development. They want their staff to ask their leaders and one another: 'What can I do to improve? Do you have any feedback for me? Here is my plan for developing this skill, do you think this is a good idea?'

But how many leaders actively tell their staff to do their duty and 'own' their development, and communicate this with a sense of urgency and conviction? Some leaders might worry that this comes across as patronising – after all, don't all teachers already want to improve? Isn't initiative self-driven? The answer is yes – but only to some extent. It is human nature to avoid seeking negative feedback. Actively creating a culture that pushes staff to seek feedback is far from patronising; it liberates and motivates staff to grow. Growth only comes from moving outside one's comfort zone. Leaders who explicitly tell their staff to do this will see their staff improve more quickly. And nothing is more motivating for a member of staff than to feel supported in becoming more proficient. In short, understanding duty helps individuals to change their mindset to actively seek feedback and flourish as a consequence. If ego is the enemy of your self-improvement, then understanding your duty is the antidote.

Authority: Progressivism vs Traditional Teaching

Prima facie, accepting the idea of authority as being a good thing is problematic. Surely history has taught us that obeying authority without question is dangerous, liable to corruption and, well, intrinsically evil?

To understand why authority is so important, it helps to look at examples where it might be easier to accept the importance of authority. Judges, for instance, have the authority to decide the fate of defendants in trial. We trust the judge to make the right decision based on all of the presented evidence and the bounds of the law. Head teachers have authority to make decisions about whom to hire. We trust that our head teachers make decisions that will best serve the interests of the pupils.

There are two types of authority that I want to discuss here: the authority of adults and the authority of knowledge itself. Firstly, there is the authority of teachers: the adults. Belief in the authority of the teacher is fundamental to accepting traditional methods of teaching where teachers stand at the front and unashamedly impart their knowledge explicitly. What gives them the authority to do this? The knowledge that they have spent years building up. Teachers tell their pupils the facts they need to know and focus on: building pupils' understanding; strengthening their pupils' knowledge in pursuit of mastery; and equipping pupils with the confidence and skill to apply that knowledge. Progressives might see pupils as having extremely valuable amounts of knowledge to bring to the classroom – and they are not incorrect. But to elevate the status of the pupils' knowledge and experience so that it is seen as equal to that of the teacher is problematic; it is to falsely view the knowledge of the pupils and teacher as symmetrical. This thinking persuades teachers to facilitate rather than drive learning. It prompts the teacher to weave between groups of pupils who are figuring out what the teacher already knows and could have told the pupils, but is holding back because they are reluctant to speak for too long and actually make use of their expertise. The overwhelming evidence favouring explicit instruction over the ineffective, misconception-prone, minimally-guided instruction is well-documented elsewhere (see for example, Kirschner, Sweller and Clark, 2006).

As the adults in our pupils' lives, we must also exercise our authority to help cultivate their habits for success. We need to teach them right from wrong. If we fail to exercise this authority, then we abdicate our duty to share this wisdom with our pupils. For example, if we do not teach our pupils to offer their seats on the bus or train, then we allow them to remain unaware of others' needs and they keep their perspective narrowed to themselves; we fail to help them understand their duty to others. If we do not implement clear rules in school with consistency, then we are failing to exercise our authority as adults. Consequently, we permit our schools to become chaotic, and allow our pupils to leave school without self-discipline.

Another habit we inculcate in Michaela pupils is gratitude. We know it is right to say thank you when someone gives us something. If we do not instruct our pupils to practise saying thank you, how will they cultivate this habit? At Michaela, teachers remind pupils to thank them at the end of their lessons. At the end of every half-term, pupils express their gratitude by writing postcards to their teachers during form time. Pupils publicly share 'appreciations' during family lunch. In all of these examples, Michaela teachers recognise that they have the authority to explicitly teach gratitude, because we know it is our duty to help our pupils become happy, and being grateful is essential to being happy.

If we were to give authority to pupils, what would it look like? Pupils might help make the school rules. Pupils might make decisions about what they learn. We might weigh up both teacher and pupil accounts about a given incident. If these sound like good ideas, then there are consequences I would consider to be problematic.

Firstly, what do you do when pupils come up with rules that are not conducive to learning? Is co-construction of rules not just a dishonest way of giving pupils a sense of buy-in? At Michaela, we explicitly communicate our rules and the rationale behind them from day one, with constant reminders to follow them.

Secondly, how well-informed are the pupils to be able to make decisions about how to direct their learning? Your expertise and training give you authority! If you do not exercise it, you are failing to help pupils make the most of the limited curriculum time and you fail to help those pupils achieve the best possible result in your subject.

Lastly, if you are taking pupils' perspectives into account when deciding which sanctions to use, you are very likely fooling yourself about how much a pupil dislikes sanctions. Pupils love the opportunity to escape facing consequences. Whilst it is worthwhile hearing a pupil's perspective, the final decision must lie with the teacher just as a referee has the final say in a football match. But if a behaviour system is based on giving equal voice to pupil and teacher, then the teacher will never be able to take the reins and lead their pupils to a successful future, never cultivate their habits, nor change their mindsets, because the pupils always have the choice to make their case, which permits them to be a victim of their circumstance.

The second way authority is important is to consider not the authority of a person, but the authority of knowledge itself. I grew up in a Hindu household where knowledge is considered to be sacred. Hindus believe in a Goddess of Knowledge, Saraswati, who is often found sitting on a lotus, holding books and tuning an instrument. This elevation of the status of knowledge to equal the status of a deity explains why I grew up revering knowledge. When I was a child, my mum taught me this idea in very concrete ways: 'You should never throw a book – that would be disrespecting all of the knowledge the book contains'. Stepping on a book is considered extremely sacrilegious because it is to shun the knowledge it contains. Why is this idea about knowledge so important to me? If the very act of throwing or stepping on a book, even by accident, makes me apologetic, then consider how I would react when a clearly knowledgeable teacher was imparting knowledge in a classroom! The very simple act of revering books elevated the authority with which I viewed knowledge itself. Knowledge became valuable; something to seek out, to treasure and to care deeply about. My relationship with books, with learning and with knowledge is one I continue to value deeply.

Whilst we don't go quite so far with our pupils, we do discuss the importance of knowledge explicitly and frequently. We talk about knowledge being precious: every lesson is important. If pupils are absent, we talk about all of the important knowledge that they need to catch up on. We narrate how empowering knowledge is: it gives us the tools to think, to critique, to understand the world, and ultimately, contribute to it. We discuss the importance of reading and how it builds up our knowledge of other worlds and other perspectives. We tie the authority of knowledge to the authority of the teachers, scientists, historians, musicians and authors the pupils study. We tell our pupils that they are lucky to have such incredibly knowledgeable teachers and access to inspiring books filled with the ideas of knowledgeable people. By hearing how wonderful and important knowledge is – inbuilt into our everyday narration in lessons and during form time – we weave a culture into the fabric of the school. We signal to our pupils that it is desirable to learn and that gaining knowledge makes one powerful.

What this means for behaviour is that pupils do not behave because they have a relationship with the teacher, but because the teacher has authority; authority precedes relationships. The teacher has the authority as an adult with special knowledge of the subject and knowledge of the habits needed to succeed. The teacher has the authority because they have the power to change the lives of the pupils in front of them. Exercising authority in this way is not a bad thing at all. Rather, it is our duty: we owe it to our pupils. We have worked hard throughout our lives to become experts in our subjects, to train as teachers and come to work every day to help guide our pupils. If we then shed all of this knowledge for fear that we exercise 'authority' and think that is a bad thing, then we fail to give our pupils what they crave: boundaries to develop good habits, and knowledge needed to succeed. It is the sense of authority that creates a culture of behaving well in school. This is not behaving out of fear, as many of our critics suggest. It is behaving out of a legitimate respect for authority, which rests upon knowledge. When relationships are built on this strong foundation, all the more respect is cultivated.

Values or Outcomes?

Why a focus on values, and not just outcomes? Both values and outcomes unify the decisions we make in our school about how we design our behaviour system, about our teaching methods and about the culture we cultivate, yet I have clearly stressed the importance of values more so than the outcomes. To understand why, it becomes important to consider the science of decision-making. Decisions can fall into two categories: rational (slow) or instinctive (fast).[1] In this chapter, I have rationally explained the importance of each value. However, when faced with a new choice, we tend to respond instinctively at first and rationally later. What if a pupil says they forgot their pen because they were at their cousin's house while their parents were abroad? Do we let them off because they were off-kilter with their routine? This is where instinct kicks in: my automatic response is to push responsibility onto the pupil – they should have been organised. Why do I have this as my instinctive reaction? Not because I am pondering the differing outcomes of my possible decisions. Rather, I can decide quickly because I believe so firmly in the value of personal responsibility.

If one of my pupils doesn't offer her seat to an old lady on the train, my response is visceral: I feel an immediate sense of embarrassment that my pupil hasn't carried out her duty. I don't observe and calmly rationalise to myself: 'I wonder why my pupil didn't offer her seat?' I don't think, 'Kids will be kids,' and roll my eyes casually. Why? Because my sense of duty is a firm part of my thinking: I am responsible for teaching my pupils, and I have failed in this instance. I would feel the urge to correct it immediately.

---

1   Kahneman, D., 2011. *Thinking, fast and slow*. Macmillan.

If we try to rationalise every decision, we may take longer than is appropriate for the situation at hand – we cannot deliberate over everything. It is important to deliberate afterwards to evaluate your judgement, but if you can hone your instincts by rooting them in your values, then you have truly and flexibly generalised your school ethos. So, by the virtue of being instinctive, values speed up decision-making compared to considering outcomes on their own.

For middle and senior leaders in schools, this is particularly important. When you are tasked with making decisions, having a visceral reaction can be extremely helpful at speeding up the decision-making process, and values are at the heart of this fast thinking. This is also helpful for an organisation: alignment is well-served by having values. That staff can flexibly apply a system in novel scenarios and agree on the decision is a mark of a cohesive school. This, surely, helps a school achieve the outcomes it chooses for its pupils, maximising its positive influence on pupils. This changes pupils' lives.

To summarise, the idea of taking personal responsibility is the centre of our ethos at Michaela. We refuse to let our pupils see themselves as victims of their circumstances; there is a huge amount they can do to succeed and transcend these circumstances. This is reflected in the decisions we make about how we operate our behaviour system. Responsibility always lies with the pupils, and we narrate this to them constantly. Implementing this requires courage, which we muster by understanding that it is our duty to help our pupils cultivate the habits they need to succeed. It is our duty to look at the long-term futures of our pupils, rather than giving them short-term gratification when we make excuses for them and allow them to abdicate their responsibility.

Our sense of duty comes from viewing ourselves as more than our own individual needs, and this is how we explicitly teach our pupils to be kind, grateful and to work hard. We narrate to our pupils that they have a duty to their peers and community to do their best. Finally, we can only achieve the above by recognising that we – as teachers or adults – have authority. Our knowledge in our subjects and our knowledge of habits that lead to success put us in a position to lead the way for our pupils by teaching them explicitly and rejecting the progressive, child-centred view.

We constantly narrate the power of knowledge, and this fosters a culture of learning and valuing knowledge, which is a form of authority itself.

These values are deeply embedded in our teachers – they develop into instinct the longer we teach at Michaela. This makes decision-making in new circumstances more visceral, allowing us to maintain our sky-high standards.

Our values allow our pupils to succeed beyond their circumstance; our school culture teaches them to flourish by transcending the negative influences present in their environment. Our values shape our school culture, which in turn empowers every child to make a success of themselves.

Is Climate Activism the True Purpose of Education?

Nathanael Smith

@NatSmith20

In 2019, we saw a worldwide 'school strike': pupils skipping school to protest against government and big businesses over their roles in climate change, some as often as every week. If you are not an educator, it may surprise you that over half of teachers (60% according to a September 2019 poll) supported the strikes.

Rather than deeming every lesson to be precious, many teachers believe that their pupils were right to forego learning in order to attend these protests. On the surface it seems like a noble sacrifice: pupils giving up their education (and potentially their futures) in order to save the planet. But I suspect that the relationship between climate change and school strikes is not quite so straightforward.

How Marxism Became Mainstream in Education

If asked to describe education in one word, which would you pick? I hope 'oppression' would not be your go-to. But to Brazilian educationalist Paulo Freire, traditional education was chiefly characterised by oppression.

Before thinkers such as Freire upended educational philosophy, the status quo was that the teacher, being the expert and source of authority, should lead the classroom. Children, as yet unmoulded by society, needed the guidance and support that only adults could provide. But Freire rejected the idea that children needed adults to shape them. Not only were children fully able to make decisions for themselves, they were not in any way 'subordinate' to teachers. Freire superimposed Marx's class critique onto the classroom: the history of education mapped a power struggle between the authoritative teacher and the supposedly subordinate learners. Freire believed that education would inevitably change, that authority would be redistributed equitably among teacher and learners, thus dissolving the categories of 'teachers' and 'learners' in one fell swoop.

Such a view has misunderstood the problem by assuming that teachers' authority is arbitrary, when really it arises from eminently practical needs. The subject knowledge, the professional experience, the wisdom of the teacher and the learner are not comparable. Therefore, of course, the teacher should be chiefly responsible for leading the learning. It does not imply that teachers are superior *people*, but it does make them better equipped to lead learning. To put it simply: teachers know more than pupils, so teachers should lead the learning in the classroom.

Alongside this, Freire posited that no educational content was politically neutral. For Freire, to state an objective fact (say, water boils at 100°C) is an ideological assertion. Freire concluded that this revelation prompts a shift in the purpose of education: the goal is for pupils to reflect independently and reach a quasi-spiritual state he called 'critical consciousness', freeing them to see the world from a more enlightened and politically radical perspective. In other words, learning facts should be replaced entirely by pupils expressing their individual opinions. By rejecting received wisdom and the traditional hierarchy of knowledge, Freire presumed, children would learn of the deep inequalities in society and the need for radical political change. Freire believed that freeing children from the shackles of knowledge and teacher-authority would prompt them to become active revolutionaries.

But as experienced teachers, we might question Freire's assumptions here. Perhaps it is the case that some children (perhaps those from homes filled with books, where their parents talk to them about current affairs and teach them about the world around them) might be able to go without traditional teaching and still garner a sufficient understanding of the world. But what of those who are less fortunate? What about those pupils who, just like many of our pupils at Michaela, are not afforded such opportunities? Freire assumes that removing the teacher's knowledge from the classroom would enable all pupils to become revolutionaries, but I would suggest that this fails to recognise the varied range of starting points from where our pupils begin their learning journeys.

It is tempting to dismiss Freire as an obscurity, but he has had more influence on university education departments than *any other theorist*. The research impact of a thinker is measured on a scale known as the h-index. Freire has amassed an enormous 138 points (not far behind Karl Marx himself on 173, and the heavyweight Noam Chomsky at 180).

Generations of trainee teachers have taken their first steps in education under such influences. It is therefore no surprise that many teachers would support the school strikes. Perhaps consciously, perhaps unconsciously, many teachers have been trained to believe in the goals Freire proposes. The climate strikes would appeal to the values many teachers shared with Freire: 1) the ultimate ideological goal was realised: pupils becoming activists, and 2) their secondary goal, that pupils would refute teacher authority, was evidently manifested in their mass refusal to attend school. The intrinsic (i.e. non-revolutionary) value of education was under assault, and so educationalists inspired by Freire celebrated.

Even some leading politicians were praising the protests. Jeremy Corbyn revelled in this inversion of the teacher-pupil hierarchy, announcing to protesting children that they had 'taught [him] a lesson about climate change'. Such a move was easy, even inevitable, for Corbyn, because progressive pedagogy arose, not from cognitive science or even common sense, but from the same Marxist principles that he holds.

Corbynites cheer when children refute 'the system' because to them schools, government and business are all parts of an amorphous, monolithic mass which is responsible for the world's problems, stated variously as 'the patriarchy', 'society' or 'capitalism'. Philosopher Slavoj Žižek evidenced this view by citing a schoolgirl who, when asked if she would be better off in school, answered 'why – so you can teach us how to destroy the planet?'. I can't imagine that any teacher would accept that this is on their curriculum. Such a worldview fails to meaningfully distinguish school from authority *per se*. Schools are not the same as big business or the government.

Teachers who attempt to implement Freire's vision know that it creates a power vacuum which the most assertive and intimidating pupils are only happy to fill. The probability of such figures leading the class productively, especially when social disadvantage is factored in, is remote. At Michaela, our pupils are able to learn because they are receiving detailed, thoroughly considered content from subject experts – nurtured in this structure, only their capacity to work hard limits them (as opposed to the uglier and more challenging behaviour that some teachers experience in some schools). When the teacher is the authority, and that is normal across the school, teachers are respected and need not resort to the short-term ploys of permissiveness and informality to manage chaotic classes.

Authority in schools, especially schools in challenging circumstances, is indispensable. The engaged, focused atmosphere around Michaela which impresses our guests would be impossible without our underpinning belief in the authority of the teacher. Our recent exam results, among the very highest in the country, would have been impossible too. We believe that if more schools were to reinstate teachers to their rightful positions of authority that the longstanding damage to education by progressivism would be stifled. Progressive ideas have underpinned the thinking in schools for decades: perhaps children's decision to skip school is another example of these progressive ideas in action. If educators refuse to stand up for learning and the authority of their teachers, then it will do nothing but harm, and none will be more harmed than the already disadvantaged.

Why the Strikes Are a Problem

On the surface, the strikes seem to be a noble and reasonable act. But I would argue that this simplifies a more complex issue.

We teachers know what kids can be like. Some of them are indeed very passionate about the environment, but many are just as passionate about having days off school for free. Wouldn't it therefore be better for children to strike at the weekend? One could suggest that this might be a more significant sacrifice for those who have just copied their friends, as teenagers are often wont to do. Or perhaps pupils could give up their phones and laptops for that week: refusing to use electricity to charge their devices would be both a huge sacrifice and a statement about their respect for the environment.

As we know, our most disadvantaged pupils are those whose chances of success are reduced further by taking time out of school. Rather than encouraging this behaviour, perhaps it is our duty as teachers to ask the pupils to protest at a time that will not interfere with their futures.

Furthermore, teachers might want to consider the impact of their own behaviour during the strikes. What are we teaching our pupils, if we allow them to take part in what was a rather belligerent and undignified act? BBC footage of the protests showed a major London roundabout blocked off entirely by youths chanting 'engines off', slamming the vans of traders and chanting: 'Whose streets? Our streets!' It was primal, territorial, like football hooligans but with skateboards and pink highlights. Kids were even holding up middle fingers to the camera. One impressionable boy was filmed bragging about his own activism and how little revision he would do that weekend, before signing off with 'see you in prison'. I cannot see how this activity benefits young people. On the contrary, it teaches them that rudeness and disruption are acceptable and that learning is something to be shunned. Again, who is most disadvantaged by this? Not the privately educated middle classes, but the poor inner-city children for whom every lesson is an opportunity to change their life chances. If we are to do our duty as teachers, we must ensure that such a culture does not infiltrate our pupils' minds.

There was nothing noble about these protests, and it is unclear how delaying tradesmen in central London played a constructive role in reducing global temperatures. The Marxist view, that all aspects of 'the system' conspire to form the arch enemy (capitalism), is the only frame through which these actions are logically coherent. If you're slamming your skateboard against a plumber's van, it may as well be the door of Number 10 or the Bank of England. I am convinced that the destructiveness of the protests betrayed their true motives: the organisers wanted power and anarchic fun. Groups like Extinction Rebellion have compared their work with the movements around Gandhi or Martin Luther King, but their comparison fundamentally misses the important messages of peace and integrity espoused by both thinkers.

Across the world today, children still contest the insurmountable odds for an outside chance of becoming properly educated. I've heard of a school in China's Szechuan province in which children climb vertically up and down a mountain every day. Elsewhere children traverse precarious bridges over gushing streams, others canoe across lakes, or brave the Siberian wilderness. They know how valuable education is, and they're grateful for it. We owe it to our own children to teach them the same gratitude.

Sadly, many British children see education as a problem: a corrupting influence and a chore to be disposed of, rather than an opportunity to transform their life chances. This isn't by accident. Of course, kids will be kids. We cannot blame children for making decisions that do not best serve their long term interests, but what we can do is guide them and help them to see that their long term success comes at the cost of short term effort, hard work, and sacrifice. The real tragedy is, of course, that many educators seem to have lost faith in the intrinsic value of education.

Education Without Activism

Education matters intrinsically — it is important to know the things that schools teach. This is something we believe wholeheartedly at Michaela: that education is more than a means to an end. Knowing about the world, its history, its people, its culture, mastering language, logic and arithmetic — none of this is arbitrary, it allows children to become intelligent young adults. It ameliorates the burden of human limitation so they can go on to live meaningful lives. This is what developing countries stake their futures on, all the while we in the west are losing touch with it.

Perhaps those who succeed can go on to tackle the world's most pressing problems; human history is, after all, a veritable litany of crises to be resolved. The activists see things differently: to them, global problems have straightforward solutions which they themselves already know, whilst they view those in power as too corrupt or idiotic to implement them. But the climate issue is bafflingly complex and requires careful deliberation to prevent the world falling apart. Should people in developing countries not go to work, and hence not feed their families, until renewables are invented and ready for them? The climate issue is a crisis spread across technology, governance, international relations, and economics. You cannot overhaul the entire economy without consequences.

Many are predicting that the climate problem will be the most complex puzzle humans have attempted to solve — why, exactly, is it better for the scientists of the future to miss school? A strong knowledge of science and geography will be indispensable. How could children claim to understand the data without a rudimentary grasp of statistics? How are they to deliver a convincing speech without studying the most persuasive writing penned in the English language? If we are to make progress with the climate issue, the leaders of the future need to be in school and university.

The soft skills children develop are perhaps as important to their education as their subject knowledge. At Michaela, we believe it would be an injustice for pupils to leave school without the attitudes and habits to operate properly in the world. We base our expectations of pupils on the importance of perseverance, personal responsibility, and gratitude because those are essential for navigating life's challenges. We give pupils frequent opportunities to speak in front of over 100 peers during family lunch, at which they eat politely and converse with visitors from across the world. They are held to the very highest standards of diligence and organisation, not for mere compliance —we are making our pupils courageous and competent. All of this is bread and butter for the privately educated, why not for all?

If there were a school that was the opposite of Freire and his convictions, it would be Michaela. Most evidently there is a world that needs changing, but education, traditionally conceived, is part of the solution, not the problem. A proper education can produce people who are informed, articulate, and, we hope, even wise enough to solve global problems. Imagine the world is a broken watch: our view is that well-educated children would go on to be master watchmakers, tweaking the tiny parts of a harmonious system with respect and care. Freire's view, that the only purpose of education is to repudiate and overthrow, resembles a vandal who tries to solve the problem of a broken watch by breaking into the workshop and destroying it. Most UK educators have sided with Freire, but a minority still believe in the traditional value of education, and at Michaela we are proud to be in that minority.

Why I am Still Talking to White People About Race

Natalie Jones
@natjone93

Where did you teach before Michaela?

I taught in a school in Kent. The demographic at my school was mainly white working class and the main issue among the pupils was apathy. For kids in that part of Kent, there weren't that many prospects after finishing school. A lot of their parents were unemployed or worked in one of the supermarkets nearby.

What are the main differences between the kids in Kent and London?

In Kent, my pupils were very apathetic. Obviously I'm generalising, and there were some children who worked very hard, but overall the children I taught just didn't seem to care about learning. Knowing stuff didn't seem to matter to them. It's not as if they had a contempt for school or anything; in fact they were quite open and easy to talk to, both in and outside lessons. Indeed during lessons they often tried to derail your teaching by wanting to just 'have a chat' with you.

The kids in London are very different. They have a hard edge. They aren't anywhere near as open and they care much more about how they're perceived by their peers than how their teachers perceive them. There's a certain dynamic in London, that isn't present in Kent, which forces lots of kids to be 'hard' just to be respected by their peers.

What about your own family?

My mum and dad are both immigrants. My mum was born in Finland and moved here when she was 19; my dad was born in The Gambia and moved here with his family when he was only 12. My dad cares very much about education and I've always felt a sense of duty to perform well academically to impress him. But his attitude doesn't nearly compare to the academic aspirations of my paternal grandparents. For 40 to 50 years of their lives, my grandparents lived in a country where free education and the prospect of university were not a given – in fact, they were very rare. As a result, the value that they placed on education was much higher. I think the longer you live in a country where education is free and comes easily, the less likely you are to value it.

What's the root of this 'edge' in London kids?

I think it stems from peer pressure from older friends, and definitely music. The force of music is interesting because the kids I taught in Kent listened to the same violent, aggressive music as kids do in London. I'm talking about rap, grime and drill. Just to be very clear about the level of violence and aggression I'm talking about, I'll quote some lyrics from popular songs in these genres:

> 'Lean out the ride trying to spray man's head back like I just finished his trim'.

Translation: I lean out of my car trying to shoot the man's head.

> 'Still got my jail shank'.

Translation: I still have my homemade blade that I made in jail.

> 'If any one of you take a shot on a track
>
> My niggas come back and put a shot in your frame'.

Translation: If one of you insults me in a song, my niggas (by this he means friends) will shoot you.

> 'Skenged up for the field cah I might buck me a python'.

Translation: I'm carrying my knife in case I see a snake. (Snake meaning untrustworthy person.)

> 'Hit with the pumpy, man down Humpty Dumpty ... I can get you shot for like one g'.

Translation: Shot with a gun, you'll fall down like Humpty Dumpty. I can get you shot for £1000.

So, kids in London and Kent alike are listening to this stuff. Why is it not such a bad influence on the kids in Kent? I think partly because they're so far away from where that music scene is happening. This music is mostly made by London artists in London. In Kent they're geographically far away from London, it's not the immediate culture where they grow up. They don't see it around them, it's not a daily reality to them. It's happening somewhere else. For Kent kids, listening to this aggressive music is like an insight into gangster life, where the danger and rudeness is quite exciting for them.

But in London, the scene described by this music is the kids' daily reality.

A lot of our pupils at Michaela know people that make this music. Even worse than that, many of our pupils know gangsters. They know people that have been grievously affected by knife crime. When I say 'affected by' I don't mean a few small injuries, I mean murdered. When I say 'know people', I don't mean their friend's uncle's sister's boyfriend, I mean their own immediate siblings and cousins. Our kids have close family members who've been murdered as a result of gang related knife crime. Outside our own school gates we've had multiple knifepoint muggings. I've seen with my own eyes, from a window in the school, a balaclava-clad gang wielding hammers and breaking into cars. In broad daylight.

So, when our kids are listening to this music that references crime, violence and murder, it's not somewhere far away, it's right there in front of them. It's outside their school gate. It's their reality. They have to learn a very different way of behaving from kids in Kent – a way that will protect them, a way that won't draw unwanted attention, or a way to make themselves the alpha figure in social situations. That's what the 'edge' is. Rap and grime and drill – at least, the kind I'm talking about – might be exciting and exotic and cool for kids in Kent; for kids in London, if they can't learn to live by that code, they are at terrific risk.

So it's clear the effect of this music differs greatly in the two areas where you've taught. So why do you think these songs, with their appalling lyrics, are popular and respected in Britain?

It's not just in British music. You find a multitude of similar lyrics in black rap music in America. I find it bizarre that it's common and seemingly acceptable to hear artists talk about killing people in their songs. Normally it's black men talking about killing other black men. It's quite disturbing that it's so normal to hear those themes in that type of black music. Imagine if Ed Sheeran started singing about killing other men – that would be weird. It's not as if these violent songs are kept somewhere in the underground, they are openly played on the radio as well, side-by-side with Ed Sheeran. Imagine if these songs referenced killing animals. No one would be okay with that, and rightly so. But killing people, is that supposed to be fine? And let's all let vulnerable inner-city kids listen to it, especially as they're surrounded by knife crime every day of the week. It's utter madness!

But why are these lyrics tolerated by society and venerated by the kids? I think it has to do with the social goals of money and power. Again, I'm generalising, but the people making the music (particularly drill) are often also involved in illegal money-making schemes like selling drugs. They have a lot of money. They brag about having that money and, for teenagers who have none, that's really alluring. If you grow up with very little, and see these 'role models' with their wads of cash and fancy cars and clothes, that's so impressive and it makes such an impact – no wonder young people aspire to be them. And if these 'artists' are involved in drugs, and known to be violent, they will have a lot of social power over others in their area.

I guess you could compare it to the respect the boys in private schools might feel for politicians or bankers. They would respect them, at least in part if not entirely, for their money and societal power. It's just that looking up to politicians and bankers doesn't reduce your chances of surviving to lead a successful life. Whereas looking up to violent, knife-wielding rappers does.

Why is your reaction to violent rap music so different to most British middle-class people? Wouldn't their view be, it's representative of a community and part of a culture, and who are we to criticise it?

The main reason I'm so against this violent music is because I witness it affecting our kids' lives every day, in school, in London. Most people can't see these effects because they don't live in London or don't have much contact with inner-city kids. These people say things like, 'Well, we all watch violent films, surely it's the same thing'. But, really, it isn't. It comes back to my earlier comments about this not being a reality for most people. For instance, I'm not an Italian mafia boss or a drug mule – that's not my reality. I don't live near or know anyone who is. If I watch a violent gang film, it all feels very far away. I can't relate to those people, so it doesn't affect me as much as it would, say, a teenager growing up in Sicily whose uncle makes money from protection rackets. It's easy to be fine with this music if you're a middle-class parent who lives in the Home Counties and you or your family don't see or feel any of its devastating effects.

Is this music 'just part of black culture'? No! Most black families would hear these violent lyrics and feel they're disgusting and awful. If I were to play drill music to my dad, who is black, there's no way he would think, 'Yep, this is just part of my culture'. He'd be horrified! So to claim that black men rapping about murdering other black men is 'just part of black culture', and should therefore be accepted, is just obscene. Imagine if Ed Sheeran starting singing about murdering white men. Would society just say 'oh it's fine, it's just white culture'? No they wouldn't. So why is it fine when it's black men?

In my opinion, most middle-class British people who think it's fine, or even actively encourage it, haven't given thought to the actual consequences. They just want to virtue-signal that they support ethnic minorities and they think they'll look bad if they criticise music made by black people. Recently, when challenged about his record on knife crime, London Mayor Sadiq Khan said 'I would rather spend money on future Daves and Stormzys than future victims of crime'. His statement already sounds absurd, but when you know a little more about Dave and Stormzy it gets even worse. Both are mainstream artists who've had many Top Ten songs in the UK Singles Chart, but Stormzy is the better known, which is why his name ends up being used as a 'catch-all' for artists who have worrying lyrics. One of his most famous songs, 'Shut Up', spent weeks in the charts and features the lyrics:

> If you got a G-A-T, bring it out/ Most of the real bad boys live in south/ If you wanna do me something, I'm about/ I'm not a gangster, I'm just about/ But you see my man over there with the pouch?/ Dare one of you man try get loud/ All of my mandem move so foul

What he is saying here is basically 'If you have a gun, bring it out. If you want to attack me then I'm ready and waiting. I'm not a gangster but my friend over there has a bag with a weapon in, I dare you to start something'. People who defend such lyrics would probably say that they are not meant literally. I'm sure that when Stormzy, whose real name is Michael, refers to himself as 'Gunshot Mike' in his album 'Gang Signs & Prayer' he would claim that it's not meant literally. If you're far away from the reality of inner-city gun and knife crime then it's easy to accept these claims unquestioningly and to continue supporting the music. It's interesting: I think Sadiq Khan, as an Asian adult, although he is geographically as close as you can get to inner-city London, is actually much further away than you'd first assume from the reality of violence than young black boys are. If you're a vulnerable teenager in inner-city London who sees and hears about genuine violence daily, then suddenly it all becomes brutally real.

Dave is also a UK rapper and, although still very much mainstream, he generally receives less media attention than Stormzy. His recent performance at the Brit Awards was very well received and described in the media as 'the most important performance in the history of The Brits'. At the end of his performance he said, 'Big up the mandem in jail'. To 'big up' someone means to express respect or approval for them. 'Mandem' means 'friends'. So, live on stage at the Brits, this 'most important performer in history', Dave said, 'I have respect for and approve of my friends in jail'.

Dave's brother is currently serving a life sentence for his part as a ringleader in the brutal murder of a 15-year-old boy, who was stabbed 15 times in the chest by a gang, dubbed 'The Samurai Tube Killers', at Victoria Station in 2010. Dave's brother's voice (taken from phone conversations in jail) features on his album, which won him the Mercury Prize. After winning the prize, Dave dedicated the album to his brother and called him his hero. So presumably when Dave said 'big up the mandem in jail' at the end of his performance, he was partly talking about his brother. I wonder what the mother of the teenager that Dave's brother stabbed to death thinks about that? Or, more significantly, about Sadiq Khan's support for 'future Daves' and his apparent lack of sympathy for victims of crime?

This is what I mean when I say often people haven't given a second thought to the consequences of supporting this music. Saying you want to 'invest in young black rappers' makes you sound good and signals to the world you're not racist. It seems not to matter to some, what some of these rappers say, or do, or glamorise. What they are actually supporting, by validating this music, the language of its statements, and the lifestyle that goes with it, is violence by black men against other black men. And, as was the case so often in London in 2019, violence against black children by other black children. But if you care more about looking as if you support ethnic minorities, rather than actually supporting ethnic minorities, it doesn't matter.

Ok, that's Dave – he's only one example. And although some of Stormzy's lyrics might be bad, he's actually helping black children, isn't he? He's giving scholarships to pay for some pupils to go to Cambridge. How do you feel about that? Black kids are being given a leg up by people in the black community, surely that's a good thing?

Stormzy is offering a scholarship to two black students a year who already have offers at Cambridge. To qualify for the £18,000 a year scholarship you have to have already achieved excellent A-level grades, have a confirmed offer from Cambridge and be fully or part black. Stormzy is assuming that the number one barrier to entry here is financial: i.e. the kids can't afford the fees. Even more specifically than that, he's assuming that the financial barrier is only at the point of entry to university. I disagree with both of his assumptions. I do accept that, by offering these scholarships, Stormzy is effectively endorsing university education, at Oxbridge in particular, and his influence shouldn't be underrated especially when a lot of black students feel or assume that Oxbridge isn't a place where they belong. Stormzy's support sends out a powerful message. But it doesn't tackle the heart of the problem – it's just a band-aid on a bullet wound.

In 2017, when predicted grades and course type were being taken into consideration for university entry to Oxford, black students were actually slightly more likely to be offered a place than other students. So if that's the case, why are they then underrepresented? Well, they were also significantly more likely to miss their predicted A-level grades, and so ultimately they didn't get in. Black students have been consistently more likely to miss their predicted A-level grades than students of any other race since 2010. In 2015, about two-thirds of black students did not secure their predicted grades, compared to less than half of white students. That's a huge issue – so why does that actually happen? And who's trying to solve that problem? Who is throwing money at that?

So, while Stormzy is giving money to students who've already got in to Cambridge and is being hailed by the media for helping fight a supposedly racist institution, he's doing nothing to help solve the actual problem. UK black students are consistently not reaching their potential at much higher rates than any other race. But of course he looks like he's helping, which unfortunately seems to be good enough for most people. On top of this, of course, Stormzy is part of and makes his money from the UK grime scene. I quoted some of his violent lyrics earlier, but as well as being violent his lyrics can be very offensive to both women and black people. In the same song where he refers to himself as 'Gunshot Mike' he also uses the N-word several times. As well as it obviously being a bad thing to encourage black boys to call themselves and other black boys the N-word, this is clearly counter-productive to encouraging young black boys to envision themselves as future Oxbridge scholars. Stormzy is also happy to collaborate with artists who have served multiple prison sentences, including for knife crime offences.

So, while it looks like Stormzy is helping, he isn't really. It's nice that he is encouraging black children to aspire to a Cambridge education, but he is part of a culture that actively prevents them from getting there.

At the same time, both Winchester and Dulwich College have turned down an offer of £1 million worth of scholarships for white, working-class boys from Sir Bryan Thwaites. Sir Bryan is a philanthropist who attended both schools on a scholarship himself – he was a white, working-class boy, and he now wants to help those in a similar situation. Given that white working-class boys are the worst performing group in schools, even worse than black boys, and are hugely underrepresented in universities, his aim seems like a fair and noble one. Winchester and Dulwich didn't think so. They said they 'do not want to put ethnic restrictions on who can benefit from financial help'. I do have some sympathy for this argument because once you start giving preference to any one group because of their race, where does that stop? What if there are mixed race boys with one white working-class parent? Are they then disqualified from the scheme even if all their other circumstances are the same? That doesn't seem fair, in the same way that it mightn't be fair that a black student from a relatively privileged background receives the Stormzy scholarship just by virtue of being black.

The point is that you cannot reconcile two contradictory viewpoints at the same time. You can't simultaneously believe that Stormzy's scholarships are great because they help black kids (even though I don't actually think they do) and that Sir Bryan Thwaites' are discriminatory on the basis of race. But that is the situation we find ourselves in. I would bet money that if Stormzy offered scholarships for black boys to attend Winchester or Dulwich, the response would have been quite different. The irony here is that scholarships to great public schools offer much more positive help to black pupils than giving money to those who have finished their A-levels. Why? Because that way, you pay for them to attend a great school and get a great education, so that they can get the good A-level grades that secure a great future. If Stormzy started offering these kinds of scholarships, he might actually help more black students achieve their predicted grades.

So, black kids aren't getting the grades to get university places. Should we then be seeing top tier universities reserve a proportion of places for them, regardless of their grades?

No. That's patronising. The minute you start saying we need X proportion of kids from Y background things get farcical. How are you really going to start dividing up these candidates? It's ridiculous. Harvard University came under fire recently for appearing to maintain a quota for the number of Chinese students it admits. It seems to be in an effort to keep their numbers below 20%, regardless of academic achievements. Harvard has also been known to have an undeclared Jewish quota in the past. Should we start to do that here, if one ethnic group ever becomes overrepresented? Of course, that happens by default if you set any kind of quota, even if it seems to be a positive quota. A target of 10% black students is the same thing as a cap of 90% for non-black students. And then what happens with mixed race kids, what category would they fall in to?

These selection strategies also assume that race is the only factor. Are rich black kids treated differently from poor black kids? You'll end up with kids who are there because they're black, not because they're good enough, and that doesn't help anyone. The minute you start to focus on race quotas rather than ability you end up with students who can't keep up with their peers. They won't be successful and they'll end up dropping out. No one's a winner in that situation. The intervention needs to come way before university level, way before sixth form level. These kids need to be taught properly in primary and secondary school.

You've said 'taught properly'. There is often debate about what kind of content should be taught in schools, especially in subjects like English and History. People often claim that there's a lack of ethnic minority literature and history taught in schools, and that teachers should be making content relevant to inner-city kids. Is there any merit in that?

As a maths teacher, I don't know much about the proportion of ethnic minority content in the curriculum. What I do know is that 'making content relevant' is patronising nonsense. We need to teach kids the best of what has been thought and said. And if the people who thought and said those things are black, fine! And if those people are white, fine! I do think a strong focus on British history and British literature is a good thing, because we live in Britain. It should not be controversial to say that. It's really important that kids in inner-city London feel that British culture is their culture and a solid grounding in British history and literature goes a long way to help that. Similar to the rest of inner-city London, a large proportion of the kids at Michaela have parents that weren't born in Britain. This means that we teach children with a multitude of different family backgrounds. When I was about 10 years old I remember asking my mum, 'what am I?' The difference between race, culture and nationality can be very confusing; especially for young children whose parents are immigrants. The answer my mum gave me has stayed with me forever. After a few moments of thought she said, 'well, you are 50% Finnish, 50% Gambian, and 100% British'. As a maths teacher I'm well aware that the numbers don't add up but the sentiment is crystal clear. I have always felt that I am British, but as my mum's wise words demonstrate, this is not at the expense of cherishing my heritage. Depriving inner-city kids of that sense of belonging, that I have been lucky enough to always have, will actively hinder their chances of success.

People that advocate for 'making things relevant' need to understand that they are actively disadvantaging children by their campaign. When I was in secondary school I remember being encouraged to write an essay on the Snoop Dogg song, 'Drop it Like it's Hot', most likely because my teacher thought it was relevant to me. I can tell you one thing for sure: the boys at Harrow aren't writing essays about Snoop Dogg songs. They're learning about Shakespeare, Charles Dickens and British history. As a 15-year-old teenager, I didn't need my English teacher teaching me about Snoop Dogg – I could have learnt about that in my own time. What I couldn't do in my own time was interpret Shakespeare. For a long time after I left secondary school the only Shakespeare play I could name was The Tempest, because that's the only one we learned at school. To this day I notice that my own cultural capital is woefully lacking, and I absolutely love that, as a teacher at Michaela, I've been able to learn poetry by heart and can now recite the English monarchs in order. The decision not to teach ethnic minority children Shakespeare because you think that Snoop Dogg is more relevant to them – that's racist. Inner-city kids in London have just as much right to feel that Shakespeare, Charles Dickens and British history belong to them as much as boys at Eton do. Deprive them of that, and you are letting them down.

It might feel nice to teach inner-city kids 'relevant content' in the moment, but as long as the private school kids are learning the material that underpins their – our – culture in this country, you will continue to widen the gap.

You mentioned earlier how important primary and secondary education is for ethnic minority children if they are to achieve their predicted A-level grades. Do you think that their education would be improved if more ethnic minority teachers taught them? For example, do you think that Michaela would be better if there were more black teachers at the school?

I used to think that it doesn't matter at all what your teachers look like, because good teachers can inspire kids, regardless of where they're from. I still think that for the most part and would never want somebody to be hired because of race rather than because they were a good teacher. However, a lot of the black boys at our school don't have father figures in their lives, so I think for them to see black men in a respectable profession, who value education, would be very good. That's not to say that the white teachers at school can't be role models for young black boys – of course they can – but I do think it would have a positive effect on black boys if they saw more black male teachers at school.

Do you think any of the kids at school treat you differently because of your race?

Yes, in trivial ways. A lot of the girls will talk to me about the hair products I use because we have a similar hair type. I've had conversations about different foods that I eat at home that they also do. Maybe I shouldn't underestimate these things, but I don't think my being a black woman has had as big an impact as if we had black male teachers. At school it seems the case that generally, black children have a black female role model – their mother. They don't have black male role models as often.

You criticise things – Stormzy's scholarships, kinds of popular music, admission quotas – that other people think of as good. Is it okay to be critical if you aren't affected by these issues of race?

It is very important to question the impact of these things. When it comes to race, more often than not, things that at first appear very nice are either not helping as you might expect them to, or are actively damaging the aspirations and life chances of black children. Stormzy's scholarships are not as helpful as the media like to make out. Teaching inner-city kids certain content because you think it's relevant to their lives can simply prevent them from broadening their horizons. Introducing positive discrimination quotas to try to plaster over the problem of poor primary and secondary education will inevitably lead to lower standards, and it's deeply patronising. Pretending that violent music is fine just because it's made by black people, or not criticising it because you don't want to offend 'black culture', just lets down thousands of inner-city kids who live in the reality where violent knife crime is right outside their school gates.

I would urge anyone who truly wants to help black children, rather than just look like they are helping black children, to stop and think about the things that they accepted unquestioningly in the past. Do they actually help? Or do they just make you feel like a really good person? Feeling like a good person is easy, actually making a positive difference is hard.

CURRICULUM

History at Michaela

Michael Taylor
@mike_taylor11

Where we have gone wrong

There are two problems with the way in which history is taught in English schools:

1. Substantive knowledge is not prioritised enough.

2. Pupils leave school without a rudimentary grasp of narrative English and British history.

Substantive knowledge should be the priority

For history teaching, if I could summarise the problem in one sentence, it would be: The 'doing' of history has become the essence of history teaching so much, we no longer teach the substantive knowledge (the historical content) with the rigour or depth that pupils need in order to engage with the complex history in the first place.

History teachers will be familiar with how this manifested itself in the teaching of sources. Source work became the history itself and as a result, became divorced from the rich knowledge base that is required to understand a source and analyse it. The obsession with sources was meant to replicate the role of the historian and the construction of historical narratives. Although well intentioned, it never did replicate what professional historians do. An academic historian already approaches the archive with a wealth of substantive knowledge.

School history is not the same as university history. The role of the history teacher is not to create academic historians there and then, but to give them the training to become one in the future. It is also the case that the vast majority of school pupils will not become academic historians and so the aims of school history teaching have to be much wider than preparing pupils to study academic history. All schools, and especially our school, which serves a diverse intake, should ensure that history lessons provide a wealth of cultural knowledge which will enable pupils to survive and thrive in modern Britain.

It would be a mistake never to expose pupils to the thinking of academic historians. It would also be problematic not to ensure pupils are situating their knowledge within the frameworks that academic historians use. However, even for those pupils who will go on to become academic historians, you do not learn how to become an historian by aping what academic historians do. In fact, you make it much less likely for pupils to become professional historians, by failing to teach the wealth of uncontested facts and concepts to pupils which will enable them to succeed as historians, and which generations of historians have had access to, and took for granted.

Although there are two different groups that school history must cater for, the day to day practice of what these pupils do while in their history lessons should be remarkably similar. For the group of pupils who will go on to become academic historians, a focus on substantive knowledge will prepare them for academic study. For the group who will not study history beyond 14, a knowledge-rich curriculum will give them an understanding of their nation's history and the broad trends in European and global history.

In order to teach in a way that breaks history down for our pupils, we need to be completely sure of the final destination we are guiding them to. Only then, can we break down those questions to the basic nuts and bolts that help us answer them in the first place. It is true that in academia, those final destinations (or the answers to historical questions) are still contested. It is also true that we need to immerse ourselves in the world of academic history if we are to have the curriculum knowledge at our fingertips so that we can teach our pupils to learn, manipulate and flex that knowledge. We also need to engage with scholarship to provide a model to our pupils and to enable us to convey our pride and passion for history.

However, if we indulge too much in that world, without giving pupils the solid foundation in the core substantive knowledge they need, then we are not preparing them to enter the volatile world of the academic historian, nor do we help them understand the country and wider world in which they live.

History and marathon training

We love marathons at Michaela. I am always amazed by how many staff members compete in 5km runs, 10km runs, half-marathons and whole marathons. Naturally, I am there to provide moral and strategic support via the safe distance of my living room. We use the marathon analogy a lot in our department. Like much of what we do at Michaela, we are inspired by others and the marathon analogy is taken, almost entirely, from Daisy Christodoulou's blog on education. She, in turn, got the idea from Michael Slavinsky and Dan Lavipour, two educators who are also athletes. In a nutshell, you do not get better at running marathons by running more marathons.

Instead, we get better at running marathons by completing a series of much smaller exercises, over a long period of time. We do shorter runs to build our stamina; exercises to develop our core strength; we change our diet; we complete medium distance runs, and eventually, we will be able to run the marathon.

I like to think the analogy can be stretched to history teaching. We are all guilty of racing far too quickly to high-level, conceptual analysis. In effect, we are getting our pupils to run marathons too soon.

Writing an essay in history is hard work and to do it well requires the pupil to have mastered a huge level of rich and varied substantive knowledge. In my first few years of teaching, I often found myself racing to the final product too soon. I do not think this is an uncommon issue. It is partly due to a culture where 'generic skills' are promoted as the pinnacle of academic achievement. More importantly for history teachers, it is because we often divorce historical analysis and second-order concepts, such as cause and effect, or change over time, from the crucial substantive knowledge that sustains both.

Training the historian – The nuts and bolts

Our philosophy as a school is that substantive knowledge can and needs to be taught explicitly, so that our pupils can flex that knowledge and bring it to bear on conceptually focused questions. In history, we think this is especially clear. I will use the example of the First World War. A pupil cannot answer a question on the causes of the First World War, a question that academic historians are still wrestling with today, unless they know and understand the following:

1. The chronology of 1870-1914.

2. The main events and their specific consequences.

3. Abstract concepts such as imperialism, nationalism, militarism and the alliance system.

4. People and personalities.

5. Procedural knowledge of cause and effect which enables pupils to discern the relative impact of certain events.

All of the above can and should be taught explicitly. These are the equivalent of the short sprints and strength exercises that I use in my marathon analogy. Only when these have been mastered, will a pupil be close to answering a question which can be objectively agreed on as a 'sound' historical argument.

So, how do we actually teach the nuts and bolts?

The teacher leads the learning

For our most deprived pupils, eliciting knowledge from pupils which has not been taught to them explicitly is a catastrophe. It is common for teachers to suffer from 'expert induced blindness'. We constantly make assumptions about what our pupils know, when actually we need to assume that they know very little.

Substantive concepts such as 'monarchy', 'parliament', 'empire' and 'feudalism' all need the teacher to spend time explaining each one with great care. At Michaela, teachers plan their explanations with a rich and carefully sequenced series of examples to illustrate each idea. Much of what we do can be described as direct instruction. Michaela history lessons are generally reverse engineered using the sequence below:

1. Design the question(s) that pupils need to be able to answer.

2. Think carefully about what exactly the pupil needs to be able to know and do in order to answer that question.

3. Create a final assessment tool, normally a multiple-choice question for ideas or substantive concepts, or written tasks for broader questions.

4. Design smaller tasks that enable pupils to master the nuts and bolts needed for the final question(s).

5. Create lesson content and a series of examples which will enable pupils to understand the substantive or procedural concepts that are being taught.

During lessons, we use thorough checks for understanding, including multiple choice questions and a variety of quick-fire methods of formative assessment. The advantage of using a multiple-choice question to formatively assess is that we can design the distractors to test whether a pupil has fully understood an idea.

For example, the multiple-choice question below is designed to test whether the pupils have fully understood the concept of 'capitalism'. The idea of capitalism is complicated and requires a careful sequencing of examples and non-examples (or incorrect answers) before pupils will understand the idea. Most but not all capitalist countries are democratic, and the idea of private versus state ownership is complex. The question below aims to test whether this broad and flexible understanding of capitalism has been understood. Even before this question is attempted, there is a whole swathe of substantive knowledge that needs to have been taught, such as 'democracy', 'elections', 'means of production' and the 'state'.

Capitalism is a system...

a. *of economic control where the state or workers own the means of production.*

b. *where people are generally allowed to keep more of their own money.*

c. *where people are free to vote in elections which decide who forms the government.*

d. *of economic freedom, where the means of production are generally owned by private business.*

e. *generally associated with forms of democratic government.*

(three correct answers)

These core chunks of knowledge are the absolute building blocks of history. Pupils need to be 100% secure on basic questions, such as 'what is capitalism?', before they answer intermediate questions, such as 'why did Truman's belief in capitalism mean that he did not want communism to spread?' This question uses a skill, namely explanation, but requires the original building block of understanding what capitalism is in the first place. To refer back to the marathon analogy once again, these are the short sprints and exercises that are needed before running a full marathon.

Direct instruction has a reputation for being dull, repetitive and far too 'scientific' for the study of a subjective discipline such as history. However, at Michaela we spend a huge amount of time practising and feeding back to each other on our ability to tell a story and engage our pupils. This is an important caveat when we say we use direct instruction. The ability to capture the imagination of our pupils and to get them engaged in a topic is a vital part of the craft of the history teacher. Often, I find myself giving feedback to members of my department on how they build intrinsic motivation for their subject; how they use their voice and how they develop their presence in the classroom, as well as giving feedback about their clarity of explanation. Critically, none of the above can be implemented at all without the teacher working hard to create an exceptional relationship with their class.

Chronology and sequencing

Chronological understanding is vital in history. Important dates and events and a sense of period throughout history are vital in providing markers for children, to help them navigate the past.

I often use the term 'coat-pegs' in our department. A date is a metaphorical coat-peg, upon which you can then hang other examples and build your knowledge. The only way you can analyse and flex your knowledge is to follow on from what you already know. You can flex something from something, you cannot flex something from nothing. Chronology provides one of the most basic building blocks for historical understanding. For those pupils who do not take GCSE History, it is even more vital that a broad chronological understanding of British and European history is secure, so that they can see the long path upon which their society was created, as well as navigate a way for the future. Chronology provides a mental framework which helps pupils organise information more easily. For those taking the subject further, knowledge is sequential. This means that everything proceeds from prior understanding which in history, by definition, must happen chronologically.

Jumping around topic by topic across different time periods makes it impossible for children to follow the narrative and understand history. The great sweep of British, European and global history is lost in a fog of thematic units and compartmentalised topics that are chosen for their relevance rather than their coherence across a larger whole.

It is true that some form of chronology will undoubtably be taught in all history classrooms. Chronological understanding features on the National Curriculum and some element of chronological understanding is incorporated into all GCSE exam boards and topics. In theory however, at Key Stage 3 teachers can select topics from a huge time-frame (such as 1066-1509) and cover a handful of topics that are as chronologically distant from one another as we are from the execution of Charles I. At GCSE, thematic units still do not provide the chronological arc that pupils need to understand the breadth of history, precisely because the thematic units are designed to shoe-horn the chronology into the theme. Units on medicine through time, ensure that pupils' understanding of English history is covered only through the punctuation marks of medical change rather than a coherent political and social narrative. In some examples of thematic units, whole centuries are omitted from study. GCSE thematic units such as medicine through time, or the history of crime, or the history of warfare are fascinating to some, just as the history of cotton production, or the history of sport may interest others. However, these themes and niche interests only make sense once pupils have mastered the metaphorical coat pegs which allow them to situate new knowledge within a framework of existing knowledge. In this case, this is a broad narrative understanding of Britain's story. Thematic units are not a sufficient alternative to learning the basics.

At Michaela, we teach the chronology of each topic relentlessly. Key dates are tested and pupils are frequently asked to situate the period they are studying in terms of the immediate chronology (e.g. knowing that Charles I was executed in 1649 as part of a unit on the English Civil Wars) but also the proximal chronology (knowing that the Stuarts came after the Tudors and that the English Civil War was happening in the aftermath of the European Reformation). All of the above can and should be re-visited constantly as part of a systematic process of retrieval and practice that ensures pupils are always being asked about the nuts and bolts that lead on to the bigger questions.

A mastery curriculum

A choice to teach a topic in history is a choice not to teach a thousand others. This is the reality of curriculum design. With a finite number of hours in which to teach history, difficult choices must be made. Choosing to teach more topics will inevitably lead to the pupils being less likely to have mastered those topics well, if at all. So, how do we choose?

Put simply, at Michaela we believe we need to do what is right by the discipline of history, but we also need to do what is right for the children we teach. Different demographics require different approaches, but I would argue that this distinction is something all history teachers need to be thinking about carefully.

On the one hand, a skills-based curriculum, that has little chronological coherence does little service to the discipline. However, it is also true that on the other end of the scale, an incredibly rich history curriculum that has huge thematic, geographical and chronological breadth and detail, even if sequenced very well, can conflict with the fact that many children will never truly be able to master topics in history if the curriculum is spread too thinly.

When designing our curriculum at Michaela, we have been careful to ensure that the content is sequenced in a way that enables pupils to understand, and critically to remember the knowledge and skills that underpin the discipline. Covering fewer topics better is preferable to covering a huge span of history, but not particularly well. It is also true that if we choose topics well enough, it will make it much easier to learn the topics that we inevitably have to leave out. By choosing a strong spine of English history to run through our curriculum, it makes it much easier for pupils to make sense of those unlearned topics, because they have a schema to fit them in. Ensuring that pupils can recount a chronological narrative of English and British history also means that they understand the country and society in which they live.

The importance of English and British history

The recent trend amongst many history teachers to move away from national history can make it more difficult for many of our pupils, most of whom come from diverse backgrounds, to thoroughly understand their country and shape it for the future.

In history, the debate over 'how' we teach is made more acrimonious by the debate over 'what' we teach. Unlike in maths, languages and to some degree the sciences, where there is a fixed body of knowledge, there is no widespread consensus among history teachers about what content should be taught.

As well as helping pupils to understand the society in which they live, a strong chronological narrative history of one geographical place also makes it much easier for the pupils to see history coherently. It also means that critical substantive concepts can be embedded over time. A strong chronological narrative also makes it much easier to understand change and continuity as a second-order concept.

There is no denying that curriculum decisions are fraught with difficulty. However, the one common feature that unites all pupils studying in Britain, is that they all live in Britain. It is therefore vital that school history ensures that pupils know the history of England and Britain, and that this is prioritised over other considerations.

When I say that we prioritise English and British history, this is not to say that we do not want our pupils exposed to European and global history, far from it. At the time of writing, just over half of our Key Stage Three curriculum covers topics that pertain only to England or Britain. However, even these English and British topics are fundamentally linked to Europe and the wider world. Religious changes in Tudor England and the English Civil War are, of course, inextricably linked to the European Reformation. It is therefore just as important that Martin Luther is covered, as well as Henry VIII's penchant for decadent food and executing his wives. One topic cannot be understood without the other.

As I mention in my chapter on national identity, there have been times in the past when British history was taught uncritically, emphasising an inaccurate picture of British exceptionalism. We think it is essential that controversial aspects of Britain's past are explored through the discipline of history and that pupils are exposed to different interpretations of the past. Understanding how those interpretations have been formed requires a huge amount of knowledge, and it is this knowledge which, ironically, is often missing in a curriculum that places a disproportionate focus on skills.

It is also right that Britain's history includes multiple perspectives and gives a voice to those individuals and groups who contributed to the national story in a huge way, but whose stories have either been explicitly or implicitly side-lined because of ignorance, ideology or neglect.

There is an increasing trend amongst history teachers to ensure that history is appropriately global and diverse. It is understandable where this urge comes from. When teaching in diverse schools, it seems to make sense to try and make history more relevant to the global citizens sat in front of us. It also happily coincides with the recent push in historical scholarship to broaden our understanding of the past and to discern connections between societies. All of this seems sensible when carefully considered as part of the big picture of what our pupils need to know and understand.

However, there is a perception that British, and particularly English history is too mono-cultural and irrelevant. A common view is that too much English and British history is being taught in schools. A leading national newspaper published a piece in 2018, with a headline which stated that the emphasis on British history was "depriving students of balance".[1] The author stated that the curriculum focused on "British wins" and that pupils are brought up learning about the "strength and heroism of this country". A small minority of commentators seem to think that rote learning of dates and kings and queens is widespread in English schools, which betrays a lack of understanding of both rote learning and what is actually happening in history classrooms. You would be forgiven for thinking that young history teachers are graduating from PGCE institutions on a metaphorical conveyor belt, reciting kings and queens and obscure 18th century British prime ministers, while preparing to decorate their classrooms with world maps covered in the colour pink.

There is a perennial concern with national history that mirrors the reluctance of many to engage with the simple fact that we all live in one country and a comprehensive knowledge of the basics of British history are actually quite important if a citizen is to be well informed and happy living here. Many see national history as inevitably falling into the trap of political distortion and propaganda, the result of which means that history teachers are encouraged to move away from national narratives. To be clear, history as a discipline should never aim to convey an unbalanced and uncritical narrative of our national story. History should never be used to bolster 'blood and soil' nationalism or encourage an unthinking reverence towards all aspects of national life.

There are undoubtedly those who argue that school history should be a long tale of British exceptionalism. However, they are just as mistaken as those

---

1   *The Guardian* (May 2018) 'Secret Teacher: the emphasis on British history is depriving students of balance'

who argue that pupils should be consistently taught topics that make them uncomfortable with the country they live in. This is especially true for pupils from diverse communities. If a child is told that at every turn, British history has been a repository of malevolence, they will never be able to identify with the place that they should call home.

There are those who say that national history will always fall victim to politicisation, while in the same breath arguing for a curriculum where diversity is the primary aim, which is a political decision. Focusing on global history is a choice which is underpinned by a desire to mould pupils into global citizens. There is nothing wrong with this, but it is undeniably a political choice. All curriculum decisions are political, and it stands to reason that a political decision to globalise the curriculum should be treated equally to a decision that ensures pupils have a deep understanding of their own country's history. In fact, I would argue that the political decision to ensure pupils know their own country's history must be more important than the political decision to make them into global citizens. Not knowing the history of the place that pupils will inevitably spend the rest of their lives impoverishes all children, but particularly those from diverse backgrounds who never grow up with a thorough understanding of their own country's story. Of course, we want all our pupils to develop a broad understanding of global history and culture. National history and global history are not in conflict. In fact, you are far more likely to develop a global perspective by building out from local and national perspectives.

Many of these curriculum problems are compounded by the focus on relevance. In order to make our history lessons more relevant, we try and adapt our curriculum to ensure that pupils can identify with the topics, or will find them more engaging. British political history at GCSE is often avoided in favour of thematic units on migration, crime, warfare, or medicine because they are perceived to be more interesting and relevant to pupils' lives. A basic understanding of narrative British political history actually helps pupils understand all of those themes more thoroughly. Pupils do not walk away from units on medicine through time as scientifically literate global citizens, they finish school confused and ignorant because they have not mastered the basics. Having mastered a good sweep of British history will be more helpful to a pupil learning about a specific thematic focus. A chronological narrative is not opposed to thematic understanding – it enables it. A focus on national history does not stop you understanding global history – it enables it.

A thorough understanding of British history will incorporate political, social and economic history, as well as the history of warfare. It is also not particularly difficult to incorporate the histories of previously marginalised groups who have contributed to our national story within a narrative history of Britain. There is no reason why the role of Commonwealth soldiers during the First World War cannot be emphasised alongside the tragic loss of the Pals' Battalions from Northern England on the first day of the Battle of the Somme. There is no reason why pale, male and stale Liberal reforms of the early 20th century cannot be taught alongside the Suffragettes. There is no reason why medieval kingship cannot be taught alongside the economic revolution of the Peasants' Revolt. There is no reason why the codebreakers at Bletchley Park during the Second World War cannot be taught alongside the tragic story of Alan Turing. In fact, a chronological narrative of English and British history does not make it harder to incorporate these stories, it makes it much easier.

It is the right of any English schoolchild to know their own country's history before they are given the choice to drop the subject at GCSE. If children are not conversant in some way with the history of their own country, then they will never understand the country in which they live. History is arguably the most important subject that shapes our view of the world, and our place in it. We live, feel and breathe our history. To feel the pulse of a country, city, or village and to draw upon a rich mental map of stories, images and controversies is what a good understanding of history gives you. This is true of every country's history, but the country that our pupils will inevitably be spending most of their lives in is England and so it is even more vital that children have a clear narrative of how their country has changed over time. Even when our national history may seem controversial, it is still the right of any pupil in our country to know about it and to be able to engage in those debates in a meaningful way.

It may seem as if I am attacking a straw man, and that it is clearly the case that British history is taught, and is taught exceptionally well in English secondary schools. Some may say that the National Curriculum for England is a British history bonanza, and history teachers are routinely in the habit of encouraging their pupils to build papier-mâché motte and bailey castles, create antique-style copies of the Magna Carta or put Charles I on trial with the legal and historical expertise of, well, a 14-year-old. There are two responses to this:

1. The National Curriculum is not followed in depth by everyone.

2. Teaching history is not the same as learning history. Even if British history is taught, it may be taught in such a thematic, or skills-based way, that the knowledge is never really learned.

At Key Stage Three, there are many examples of schools following a hybrid Humanities programme of study, or who make relevance the priority in determining the choice of topics. An example I saw recently, was a curriculum where the only English history that was covered included the Normans, migration, Elizabeth I, slavery, and the Industrial Revolution before pupils were given the option to drop the subject. At GCSE, units on medicine, crime, migration, and warfare convey a British history narrative divorced from the over-arching political story that ensures these themes make sense. As part of the warfare British breadth study, it is entirely possible to study the tactics of the Parliamentarians at Naseby without knowing what they were fighting for. It is entirely possible to study the Battle of Agincourt without any knowledge of the Hundred Years War. At the time of writing, there are only two exam boards out of the four principal ones in England and Wales which offer a chronologically coherent political history of England and Britain. One look at the British thematic units which are chosen by the leading publishers of revision guides is enough to highlight which units are the most popular, and they most certainly are not the units which offer a broad and coherent political history of Britain.

A conversation with the average school leaver will disabuse you of any sense that they have a broad and flexible understanding of England's story. In a report entitled 'The Strange Death of History Teaching', Professor Derek Matthews cites a survey he organised for first year undergraduates at a prestigious Russell Group University, in which they were asked relatively simple history questions. Only 11.5% of the undergraduates could name a single British Prime Minister from the 19th century. This rose to 30.6% of students who had studied A-Level or AS Level history. 34.5% of his undergraduates could name the reigning monarch during the Spanish Armada, rising to 49.2% of students who had studied history at A-Level or AS Level. 30.6% knew the location of the Boer War, rising to 55.4% of students who had studied the subject post 16.[2]

---

2   Derek Matthews, *'The Strange Death of History Teaching'* (Cardiff, self-published, 2009)

Of course, individual facts in the style of a pub quiz do not constitute a coherent history curriculum. However, a failure to name any British Prime Minister from the 19th century, Elizabeth I or South Africa as the answers to the aforementioned questions betrays the fact that pupils would not have been exposed to 19th century British history, the Tudors, or the history of imperialism in Africa in a meaningful way at school.

There are, no doubt, many who see the whole idea of national identity as problematic. It is a position that does huge damage to those living in diverse communities. The nation-state exists, and education must prepare pupils for life in modern Britain. State schools are funded through general taxation, and so it is our responsibility so that pupils are prepared as best they can to succeed in this country. It is right that we design our curriculum to ensure that it prepares pupils to study history post 16 and at university. However, it is also right that we help them understand the country they live in. The push to globalise history may make sense to those who work in academic circles, but this is directly at odds with what is required, ironically, to make pupils understand the world around them, as they leave school confused and with no framework to fit these geographically disparate topics into. More damagingly, it encourages a dilution of the chronological narrative of England's story, which inhibits pupils from understanding the country and society in which they live.

At Michaela we believe it is the right of every one of our pupils to leave school knowing the basics of English and British history. Everyone in this country deserves to know England's story, from the fall of the Roman Empire to the present day. Those on the extreme left who argue that teaching English history is an act of oppression against those who may not want to identify as English or British are just as bad as those on the extreme right who wish to deny English history to children because of the colour of their skin. English history belongs to us all, just as England belongs to us all.

Geography at Michaela

Grace Steggall
@gracesteggall

Introduction

Geography is a vital feature of our curriculum because it is uniquely focussed on our sense of place. It is the main way in which we teach our pupils about the Earth that they live on, but it is also where we teach pupils about their home and the country of which they are a part. This is even more important in an area such as ours that is incredibly diverse and where we educate pupils who have varied and diverse heritages. This chapter will explain why geography is so important to us as a school, what we teach and give you a little insight into how we teach it at Michaela.

The importance of place

Cultural knowledge of the world

Geography is important because it teaches pupils how to understand and appreciate the world around them. This includes both our own country (with its many regions, cities and towns) and those beyond our shores. We desire two main outcomes from our geography curriculum. Firstly, that our pupils can enjoy the cultural capital and knowledge of the Earth that is taken for granted in more affluent settings. Secondly, that our pupils, regardless of where they or their parents come from, feel a sense of belonging and connection to England and the United Kingdom.

One of the ways in which we achieve this is by introducing our pupils to a sense of place. Place is a central concept in geography. Whereas *location* describes where something is physically situated, place ascribes meaning to that *location*; it is where the physical meets the human. Our view is that a child who has left school at 16 without any knowledge of *place* has been dealt a great injustice: such a child will have only a very narrow field of experience and will be oblivious to the world's varied cultures and landscapes. What is the point of education, if not to help a child learn more about the world beyond their own limited horizon?

However, it is just as vital that we take time in our geography curriculum to pull our pupils together as one community, particularly as our pupils' heritages span the entire globe. It is important for our pupils that the UK is not merely one location among many, but a place with which they have a deep and particular connection. How can anyone feel at home in a country they do not understand?

Socialisation

Therefore, the geography curriculum is an indispensable way in which we pull a diverse range of pupils together. The result is that they have at least one common story and they feel part of the 'we' that is England and the United Kingdom. This is not to erase or dismiss our pupils' diverse and varied heritages: just like Mo Farah, our pupils learn that they can be proud to be Somali, or Jamaican or Brazilian, as much as they can be proud to be English and British, too.

In our view, the humanities offer the perfect opportunity to nurture in pupils an understanding of the country in which they live. Through religion, pupils can see the spiritual foundations of Western thought, and draw parallels to other cultures; history allows pupils to participate in British cultural heritage, and understand Britain's historical context; geography equips pupils with an understanding of Britain as it is today. Together, the humanities provide crucial knowledge for pupils to draw their own conclusions about the world in which they live.

Whether we like it or not, teachers have a social and ethical responsibility to act as agents of socialisation. We must be more than mere curriculum dispensers, realising that the knowledge with which we equip pupils forms the basis of their lives. Geography, given its contemporary emphasis, needs to be at the heart of an education which aims to foster a common identity.

How is geography misunderstood?

Where we are

Some people argue that pupils need not be taught geography at secondary school at all. Some will say that 'they've done it all in primary school' or even that teaching pupils the continents and oceans is too easy because they know it all already. Whilst it is debatable whether year 7s do arrive at secondary school with all the essential geographical knowledge to progress in the KS3 curriculum, there is no harm in over-learning this essential global knowledge.

Confidence in knowing key nuggets of information about the world (like continents and oceans) is valuable, but also works to contextualise their learning of the United Kingdom.

There is an embarrassing lack of geographical literacy amongst Britons. This is partly the consequence of some very damaging pedagogical ideas. In geography, 'progressive' contemporary curricula have felt unable to prioritise regional/national geography – the geography of England and the British Isles – but have instead been at pains to emphasise a diverse and global outlook. Many teachers may ask: 'Why teach about our country when it's just one of many? Why spend more time on Britain than Bolivia?' But, in our view, this is to forsake one of the essential purposes of education – to create and nurture a sense of 'we' and home. By no means does this mean compromising the global literacy of our pupils; we give them an overarching understanding of the world in which to contextualise their own country.

Prioritising geographical literacy

Case studies and examples are an integral part of geography as a discipline. As a lecturer of mine used to say: 'you are learning about the geography of *somewhere*, not just the geography of *anywhere!*' Pupils should learn geographical principles first and foremost: key concepts, places, cultures, landscapes, and relationships between countries. Once mastered, teachers should then use an example or case study to contextualise the already mastered core content. The case study should not be the first time in which a pupil encounters a central concept! In a child's head, if they are taught the content through a case study, the information will always be learnt as an attachment of that case study, rather than more fundamental knowledge that might apply to other places in the world.

Unfortunately, geography is often taught with the more 'racy' information leading the discipline, but without the underlying place knowledge to contextualise new content. This is especially important in geography: with its natural split between physical and human, separate units can feel totally unconnected to each other. Pupils may be taught a topic on volcanoes, then one on development, then rivers and so on. This renders pupils unable to make wider connections across the curriculum because they have been taught isolated blocks of disparate content. If global and national literacy is promoted across the KS3 curriculum, pupils will have a better understanding of geography as a whole and make connections more easily.

Misconstrued 'backwards planning'

In maths, it would be absurd to teach pupils to solve simultaneous equations before they learn their times tables. For some reason, few schools carry this logic over to geography: I have seen schools teach case studies about the Nepal earthquake before pupils have any proper understanding of earthquakes *or* Nepal! This leaves pupils snookered when it comes to understanding, for example, the Nepal earthquake in the context of earthquakes more broadly. This forces geography teachers to teach sentences about case studies by rote. The value of geography is missed entirely in such approaches, even if pupils succeed in stringing together exam answers (which many do not). It is deeply ironic that the progressive insistence on the superiority of project-based learning (which led to a preference for teaching *through* case studies) has resulted in an *increased* prevalence of rote learning in schools.

Many schools in Britain follow a 'backwards planning' curriculum. This means they acknowledge the desired result and work backwards from it. This is opposed to a traditional curriculum which starts with key curriculum content. Deciding where you hope to end up and reverse engineering is not necessarily bad (in fact, it is often the basis of very good planning). The problem here is where the backwards planning begins at the GCSE criteria and thus constricts KS3 to become a narrower version of the GCSE. Some schools have reduced education to GCSE outcomes (important as they are) and construct their curriculum accordingly (only focussing on the GCSE specifications). In fact, I have heard of geography being called a '5-year GCSE' (and even more extreme, a '7-year A Level').

This overlooks the hierarchy of knowledge around which we base our curriculum: central concepts are taught independently so that case studies can be inserted into a secure and rigorous knowledge base. For example, most GCSE specifications require a case study of an emerging country (such as Brazil). Some schools will teach it in year 7, potentially again in year 8, and again during KS4. For many, they will double up their 'urban' unit by teaching from the same country (for example, Rio de Janeiro). Having hamstrung themselves on a narrow curriculum, they are forced to miss out on the opportunity to teach about different countries.

The hinterland of knowledge

The central knowledge in geography needs to be taught directly, not shoehorned indirectly through an example or case study. There is so much technical language in the new geography GCSE that pupils will be left floundering without structured guidance, especially if taught at KS3. Take this GCSE sentence as an example: *'Nepal (low income country-LIC) was unable to prevent some serious effects of its earthquake because the infrastructure was not stable enough to reduce fatalities.'* Pupils may be able to read this but wholly unable to comprehend it. Pupils need to know lots about Nepal, about LICs and their characteristics, an implied knowledge of 'economy', what an earthquake is, what an effect is, which effects were specific to the Nepal earthquake, what infrastructure is, how better infrastructure could have prevented some of the effects, what fatalities are, and much more! It becomes obvious that a clear and well-connected curriculum (not focussed just on the Nepal case study) is required for pupils to access even this one sentence.

The irony of the misconstrued 'backwards planning' curriculum: it sets its desired results as improved GCSE outcomes, but actively *impedes* GCSE success by ignoring a hinterland of necessary knowledge to succeed. KS3 is an important period in which pupils should be able to enrich their understanding and create a deep network of national, regional and global place knowledge. A pupil equipped with this will see the GCSE content as meaningful, and will not only succeed academically, but will be really enriched by it.

Geography at Michaela

In order to create a meaningful curriculum at Michaela we had to start with some questions: what is worth learning, and how should it be structured? Our vision for pupils is that they have enough geographical literacy to travel anywhere in the UK and understand its cultural, physical and historical heritage – to *feel* it is part of who they are as British citizens.

KS3 curriculum

Our KS3 curriculum focuses on place knowledge. Initially, pupils learn about all seven continents and ten major physical (natural) and human (man-made) features in each. This is taught continent by continent, starting in Europe and ending in Antarctica. We teach key capital cities, major rivers, major mountain ranges, different landscapes (savannas, plains, deserts). Already, this provides pupils with a global literacy to rival many adults! Later, when we teach geographical concepts like earthquakes, pupils have this hinterland of knowledge to contextualise new information, rendered meaningful and free to be directed towards different questions.

Once we have toured the globe, we focus on the United Kingdom, Great Britain and the British Isles. You may be wondering the difference between them all, or why we even have so many names... ask our year 7s and they'll tell you! We teach counties, cities, coastal regions, mountain ranges, rivers, and even focus on cultural differences between Wales, Scotland, England and Northern Ireland. The kids truly enjoy it, enabling them to relate to their country on a deeper level.

GCSE

During our lessons, we home in on key features, identify location and significance, and provide maps where pupils label and learn the places. As starters in lessons, we draw up blank maps and quickly quiz pupils on different mountain ranges, rivers, or cities etc. Once the pupils have this knowledge, we continually embed this through the GCSE. It is useful information in its own right; it is the cultural capital which the privately educated take for granted; it is a way of encouraging pupils to feel proud as knowledgeable citizens of their country. *Our* country.

By the time our year 10 pupils begin their GCSEs, they have developed such strong background knowledge that they are hungry to learn about the world and ready to succeed. Only some of this background is specifically required by a GCSE specification (though it does make the course easier) – we simply believe it to be important. We know it will help them to belong to the UK on so many levels. We know we are doing our jobs as teachers to prepare our pupils for the world outside Michaela and are setting them on a good footing for life.

Conclusion

A varied KS3 curriculum is a springboard for GCSE success and a way of teaching pupils valuable global and national knowledge. Not only this, but a way of creating a sense of belonging and identity for our pupils who come from diverse backgrounds. We explicitly teach fundamental concepts, processes and places so our pupils have a contextual understanding of the world and our country. All in all, the way we prioritise these things means pupils can carry this understanding with them for life, taking it around the country and world with them.

Religious Education at Michaela

Sarah James

Introduction

Growing up, one of my favourite films was 'The Prince of Egypt': I loved the flamboyant musical numbers, I despised the Pharaoh's magicians, and secretly I wished I had the sass and poise of Moses' wife, Zipporah.

However, amidst my brother's and my comic attempts to 'dance like Egyptians' lurked some more profound messages. Re-watching the film the other day, I was taken by the idea of humanity as a beautifully and skilfully made tapestry. In the song 'Through Heaven's Eyes', Jethro sings: 'a single thread in a tapestry, though its colour brightly shines, can never see its purpose in the pattern of the grand design.' Taken as metaphor, this 'grand design' can be viewed as the 'big picture' of human civilisation. The threads in this tapestry of humanity represent different cultures, faiths and periods of history that must be clearly understood so that we might see the intricacy and beauty of the rich tapestry of life.

This explains why religious education is so important to us at Michaela. We know that, if children are truly to see this tapestry in all its rich pattern and beauty, it must be brought out in front of their eyes. Good religious education helps young people to see this tapestry as a complex, intricate and richly fascinating network of ideas and practices that bind people and peoples together.

This chapter therefore will attempt to explain why religious education must form a key component in any knowledge-rich education. It will try to give those who haven't visited the school some sense of how that is achieved.

The state of the subject

Teachers up and down the country strongly disagree about what good religious education looks like and how it should be taught. This can be seen in the plethora of names given to the subject: Religious Education (RE), Religion, Philosophy and Ethics (RPE), Worldview Studies, Citizenship and Religion (RZ) and Religious Knowledge. In schools across the country, religious education is often an uneasy hotchpotch of different subject areas including citizenship, government and politics, general studies, sometimes with only a sprinkling of religion in order to fulfil the legal requirement that all pupils between the ages of 5 and 18 receive some form of religious education. Within some classrooms, we see children building mock temples to 're-enact Buddhist meditation practices' and creating mock political elections to vote for a particular Sikh Guru. A small number of teachers have even taken to dressing up in religious clothing as a way of teaching children about religious dress. It appears that there is no consensus about what we should teach nor how we should teach it.

The consequences of this disciplinary confusion are starting to come into view. In the last eight years, the number of pupils taking religious education has decreased by 42.6%[1] and the number of pupils taking religious education into A level has dropped by 22%.[2] With fewer pupils taking religious education at GCSE many schools have stopped providing the subject at all. The Final Report of the Commission on RE found that, in 2016, 33.4% of schools did not offer any religious education at KS4 and a further 23.1% didn't offer any religious education at KS3.[3] This is despite the subject being a statutory requirement for all children in state maintained, academy and free schools.

Moreover, the effect of such growing religious illiteracy on our society is striking. A survey report[4] by the Bible Society showed that 27% of the British population believed Superman was or could be a biblical story. Included among these 'biblical stories' were the Hunger Games and Harry Potter. Perhaps unsurprisingly, therefore, in October 2013, Ofsted found that the quality of religious education in around half the lessons seen was less than 'good'[5].

---

1 https://www.religiouseducationcouncil.org.uk/news/religious-studies-gcse-entries-fall-despite-popularity-among-pupils/

2 https://www.religiouseducationcouncil.org.uk/news/religious-studies-a-level-entries-decline-by-22-8-as-the-subject-is-squeezed-out-of-the-curriculum/

3 https://www.commissiononre.org.uk/wp-content/uploads/2018/09/Final-Report-of-the-Commission-on-RE.pdf

4 https://www.biblesociety.org.uk/uploads/content/projects/Bible-Society-Report_030214_final_.pdf P13

5 https://assets.publishing.service.gov.uk/government/uploads/system/uploads/attachment_data/file/413157/Religious_education_-_realising_the_potential.pdf

Whilst our primary motivation for teaching religion at Michaela is to expose children to these diverse and binding threads of the human tapestry, religious illiteracy continues to taint the overall story of our society. This illiteracy is potentially very dangerous. It would be naïve to suggest that inadequate religious education is the cause of religious discrimination and hatred in this country. However, we shouldn't underestimate the power that knowledge has to defeat prejudice. We should teach children about religion because religions, and the ideas and assumptions that they contain, are part of the rich and fascinating tapestry of humanity. But shared religious understanding has practical benefits, too. By learning about the assumptions that inform our different worldviews, we can often knock down some of the barriers that seem to divide us. It is easier to love our neighbour when we know who they are and what they hold sacred. By teaching children about what others most value, they are able to see not just the diversity of the threads in this tapestry, but the way in which these threads are interwoven, binding us together.

What do we teach at Michaela?

At Michaela, we have a clear sense of what should be studied in religion and how our teachers should go about it.

For us, the study of this rich tapestry starts with the Judeo-Christian tradition which forms the traditional bedrock of ideas and assumptions both in Britain and the West. Regardless of the personal beliefs that our pupils may or may not hold, it is our responsibility to help our pupils understand the ideas that underpin the country and the culture in which they live.

Such ideas are an important aspect of our culture, permeating our artwork, literature, and even our language, in powerful ways. The GCSE set text, 'An Inspector Calls,' captures the Christian emphasis of *agape*, the unconditional love for one's neighbour, whilst the death of King Duncan in Shakespeare's 'Macbeth' echoes the crucifixion of Christ. In history, the abolition of the slave trade and the song 'Amazing Grace' are inexorably entwined with non-conformist Christian history. The lyrics 'I was lost and now am found' are so much more intelligible when a pupil has learnt about the Parable of the Prodigal Son and the doctrine of Grace.

British history and Christianity are also inseparable: The Crusades, the Break from Rome, the English Civil War all serve as examples of the way in which history and belief are intertwined. As the philosopher

Larry Siedentop has argued in his book, *Inventing the Individual,* even the West's attachment to liberal individualism is rooted in the revolution of ideas that took place around the Mediterranean in the first century CE. More recently, the historian Tom Holland has drawn public attention to the Christian underpinnings of much of contemporary society, pointing out that even our understanding of secularism – a word drawn from Christian understandings of the 'saeculum' (roughly, 'our span of living memory') – points to the influence of Christianity on these isles. As a non-denominational school, our role is not to make judgements about whether this influence was, or remains, a good or bad thing. However, we do believe that learning about Christianity is a vital component in understanding this country's cultural heritage.

Religious knowledge is also fundamental to accessing other subjects in the curriculum. A child who lacks any knowledge of Genesis, The Fall or the Crucifixion is greatly disadvantaged in appreciating great artwork, literature, and the history of Western society. If we do not acknowledge the seismic changes and influence upon civilisation of this tradition, we fail in our responsibility to depict the 'tapestry of humanity' as vividly as we should.

However, we also know that the rich tapestry of human civilisation requires us to look beyond the tradition of ideas in this country. To be British today is to live alongside people of all faiths and none at all. Our neighbours are Christians, Muslims, Jews, Hindus, Sikhs, Buddhists, atheists and many more, and being part of British society is to learn to live amongst the familiar and the unfamiliar with love and acceptance. For this reason, we also devote significant curriculum time to world religions such as Islam and Buddhism, so that our pupils can appreciate the breadth of ideas from around the globe as well as being familiar with the ideas and practices that predominate closer to home. With this in mind, we also give our pupils an introduction to those philosophers whose legacies are most keenly felt – Plato and Aristotle from the pre-Christian world and sceptics, such as Bentham and Hume, whose contributions to the rich tapestry of civilisation are so significant.

Although we still have a lot to learn, we believe that our pedagogical philosophy is bearing fruit. In our most recent set of exam results, 83% of our pupils achieved grade 9-7, a particularly strong set of results given that almost the entire year group take the subject. Nearly 1 in 3 of those achieved a grade 9, placing them in the top 3% of all candidates nationally. Whilst we are so proud of the hard work of both pupils and staff, we hope to build on this success by continuing to develop our curriculum and teaching practice with each passing year.

How do we teach religion at Michaela?

What distinguishes the teaching of religion at Michaela is not just the 'what' but the 'how'. There isn't space here to discuss all of the various techniques we use to make sure what we want to teach 'sticks', but there are a few that are worthy of further explanation.

Stories

'Stories are a communal currency of humanity.' –Tahir Shah, Arabian Nights

At Michaela, we create our own booklets for each of the topics we teach. There are several benefits to this, but perhaps the most notable is that it helps our teachers to tell the story of religion so that our pupils can see how individual units fit within a greater narrative arc. In the same way that our history department teaches about the Anglo-Saxons before the Norman Conquest, and the First World War before the Second World War, we aim to teach our pupils about the stories of the Hebrew Bible or Old Testament before the New Testament, or the Night of Power before the Battle of Karbala. We believe that helping our pupils to see the story of a religion, as they proceed from Year 7 to 8 to 9, is one of the secrets of our success.

The pedagogical benefits to this approach cannot be overstated. It is almost impossible to explain to a pupil why Jesus' crucifixion is of such significance to Christians, unless they understand why Christians believe such a sacrifice was necessary and where the act of crucifixion sits in the wider Christian story of God's relationship with humankind. For this reason, all our pupils begin Year 7 with Genesis and the story of the Fall. They learn that Christians believe that the death of Jesus was necessary in order to atone for humanity's sins and reconcile human beings back to God. In the same way, a pupil cannot properly understand the significance of fasting during the month of Ramadan until they have been taught about *'Laylat al-Qadr'* – the 'Night of Power'. This was the night in 610 CE when Muslims believe the Angel Jibril appeared to Muhammad and he first began receiving the Qur'an. The present-day practice of fasting during the month of Ramadan in order to draw closer to God and reflect on the miracle of this revelation cannot be fully understood outside of this. A religious practice makes much more sense once the reason for its practise has been clearly explained.

This emphasis on the wider story of a religion recognises that the study of religion is often both cumulative and hierarchical. Most topics cannot be understood in isolation or in an order that is haphazard, for the same reason that learning Pythagoras is impossible without first learning basic addition and subtraction. Rather, topics in religion must be placed within a broader narrative arc or 'story' of the religion, which accepts that mastery of one topic is often required before moving on to another.

This overall story of the curriculum is reinforced with recap tasks at the beginning of each lesson, which prompt the pupils to draw from their knowledge, not just of previous lessons, but of previous units, sometimes going right back to their very first lessons at the school. This way pupils at Michaela are constantly being asked to retrieve what they have already learnt about a religion or a set of ideas, keeping it fresh in their minds, and helping them to access new ideas that may well depend on a thorough understanding of topics that, otherwise, would be long forgotten.

Drills

The idea that pupils should be 'drilled' is unpopular in contemporary Western education. Drills, and other repetitive tasks like them, cut against all the values championed by teachers who argue that children should be more spontaneous and lead their own learning, without the overbearing influence of adult authority.

However, at Michaela, we believe that some drilling, used moderately and judiciously, can make learning, in the long run, much easier for pupils. We know that by drilling the component parts of a more complex task, just as instrumentalists do with scales or arpeggios, we can free up our pupils to devote their working memory to the parts of the task that are most abstract or complex.

In the study of religion, a good example of this is the drilling of quotations. By memorising quotations, pupils are freed up to spend time thinking about what they really mean and to be able to apply them to more complex questions. The purpose of drilling is not to create robots of our children. Drilling enables children to grasp the building blocks of religion with the purpose of going on to use these building blocks to understand more intricate ideas.

Any scholar of religion – and particularly Abrahamic religion – knows that scriptural knowledge is fundamental to a comprehensive knowledge of a religion. Buried beneath any discussion between the Abrahamic faiths, and certainly *within* them, are disagreements about how to interpret this or that line of revelation. Knowing your scripture, then, is a vital component in knowing religion.

The process by which we teach the pupils to become familiar with this scripture involves some drilling, which we break down for the pupils into a series of stages:

Stage 1

We begin with inflexible knowledge. Pupils spend time memorising the quotation. For example:

"He is God the One, God the eternal. He begot no one nor was He begotten.' (Surah 112: 1-3)

They do this using drills such as the one below:

Which words are missing from the quotations?

"He is God the One, God the *******."

We make these drills harder by removing more words until pupils are required to write the entire quotation from memory.

At this point, all pupils have memorised the quotations. We've found that these quotations act as a 'hook for knowledge.' For example, a child remembers the quotation, 'He is God the One, God the eternal. He begot no one nor was He begotten.' They then remember that the oneness of God in Arabic is called tawhid, which is part of the Six Articles of Faith, and that rejecting or turning away from the oneness of God is a grave sin in Islam known as 'shirk'. For pupils in the exam, one quotation can act as a 'hook' or memory aid for a number of other concepts they have learnt in class. An essay paragraph can be formed around this quotation.

Stage 2

When pupils have mastered this, we increase the level of challenge by asking pupils to match quotations with the beliefs the text supports. This helps pupils to formulate point sentences. For example:

Give a quotation to support the following Islamic beliefs:

1. Muslims believe in the oneness of God. This is known as 'tawhid.'

For this belief or 'point sentence' pupils should choose:

"He is God the One, God the eternal. He begot no one nor was He begotten." (Surah 112:1-3)

We also include multiple choice drills where pupils have to choose the correct point sentence for the quotation that will follow.

Stage 3

The final stage is to move onto explanation drills where we practise explaining what the quotation means. The point sentence and explanation drills can be done in isolation depending on the strengths and weaknesses of the class – or they can be done together to help structure paragraphs as a class.

We've found these drills to be invaluable both in providing hooks for knowledge through the simple memorisation of a quotation, but also in piece by piece building deeper understanding of the quotation, which can then be manipulated by the pupil in an exam context.

Weekly Quizzing

Anyone who has ever taught a class with lower prior attainment will be familiar with the emotional rollercoaster that accompanies weekly lessons. One of the great frustrations for a teacher is finishing a lesson feeling as if a class has really grasped a story or a concept only to be greeted by blank faces the following week. Just as frustrating is the feeling when a pupil seems sparky and ebullient, proudly showing off her knowledge to the rest of the class, but later bombs an upcoming mock exam.

One of the biggest barriers to our children flying in religion is their seeming inability to remember information from one week to the next, as well as the challenges they have manipulating that knowledge in a way that will enable them to answer unseen exam questions.

We try to address these barriers through weekly quizzes in which we test the substantive knowledge – the 'nuts and bolts' – that pupils need to grasp before they can move on to more complex ideas and discussions.

For example:

1. *What word means 'the belief that there is one God?'*

2. *How were the Israelites different from the Canaanites?*

The questions often surprise teachers who visit, who are unused to seeing such seemingly simplistic questions posed to pupils of reasonably mature age and ability.

However, what they often miss is the very deliberate way in which the knowledge demonstrated in one question is built upon the understanding shown in another. Here, for example, the answer to the first question helps 'unlock' an answer to the second. The pupil explains that the belief in one God is known as monotheism and *then* can say that Israelites differ from the Canaanites because, whereas the Israelites were monotheistic, the Canaanites were polytheistic.

In this way, we build pupils' understanding by connecting 'nodes' of knowledge and understanding together piece by piece. Such deliberate sequencing, and the weekly testing that accompanies it, creates an overall understanding of the theology of Judaism and the history of the Israelites which is carefully and deliberately built up week by week.

Of course, the quizzing of these 'nuts and bolts' on its own would not constitute a very good education at all. However, weekly testing of these fundamentals, much like the weekly drilling of quotations, leads to much greater fluency and ease in more abstract tasks.

Here, you can see how we blend together these different forms of assessment so that, each week, pupils are mastering the 'nuts and bolts' at the same time as they apply their knowledge to longer and more conceptually challenging questions and discussions.

Task	Date set	Date due

Section A:
Plan each of these questions. You should fill one A4 page per <u>12 mark</u> essay- in the same format as the template on the back of this document.
 	
You will be quizzed on one of them the lesson your homework is due.
 	
Existence of God and Revelation:
   1. 'Special revelation does not prove that God exists.' [12]
 	
Crime and punishment:
   1. 'The death penalty is always wrong.' [12]
   2. 'All crime is caused by greed.' [12]
   3. 'Reformation is the most important aim of punishment.' [12]
 	
War and peace:
   4. 'Violence is never justified.' [12]
   5. 'There are no good reasons for countries to possess nuclear weapons.' [12]
 	
Section B:
 	
Revise all quotations from Peace and Conflict for a short quiz on Monday.		

Section A tests the ability of pupils to manipulate what they know to answer an exam question. This gets to the heart of how well a pupil has understood something and whether they can apply it accurately in an exam context.

However, Section B tests the substantive knowledge – 'nuts and bolts'. Can pupils remember the quotations that they will need to support their answers in more abstract tasks?

We do this weekly quizzing for the same reason that we drill quotations. An excellent understanding of the 'nuts and bolts' unlocks the more complex and nuanced world of religious thought and interpretation. This is not the same as rote learning. As a department, we haven't been successful if knowledge comes without understanding. We drill and quiz the basic concepts so that pupils can understand the more complex concepts. The two must go together. By checking that the basics have been mastered, at the same time as checking that the basics can be manipulated and applied across different contexts, we better prepare our pupils to engage with the most complex conceptual questions thrown up by the subject. Thus, our assessment of the basics *and* the more complex go hand-in-hand.

Conclusion

As a department, we are still learning and making changes all the time. These are just a few of the techniques we use to convey the tapestry of humanity to our pupils in a way that will serve them well, both for their exams and for their lives to come.

As teachers of religion, our job is to give children the tools and the knowledge to understand the religions and ideas that surround them, as well as to access their cultural heritage. Equipped with this knowledge, it is for them to decide what their purpose or identity is in the 'grand design' that Jethro sings about in 'The Prince of Egypt' and which so fascinated me as a child. My hope is that our pupils, and pupils across our country, can learn about this 'tapestry of humanity' in all its beauty. With knowledge and understanding of what has come before them, and the ideas and assumptions that have shaped civilisation, they can see themselves as valuable, complex and unique threads of the 'tapestry of humanity' which they are continuing to weave.

Why Stormzy Could Never Replace Mozart

Pritesh Raichura

@Mr_Raichura

Three years ago, I knew next to nothing about western classical music. The extent of my knowledge was that I had heard of Beethoven and could recognise his famous fifth symphony, 'dum dum dum dum...', and I had learned to play the beginning of *Für Elise* on the keyboard in Year 9 at school. Who was Vivaldi? Gustav Holst? I'd never heard of them. Chopin *who*? I couldn't recognise a single one of Tchaikovsky's pieces and couldn't even tell you Camille Saint-Saëns was a composer.

Then I became a form tutor at Michaela. Every morning during term, like all form tutors at Michaela, I receive an email from our Head of Music. The email contains a hyperlink and some basic facts about a famous piece of classical music that we can play to our form as they come into class. Grieg's 'In the Hall of the Mountain King', Vivaldi's 'Spring', Tchaikovsky's 'Waltz of the Flowers' and Gustav Holst's 'Jupiter' are among the regulars that feature.

Every single day, five minutes at a time, I have been exposed to these beautiful pieces of art. These evocative sounds of the human imagination and spirit have poured into my ears, awakening in me, at first, just a passing interest, and then a deep passion for classical music. What impact has this had on me? I am now an ardent listener of Classic FM; I have spotted countless references to classical music in literature, news articles, podcasts and in conversation that I once would have missed; now, I *actively* seek out the opportunities to experience this music played live. In short, this newfound knowledge has opened up a multitude of experiences for me.

If this is the impact of a simple morning routine on *me*, what impact could it have on my *pupils*?

Come May 2019 and a debate on Twitter fills my timeline: 'Stormzy should replace Mozart in music classrooms'[1]. My instinctive disagreement prompted

---

1   Stormzy Should Replace Mozart in UK Music Classrooms, Study Says. Sky News. Available on: https://news.sky.com/story/stormzy-should-replace-mozart-in-uk-music-classrooms-study-says-11725859

me to put pen to paper and share exactly why I think this is completely misguided. It's not just the idea that grime should replace classical music that I find saddening, but the wider beliefs about curriculum, powerful knowledge, engagement and authority that this Twitter storm (excuse the pun) reveals. I should add that my gripe is not with Stormzy himself. I use Stormzy purely as an example to illustrate the criteria for excluding certain music from the curriculum: music should not be chosen simply for the sake of relevance. Nor should it include music where the artist is an active negative influence in our pupils' lives. What absolutely must be present in the curriculum is music that has endured for centuries.

Powerful Knowledge

Conversations about music must involve Mozart; knowledge of his work constitutes powerful knowledge in music, which liberates pupils from their everyday experiences.[2] An excellent curriculum in any discipline ought to be a curated tour of the most influential creators of the knowledge that contributes to that particular discipline. In literature this must include Shakespeare; in physics, Newton; in music, Mozart. These thinkers' works have endured for centuries. Time and time again, they have been hailed as being remarkable contributions to our civilisation. This is why knowledge of their works constitutes powerful knowledge.

So, what are the arguments of those teachers who insist Stormzy should either replace or sit alongside Mozart in the curriculum? There are two main arguments: pupil choice and pupil engagement.

Pupil Choice

Should pupils – rather than teachers – elect the genres and composers to be studied in the music curriculum, like some sort of democracy? My answer is a resounding, 'No'. Pupils cannot choose to learn about composers they have never heard of. They do not have a bird's-eye view of the whole of the musical domain. Pupils making curricular decisions results in a curriculum becoming a conduit for exploring pupils' existing interests and knowledge rather than broadening them. If we only indulge pupils' existing tastes, we deny them the opportunity to access something beautiful that they wouldn't otherwise

---

2   Asbee, Ruth (2018) https://rosalindwalker.wordpress.com/2018/12/05/the-language-of-curriculum/

be exposed to. It is this new knowledge that will allow pupils to participate in conversations about what constitutes the 'best music'; to deny knowledge of Mozart is to exclude our pupils from these conversations.

The same applies to every subject: we have a duty to curate the most powerful knowledge that exposes our pupils to the very best that has been thought, said, and composed in our respective disciplines' curricula. Access to this knowledge has to come from somewhere: it will either come from the pupils' parents (which will be true of pupils from advantaged backgrounds), or it will come from the school curriculum we consciously design.[3] Only the latter ensures every single pupil receives their entitlement to this knowledge.

Pupil Engagement

What about engagement? Surely, pupils who love Stormzy will be more engaged learning about his work rather than Mozart's? To think pupils find Mozart irrelevant is to be mistaken. How can we be so presumptuous as to believe that a composer, whom people around the world have admired for centuries, would not speak to the souls of the pupils in front of us today? As teachers, we should revel in the opportunity to share the delights of Bach and Tchaikovsky with our pupils. We can engage pupils by expressing our sheer excitement when we teach about the greatest and most influential composers of all time; our joy fizzing and bubbling on our animated faces when we react with sheer delight listening to their works.

More broadly, critics of a curriculum that includes lots of 'dead white men' entirely miss the point: an artist is more than their race. Shakespeare doesn't need to be Asian for Asian pupils to relate to the profound ideas about the human condition contained within his works; Mozart doesn't need to be black for black pupils' hearts to soar listening to his symphonies. Maya Angelou famously said she believed Shakespeare could only be a black woman. As a science teacher, I would never dream of dropping Newton's laws of motion from my curriculum because I suspect my pupils might not relate to him or find another scientist's work more interesting. So why should this happen in the arts?

3   Young, M., Lambert, D., Roberts, C. and Roberts, M., 2014. *Knowledge and the future school: Curriculum and social justice.* Bloomsbury Publishing.

If these arguments about pupil choice and engagement have left you wondering why Stormzy couldn't sit alongside, rather than instead of Mozart in a curriculum, then there are two main factors to consider: what influence does Stormzy have on our pupils and what are the opportunity costs?

Pupils find grime artists like Stormzy cool. These artists boast about living lavish and indulgent lifestyles and exert a very real influence on our pupils. They regularly feature in the charts and in mainstream media. They have the capacity to influence the way our pupils think. Unfortunately, their songs contain lyrics that are both violent and misogynistic. The potential for their music to act as a negative influence is therefore significant.

It is important to remember that we have limited time with our pupils. There is a potential opportunity cost with every decision we make: choosing to spend time learning about Stormzy – even if it is to challenge the content of his songs – is time taken away from learning about Vivaldi and Tchaikovsky.

This is not to say that our curriculum consists entirely of classical music pieces. More modern music is featured if the artists do not encourage a lifestyle that is extremely dangerous for our young people.

Institutional Racism

In his TED talk, 'Black Murder is Normal', Michael Smith argues that indeed, 'black murder is normal' in America[4]. He links the disproportionately high homicide statistics amongst black communities to the societal expectations for black Americans to reference killing each other in their music. Criminality, he argues, is inherent in society's misguided view of 'blackness'. Nobody questions the black artist who raps about drive-by shootings; it is viewed as normal because the artist is black. The fact that the music industry condones this stereotype constitutes institutional racism. Consumers are complicit too, since the music industry is ultimately driven by their choices. Smith takes his argument further when he says that the artists who write violent lyrics also succumb to this tragic stereotype, making them victims of systemic racism themselves. This on its own is a compelling argument to exclude music, like the type I describe above, from our curriculum. But of course, we see the everyday effects of this type of

---

4   Smith, Michael, 2015 – Black Murder is Normal. https://www.youtube.com/watch?v=1DxH L2i3cZo&feature=youtu.be Accessed 11th April 2020

music all the time. It manifests itself in seemingly insignificant traits: in the gait of our pupils; their sartorial choices; their gun-sign gestures. But these traits are a part of the very same culture that Smith describes as making black murder normal. The power of this culture's influence is not to be underestimated. It is heartbreaking how this music is part of a culture that can destroy our pupils' lives.

Powerful Knowledge Must Come from School

Our pupils have the right to inherit the culture of our wonderful civilisation. For millennia, humanity has built up, discovered, composed and constructed beautiful and elegant knowledge, be it in the form of poetry, literature, scientific theories, mathematical proofs, symphonies or works of art. The goal of a curriculum is to curate the outcomes of this human endeavour so that our pupils can marvel at, understand and appreciate these pinnacles of human achievement. Let's not take that away from our pupils.

I was born and raised in the London Borough of Brent – the same borough as Michaela Community School. I know first-hand what sort of music pupils here choose to listen to. I cannot recount a single instance from my childhood where my friends and I talked about classical music. Why would we, given that 50 Cent (Get Rich or Die Tryin') and Akon (of Konvict Music, alluding to the fact that the rapper has spent time in prison) were on the scene releasing high-octane songs? The works of these rappers do not need to be taught in music classrooms for them to be discovered or appreciated. I discovered the work of Stormzy without any help at all – as will my pupils. My discovery of Mozart, Tchaikovsky and Bach came about when I was purposefully exposed to their works. How would have I come across them otherwise?

It could only have been at school where someone could have said, 'Listen to this – this is music that isn't in the charts and it hasn't been popular for just a few weeks. It is music that has been loved for over a hundred years and continues to be admired all over the world', for it to even register as something worth appreciating. My love of classical music blossomed through purposeful exposure during Michaela form time. My curiosity to learn more about classical music emerged from my newfound knowledge – not the other way around. I now always have my ears open for references to classical music because knowledge is sticky. Such a permanent transformation is no accident: it came from a carefully curated tutor-time activity. Luckily for

Michaela pupils, in addition to this excellent tutor-time curriculum, they have a remarkably designed music curriculum. Take a look at a segment of the KS3 curriculum below and imagine how much more knowledge and curiosity Michaela pupils have than I do. They are incredibly lucky.

Era	Composer	Work
Baroque (1600-1750)	Vivaldi	Spring (Allegro) from Four Seasons
		Summer (Presto) from Four Seasons
	Bach	First prelude from The Well-Tempered Clavier
Classical (1750-1830)	Haydn	Andante from Symphony No. 101 (The Clock)
		Andante from Symphony No. 94 (Surprise Symphony)
	Mozart	1st movement (Allegro) of Eine Kleine Nachtmusik
		2nd movement (Romanze) of Eine Kleine Nachtmusik
	Beethoven	Symphony No. 5
		Symphony No. 9 'Ode to Joy'
Romantic (1830-1900s)	Wagner	Ride of the Valkyries (from 'The Ring')
	Tchaikovsky	Swan Theme (from 'Swan Lake')
		Dance of the Sugar Plum Fairy (from 'The Nutcracker')
	Saint-Saens	The Swan (from 'The Carnival of the Animals')
	Brahms	Hungarian Dance No. 5
	Grieg	Piano Concerto in A Minor
		In the Hall of the Mountain King (from 'Peer Gynt')
Modern (1900-)	Prokofiev	Montagues and Capulets/Dance of the Knights (from 'Romeo and Juliet')
		The Cat (from 'Peter and the Wolf')
	Gershwin	Rhapsody in Blue
		Someone to Watch Over Me
	Bernstein	Somewhere (from 'West Side Story')

Michaela Misconceptions

Tom Kendall
@tkendalluk

There are many misconceptions about Michaela, not least when it comes to our 'didactic' approach to teaching and learning.

Take John, for example, who is in his second year of teaching. Last year he had a tough time applying what he had been told to do during his teacher training. He spent hours putting up displays and neatly setting up his resource corner for independent learning. When planning his lessons, he carefully noted how he was going to differentiate for each type of Special Educational Needs (SEN) pupil present in his classroom (and don't forget the pupil premium kids either). He did plenty of group work. He spent hours trying to get to know all his pupils, handing out surveys for them to complete at the start of the year and regularly getting them to give feedback on how they felt they were learning. He marked their books once a week and was sure to give every pupil a next step to which they had to respond.

In short: he was knackered, the pupils he taught didn't seem to learn that much and, to make matters worse, some of his classes treated him like dirt, even though he was spending every waking hour trying to figure out how to help them.

It was obvious to John that what he'd been taught on his Postgraduate Certificate of Education (PGCE) was not only unmanageable but ineffective. Searching for answers, he looked to Twitter, where he heard about a controversial school called Michaela: a school that seemed to reject everything he'd been told was sacrosanct. After researching the school and its approaches, he went back to his own classroom with the following 'revelations':

1. Just teach 'facts'.

2. Textbooks are your lesson plan.

3. AfL (Assessment for Learning) is just another progressive fad.

4. Lessons don't need joy.

But was John right to assume that these 'revelations' accurately depict what we do? In this chapter I hope to suggest that they are a gross misunderstanding of our approach.

Misconception 1: Just Teach Facts

Truth: Facts are the first step to understanding

At Michaela we unashamedly get our pupils to memorise facts so they are stored in their long term memories. Why we do this and how we do this is given plenty of explanation in our previous book and by great writers such as Daisy Christodoulou and Dan Willingham. However, there is a temptation for some teachers to hear this and think, 'Well, now my lessons are just going to be filled with quizzes based on their knowledge organisers. All they need is some good old-fashioned rote learning.'

This is very tempting because not only is it easy to do, it is also the easiest way to make your pupils feel successful very quickly, which in turn makes you feel successful. How does this work? In History for example, you may get them to memorise an analysis containing plenty of interesting concepts. In English, you may get them to learn a linguistic term that normally only undergraduates use. In my own subject, Maths, something I am ashamed to say I've done in the past is to train a class to answer one specific tricky Maths Challenge question. This one question took about half a lesson to get them to do.

Training pupils to spout a single esoteric historical analysis is not enough to get them to understand history. When maths teachers learn words like 'esoteric' and throw it into their own writing, it doesn't make their writing better, it just makes them sound more pretentious.

The time we have with our pupils is our most precious resource and we must strive for a position where the knowledge we get our pupils to commit to their long term memories is the most enabling or 'powerful' (Young: 2013). Moreover, all knowledge exists on a scale, from flexible to inflexible (Willingham: 2002). Roughly speaking, flexible knowledge can be applied to other contexts. Inflexible knowledge on the other hand cannot.

If for some bizarre reason you wanted to learn the fact that, 'the cost of intangible assets can be written down by amortisation', you could do so. Just repeat it every morning whilst you're in the shower. This would be pretty inflexible knowledge, unless of course you are studying to become a Chartered Tax Advisor (in which case I've heard it's quite a thrilling fact). But otherwise, what use is this fact? I have no idea what it really means, nor do I know how to go about applying it in context.

As a Maths teacher my knowledge of Pythagoras' theorem means that not only can I find the length of the hypotenuse of a right-angled triangle, I can also extend that piece of knowledge to calculate the distance between two points on the Cartesian plane. This is because my knowledge of Pythagoras' theorem is quite flexible in application. The pupil who just knows that you have to square the short sides, then square root the answer to find the length of the hypotenuse, has pretty inflexible knowledge of Pythagoras' theorem. At some point in the past, my knowledge of Pythagoras' theorem was inflexible: whilst that might have been fine at first, eventually that knowledge must become flexible. This can only be done through learning how Pythagoras connects to *other* pieces of knowledge, and how it can be applied in a range of contexts.

Yet, even if we do choose to ask our pupils to memorise some of the most powerful knowledge by rote, that alone is not enough to make that knowledge flexible. Several steps need to take place to make the inflexible, flexible. For instance, pupils need time in history lessons to write extended essays comparing different ideas. In English, they need chances to offer varied analyses of texts. They need to see Maths problems where they can apply the processes they've already learned in new and different contexts. It takes time, and therefore pupils must be given opportunities to look at the same piece of knowledge from different angles, and then to manipulate it, so that it then becomes flexible in their minds.

Manipulating knowledge and seeing it in a range of contexts should not be confused with Bloom's 'Taxonomy' of skills. I wouldn't suggest for a moment that knowledge is less important than 'evaluation' or other such skills. Instead, I would suggest that a piece of knowledge should be handled in different ways until the pupil is able to use that knowledge flexibly to evaluate or analyse.

The art of good teaching lies in finding the balance between learning things by rote and the practice of applying them. As a rule of thumb, this is what we do at Michaela when teaching something new:

1. Tell them/show them examples of something new.

2. Tell them/show them where this thing fails to work (non-examples).

3. Ask them questions to check they have got some grasp of this new thing.

4. Ask them questions linking it to other things they already know.

5. Get them practising using the new thing, starting in pretty standard scenarios and progressing to the more weird and wonderful.

It's not that radical really but it is definitely far beyond just teaching facts.

Misconception 2: Textbooks Are Your Lesson Plan

Truth: Lesson planning is thinking through how you're going to teach

'Textbook teaching' is often viewed with derision. Throughout my career I have heard it portrayed as the epitome of bad teaching. Because of this, we have a situation where only around 10% of teachers in England use textbooks as the basis of their instruction (Oates: 2014). This means that many teachers up and down the country find themselves having to create new resources for their own lessons, day in, day out. More experienced teachers generally have a hard drive full of resources that they know how to navigate so they can draw on lessons they've resourced previously. On the other hand, less experienced teachers are generally left searching for their own resources. Sometimes this search involves looking through a shared drive at school; often it ends up on Google hoping to draw on a resource someone else has kindly shared. When neither of these strategies work, teachers must spend their time creating the resources themselves.

At Michaela, teachers unashamedly use our own *centrally* prepared textbooks, but we firmly understand that these resources themselves are not a lesson plan.

Your lesson planning should be a *mental* activity, where you think about how your lesson is going to go. Thinking about how you are going to use the booklet or textbook is a big part of this. This is time much more valuably spent than creating resources from scratch for each lesson, or worse, spending time scouring Google for a decent PowerPoint visual you can adapt. The key problem with this is that, unless you are some sort of superhero, by the time you have resourced the lesson, you don't really have the mental energy left to actually *plan* your lesson.

At Michaela, our ideal lesson-planning thought process would incorporate all of the following:

1. The Big Picture

2. The Next Booklet

3. The Next Lesson

4. Reflections on Previous Teaching

5. Misconceptions, Explanations and Examples

So whilst on the surface it might seem that having centrally planned booklets readily available might save the teacher time, it does not follow that teachers should then merely turn up to the classroom, ask the pupils to turn to page 22 and start reading. The teacher's job is to take the resource and consider how to adapt and use it as a dynamic tool for teaching their class. This includes thinking deeply about how best to explain a new concept to the kids in front of you, how best to ensure that you check rigorously for understanding, and how to ensure they spend enough time practising the right range of applications.

Do Michaela teachers use textbooks? Absolutely. Do we simply pick them up and start teaching without giving the mechanics of the lesson a second thought? Absolutely not.

Misconception 3: Checking for Understanding: Assessment for Learning (AfL) is Just Another Progressive Fad

Truth: Teachers must strive to have as good a picture as possible of what is going on in their pupils' heads

'Just tell them!' declared my brilliant colleague Olivia Dyer at one of the Michaela events a few years ago. Why was it necessary for Olivia to say this repeatedly? Because one of the most common mistakes new teachers to Michaela make with lessons is to play a game of 'guess what's in my head'. This is where the teacher asks a question to the class that encourages the pupils to guess, but without their having the relevant background knowledge to get anywhere near the right answer. For example, a teacher may ask, 'Does anyone know what the witches tell Macbeth?' Perhaps some of the pupils may have learned the play in primary school, and perhaps some of them might remember those details. But it's most likely, of course, that most of the class won't have a clue – so those pupils sit avoiding their teacher's eyes, and sit waiting for someone else to give the answer.

As teachers we need to ask ourselves: what is the point in asking this question, if most pupils in the room are unlikely to know the answer? The 'Just Tell Them' approach instead recommends that we shouldn't waste time asking pupils to guess what's in our heads, but instead give them some direct information they can then learn and, later, manipulate and apply to different contexts.

Not only does this approach save pupils' learning time, but it aids deeper learning. Once the child has learned a new piece of information, he can start thinking about it in different ways and contexts. For instance, in the case of Macbeth's ambition, the teacher might explain that the basic action of the play is that three witches tell a Scottish nobleman he will one day become king, that the idea will start to grow in his mind until it eventually consumes him and leads to tragic results. The teacher could *then* ask, 'What do the witches tell Macbeth?' and the pupils would likely respond, 'that he will become king one day'. Once pupils have learned this basic idea, the teacher can use it as a foundation on which to pin more and more detail about the drama. So next, pupils might learn exactly what the witches' three prophecies were, how Macbeth reacted to them, and so on. So in this example, the teacher doesn't ask pupils to guess what is in their head, but 'just tells' the pupils what they need to know before gauging their subsequent understanding.

Those who take the 'just tell them' philosophy too literally, however, would not do what I describe above. With those who have misinterpreted the Michaela 'Just Tell Them' method, the teacher might instead simply ask pupils to repeat back whatever the teacher has just said. For example, a teacher could say, 'Macbeth can be described as ambitious. How could we describe Macbeth, Abdul?' and the pupil might reply 'ambitious'.

In this example, unfortunately, the teacher did 'just tell' the pupil what he needed to know, but without investing any real meaning, so that here the teacher's check for understanding is extremely shallow. How does the teacher know whether Abdul understands what ambition actually is? Does Abdul even know who Macbeth is? Does he know what Macbeth's ambition relates to?

So whilst on one hand we do want teachers to 'just tell' kids what they need to know, we must tell it in a way that still requires the child to think deeply, to link the new knowledge to previous knowledge, and to understand how the knowledge should be newly applied in different contexts.

As a teacher, trying to understand what's happening in the room should be a constant pursuit. Our headmistress Katharine talks about how, as a teacher, *you* are driving the bus. You are moving the class through the material, constantly challenging them and pushing them to achieve more than they ever believed possible. However, to drive them forward effectively you must make sure they are actually with you on the bus.

Assessment for learning (AfL) is talked about an awful lot. In the past, there have been huge government-led pushes to encourage more AfL in UK classrooms and, from my own experience, I think it is the single topic that I've had the most training on throughout my career. In short, AfL has the emphatic support of the educational establishment. This alone has perhaps made people think that Michaela would be anti-AfL, given that we are anti many of the other pronouncements of the educational establishment. However, this could not be further from the truth.

At Michaela, we never just lecture the pupils in lessons. Every explanation is peppered with questions, to constantly check our pupils are on the bus with us.

There is an awful lot of great work written about AfL which I am not going to attempt to do justice to here. Rather, I suggest you check out the brilliant work of Paul Black and Dylan William (Black: 1998), Harry Fletcher-Wood (Fletcher-Wood: 2018) or Daisy Christodoulou (Christodoulou: 2017).

We cannot ever see learning *happen*, as learning is the process of effecting a change in the long-term memory and thus occurs over a longer period of time. AfL is essentially an attempt to see what's happening in our pupils' minds during the lesson, to give us a better sense of whether learning will be achieved or not.

A lot of the strategies that we use at Michaela are covered in great detail in the section on 'Checking for Understanding' in the book Teach Like a Champion (Lemov: 2015). However, there are some other unique and specific Michaela techniques that we use.

Firstly, every teacher has 'post-it note pupils'. These are around three pupils in each of the classes that you teach, whom you have identified as struggling in your lessons from their recent quizzes. Every teacher has the names of the pupils on a post-it note and stuck on their computer. The idea is that you check in with these pupils even more regularly than you would the rest of the class because they are struggling.

Secondly, in maths we use mini-whiteboards all the time. I will go so far as to say that I don't know how I would teach without them now. Every pupil is expected to have their own dry wipe pen as part of their equipment and in every maths classroom the whiteboards are out permanently on the desks. As a teacher all I have to do is write up a question and say, 'On your whiteboards. Go,' and seconds later I can see exactly who didn't have a clue what I was talking about in the previous minutes.

Finally, another key technique that I often find neglected when talking about AfL is reading the room. It's less precise than using whiteboards and asking questions, however, it is still an incredibly important thing for any teacher. When you know your class well, you must constantly be reading their facial expressions as this often gives you a pretty good sense of whether they're with you or not. Having pupils put their hands up when they think they know the answer to a question also gives you data on the confidence of the room —and as a teacher all rapidly gatherable data in lessons is very valuable.

In summary, at Michaela we do not get pupils to guess at answers but neither do we lecture them with answers. Throughout every lesson all Michaela teachers strive to use techniques to capture as rounded a picture as possible of what's going on in the wonderful world of our pupils' minds.

Misconception 4: Lessons Don't Need Joy

Truth: Lessons should be filled with joy

It almost goes without saying that at Michaela we are very strict on discipline and self-discipline. From this people sometimes draw the conclusion that Michaela teachers are all joyless, stern, Victorian-schoolmaster types, stood in front of rows of unsmiling urchins.

In fact, the opposite is true. Because we are strict, it is even more important that we also create joy. Warmth vs Strictness is not a one-dimensional scale like this:

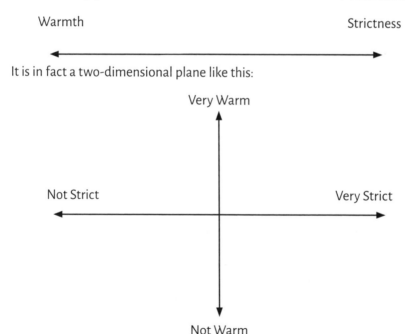

It is in fact a two-dimensional plane like this:

No teacher's role is to be an entertainer. Our job is to get our pupils to learn as much as possible. The crux of this process is that if your pupils hate you, they aren't going to learn very much from you. Of course, it doesn't mean that if they like you, they will learn from you either.

A sense of success is the key motivator. Pupils will get joy from coming to your lessons and feeling successful. As a teacher, your sincere praise for when they have done well is hugely important (don't try to fake it too much; cynical teenagers see through that pretty quickly).

On top of this, you must aim to make them feel that you know them as an individual and care about them as an individual. This is hard when you have a class of 32 pupils in front of you. Smiles and greetings as they enter the room are key. Having nicknames for individuals in your lessons is also a nice touch. A nod and a thumbs up here and there when pupils have done something well, smiling and showing genuine delight when they succeed are all central to building good relationships. These are all things that we look for in lessons at Michaela – just having clear explanations from our pupils is not enough.

I have been known to pretend to vomit every time a pupil missed off their units in an area question and even to do a dance in front of my form when we've had a detention-free day amongst other things.

It would be lovely if all our pupils were intrinsically motivated to succeed at school but we know this will not automatically be the case. Often pupils may not be willing to put the work in for themselves, but they will be motivated to work for you, their teacher, if you've built up a good relationship with them.

When faced with particularly 'challenging' pupils, it is fair to say that building up a positive relationship can be challenging. But never lower your standards in pursuing this relationship. If you do, then you risk undermining the relationship in the long run as it will gradually become clear to the pupil that you don't believe they can achieve as much as others. Letting them off for not having done their homework one night or for having forgotten their whiteboard pen another day will win their favour in the short term ('Miss is proper safe' and the like). However, they will grow to expect preferential treatment that will widen a gap between them and the rest of their classmates.

Instead, you must apply the rules unflinchingly. You must explain constantly *how* they broke the rule and why that rule is necessary. You have to spend time talking to them during detentions to rebuild the relationship and show them that you care about their success. You need to speak to their parents. And in every interaction you have with them, you have to persuade them that you really care about their future and their present: harping on about GCSE results or job prospects is a start, but often it is not enough.

The process in operation is a paradox: ensuring that joy permeates every lesson then actively supports your strictness. Enforcing the good behaviour that a strict classroom creates, concurrently allows your own personality to shine through much more. If you are concerned that Kain in the corner might kick off at any moment, it's very difficult to crack a joke. If, on the other hand, you know that even after some rapturous laughter, you can just say '3, 2, 1 and SLANT' and you'll have 32 pupils sat in silence with their arms folded, then you are much more likely to be cracking the jokes. Our corridors may be silent during transitions, yet during lessons they are often filled with the sound of laughter. Being a traditional teacher does not mean being a joyless one.

Conclusion

At Michaela we are very open and vocal about what we do. We write tweets, blogs and books, and encourage visitors to come and see us every single day. Nonetheless, what we share is often misinterpreted. I hope I have fully addressed here four misconceptions about Michaela and our approach here to education.

We are *not* all about rote learning. We are *not* about strictly following textbooks. We are *not* about lecturing our pupils. We aren't about joyless lessons, and we aren't trying to take education back to some undefined glory era. We are doing something far more radical and exciting: taking what works from the eras past *and* present to create rigorous, joy-filled lessons where teachers can instantly assess and correct and encourage pupils. We are definitely working to change our pupils' futures.

References
Black, P. & Wiliam, D., 1998. *Assessment and Classroom Learning, Assessment in Education: Principles, Policy & Practice*, 5:1, 7-74, DOI: 10.1080/0969595980050102.

Christodoulou, D., 2017. *Making Good Progress*, OUP Oxford; New edition edition (2 Feb. 2017).

Didau, D., 2015. *What If Everything You Knew About Education Was Wrong?*, Crown House Publishing Limited, First Edition.

Fletcher-Wood, H., 2018. *Responsive Teaching: Cognitive Science and Formative Assessment in Practice*, Taylor & Francis Ltd.

Lemov, D., 2015. *Teach Like A Champion 2.0: 62 Techniques that Put Students on the Path to College*, Jossey Bass; 2nd ed.

Oates, T., 2014. *Why textbooks count. A policy paper.* Cambridge: University of Cambridge.

Wiliam, D., 2011. *What is assessment for learning?. Studies in educational evaluation*, 37(1), pp.3-14.

Willingham, D., 2002. Ask The Cognitive Scientist URL: https://www.aft.org/periodical/american-educator/winter-2002/ask-cognitive-scientist.

Young, M. and Muller, J., 2013. On the powers of powerful knowledge. *Review of education*, 1(3), pp.229-250.

LEADERSHIP

Servant Leadership

Katharine Birbalsingh
@Miss_Snuffy

'Do nothing from rivalry or conceit, but in humility count others more significant than yourselves. Let each of you look not only to his own interests, but also to the interests of others.' –Philippians 2:3-4

You don't necessarily need to believe in God to follow His advice. I'm not sure whether God exists, but I find it helpful to behave as if He does. I imagine Him gazing down on me from heaven, judging everything that I do. I hope it keeps me humble. I know it keeps me striving to be better, even – and perhaps especially – when no one else is looking.

If we choose to, we can all try and behave as Paul in his letter above suggests we should. We might not always manage it, but we can try. We can try to serve our family, our community, even our country, and we should do so expecting little in return. If there is any satisfaction, it is the feeling that comes from knowing that you gave enough to have had an impact. Lying on your death bed, you can die in peace, assured that your life was worth living, and that, in your own small way, you've contributed towards something bigger than yourself.

Servant leadership is about the challenge of putting the needs of something bigger than you above your own needs and the needs of any one individual. That's what makes servant leadership so hard: making decisions for the good of a family, or a business, or a school, often means making decisions that are unpopular, or that individuals in the group find difficult to understand.

Getting leadership right is hard. This chapter is about how I try to lead, the main things that matter, and the values of servanthood that hold us all, including me, to account.

Judgements

As Headmistress, I feel as if I'm making a hundred judgements or more every day. This can be overwhelming, especially if one isn't always certain of what judgement to make. It is easy to make mistakes. For any Head, this is a huge responsibility. At Michaela so much is riding on my decisions. Not only do the staff do me the honour of trusting my judgement and believing in what we do, despite much of it feeling unfamiliar or a little scary, but many people on the outside are watching our every move. Some have been waiting for us to fail, although I think many of them these days have given up on that dream. But others still would take delight if things didn't go quite right for us. This is very sad when you think that, if things went wrong, the main people who would suffer are the children at Michaela.

I always feel as if I am morally obliged to repay the staff for their trust by getting it right and that can require me making judgements of *them*. Too often in schools, I think leaders shy away from making judgements of people altogether because it seems 'mean'. It is hard to make judgements, not just because it is difficult to get them right, but because so many others would prefer you not to make them.

Not that decisions and judgements at Michaela are made on my own. It is extremely rare for that to happen. I might be speaking one-on-one with a teacher and we decide together that something is a good idea. But I won't make the decision then and there. I'll always tell the teacher that first I need to check with the senior team to see if they will approve.

Senior team meetings

The senior leadership meetings we have each morning are always focused on trying to do what is best for the school. We're always mindful that the decisions we make will significantly impact the whole community. We plough through stuff that needs deciding, often from the previous day – but sometimes we'll look at more long-term issues like who will have a tutor group in September, or staffing issues. Most whole school decisions are made in these meetings. It may seem excessive to meet daily, but that's what is required if you want your senior team to know what is happening across the school and if you want to move quickly. One might think that servant leadership would be to allow one's senior team to meet less often. That seems 'nice'. But servant leadership isn't about being nice. It is about doing what is required to lead well.

I don't think it is the most efficient or effective use of time when senior teams meet weekly and have various senior staff give presentations to each other with photocopied sheets or power points. Colleagues tend to glaze over and the meeting becomes about ticking a box, or allowing the presenter time to shine in front of the others. But, for what purpose is this show happening? I always ask the purpose of any activity. If a specific goal isn't being achieved by an action or event, then maybe it shouldn't be done. If it is going to be done, then it needs to have a purpose and it needs to be done fast.

I do wonder how often meetings are had across some schools for the sake of having a meeting. Or sometimes tasks are given to people to flatter someone's ego. Other times, perhaps an assistant head or deputy head is allowed to run with something that will require collecting lots of data from other staff, wasting everyone's time, essentially to help that individual do a project they thought would be a nice idea. But why are they allowed to do it if the project isn't moving the whole school closer to fulfilling its vision? What is the point?

I am pretty ruthless about saying no to things that I think will waste people's time or take us off track. That can be a hard judgement in the moment but good leaders do this. Of course nowadays at Michaela, because it has become normalised to think in this way, it is very rare that anyone would ask to do something like that. I see it as my role to help hone the thinking of my senior team so that Michaela's vision and culture is pumping through their veins at all times. It helps anchor their own decision-making and ensures consistency is always coming from the top. When they then run their own meetings with middle leaders, a similar culture embeds.

That's why I involve them in every decision I make. If I ever decide something without them, I always email to apologise and explain that a decision was needed immediately so I couldn't wait for their input. I am beholden to the senior team as much as anyone else. While the last word always lies with me, I can't tell you how much my decisions are influenced by my senior team. They argue with me, tell me I'm wrong, question so much of what I think. I go to them constantly because I know that whatever decision is made after we have discussed it, it will be far better than me having made it on my own. They'll remember things I've forgotten. Different personalities around the table will have different opinions. Tossing the issue about like bears tearing at raw meat, means that we try to put the school's needs ahead of our own. We sacrifice the temporary pleasure one might feel in presenting an idea to the team just so that others can nod and give their approval. This means that senior leadership meetings are entirely directed towards the needs of our little platoon – which Edmund Burke describes in the quotation at the beginning of the book.

Meetings across the school

My senior team muck in and do whatever is necessary to run the school. There is a data guy. There is a pastoral one too. We have a Head of Sixth Form and someone in charge of Safeguarding and SEN. One of my deputies takes on whatever I ask of her. She miraculously transforms into whatever is required. They are the best team a Head could hope for.

The pastoral one runs our Heads of Year. We tend to have one Head of Year per year group; although we have been known to split year groups if they are tough to handle. The deputy meets with the Heads of Year every week, sometimes twice a week and speaks to them constantly to keep consistency on the pastoral side of things.

I meet with the heads of department once or twice a half term, depending on what is required. Just like with the senior team, I don't have an agenda. What I mean is that I don't email or print out an agenda in advance of our meeting. I feel they restrict and aren't fluid enough. One should be flexible enough to go with the flow but at the same time have a list of things that needs to be discussed. A list isn't an agenda. It is just a list. Of course for this to work, there needs to be high levels of trust. Staff need to believe that your list isn't going to waste their time. They need to feel happy with not having seen the list in advance because they trust you to lead the meeting well.

I also think minutes are problematic and waste time. You might say minutes are needed in order to hold certain people to account. But it is far more powerful to send an email immediately after the meeting to confirm what was agreed *only* to the individuals you know cannot be counted on to deliver. I can then tell that member of staff that the hope is that we can get to a point where we don't have to do that anymore. I always say to staff, don't be that person who makes my or your line manager's 'to do' list even longer. Don't be an extra stress that we have to worry about to chase. Be that person of whom I can ask something and it just gets done, as if by magic, making my life easier, not harder. In fact, be even better than that and be pro-active, take the initiative and help to lead the school.

By giving everyone minutes and an agenda, you are treating everyone the same. But not everyone needs confirmation in writing of what needs doing. So let the good staff get on with things instead of bombarding them with paper. When you reduce the amount of useless paper given to staff, it means that when staff are given a piece of paper, they are far more likely to take note of it. They are also more likely to trust you.

One is then freed up to hold others to account by letting them know directly that they are letting you down, letting their colleagues down and making themselves look bad by being unreliable. If you don't do this, they will keep on doing it. Be straight with people. Tell them what to fix and be clear about it. Doing the harder thing and being honest is more difficult and follows the course of servant leadership. Then, if the staff member doesn't fix it, they have no one to blame but themselves.

I meet with all of the staff, twice a week. We meet on a Monday morning for Briefing and on Tuesday afternoon for CPD – Continuing Professional Development. That lasts about 1.5 hours. It tends to be partly about practical things in the school that need discussing. Heads of Year for instance will take this opportunity to talk about their naughty kids in the school or their special cases (if a child has had a death in the family or needs tender loving care at the moment). These meetings make sure the entire school knows what's happening with those children so that our approach will be consistent across the staff.

Getting consistency across the staff should always be a key goal of any meeting, so that our shared vision of the success of the school is viewed as more important than our own individual needs. I am always trying to make sure as many people know as much as possible about what is happening around the school. We over-communicate. We say it in emails, then at Briefing, then at CPD. Then I ask the Heads of Department to say it again to their teams during their weekly catch ups. If X is going to happen, it is imperative that ALL staff are doing X. In fact, if it's not being done by everyone, it's preferable for it not to be done at all, because then we don't look disorganised and directionless in front of the children or the parents. Do that one too many times and the children and parents start to lose trust. Then the next time we ask them to follow us into battle and take away their child's smartphone, or ensure homework gets done, they won't do it because they don't believe in the school.

You want people's trust? You had better deliver. Not just once, but every time.

Why is consistency so important?

In 2020, society is wrong about a lot. One fundamental thing it gets wrong is believing that creativity comes from lack of structure and lack of consistency. Jonathan Porter's chapter 'School of Freedom' talks about different types of freedom. He says, 'some constraint and some direction frees our young people to be the best that they can be'. That's true.

It is the same with staff. If teachers have the freedom to do 'whatever they want', making hundreds of resources on their own or planning thousands of lessons, then what takes place in each classroom will differ wildly. One child might get lucky one year and get a good set of teachers. The next year could be very different. Two children in the same school can have extremely different experiences, depending on the teachers they so happen to get. So children's futures are left to chance. We tend to think that this is normal in schools. Some teachers are good, some aren't and that's just the way that it is. But it doesn't have to be this way. Consistency is not restrictive. It is liberating.

When visitors go into *any and all* classrooms at Michaela, they cannot tell which teacher is a newly qualified teacher and which one has been teaching for years. Consistency means that all of the classrooms reach a certain standard. Even teacher visitors cannot tell the difference. Very experienced teachers might know the difference when observing over time at the back of the classroom. In some classrooms, the teacher will make teaching bottom set Year 9 or 10 look like it is top set Year 7. The teacher makes it look easy because they are very good. But, one of the remarkable things about Michaela is how the systems ensure that all teachers are able to perform at an incredibly high standard while their personality shines on through. It is simply a mistake to think that making sure all staff teach well is to somehow rid them of their quirks and relationships with the children. Think of all the expert tennis players. They are all very good without all being exactly the same.

Imagine if your chances of surviving or dying in surgery were just as great as the chances of you getting a good or bad teacher at school. Imagine if there was little consistency between surgeons and how they perform their craft and that whenever anyone went into surgery, they would cross their fingers and just hope they got a good surgeon. Good one? Great. Bad one, whoops I suppose you might be heading for the morgue. We would be horrified. But with teaching, parents and children expect so little of schools and in particular of leadership in schools. They think the Head is there just so they can complain. But the Head and senior team are meant to set the school's culture and bring consistency across the school. What's worse is that teachers themselves don't want the senior leaders to bring about consistency. They demand absolute freedom to do 'whatever they want' because they think that absolute freedom improves their lives. But they are wrong. Consistency and teamwork make everyone's lives so much easier because everyone benefits from everyone's hard work. True servant leadership from the top can make it so that it is no longer every man for himself. At Michaela, we talk about being a Michaela family and as such, we look after each other, putting the needs of our little platoon first.

Teamwork

A team should work like a team. Not only can detentions be shared, but teachers in each department can plan together, resource together, and share each other's hard work. Not only does this reduce workload massively, but this brings consistency to teaching across the school and helps everyone work as a highly functional team. Staff grow to depend on each other, to know each other's work habits well, to feel like they belong to something bigger, ensuring that no one person ever wants to let their colleagues down.

Whenever I am interviewed about Michaela, I get the inevitable question, 'Yes well the school seems wonderful, but aren't all the children being turned into robots? Aren't the staff all robots too?'

But having a strong culture of consistency does not mean that everyone is exactly the same. I can honestly say that in my entire career, I have never been challenged so much by staff as I have at Michaela. Again, in my whole career, I have never encountered children so curious about the world, so clever at arguing their well-informed points of view. Perhaps in some eastern countries, encouraging a strong culture would be a worry because a stronger culture of conformity to the group already exists. In some eastern countries, people don't want to stand out and are actively encouraged not to. But in western countries, the exact opposite is the case. Our more individualistic society is about making a name for oneself, standing out of the crowd. In fact, at Michaela, we have to work hard to overcome the temptation to regard oneself as a 'hero teacher'. Too often western teachers enjoy the feeling of being the only one who can control that challenging class. We've all heard in our careers, 'Well they never behave like that for *me*.' We work hard with staff to ensure, as Paul suggests above, that 'we look not only to his own interests, but also to the interests of others'.

Being immersed in western culture, Michaela's routines and strong culture ensure that we deliver from a position of strength. For both staff and pupils, their natural western characters are always shining through. Working together and using similar routines in the classroom doesn't mean you lose your individual thought processes or personalities. This book demonstrates exactly this. Nearly 30 Michaela staff have written about their own chosen topics. Two support staff have contributed to the book. The staff at Michaela have written two books! This doesn't normally happen at a school. If we were all robots, we would never be able to do such a thing. Not only that, but we take risks, taking on board viewpoints that are unpopular. Creativity is in abundance at Michaela.

We are very much a team but in looking after each other, we find strength to think differently and step outside the lines. We don't tend to spend our energy trying to 'manage each other' or trying get round a difficult member of staff who has been allowed to get more and more difficult over the years. This book, *The Power of Culture*, is filled with radical thinking and is a product of the strength of unity found at Michaela. There is always a balance between the individual and the team but, by emphasising and uniting the group towards a common understanding, in a way that is often counter-cultural in the West, we are able to achieve more together. In this way, we keep our individual identities, the 'I' and the 'me', while also feeling that the 'we' is contributing towards a shared vision. That shared communal strength, and shared identity, has allowed us to be more radical than any individualistic culture would allow.

There are many ideas that have made Michaela what it is. But no one individual tries to own any of those ideas. As Harry Truman said, 'It is amazing what you can accomplish if you do not care who gets the credit.' We are just happy that these ideas work for the whole. We don't have members of the senior team collecting information from staff so that they can show off their pretty project. We do our best to put others before ourselves. That is, after all, why we have written this book: to share our ideas with you. It is why we open our doors to over 600 visitors a year: to help spread the word. It should be, as Paul says above, 'Do nothing from rivalry or conceit, but in humility count others more significant than yourselves.' This is all the more important for those in positions of leadership. Because we have power, we have a duty not to abuse it. We demand a lot from those staff below us and we are bound by duty to do what is right by them as they are bound by duty to do what is right by the children.

Candour

That doesn't mean that things are easy at Michaela. We are honest with staff and hold them to account in ways that they might not find elsewhere. This means giving them direct feedback and being clear on expectations. It means they will improve very quickly and for the right people, it works beautifully. Staff will tell you that they learn more in 3 weeks at Michaela than they learn in 3 years elsewhere.

When staff join Michaela, I am very clear about how different our culture is and how one should leave one's ego at the door. One isn't going to be able to march around saying 'look how brilliant I am'. It won't fit with our culture. One cannot be the hero teacher. I tell them they will get more feedback in a week than they have had in their entire careers so they had better find the backbone within to handle it. In fact, I tell them this on their interview day and some people decide this environment is not for them. I prioritise the needs of the group over individual needs even if it makes me unpopular.

Leaders often shy away from candour because it is naturally unpopular and threatening. But it is required if you want real improvement. Servant leadership requires leaders to have the backbone to give candour (as well as the backbone to receive it!) It requires an understanding that leading well often means making decisions that are difficult, and therefore a leader should focus on being respected rather than liked. If, in the end, you are successful at doing what is best for the whole community – the parents, the staff *and* the pupils – you will get your teachers' respect. They will understand that you have done the difficult thing of putting the group's needs ahead of any one individual's or your own. But such decisions cannot please all the people all the time. So, if your *aim* is to be liked, servant leadership is not for you.

Our culture at Michaela is one where staff regularly feed back to me and the senior team about what might not be working at the school. They pop into my office all of the time to talk to me and tell me what needs to change. They also email. I get half a dozen emails every week with suggestions about how to improve things around the school. I have many conversations with staff every week where they explain what might not be working and give suggestions on how to improve. I'm not saying I will always do what they say. As a leader, the final decision lies with me. But I'm interested in their ideas and I am clear that because they are on the ground in a way that I am not, they have knowledge that I don't have.

When you read Abi Smith's chapter, 'The Culture of Feedback', you might think it isn't possible that people would be so happy to be faced with constant criticism. But that's because we don't see it as criticism. I don't see it as criticism when staff feed back to me on what isn't working in the school. In fact, staff constantly seek out feedback from their colleagues, always wanting to improve. There are no grades and the feedback is so frequent and informal that it can be used as a genuine tool for improvement. Staff are motivated by not wanting to be the weakest link because they put the good of the whole team above their own interests. We have high levels of trust. We work as a team and try to be as consistent and as honest with each other as possible. Honesty doesn't mean being horrible. Accurate feedback can be delivered in a caring way. But at Michaela, we don't shy away from the truth. Because not telling someone that they're letting down their colleagues may be easier for the *individuals* concerned but it's rarely the best thing for the team. Fudging the truth is always easier for the *leader* (because giving critical feedback is hard), but it isn't easier for the dozens of other staff who are routinely let down by someone who is underperforming. And it isn't the best thing for that member of staff either: they might have improved if only the leader had been straight with them in the first place

Ultimately, I believe that is why we are able to write the chapters you find in this book. They speak the truth as we see it, and we aren't afraid to voice it. I have a quote by Thomas Sowell in my office that all staff are aware of that says, 'When you want to help people, you tell them the truth. When you want to help yourself, you tell them what they want to hear'. We live by this mantra at Michaela.

How do we hold people to account?

Staff at Michaela are excellent. By staff, I don't just mean the teaching staff. I mean everyone. As I say in the introduction, the thing I am most proud of is how I have managed to put all of these amazing people into one building. I have the best caretakers, the best office staff, the best kitchen staff and the best teachers. To thrive at Michaela, you have got to be good.

Michael Gove was a great believer in performance related pay. So are many people in business. In teaching, or in any job where you need people working in highly functioning teams, I believe performance related pay is a bad idea. When you read Simon Virgo's chapter, 'Something worth fighting for', you will understand why Napoleon didn't pay those men to stand at that gun battery. You will also understand why, if he had, Napoleon would have lost the battle. This is because the motivational pull of the needs of the group is far greater than the motivational pull of the individual. Sadly, performance related pay assumes the opposite and encourages an 'every man for himself' mentality, destroying the camaraderie and togetherness of the team. Similar to those soldiers, performance related pay misunderstands everything about what motivates dedicated and enthusiastic teachers who want nothing more than to better the lives of the children in their charge.

When other heads or deputies visit Michaela, they often ask how accountability works at Michaela. Does performance management work as it does at other schools? No. We don't do targets unless someone is underachieving. Remember the point about letting good staff just get on with the job? You don't want to treat all your staff in the same way, just as you don't want to give certificates to all of the children for having 'participated'. The concept of 'prizes for all' having a negative unintended effect applies to staff too. 'Prizes for all' means that no matter how well you performed, how much effort you made, you will get the same prize as a child who did little to prepare and who performed badly. The problem here for the child is that it affects their motivation. Why work hard when you cannot be seen to do well and will be seen to be just like everyone else, including children who aren't very good? The same applies to staff. While it is true you don't want staff competing to be the hero teacher and not working as a team player with their colleagues, you also don't want staff to feel that no matter how good you are as a teacher, you are treated in the same way as a teacher who perhaps doesn't make much of an effort. Why do well at one's job if one is going to be subjected to the same target setting and performance management that the struggling teachers have to do?

Why write down targets in September so that staff can scramble around in June before their performance management meeting looking for those targets so that they can make up reasons for why they have achieved them and tick that box with their manager? It is all a total waste of time in my opinion.

I find that too many accountability structures in schools are about ticking boxes and making us FEEL as if we are being leaders. They make us LOOK as if we are holding people to account for what they do, but in fact we are simply holding people to account for LOOKING as if they are doing the right things. So performance management discussions about targets aren't really about that staff member actually improving. They tend to be about that staff member proving that that they LOOK as if they are improving. As always, I ask what is the point of that activity? If it is wasting people's time, then we cut it.

That then leaves you with the time to use target setting for staff who are in desperate need of it and you can really monitor those targets regularly, meeting every couple of weeks with tight feedback loops. Normally, performance management is so unwieldy across a school that it becomes utterly meaningless.

So we try to find ways which genuinely help people to improve. As Abi Smith talks about in her feedback chapter, real feedback not only allows the staff to improve, but as a staff body, we have a real sense of what is going on in lessons across the school. Middle Leaders have a REAL grasp of what is going on in lessons. We don't do performance lessons for observations. Everyone is in and out of each other's classrooms so often, we have real visibility of what is going on. Our systems of accountability are all the more real for not having the appearance of tick boxes. We only do what works. We don't do what LOOKS like it works.

That is the point. REAL accountability and REAL improvement is what motivates people. When you deliver this, staff will trust you in return. Giving someone a bonus at the end of the year is meaningless, as is ticking off some stupid targets. I was given targets all my career. I never tried to achieve a single one of those targets. Why would I? I was too busy trying to be an excellent teacher. So the question to ask there is, what is the motivation for *that*? Why does someone choose a job that doesn't pay that much, is pretty hard-going, long hours and is generally denigrated by society? We teachers choose teaching because we believe in something better. We believe we have a duty to the world to make it into a better place.

That sense of duty is the best accountability tool you'll ever find. People hold themselves to account because they don't want to let their colleagues down. They don't want to disappoint the children. They have a sense of shame in not wanting to be selfish when the group requires their hard work and commitment. They put the needs of the group above their own. This is far more powerful than a performance management set of tick boxes. The key is to unlock that sense of duty in the staff and accompany it with bureaucratic processes that are very light touch. You will then create a strong culture of trust and accountability rooted in a sense of everyone being driven towards the same goal.

Servant Leadership

I first had the idea of Michaela at the end of 2010. It has been nearly 10 years that I have been dedicated to this project. That's rare in free schools. Many free school heads spend a few years in the position before moving on to something else. But the idea of moving on from Michaela has always seemed preposterous to me. This is partly because I see it as my duty to stay, but also because I find myself deeply attached to the community that I've spent 10 years trying to build.

In his letter to the Philippians, Paul tells us what servant leadership looks like. He says that 'we should not look to our own interests but the interests of others'. Just like the staff at Michaela, I feel it is my duty to do what is right by my colleagues and our children and put the needs of the school above my own. A bigger salary or promotion are meaningless in the larger scheme of life's priorities. Being able to contribute to a larger endeavour injects meaning into your life. This requires keeping in your mind's eye the goal of the whole project: that we should deliver an excellent education to these children and that we should play our part on the national stage in trying to move education forward in our country.

I ask the children and the parents to do their duty and follow our rules, do our homework, turn up on time, be well behaved, work hard, be kind and so on. I ask the staff to look after the children, to take on the same values that we ask of the pupils, to hold ourselves to high standards and live and breathe the school's values. So then in turn, the governors ask of me to do my duty and fulfil my responsibilities at the school, by ensuring that I take care of the staff and the children to the best of my ability.

This duty of care works both ways: they have a duty to me as I have a duty to them. Staff want to work for me because I want to work for them. We all try to do our best while keeping the needs of the school at the forefront of our minds.

Everything we do at Michaela is real. Staff work hard but every bit of the work they do has impact and is for something. There isn't a single staff member at Michaela who is just 'doing a job'. Everyone believes in the bigger picture, not just the teachers but the support staff as well. Everyone believes that we can change the world. I fundamentally believe that this is why all teachers became teachers in the first place. Leaders just need to unlock that passion.

I want to be able to lie on my deathbed and look back over my life and feel I lived well. All of us will die, but we must ensure that by the decisions we take in life, our behaviour, how we treat others, that at the end when we are about to die, our lives demonstrate that we also truly *lived.*

I still haven't decided whether God exists. But, if He does, I hope that He thinks I've done my very best to follow His advice.

Michaela 6th – What's Stopping You?

Jessica Lund
@JessicaLundx

Michaela opened its Sixth Form in September 2019. Our stated aim is to prepare students for entry to, and success at, the best universities in the UK and abroad: our shorthand for that is "Oxbridge and Russell Group". Nearly half of our year 11 cohort have stayed with us into the Sixth Form. We also have 14 students who joined our Sixth Form having taken their GCSEs at another school.

As Head of Sixth Form, I spent a lot of time prior to opening thinking about how we would prepare our students for the challenge of university entrance. I read about "aspirations" and "widening participation" and "barriers to entry". I talked to the people who run some of the best Sixth Forms and colleges in the country. Michaela is unique, but it is not unique with respect to the community it serves: inner-city London, predominantly BAME with high indices of deprivation, and students who, in the main, will be the first of their family to attend university.

The experience of trying, with the help of my excellent colleagues, to figure out our students' ambitions and help them to "aim higher" has been eye-opening. I thought I was in a good position to do this because of my own background. I grew up on a council estate. I received free school meals. I'm a non-white female. I got into grammar school by the skin of my teeth and worked my way to a place at Oxford. Surely if I could, they can!

It is so tempting to rewrite your story so you are the hero. When I relate the "facts" of my journey to Oxford, it all sounds so inspirational. I do it in assemblies all the time – if I can, you can! And that may be true. But I cannot ignore the many, many circumstances which were so heavily in my favour. My mother was at home, and taught me to read and write before I went to primary school. My father spoke French to me. I travelled a lot. I went to a superb primary school, with excellent "school ma'am" teachers who did not suffer fools and pushed me constantly (if you're reading this, Mrs Smith, I'm so sorry I butchered your Fray Bentos pie with my compasses when we were doing that 'how many ways can you draw a circle' lesson). When it was time to apply for secondary school, my grandmother paid for me to receive tuition for the 11+. I went to a grammar school, where I was surrounded by teachers who knew their stuff, and highly competitive girls who *wanted* to know that stuff. I didn't have social media, or even a phone until I was 13, and even then it was a Nokia 3310 and "Snake" wasn't all that thrilling after the first hour. It was a big deal when I made the switch from my Children's Encyclopaedia Britannica, to Encarta, to the internet. When I was 14, my mother told me that my grandfather (who died before I was born) had always wanted to study Theology at Oxford, and so Oxford became my goal. I had teachers who talked me through the process: a wonderful Classical Civilisation teacher who gave me a mock interview about a brillo pad holder; an Oxbridge advisor who gave me a list of colleges I should apply to (I didn't listen, because I was insufferable, but I got lucky)... I had everything in my favour.

Our kids don't. There are more factors than I could ever have imagined that would prevent students from aiming for the best universities in the country (or the world). The educational landscape is completely different from the one I navigated in my teens with my teachers. I have spoken at great length with the majority of students about the "barriers" they face: I present them to you here. Some – those of geography, academic calibre and course choice – apply to all Russell Group universities; others are Oxbridge specific.

"My heart and soul are not set on going to Oxbridge or the Russell Group." – J, 12E

Let's start with an easy one. "Oxbridge and the Russell Group" is not for everybody. Of course it isn't! It is foolish to pretend that it is. We tell our pupils in the lower school, right from Year 7, that they can all aim for the top universities, and they can – but just like aiming for the top in any sphere, only a few will actually get there. And even if a student is very bright and very motivated, that doesn't necessarily mean that this is the right destination for them – perhaps the courses aren't right, or the environment, or anything else.

What is important is that we understand *why* the student in question feels like that. If it's the courses, fine – J wants to study Art, and is better served elsewhere. She is *very* bright, and loves academic study, but Oxbridge just isn't her thing – she appreciates the benefits, and has made an informed choice. The problem is that there are many students who will *say* "oh, the courses aren't right" or "I'm not too keen on the environment" when they mean something else. "I don't want to apply to Oxbridge" is more often than not shorthand for:

- "I don't think I'll fit in socially"

- "I don't think I'm clever enough"

- "I don't think I'll get the grades"

- "I'm scared of the exam or interview process"

- "I'm worried about how hard I'll have to work"

- "I don't want to leave my family"

It is also, occasionally, the stock answer given when a student does not really understand or realise the impact of attending an elite university. This is understandable. For those students, it doesn't matter how much I or my colleagues talk about the amazing experiences we had and how many doors were open to us as a result of attending such and such a university. We're just teachers – none of my students want to be teachers (well, one does, but he has always been weird). They don't know anybody who does a job they want to do – doctors, bankers, lawyers, etc. – who has been to these universities and has a similar account of the extraordinary benefit of so doing. It *does* open up wonderful opportunities for students: that's why, in the words of Hector in *The History Boys*, "[all the] other boys want to go there. It's the hot ticket, standing room only".

"I don't think I'll fit in socially." – R, 12B

R is a smart cookie. He hasn't always been the hardest worker, but pulled out some blistering GCSE results and, now that he has found his academic niche at A-level, is doing very well indeed. He is popular, charismatic and articulate, and he has enormous potential. When he says he doesn't want to apply for Oxbridge, he means that he doesn't think he'll fit in. He doesn't know anybody, outside of school, who has been to an elite university. He does know people – competent people, smart people, role models, people with good jobs and good salaries and nice houses – who have not been to Oxbridge, so he doesn't really see the point. The people he does know who are Oxbridge-educated are, in his mind, *very* different from him. Why bother, when he can set his sights elsewhere and be more comfortable?

Comfort and safety are key concerns for our kids. They are more risk-averse than I would ever have imagined. The idea of leaving their comfort zone is deeply undesirable for the majority, and *that* is one of the principle challenges of getting them to aim high: how can we persuade them that aiming for the best universities is worth the risk and discomfort of putting themselves out there?

We talk a lot about the variety of people that there are at Oxbridge. In the lower school, we run an annual trip to Oxford so pupils can see it in action, and we can demystify its dreaming spires. We invite speakers to the Sixth Form, many of whom are graduates of elite universities and also represent a huge variety of backgrounds. It is truly wonderful that we have had so many high achievers giving up their time to come and inspire our students.

Will this be enough to persuade R to burst out of his comfort zone and try for the Russell Group? I don't know. I hope so: I hope that the appeal of being not only the first in his family to go to university but the first in his community to go to Oxford will win out. I find that boys, in particular, care about being seen as leaders in their community – I just hope they will be able to make the tricky choices that this entails.

"I don't think I'm clever enough." – L, 12C

The other, less nebulous, part of "fitting in" is the concern that many of the kids have that they will not fit in academically, i.e. while they may get the grades, they are not academic in the way that students at elite universities are. In some cases, it doesn't matter how many "As" they see on their essays or 100% scores in their quizzes, they are convinced that Oxbridge students are somehow other and that they would be far better off somewhere with normal people.

Different students respond to different kinds of encouragement in this regard. It is helpful that I have an Oxford degree and am, in many and very visible ways, a deeply flawed human being: my students get to see my normality (and weirdness) on a daily basis. They are also taught almost uniquely by Russell Group graduates – I think this has the effect of normalising their achievements, rather than putting them off being 'nerds' like their teachers.

We are, however, realistic about the challenges of getting into *all* of these excellent universities. This is a real double-edged sword: we need students to understand that they are competing with thousands of excellent students across the globe, because they need to understand that getting into these universities is often the result of working harder and better than others. We hold up the students of Eton and Harrow as "the competition" and talk to them about the structural advantages that private school students have as a way of showing them that, in order to succeed, they have to go above and beyond. Some of our students hear that and say, "bring it on!"; others, of a more sensitive disposition, hear that and think, "oh dear, with those advantages and those natural smarts, how can I possibly compete?!" (although we don't talk about natural smarts, that is what they assume).

Some students need constant reassurance that they are on the right track, and are intellectually capable of holding their own: for this, they have the constant input of their form tutors, who offer regular advice and encouragement to all students, whether or not they have Oxbridge in their sights. Again, only time will tell whether those who are capable will, when push comes to shove, list Oxbridge or Russell Group universities in their UCAS application: I suspect they will, but there will be a lot of conversations with nervous kids beforehand!

"I'm scared of the interview process and the exam." – A, 12D

This is not a concern I hear too often, but I'm sure that some of the students feel it. Some of our students are very confident in their interview skills (and rightly so); others are less confident, but know that they can improve when they need to and that we will support them to do so. We use tutor time in the first two terms of Y12 to explicitly teach and practise public speaking, interview and debating skills: our students deliver presentations on things that interest them, and on areas of their subjects that they find fascinating; they also do "hot seat" activities in which the tutor interviews the student and the others give them feedback on their performance. One tutor group turned this into an *Apprentice*-style "hired or fired" activity which, counterintuitively, worked extremely well!

We also prepare them for the required entrance examinations, but in a very softly-softly way: a few sessions after school with expert teachers who run through the exam rubric and set and mark a few mock papers. Our students are used to being examined and to taking assessments very seriously, so the prospect of an additional hurdle for entry to Oxbridge and the Russell Group, or for competitive courses such as Law and Medicine, does not faze them.

"Isn't Oxbridge racist?" – K, 12E

K is an extraordinary person and will, if there is any justice in the world, be taking up her seat in an Oxford college from 2021. When she applied to join Michaela6th, I spoke to her about her ambitions for university. She, like I, had decided early on that Oxford was her goal, to study something related to (but not necessarily) Medicine. Her academic pedigree is superb, and her potential is clear.

The first question she asked me when I told her I went to Oxford was: "Miss, isn't it true that Oxford is racist?"

At Michaela, we hold sacred a number of values. One of those values is that of rejecting victimhood. We encourage our students not to fixate on the things in their lives that might stop them from being successful, or make success more difficult to achieve. We tell them not to focus on sex, race, or any of the other immutable characteristics they might have. We recognise that while *statistically* things might be a bit more difficult if you are a black, Muslim woman, you do not *have* to consider yourself limited by these things, nor should you *act* as though you are limited by these things. As far as we are concerned, the prizes are there for the taking by anybody willing to work hard.

And yet, K and others have asked me, their teachers and the guest speakers who have come from Oxford and Cambridge, whether these universities in particular are institutionally racist. They read the news; they hear the commentary from prominent public figures like the MP David Lammy; they see the pictures of the few Afro-Caribbean male students admitted to Cambridge in a given year. They have no good reason, before talking to us, *not* to believe that they are at a disadvantage because they are BAME.

I don't get angry at much, but I do get angry at the media presentation of Oxbridge as racist. Many wiser and more eloquent people than I have written on this subject, so I won't add too much, except to narrate what I and others at Michaela have told our students:

 ♦ It is possible that, among the many admissions tutors and academics at Oxford or Cambridge, there are some who consciously or unconsciously favour students of a particular colour. It is also possible that they might prefer you for being BAME. They might prefer you being short or tall. What does it matter? You apply regardless.

- It is undeniable that Oxford and Cambridge have not, historically, admitted as many young people of colour as they have other groups. Does this mean this trend will continue inexorably? No – past performance is not necessarily an indicator of future performance. In fact, Oxbridge are painfully aware of this fact, and are going out of their way to advertise themselves to BAME students. There has never been a better time to consider Oxbridge if you are young, bright and BAME.

- The people who claim in the media that Oxford and Cambridge are racist do so with good intentions: they want to ensure that the universities are doing everything in their power to ensure that there is *not* institutional racism in the admissions process. They perceive an injustice and are fighting it – fair enough. What they don't see is the profound impact that this has on the young BAME students who may not even have *considered* that they may be at a disadvantage when applying. All this narrative does is reinforce an incipient sense of victimhood, which leads to the following conclusions:

"If Oxbridge is racist, I don't want to put myself out there and risk being rejected."

"If Oxbridge is racist, they won't want me so there's no point in applying."

"If Oxbridge is racist, everyone there will be of a type and I won't fit in, and I don't want to stick out like a sore thumb."

Or even, post-application:

"Oxbridge rejected me because I'm BAME" (rather than other possible, constructive explanations that would encourage the student to work on what they *can* change, such as academic interests, rather than fixating on what they can't, i.e. the colour of their skin).

The emphasis on law and medicine in the community that Michaela serves is also a major factor in the perception that certain universities are racist. Law and Medicine are two of the most over-subscribed subjects at universities across the country. It therefore follows that a larger proportion of BAME applicants to those courses don't get in, because there are far more applicants for those places. Nothing to do with race. Yet when analysing the question of institutional racism at elite universities, very little is made of the fact that BAME students would fare far better if they were applying for less competitive courses.

Why do well-heeled private school students make up 100% of the cohort studying Anglo-Saxon, Norse and Celtic at Cambridge? Not because they are the only people who could ever be enthused by such subject matter, but because they and their peers come from schools that are very well-practised at playing the numbers game when it comes to course and college choice. This is why my Oxbridge advisor told me which colleges to apply to, and to apply for Classics rather than Law – I was statistically more likely to be successful. But it is very difficult to persuade students that they should consider a different subject because it will improve their chances of getting into an excellent university.

We have on our staff, and have been visited by, high-achieving Russell Group graduates who are also BAME. Our students are now, after many conversations and "debunking" sessions, convinced that their application to Oxbridge is as worthy of consideration as any other, and will be considered like any other. Whether that is in fact the case (and I think it is) is almost beside the point: they must not have their ambitions stifled either by prejudice or by the perception of prejudice, and to allow them to be so is unconscionable.

"I can't decide if I should be a doctor or a lawyer." – N, 12E

It is no surprise for our students that some courses – Law, Medicine, PPE – are more competitive than others. The challenge is opening their eyes to the huge variety of courses that are *not* law or medicine. The majority of students began Year 12 at Michaela6th with the following shopping list of potential professions: lawyer, banker, doctor, solicitor (they don't know this is like 'lawyer'). Why?

Many are from families with a clear, but narrow, view of what 'professional success' looks like. In a lot of cases, this is just accepted wisdom: doctors and lawyers, whether or not you know any or know *of* any, are respectable and successful, and therefore those are the professions for which to aim. It is far from clear to these families and their children that studying academic subjects which do not have a clear vocational link is valuable and worthwhile for their future (even before we get into any argument about the intrinsic beauty and value of knowledge).

We talk to our students regularly about picking a course that they think they will enjoy, as opposed to one that leads to a particular career. We tell them about how many options will be available to them if they study non-vocational courses for the sheer love and enjoyment of the subject. We have dozens of copies of simplified course guides of certain universities strewn around the Common Room – students pick them up and browse in the hope of happening upon a course that they like the look of, rather than one they feel they "ought" to do. Our speaker programme exposes them to people from a wide range of fields, who have studied a variety of academic subjects, all of whom are very successful, and who have encouraged our students to think about fields outside "the professions".

It is another task entirely to persuade families of this. One student, whose parents were adamant that she should become either a doctor or a lawyer or there was no point in this education malarkey (such is the rhetoric received in the media), was incredibly brave in going against their wishes to study the subjects that she really wanted to study, as opposed to the ones that would lead directly to law or medicine. She is a rarity: more often, students are reluctant to go against their parents' wishes. It may be that, when students choose courses, I and my colleagues will have more meetings and conversations with parents to persuade them of the value of non-vocational courses.

We want to persuade students and their families to look at as wide a variety of courses as possible, with a view to choosing something that they would really enjoy, as well as something that would serve them professionally. It is helpful, in that respect, that law and medicine are so popular: we can explain that the chances of getting into those courses are limited compared with others. Of course, we have no desire to divert a child from studying what they really care about. We are, however, *very* clear: if you want to study a competitive course, you have to really *want* it, and you have to be prepared to go well above and beyond what might be necessary for a less competitive course. If you don't, you should look around – it may be that Biochemistry is more your thing than Medicine, or you might prefer three years of Ancient History rather than three years of Tort and Contract Law. And when it comes to applying, while two of their choices might be orthodox, I hope that two or three will be outside of the box.

"I don't want to leave my family." – 90% of them

For every student who is desperate to flee the nest and experience the freedom and independence of university life, there are nine who are very resistant to the idea. I find this sad, because it means that those students are cutting themselves off from the world of opportunities that exist outside the M25, without really having thought about the life-changing implications of such a choice. Of course, there is nothing wrong with wanting to be close to your parents and support networks, particularly now when the financial burden of university study can be so much greater than it was. Yet one cannot deny the wealth and breadth of experience that students might have at the full range of universities in the UK and abroad. How on earth do you go about convincing students to at least *consider* universities outside of London?

One of the biggest concerns is cost. Living at home makes the extraordinary expense of university seem slightly more palatable – that way, you are only concerned with repaying tuition fees and travel expenses, as opposed to taking on an additional £15,000 in debt to pay for living costs during your degree. I had expected that the cost of university would be a big factor in students deciding either not to go, or to go somewhere close to home, but they all seem to understand that there is plenty of financial support available, and that repayments are reasonable. This is a triumph of narration from the universities. Of course, it may be that they just don't think long-term enough to worry about paying back the debt they will incur – who knows! They also believe that higher education is worth the investment, which is a triumph of narration from both school and family.

However, living at home does reduce costs. What is more, there are several exceptional universities on their doorstep in London – why go elsewhere? This is a particularly acute question for our girls, many of whose families are very protective of them and reluctant to part with them for university. The stronger-willed are engaged in a lengthy battle with parents over how far they are allowed to go for university. Some of them have been inspired by presentations from our teachers about their university experiences in far-flung institutions like Bristol, St Andrews, Durham and Warwick. They see the beautiful surroundings and architecture of these non-London institutions. They hear about the extraordinary academic experiences available at a whole variety of institutions. Teachers talk to them constantly about the peculiar joys of being away from home – the independence, the living with strangers, the elusive "cleaning rota", the friendships forged, the terrible (but formative) decisions... All of it!

Our responsibility, when faced with this question, is to ensure that the decision to stay at home and go to a university that is near family is made for the right reasons. If it is a legitimate concern about money, that they are worried about repaying vast sums, and we cannot persuade them of the ample financial support that is available, then fair enough. If the student is needed at home to take care of family members, and we are unable to help the family to arrange things such that the student might consider universities away from home, of course that is the right choice. If it is tradition that the student remains at home... I find that difficult to accept, but accept the wishes of parents we must (although not without discussion). But our duty is to ensure that the decision is not rooted in fear – of distance, of the unknown, of anything. In the same way, we have a duty to ensure that the decision to *leave* home is made for the right reasons as well. We are realistic and open with students about the challenges of studying away from home – they know it is more of a risk, and that greater risks *can* yield greater rewards.

I do wish that we could do more to expose them to the beauty and benefits of studying in some of those further-away places. I know that many of our students' ambitions were shaped by a visit to Oxford in year 9. The expense and time-cost of making trips is, in most cases, insurmountable – I wonder if, in future, universities might direct more of their widening participation funding to allow more schools to bring students to visit them. Just a thought.

We will see in 2021 whether our wonderful students are successful in their bids to be accepted to the Russell Group (and, indeed, the Ivy League). We will continue to interrogate their doubts about the unknown, and ensure that their decisions are based on what is right for them, as opposed to what they fear. It is my sincere hope that some will leave London for elite universities across the country, will find the joy of learning and new friendships and acceptance in wholly unfamiliar environments, and will do so confident in their ability to navigate the academic and personal challenges of the best universities in the country. I hope our students know: the only thing that can stop you is you. What an unbelievable privilege it is to guide them in one of the most important decisions of their lives.

Being Head of Year for Our First Year 11

Hin-Tai Ting
@HinTai_Ting

Being a classroom teacher is nothing like being a Head of Year.

A classroom teacher has a defined schedule, a defined amount of content to teach, a defined set of techniques and methods for teaching it, a defined learning objective for each lesson. 'Welcome to Michaela! Here's your year 8 class – you'll see them at these times – they're going to be learning the fundamentals of algebra this year – here are all the booklets you'll be teaching from – watch these three teachers in particular to see how we teach algebra here.'

In contrast, a Head of Year has an unpredictable schedule – 'Mr Ting, we've just had a parent phone in about an issue at home, are you free to talk to them?' A Head of Year has an overwhelming objective – my job was to embody and set the culture – to get each and every child in my year group to work very hard and be very kind. A Head of Year has no easily defined method of achieving this: I remember well when Katharine described the role to me: 'you just need to inspire them and lead them into battle against their GCSEs!' Being a Head of Year is a bit like being a dad, except you somehow find yourself with over a hundred children, and you missed out on the first 12 years of their life, and you're desperately trying to play catch up in what time remains.

Much of what we do at Michaela is easy to scrutinize. Visitors watch lessons, they see merits and demerits, they flick through booklets, they take part in family lunch, they listen to an assembly. But it's much harder to see the real work of Heads of Years. It's the inflection in the voice when dealing with a particularly tricky customer; the winks and pats on the back during a good day; the shoulder-sagging disappointment after a pupil's just let himself down; the knock on my classroom door after school, with a pupil asking 'sir can I speak to you about something?'; the phone call to mum in the office at 5pm; the restlessness in bed at night, desperately running through an assembly. While harder for visitors to see, this presence is vital to the culture of the school. If anything, as several other chapters in this book explain, they're especially vital at Michaela, so our pupils can see, without a shadow of doubt, the love behind our 'tough love'.

Similarly, it's much easier to see whether your classroom teaching has succeeded, than whether your pastoral leadership has made any impact. Our classroom methods were vindicated on Results Day 2019, but even before that, there were clear signposts of success with every classroom quiz, every homework, every mock exam. But when being a Head of Year means helping each child on their journey to become the best version of themselves – well, it's very hard to appraise how I did in my role, even now, many months after I've stepped down. To be sure, the real results won't really come in until my year group have started to find their own feet as adults.

But don't get me wrong. Being the Head of Michaela's first ever Year 11 cohort has indeed been a unique challenge, but only because it's been one of the greatest privileges of my life. As a maths teacher, I focused on handing down precious knowledge, skills, and the joy of learning – all of which are deeply significant. But as a Head of Year? My focus was on one hundred and seventeen children, all born somewhere between September 2002 and August 2003, on the joy and sorrow and richness of their lives thus far, on how to amplify the joy and help them overcome – or at least deal better with – the sorrows.

I'm glad to be writing this chapter now, nearly a year after that cohort has left. Several stories spring to mind. Every time I bump into a former year 11, I'm delighted. I think of one meeting at the tube station, heading home during the darkness of the depths of the winter term. I'm about to tap in with my contactless card when I hear a loud and insistent 'Mr Ting! Mr Ting!' I look up and see Trevor, a former year 11. He stands up tall – taller than I remember – takes off his hood, even though it's raining, takes out his earphones, shakes my hand, looks me straight in the eye, and starts chatting with me. He's doing well, he says, as are his mum and dad. He's doing an IT course at a local college, he's enjoying it, he likes his teacher, he's working hard (though he's not sure about some of his coursemates...) When I ask him, he's even willing to admit that he misses his teachers from Michaela. As we head off, I tell him it's good to see him, and that I'm so glad he stopped me for a chat – he replies in kind.

To a passing commuter trying to get home from Wembley Park station, that encounter would have seemed entirely unremarkable. Yet to me, as I type it out, I can't help but smile. Trevor was a quiet, mild-mannered lad, who scraped his way through with minimum effort in his lessons and his homework. He just wanted to keep his head down, and he hated hassle and attention. (So much so that on results day, he took his envelope, refused to open it there and then, and left with it immediately after picking it up and saying a few unavoidable hellos). I managed to slightly bond with him through a shared love of basketball, though 'bond' is perhaps a stretch. Over the years, I tried to encourage him to participate more in lessons. I tried to help him see that beyond the hassle, his teachers got on his back because we cared about him. Yet I was never particularly sure that I had ever gotten through to him.

Yet here he was, pleased to see me, chasing me down before I headed through the tube barrier. Here he was, interacting without being asked. I think back to the times I welcomed him at the school gate after a holiday, with a handshake, telling him to put a bit more welly in his. I think of the times I sat with him in side offices, reminding him to make eye contact, to speak and sit up a bit. I think of the meetings with mum about his general effort levels, and his tired and defeatist attitude throughout.

Yet here Trevor was, standing tall, standing in front me, shaking my hand, talking to me, telling me about his future plans – like a responsible young man, no longer a year 11, ready to make his way in the world.

I had a similarly surprising experience in Michaela's sixth floor stationery cupboard a few months ago. I open the door, looking for a stack of A4 lined paper. 'Ouch!' says a bump behind the door. I peer down – it's Sophia! 'Hi Sophia! What are you doing here?'

'Hi sir!' she replies, in a breezy and happy way. 'I'm doing work experience, helping out in the office!'

I ask her her plans – she's always wanted to go into healthcare, perhaps as a midwife. She's enjoying her BTEC at college but finds the atmosphere a bit distracting, so based on her research, she's hoping to transfer to a Sixth Form to do A Levels instead. I tell her I'm surprised to see her back! Does she miss Michaela? Yes she does. She likes seeing her teachers and she likes being back in the building. She knows her teachers cared about her here. It's nice and quiet, she says – a luxury she didn't appreciate before, but now she definitely does.

I have to get ready for my next lesson, so I say my goodbyes. But as I walk to my classroom, again I think back to Sophia in Year 11. I remember multiple chats with her about the importance of each school day, the importance of showing up, as her attendance was on the worse side of the year group. Yet here she was, spending extra days at Michaela, voluntarily. I remember one holiday, where she tried to pass off old homework as her holiday homework by gluing her old homework into her new book. (I was very pleased to catch that one.) Yet here she was, happily reorganizing the stationery cupboard, with ambitions for her future and a plan to get there.

As I mentioned above, the goal of being a Head of Year at Michaela is very simple to define – all you have to do is get the kids to become people who work hard and be kind. But how you achieve that goal is a different question altogether. After endless assemblies and sermons, daily parent meetings and phone calls, Excel spreadsheets galore, a fantastic team of form tutors and classroom teachers all pitching in, parent evenings, breaktimes and lunchtimes spent moving around the yard chatting and joking and sympathising and exhorting, devices handed in, homework support arranged, pulling kids out of form times and lessons – only time will tell how successful we've been at achieving this goal. After all, as with teaching a subject, one of the keys to being a Head of Year is AfL – did they get it? How do I know if they got it or not?

Trevor and Sophia are just a couple of snapshots. But as I bump into more and more of that cohort, as I teach some of them in Sixth Form, as I see them on the streets and stop for a pleasant chat, I find myself bumping into polite, kind-hearted, warm young men and women with the world at their feet.

Ultimately, though, one of the best ways to AfL (to judge whether what you've taught the pupil has had an effect) is to see what the pupils themselves understand and produce. Towards the end of our final exams I had the privilege of interviewing a spectrum of our year 11s. My chapter will end, appropriately, with their own words. Some of these interviewees are still with us, in our Sixth Form. Others have since moved on to other colleges. As you'll see, they come from a diverse range of backgrounds and experiences prior to arriving at Michaela. But their memories and impressions of Michaela share some common themes, and it's deeply moving to read them all. My one regret is that I didn't interview the whole year group.

I'll say it again: the real highlight and privilege of being a Head of Year is in getting to know these children, and so it's an absolute pleasure to be able to share something of that privilege with you, through their words.

Testimonials

Charlotte

Coming to Michaela was nerve-wracking. I barely knew anyone from my primary school. My behaviour in primary school was bad. I often got involved in arguments and was in a lot of fights. I was quite a violent person. In primary school, everyone was mean. It was normal. There was this girl, and she wasn't very talkative, but people would find it humorous to pick on her for certain things. When one person started to pick on her, everyone else did too.

But at Michaela, the strict rules meant that if someone was getting picked on, teachers would stop it immediately, and it wouldn't be that much of a big deal. The teachers taught us perspective. At Michaela, I learnt that bullying, drama, and arguments were not right. You should go out of your way to help others.

In primary school, because I'm dyslexic, some teachers would let me do what I wanted, and I wouldn't really learn. It was an excuse for me not to do anything. I would use it as an excuse not to do my homework. Now I'm at Michaela, I make sure I go out of my way to make up for all the times I wasn't learning in my other lessons in primary school. At primary school I could barely read – reading in front of others was nerve-wracking. However, after five years of Michaela, now and again I have a few difficulties with being fluent, but it's not really a big thing – I just have to stop and think about what I'm saying. I think my reading is great now! I even enjoy reading the Bible at church now, even though there's lots of tricky words.

Michaela can be difficult to adapt to. But even though it's stressful, and sometimes you feel like you don't want to be here anymore, in the long run it helps you become a better person – you are educated and also just a nicer person in general.

Assad

Despite being born in the UK, I spent most of my childhood in Iran, and only returned to London at the very end of year 6. English wasn't my first language, and it was very difficult – not only learning English, but also learning other subjects through English. As a result my primary school put me in the bottom set. My English got slightly better in year 7, but new difficulties came – like learning French, a new foreign language, via English!

In year 8 I joined Michaela. I instantly found it a much calmer environment. Classes were peaceful, even though that shouldn't have to be a term to describe a classroom. I joined in the third set, but within a few months, thanks to the quality of teaching, my English dramatically improved. I had reached the top set by the end of year 8.

When I moved to London, I was a silent kid, after experiencing some difficult events in the Middle East. This continued until I joined Michaela. Attending Michaela helped me become more open. The teachers and pupils alike never gave up on me, and they gave me lots of advice on how to open up and contribute more. I had told them I preferred to be silent, but they saw my potential, and wanted me to flourish and benefit others.

On top of school work, my life in the last few years has very busy with religious commitments, helping my father, and extra language lessons in Arabic and Farsi. I've really appreciated the support of my friends and teachers in helping me stay sane and focused on my future goals.

Nina

In May 2018, I was at a Pupil Referral Unit for having gotten into a fight at my previous school. I joined Michaela one month later. It was a rocky start at first: I didn't think the teachers were serious about the homework, the rules – about anything! I didn't think they were actually going to enforce all the rules. I spent the first few weeks picking up loads of detentions and demerits for homework, and for not paying attention.

I just realised that how I was acting was affecting my family, especially my mum and my younger siblings, and I wanted to be an example to them all.

At Michaela it's not cool to misbehave or miss out your homework – my friends would look at me and say ‹what are you doing?!› Michaela takes all the fun out of misbehaving. When I came to the school I went from not doing a single piece of homework, ever, to spending two hours a day on it. Because Michaela lessons were so fast paced, I felt like I HAD to do the homework to keep up.

I remember when I was struggling in science, Ms Dyer would give me extra help in lessons to help me catch up with everything. I soon started to realise that the teachers at Michaela really cared about me.

I've recently struggled in maths. When I came to Michaela, the teaching was really clear, and teachers would give me extra help when I didn't do very well in a test. I started to realise that I could actually do well if I worked hard. As long as I tried hard in lessons, and tried hard at home, I would succeed. Friendly competition with my friends also helped me to push myself.

I remember when it was the one-year anniversary of the fight that got me kicked out of my last school. I thought about how much I had changed in that one year. Before, all I used to care about was my social standing, and drama at school. Now, my friends and I at Michaela are all focused on our education and supporting each other to reach our potential.

I find it strange how something as negative as a fight meant that I had the opportunity to come to Michaela and see my life changed in so many ways. I'm so grateful for how things turned out.

Mustafa

In year 7 I was terrible. I used to be in detention or referral every day. I didn't have any discipline. I didn't listen to anyone or take on board anything anyone told me. In primary school I had friends who were a bad influence on me. When I first came to Michaela, I wanted to leave! However, because I kept getting called out for my behaviour, I started to realise that I wasn't a very nice person. I compared myself to others – both academically and personally – and was embarrassed. I started to want to change. I also became friends with my classmates who were a really positive influence on me. Gradually, I became more self-disciplined, and listened more to what teachers were saying to me.

For the last few years, my experience of school has completely transformed. I didn't use to like how teachers pushed me to contribute, because I was really arrogant – but now I'm unafraid to give answers, even if I think they're wrong, because I know no-one will laugh at me in lessons. I really enjoy my lessons. I used to think science was boring – but now it's one of my favourite subjects. I used to disrespect teachers, but now we get on – they trust me a lot more.

At Michaela, if you think things are tough, stick with it, because you learn skills like self-control that will be invaluable throughout your life. And it's not just skills – it's how to become a better person. I look back at myself in year 6 – I used to be a bully! But now I try to be as kind as I can, and as good a person as I can.

253

Patman

At my last secondary school, I bought a knife into school. I wasn't thinking straight. You know what I'm like. I have a brain but I wasn't using it properly. I thought if I bring a knife, people would be scared of me, and wouldn't want to fight me. So I got kicked out of my school.

I was at a PRU in West London. PRU changed me a lot. I met people who had been in prison. I didn't want to end up like them. I got the chance to go to Michaela at the end of Year 9. No other schools would take me because of what I did, but Michaela gave me the chance.

Michaela was rough at first. It was boring at first. My first lesson in maths, I just stared at the clock, but the time got longer and longer. I went to sleep and got sent out of the lesson.

But after a few months, my perspective changed, because I knew I wanted to get a good job. I realised that I had gotten cleverer during my time at Michaela. I learned a lot more here than at my other schools. The classrooms are silent, there's no messing around, and I pay total attention to the teacher. At my old school, whenever anyone messed around, I would join in, everyone would join in, and it was chaos. Teachers would call other teachers to try and sort it out and we would just walk out of lessons. At Michaela, pupils don't even try to mess around.

At Michaela, I knew I could work hard and focus. At my last school, I never did any of my homework. I remember my first piece of homework at Michaela. I didn't do it. The teacher was not happy with me. I quickly learnt that I had to do all my homework, and I've been a lot better at doing my homework. Sometimes I even did optional English homework – at Michaela I learnt to love writing. I felt like my head was full of ideas and I wanted to write them all down.

At my last school, I had enemies at other schools and I would go looking for a serious fight with them. I think I've become a nicer person at Michaela. I've calmed down a lot. The atmosphere at Michaela is quiet and calm. Pupils are much nicer here. I've realised drama and fights and arguments aren't worth it. Causing trouble makes you look like a clown.

If I hadn't gone to Michaela, I believe I would be in prison or in jail right now.

Jamie

When I started at Michaela I was only focused on messing about. I would find ways to be sneaky and misbehave when I was bored - it was just who I was.

In Year 9, when I realised how far behind I was compared to some of my friends, I stopped and started to focus more on school.

I felt that Year 10 was a setback because I felt that I was trying really hard, but I wasn't getting enough recognition from teachers. But after a low point, I had a talk with Mr Ting, my Head of Year, who taught me that life isn't about trying to impress people. What's more important is simply doing the right thing because it's right. I came back from it a changed man, determined to be a better person.

The teachers have always had faith in me. They always told me how much potential I had. I didn't like how they saw me as wasted talent. I knew it was time to buckle down and realise that potential.

The high standards at Michaela are going to be a struggle at first, but stick with it, and it gets better. Michaela helps you keep your future in mind. Wherever you see yourself in a few years, Michaela will help get you there. Tell a teacher what your goal is, and they will do everything to help you get there.

Teodora

I arrived in London from Romania in year 9. I only knew the phrase 'could I have some water please?' in English. I didn't even know how to spell my name in English. For the first two months, before I could speak English, it was hard. Every time I was asked questions in lessons, I just didn't know. When I started to talk to friends in my form, my English fluency and vocabulary started to improve. I also had hours of individual support with Ms Widdowson in the library, and that really helped my English. I was working my socks off.

After my English had improved, I realised how good Michaela is. I was shocked by my science lessons – in Romania, I thought I was terrible at science, but at Michaela, I suddenly realised that I understood the chemistry, biology and physics lessons, even though the lessons were in English! The teachers were so good at explaining things so that I could understand.

I love how everything is organised – the discipline – everything. I was all over the place in Romania. I literally knew nothing. I didn't know what was going on with my life. Michaela taught me to be disciplined. I feel like I've found myself at school. I've started to grow up and become mature here. My brain has developed so much.

If I stayed in Romania, I know that I would have failed my exams. Here, at Michaela, I feel confident to face my GCSEs. I have the hope of a better future. Now I feel that I can use my education, and use everything I've learnt, to change the world.

Kehlani

The last five years at Michaela have been a journey, in a way. When I first started, I felt shy, and I didn't know anyone else in my year group apart from Cayley. However, on my second day, I decided to lead a chant in my class, and led it loudly! I realised there was no need to be shy.

Michaela taught me stoicism. I remember seeing how the teachers modelled stoicism – and kept on going, even when they were tired. Stoicism was an important lesson for me personally because I have really bad asthma that often means I have to be treated in hospital. When I'm in hospital the doctors and nurses are always surprised to see past papers and homework on my hospital bed dinner tray. I also can have quite a sensitive personality, so stoicism plays an important role in my life in helping me to calm down.

Recently, I have really appreciated how the teachers work endlessly to make sure that we achieve the best grades possible and fulfil our potential. For example, Mr Ting is always happy to keep me behind til 6 o'clock even if we are working on one maths question, which shows how much he cares.

To summarize, basically, Michaela is a school for those who want to learn how to work hard and be kind.

Sharraqah

I arrived in London from North Sudan at the beginning of year 6. Starting school wasn't easy, especially as I didn't understand a word of English (except 'miss', 'thank you', 'please' and 'excuse me'), but I was eager to discover and learn this new culture. It took me a long time to get used to the differences in education – mixed classes, new subjects like history. I didn't really like primary school. I didn't know anything – subjects, people, everything!

When I first arrived at Michaela in year 7, it was still hard to adapt, but I still remember my second week: it was the first time I formed really close friendships. Bootcamp in year 7 really helped me get to know new friends and new teachers. Everyone was kind at Michaela and teachers encouraged us to speak up and expand our friendship circles. We soon got to know all the characters in our year group!

My dad has always inspired me to think of how I could do better, how I could improve myself, and never to settle for anything less than 100%. This was perfectly reinforced at Michaela. Both Ms Birbalsingh and my dad told me the story of Dr Ben Carson: how he started life in a very poor family, with life stacked against him; but because he worked so hard, he eventually became the first doctor to separate conjoined twins. His story inspires me to want to become a doctor too. The teachers always encourage us to persevere, even when it's difficult, especially when it's difficult!

The teachers at Michaela are willing to dedicate their time to everyone, no matter where you are in your education.

Zahra

At primary school I was often behind in my lessons. I was a late developer – I had glue ear, which meant I had hearing problems until I was 6, so I didn't start speaking until Year 3. (In year 1, because I couldn't speak, my teacher assumed my parents were illiterate, and that my family had just arrived in this country. This was not true!) This meant that I really struggled to catch up on the years that I missed.

At Michaela, the teachers really cared about me, and made sure that I could catch up. I remember having small group sessions in Maths after school to help me understand things that I didn't understand in lessons. Teachers would also contact my parents to let them know how I was struggling, and how they could help me. In lessons, teachers paid attention to every pupil, and made sure everyone understood before moving on to the next topic. There weren't any distractions, and the quiet environment really helped.

In the last few years, I caught up in all my subjects and am able to understand so much. I feel that at another school I would still be behind and wouldn't be at the level I'm at now. I feel like I've made a huge improvement. I can still stay behind after school and ask for extra help, and teachers are really happy to help me. I've really appreciated all the special resources the teachers have made too – my friends at other schools are stuck with YouTube revision videos and CGP guides, but I've benefited from so much tailored revision help throughout my GCSEs. Now, at the end of my GCSEs, I feel that all my exams went really well, because I've been revising hard for a long time.

Being at Michaela has made me more confident and a better person. I was very quiet in primary school, and also a bit mean – when people were rude to me, I was rude right back at them – that's what everyone did. I just copied what everyone around me was doing. Michaela has taught me that in order to succeed, it's not just about working hard, it's also about being kind. You don't know what's going on in other people's lives and what's making them struggle. The teachers here are perfect role models who show us kindness, responsibility, and how to treat others. They are also strict on unkindness and bullying, and that's taught me how it's just not acceptable. So the pupils here are welcoming – we just mix with each other instead of staying with people who are like us.

I would recommend Michaela to others, because I know how much it's made me improve as a person, both academically, and in my character.

Jaevon

I don't even know where to start.

In year 7, I left primary school and started at secondary school. It didn't go too well. I lasted 6 weeks. I was kicked out on October 23rd, 2014 – I remember that date! Fireworks were set off right outside that school, and I was found with fireworks in my bag.

I was then sent to a PRU in Lambeth North. I barely went because it was too far and I didn't learn anything there. I stayed at home, not doing anything, until I was given a 6 week trial at another secondary school. I failed the trial 4 weeks in – I was swearing at teachers and had a fight with another pupil.

I went to another PRU in Hammersmith for about a year and a half. I did okay at the PRU and was about to go back to school. But I never made it to the Fair Access Panel because I got arrested under Joint Enterprise for shoplifting. The PRU excluded me for two weeks. After that, I behaved well, and was about to be sent to another school, but I again didn't make it to the Panel because I was bag searched and found with a knife. I was excluded again for two weeks. After that, I came back, and managed to behave well for a month or two. I finally made it to the Panel and was accepted to come to Michaela. I was desperate to come to school so accepted the place.

I arrived at Michaela at the end of year 8. I remember I got a detention on my second day for not doing my homework – I was so used to not having any homework. But it was a new school, and I wanted to stay out of trouble. Year 9 mostly went really well. I started to get it. I started to understand the importance of behaving well. The strict rules meant that I was kept in line. At my other schools, if anyone tried to give me a detention, I would bunk it. I would walk out of referral. At Michaela, I stopped doing all this. I knew this was my last chance, and I knew that teachers took my behaviour seriously, and wouldn't overlook this.

At my other schools, I would go to sleep in lessons. Teachers would wake me up and I'd go back to sleep again. My friends and I would muck around in lessons and we didn't learn anything. At Michaela, everyone wants to learn. The lessons are quiet. No one is mucking around. This meant I stayed out of trouble.

At the end of year 9, I started to hang around with some badly behaved pupils, so I started to change. In year 10, I started going to referral again for being rude to teachers. I skipped school twice and went into referral. Sometimes I wouldn't do my homework. I often came late. I started to dislike school and got into arguments with my mum about going to school. I didn't care about my grades and wanted to leave. But my teachers and my dad would always get on my back. They would help me see the bigger picture – my long-term goal – to be successful. And you can't be successful unless you have good GCSEs.

Year 11 has been better. I barely spent any time in referral, and got into better habits. I gave up my phone to the school and to my mum. In one of the half terms, I didn't even receive a single homework or quiz detention. I remember when it was 10 weeks until the end of GCSEs. Now I've almost finished them all. It's gone so quickly. A whole month of exams sounds long – but it's flown by.

There have been a lot of ups and downs. There've been times when I've loved it, and times when I've hated it. But overall, it was worth it. Michaela saved me. I remember in year 10, I told my mum, 'when I finish school I'm going to protest, and make sure no one ever sends their kid here again!' But now, I know that Michaela has kept me on the straight and narrow. Short term pain for long term gain.

Nora

There's so many ways I feel like I've changed. I'm obviously 5 years older than when I started. But more importantly, many of the things that I value now, I have learnt a lot of them from Michaela. For example, my family have always taught me how important hard work is. But it's hard! It's called hard work for a reason. However, teachers at Michaela always tell us to learn to love hard work, and it won't seem as bad. It's a hard lesson to learn, and it takes a lot of maturity, and I'm not there yet! But I value hard work now.

The school motto is the most important – 'work hard, be kind'. It's not enough just to get the grades – being kind is what really makes you a good person, and what will make you be remembered by other people. If you work hard but are a terrible person, you might get respect for your hard work, but no one will like you. As teenagers, it's so easy to be mean, because everyone does it. It's tough, because you want to fit in and be part of a group of friends, and you don't want to be seen as an outsider, but when you really think about it, you know you shouldn't be doing it. Just because someone else does it, doesn't mean it's the right thing.

But I've always felt really safe at the school, and I feel that's something I have really valued at Michaela. When I talk to my friends from other schools, they can't believe that there's no bullying here. But I know that teachers will take things really seriously and we trust that they will do something about it and make sure there are no issues.

When I came to the school in year 7, I was not reliant on technology at all. I didn't have a laptop, phone, or social media. I was really proud of that fact. I remember sitting in an assembly once and Ms Birbalsingh asked us how long we could go without using technology – could we go a night? a whole day? a whole week? At that time I remember feeling proud – I knew I could go a long time without using any technology.

But that's completely changed in the last few years. I got my first proper phone in year 8. And then I got social media and Netflix in year 9. That's when I started to become more addicted to technology. At home, by myself, I chose Netflix over my homework and my revision – the stuff that I really need to do. In year 11 it got really bad – I just kept coming to school late and didn't do my homework properly. Binge-watching Netflix kept getting in the way of sleep and homework. I would get to Friday mornings feeling so, so tired. My grades got worse and worse.

So, in March, I was actually so happy when my mum came for a meeting with my Head of Year. Mr Ting blocked all social media apps on my phone, and he blocked Netflix from my laptop. The change was dramatic! I got much more sleep, came to school on time, and my homework and revision got a lot better. One time, I remember feeling so happy, because I realised that my sleep quality was much better than it used to be. Netflix had made it so hard for me to fall asleep, and that all changed after it was blocked.

Michaela has been so helpful for teenagers like me, who need that push to work hard and fulfil their potential. I don't know what I would have done or who I would be if I hadn't come to Michaela.

Lamarcus

I found Michaela very hard when I first came here, but I found it easy to adapt to – I come from a strict family so I adapted very quickly. For example, my big brother is such a motivation to me. He is very disciplined. He taught me to restrict myself to work for a better outcome, whether in the gym, or anywhere else. So I didn't like Michaela's discipline at first because I was hoping to have a little bit of fun at school, but then I realised Michaela was just the same as home, so I stuck to it.

My attitude towards things has changed. I've become more responsible. When I used to go out with my friends, I noticed they had a different mindset to me. I would be thinking 'okay, I'll have to get home by this time, because I've got to revise for a test this week', but my friends would often try and get me to stay out later. Now, I feel I've passed on my responsible mindset to them, and they've become stricter on themselves too!

From the middle of Year 9, every Thursday I would leave school at 10am to train for QPR Academy. The discipline I learnt at Michaela helped me at QPR. You always have to stay focused, whether at school, or on the football pitch – always. On Wednesdays I would go to all my teachers I was missing a lesson with and ask them what we would be going through on Thursday. I would then make sure I caught up with work around my football commitments. It was often difficult to catch up – I had training sessions 3 times a week, and it was a long journey there and back too. I would revise on my way to training and on my way back home. I'd get home late and then stay up late to revise and go over my schoolwork. It was very hard. But my teachers helped me – they let me stay back after school to help me catch up, or they would give me some extra work to do.

I used to be vulgar with my language on the football pitch – and everywhere else. I used to be aggressive sometimes too. I remember in lessons I used to have a grumpy face, all the time. But after conversations with teachers, I realised I had to change. My attitude in the classroom affected my attitude on the football pitch. Now, after many conversations, I've become much more responsible and mature.

I remember when I got my 2-year scholarship to continue playing for QPR. It was lovely! I don't even know how to describe it. I've been brought down so many times in my football career, and it was the first time I've achieved something in football. It's made me more confident. I've realised that working hard is good: when you work hard, you will achieve your goal.

Conversations with teachers helped me balance my football commitments with school. School is also very important. Even though I have my scholarship, I still have to get good grades in order to get onto it, as I'll be doing a BTEC Level 3 in sports at QPR. Later on in life, say if my football career ends early, my grades mean that I have options that I like that I can jump back on.

Michaela teaches you so much self-discipline, especially the teachers. Because they consistently remind you what to do, and what not to do, you start to get used to it, and it turns into a good habit.

Keep your mind on the goal you want out of life. If you keep your mind to it, all the distractions around you won't affect you. You have something other people don't, and you can put that to use. My big advantage was my work ethic. As my mum always said: 'keep working hard, and you will achieve your goals. Don't let anyone affect your ambitions.'

Munisa

Michaela Community School. In the summer of 2014 that was nothing but a name to me. It had no meaning to me and I certainly didn't know the magnitude of the impact it would have on me. I have come a long way from September 2014 and I can say that I have Michaela to thank for this.

I started as any pre-teen going to secondary school. On the very first day we had an assembly from Ms Birbalsingh which I can still recall word for word. She spoke about hard work, behaviour policies and obviously, phones! This was the first time I began to change. I was terrified. Surprisingly, high school was not all fun and games. Over the next week I was introduced to stoicism, kindness, and personal responsibility. Then I found out about GCSEs. I had never heard of them and at Michaela it was all that we were talking about. After this I knew that I had to work for my future and that it wouldn't just be handed to me. Year 7 was the year of revelation for me. I had a glimpse into the real world of hard work- even though there was much more work to be done.

Over the next few years I became accustomed to exams. We had regular exam weeks and with this came another change. Being introduced to exams very early was very good for me as I really learned what hard work was. There was no magic spell. I had to open my knowledge organisers and do revision or else I would fail. In Year 8 and Year 9 I learned the importance of revision, hard work and how success came about.

Year 10 and Year 11 have been the hardest years I have had to date. Exams went from twice a year to once every week. Homework went from one subject a night to two. Although the pressure was mounting, the support I got from my teachers was immense. They set up subject clinics after school for any additional help we may need. It was a constant uphill battle trying to balance life and school work. In my opinion, the real work begins in Year 10. This is when taking a day off is like taking a week off in the other years. These are the most crucial years of my life and all I will do is keep running as fast as I can to that finish line.

As a person I have changed a lot as well. Starting secondary school, I wasn't the most sociable and confident person and although I can still improve, I have come a long way. Appreciations and my teachers always telling me to project helped boost my confidence. Also, I never saw outside my own world.

Now I consider others and I now know how my previous view was damaging not only to myself but also to everyone around me. Although I was initially a very insulated and self-absorbed person, I have now come to realise the importance of being more social. Michaela taught me this.

Michaela Community School. Now these are the three words that I will remember forever. This is where I have spent my most important years and I still have a few months to go in secondary school to continue to learn, grow and change. I have learnt so much at Michaela and many of these things will stay with me forever. Thank you, Michaela Community School.

My Year 11 Nurture Group

Cassandra Cheng
@casscheng2

Growing up in Wembley can be tough. I know this as a teacher and as a teenager who grew up here. I was born in the same hospital as some of our pupils, attended my local comprehensive school, shopped in the local supermarket and ate regularly at Sam's Chicken. In short, I am aware of the significant challenges our pupils face. For me, working at Michaela is not just an exciting professional opportunity, it is also an important personal chance for me to give back to the community in which I grew up. My aim for this chapter is to provide an insight into what it is like to be a form tutor at Michaela.

'Apollo' are a small class of 15 and they are our nurture group. A number of pupils have Special Educational Needs (SEN), and many of them have complex pastoral issues. When I inherited this form, I knew that I would have to do more than simply take the register every day. Being Apollo's tutor was going to require a lot more input on my part.

There are a number of interesting characters in the class and here are some anonymised descriptions of my lovely form:

- Abel joined Michaela in Year 7, with a statement saying he was only able to recognise colours and three letter words. Now he is flourishing in his subjects (relative to his academic ability). For example, he is now confident factorising a quadratic expression in maths.

- Masih joined in Year 9 after being excluded from his previous school and spending a few months in a PRU. He is capable of great work, but sometimes underestimates the effort and focus required to really master content. Masih wants to be a plumber.

- Duong is a lovely, timid boy, who only began speaking English around four years ago. He works hard, but finds it difficult to communicate. He also has emotional and cognitive learning difficulties.

- ◆ Leah is a polite, well-mannered pupil. She usually works hard in lessons but can let herself down with missed homework deadlines. Leah is keen to be a mental health professional.

- ◆ Jayla joined Michaela as a selective mute, but has produced the most wonderful artwork and has made some really supportive friends.

Like all teachers in the profession, we care about our pupils' happiness, their well-being and their lives beyond the classroom. We want to have a positive impact on their lives. So, when I took them on as a tutor group, Apollo needed to know that my expectations of them were unapologetically sky-high. Apollo needed to know that growing up in Wembley does not diminish your life chances or choices. Apollo needed to know I care not just about their academic progress, but I also care about them as people. When they do well, I am filled with joy. When they misbehave, I am disappointed. Over our three years together, there have been many times when pupils have come to me seeking reassurance, or because they have been struggling both personally and academically. As with many of the pupils we serve, the pupils in Apollo come to school every day dealing with serious challenges and circumstances beyond their control. Therefore the considerable tutor time established at Michaela means that we get to know our pupils so that we can support, nurture and guide them.

Tutor time at Michaela

Every day, pupils have 45 minutes of tutor time, double the amount of tutor time compared to my own secondary school experience. As a pupil, I mainly remember tutor time was an opportunity to have a catch up with friends or complete unfinished homework. Most days it was simply a matter of the teacher taking a register before everyone went their separate ways for the day.

At Michaela, I see Apollo once in the morning for twenty minutes and again at the end of the day for twenty-five minutes. In the morning, pupils come into class and read silently. We have classical music on in the background, selected each week by our Head of Music. Next, a quick equipment check is completed to ensure no lesson time is wasted with pupils asking for pens, rulers, calculators etc. Then, it's time for my favourite part – trying to motivate this lovely bunch with a pep talk. This can take many forms:

1. Reminding them of the Michaela values, such as maintaining their self-control when being given a consequence or showing gratitude to every teacher by thanking them as they leave the classroom at the end of a lesson.

2. Reinforcing messages given in assembly – for example, their Head of Year gave a fantastic assembly about avoiding the use of mobile phones whilst doing homework. Once back with Apollo, I explained: "being an adult means doing what is important instead of what feels good in the moment. Adults choose the short term pain for long term gain. Do give up your phones completely before your GCSEs or start with giving your phones to your parents whilst completing your homework. It means you can completely focus without any distractions and notifications buzzing away!"

3. Looking at the big picture – "there are 50 days left to your GCSEs – make each lesson count! Put 100% effort in class; what you learn in maths today may come up in your exams. That might be the difference between a Grade 3 and a Grade 4, and that Grade 4 means you will get into your level 2 course and not a level 1 course."

At the end of the school day, it is time to check in with the pupils again. We discuss how the day has gone for the form, basing this assessment mainly on the merits and demerits they've earned throughout the day. This is a chance both to congratulate those at the top and to have conversations with those who are struggling. This is also a good time to check what homework pupils have to complete that evening. Finally, notices and announcements are read out, including the detention list. Whenever I read out the list, I always use this as an opportunity to invite the pupil to re-visit the particular mistake they made that day, and to reflect on what they could do differently next time. These conversations have been really impactful – I frequently notice that pupils will stop repeating the same patterns and have learned how to stay away from detention.

Keeping an eye on their progress every day

I am really grateful that at Michaela I get to maximise the time I spend with the pupils every day. The school's Senior Leadership Team (SLT) recognise that the tutor is a central pillar to their class's success, and usually they engineer the timetable so that tutors also teach their form groups. (All classes are streamed so that pupils are taught in their form groups: it helps to build a sense of team camaraderie, and makes it easier for tutors to follow their tutees' progress). Moreover, whenever we have lunch time duties, the SLT organise the rota so that form tutors are in the same areas as their form groups. These are great opportunities for me to check in with my tutees. I try to circulate and speak with individuals, but also make myself present so they can come and speak with me if they need to. Sometimes I will try to score a hoop at basketball or have a table tennis match with Masih (I usually lose!). Having these slightly more informal interactions with my tutees means I can get to know them as individuals, not just as learners.

As they are streamed, they move from class to class together. This means they are all in the same group for English, Religion, Maths, and so on. With Michaela's wonderful open door policy, I can pop into any classroom at any point and watch Apollo working in lessons. Apollo know I'm watching, ready to find them at break or lunch to give them praise, such as "Jayla, you were on fire last lesson, lots of hands up!" Or "Abel, that was a fantastic Macbeth quote you gave!" These frequent interactions are so important to our school culture; they remind the pupils that I care about them and their success, and that the teachers are one team supporting each other.

Of course, it isn't always possible for me to pop in to their lessons; I am a full-time teacher. Luckily, communication is really strong at Michaela. Even when I can't pop into a lesson, my colleagues often drop me a quick WhatsApp message to let me know how my form did in their lessons that day. This maintains the illusion of my omniscience for the pupils. Even if I never appeared in the room to observe their lesson, I can still say things like: 'I hear you worked hard at surds in Maths today, Abel'.

This form of communication is also very helpful when the pupils in my form make mistakes and get detentions. For example a teacher might pop me a quick message to let me know something simple, such as: "Masih has a detention for making silly noises in class". This allows me to find him at break to have a conversation with him about his choices. I will then try to help him understand how to avoid making the same mistake again. These conversations are never angry, and I never show any frustration. Rather, they are an opportunity to build a relationship and help the pupil to get back on the right track. I want to help them to understand the reason for the sanction, and to support them so they do not make the same mistake again. This also reminds them that their teachers are working together to help them.

Anecdotally, I've found that these chats do tend to reduce the number of detentions they receive overall. And of course, when they do manage to avoid getting detentions or making mistakes, I'm able to tell them how proud I am of their progress.

Approaches to praise

Praise at Michaela is important. We hold all our pupils to sky-high expectations. Some have said that these expectations are too high. Yet every single day, most of our pupils meet them. This is certainly deserving of praise. At Michaela, there are many ways to praise pupils – verbal feedback, merits, postcards, phone calls. Form tutors across the school are encouraged to create their own personal ways of praising their pupils. I introduced a 'star pupil' for each lesson. Teachers in each of their classes would tell pupils who their 'star pupil' was, based on the number of merits or how impressive they had been that lesson. I was surprised how much the pupils liked it. They wanted that pride and recognition. I had pupils come and find me at break with a beaming smile and say "I got star pupil, Miss" or as Abel likes to call it "I got man of the match, Miss!"

This recognition gave a nice confidence boost for pupils like Duong. When Duong arrived in year 9 at Michaela he was really timid and scared. He had just moved from the Far East to a new country and new culture. In addition, he had severe health problems. I remember meeting Duong for the first time and he greeted me with a beautiful smile. At break and lunch he would be found in the yard by himself or in the library reading. I tried to integrate him with other Apollo pupils but he would be back on his own the next day. When I introduced star pupil, Duong was getting the most stars every week. Other pupils would ask how he did it and it was lovely to see him tell the class "by answering questions and completing my homework". Over the next two years, he made friends with pupils in the form and this summer he is going to the school prom with his friends. For me, it has been wonderful to see him change. He is now so much happier than before, is thriving in school, and is going on to study art in college.

Cultivating Curiosity

Part of cultivating academic excellence in our pupils is encouraging them to be inquisitive. Michaela form tutors are given broad autonomy at form time. So, once a week, I had 'Miss Cheng's questions'. It was time for pupils to anonymously ask anything they want (within reason) on a piece of paper. I would always pre-empt this by saying "I trust you to ask respectfully or you won't be able to ask any more questions for the next few weeks." To see what questions they asked was eye-opening to say the least. Some example questions from the pupils included:

◆ Do fish drink water?

◆ How long are elephants pregnant for?

◆ For a crime you didn't do, would you rather go to jail for 10 years or send a family member for one year?

◆ If there was a reunion in 10 years, would you come?

◆ Would you rather read minds or know everyone's next move?

◆ You know energy transfers to another place every time and humans have energy inside, so when we die do we transfer to another place?

Of course answering these questions fuels more questions, and over time pupils would also begin conducting their own research. I found that this was very important in building their social interactions, and eventually even helped with projects such as choosing topics for the speeches they had to research and carry out as part of their GCSE English Language qualification. For example, Leah chose to discuss whether all humans should be vegetarian and another pupil discussed if voting should be lowered to 16 – topics they had developed an interest in through being given the opportunity to engage regularly in discussions with myself and each other.

I also chose to regularly discuss the non-academic tools needed for success, and it was amazing to see how little pupils knew about the 'real world' and how it works. Once a week, I gave them mini introductions to basic first aid, driving tests, mortgages, taxes, and even something close to my own heart: Chinese culture. Pupils also suggested their own topics, and we discussed subjects such as setting up a bank account and college admission interviews. It was also really enjoyable for me to illustrate these discussions with examples from my own life experiences; I would share anecdotes such as my time at Scouts and my various triumphs and disasters cooking in the kitchen!

Gratitude

Gratitude is one of the things I love most about Michaela. While this may at first sound strange, we explicitly teach our pupils how to be grateful. We want pupils to buy in to our school ethos and to appreciate how lucky they are. We tell them that they have won the golden ticket by getting a place at Michaela. I asked how the school has changed their lives, and some of their responses included:

- "Michaela has made me improve my behaviour and work ethic. I am grateful for my place."

- "It has made me sociable" – Jayla

- "I now work hard and care about my future" – Masih

- "If it wasn't for Michaela, I wouldn't make eye contact with teachers"

Like many schools I've previously worked at, I give out postcards to pupils and make phone calls to parents. At Michaela we also get pupils to write postcards to their teachers. There is no prescribed way of writing the postcards and hence, when I first read them, it is often hilarious and always heart-warming. Here are some example postcards I have received from Apollo.

Postcards

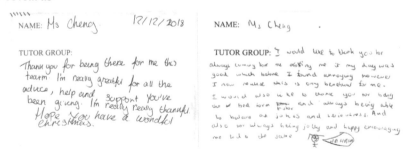

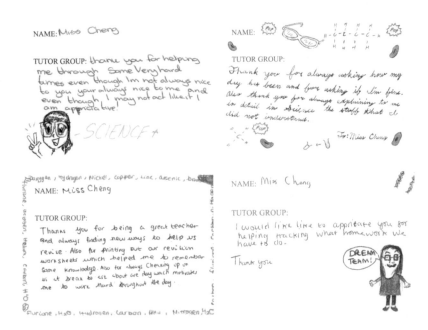

NAME: Miss Cheng

TUTOR GROUP: thank you for helping me through some very hard times even though Im not always nice to you your always nice to me and even though I may not act like it I am appreciative!

— SCIENCE —

NAME:

TUTOR GROUP: Thank you for always asking how my day has been and for asking if Im fine. Also thank you for always explaining to me in detail in science the stuff that I did not understand.

For: Miss Cheng

NAME: Miss Cheng

TUTOR GROUP: Thanks you for being a great teacher and always finding new ways to help us revise. Also for printing out our revision worksheets which helped me to remember some knowledge. Also for always cheering up ur us at break to ask about are day which motivates me to work hard throughout the day.

NAME: Mis Cheng

TUTOR GROUP: I would like like to appreiate you for helping tracking what homework we have to do.

Thank you

DREAM TEAM!

Team Culture

In the previous schools I taught at, I found the biggest problem with bottom set classes would simply be their behaviour. My whole job seemed to revolve around making sure the pupils were sitting in their chairs, making sure they were all focused in class, and indeed that they attended lessons at all. I remember when I first visited Michaela I was in awe of the impeccable behaviour: the pupils were polite and enthusiastic. As a teacher, I am very lucky that the behavioural systems are so tight. My colleagues and I are all 'rowing together'. I feel the pupils are more focused in class, more productive and achieve better outcomes. This allows pupils like Duong to be heard in class and not get laughed at when he answers. It means that if pupils like Masih are disturbing learning there are consequences. Most importantly, we are a team! I want our form to be the best – to get the most merits and the fewest detentions. Each pupil plays an integral part in the form and the success of the form relies on the success of every individual.

I feel like a mother figure for Apollo, championing and praising them when they do kind things. Over time, I have noticed that the class have all become closer as a group and, as they approach the end of Year 11, they are beginning to support each other too. Often it's just simple things. For example when

Leah once stayed behind after school to help Jayla sort out her work pack and put her homework in order. Or on another occasion, when Masih recommended that we watch an inspiring video he hoped would motivate us all to do more to help those in need. As a teacher there are few things that bring more delight than watching your pupils become Good Samaritans.

I say goodbye to my tutor group this year as they all take their GCSEs. I certainly will miss them, and I hope that they will achieve wonderful things in their respective futures. At Michaela we take on pupils with challenging circumstances. Sure, growing up in Wembley can be tough but still, at Michaela our expectations are sky-high. We use tutor time to teach our pupils that they are masters of their fate, and that they must go forth and dream big. We use tutor time to urge them to aim for the moon so that even if they don't reach it, they will fall among the stars. I very much hope Masih becomes a great plumber and that Jayla continues to excel in her art. I hope that Leah achieves her dream of working as a mental health professional. I hope that all 15 pupils of Apollo will grow to be kind, responsible and successful adults that Wembley can be proud of.

Getting the Culture Right in Year 7

Alexandra Gazi

@AlexandraGazi

Why worry about behaviour and learning habits in Year 7?

It is a truth universally acknowledged that Year 7 is the year that pupils are best behaved...and that as they get older, their behaviour gets trickier.

Dramatic as it sounds, for some of these children, choosing poor behaviour at the start of secondary school is just the first step on a dangerous path towards worse behaviour, violence and exclusion, not to mention poor – if any – GCSE results.

Year 7 is when our cute, eager-eyed pupils in their too-big blazers are most impressionable and when they most look up to us. Year 7 is therefore the most important time for secondary schools to prevent any descent into poor behaviour.

7 Jupiter: The Nightmare Class That Wasn't

'That is the hardest class I've ever taught at the school... They are really tough.'

The quotation above is from an exchange I had with one of my most experienced colleagues on the first day of "Bootcamp" (our week-long induction) in September.

7 Jupiter had just experienced their very first lesson. I vividly remember standing in the doorway as the lesson was ending, watching the class that would become my form group. If they were this difficult now, what would they be like further down the line? The sweet Year 7 class I had envisioned was fast disappearing into a puff of smoke.

Over the next two days it seemed that every teacher who taught 7 Jupiter used words like *tricky* or *tough* to describe them (or even worse, the euphemistic phrase every teacher dreads, *interesting characters*). As a class, they were unfocused and distracted, and the problematic behaviour wasn't restricted to just a handful of children; it was spread throughout almost the whole class. There was constant turning around, calling out, fiddling, not listening to the teacher, among a whole host of behaviours that were either rude or prevented learning. There was no denying it: they *were* tough. And this was in their first few days at secondary school.

However, if you ask any Michaela teacher what their impression of 7 Jupiter is now, you will hear 'they're delightful,' or, 'they're my favourite class'. It is not an exaggeration to say that they are a far cry from the nightmare class that everyone believed them to be at the start of the year.

I believe that their transformation was about more than just good behaviour systems. It is a testament to the successful culture we have established in Year 7. We don't have all the answers – no one does. But these are some of the values that we have focused on instilling in 7 Jupiter, which have helped make them the lovely class that they are today.

Asher: High Expectations

What you permit, you promote.

When we look at our pupils, we should see beyond their angelic-looking faces to the young adults they are on their way to becoming, should their current behaviour continue. It is all too easy to fall into a trap of telling ourselves it is just 'kids being kids'. As a result, we let misdemeanours go unpunished, and therefore the children cannot learn how to improve.

Imagine a boy throwing a pen at another pupil in your classroom. It may seem relatively harmless, but he is flouting the school rules and seeing what he can get away with. If he goes unpunished, he knows he can do the same again, and more.

That girl refusing to speak to you politely is testing your authority – she thinks she can be exempt from following the rules. If she is allowed to continue in this way, she might soon be making her own rules. The Year 7 shrugging at you is one step closer to becoming the Year 10 swearing at you.

I understand that this may sound extreme but consider these statistics from a 2019 NASUWT survey of teachers:[1]

- 89% had experienced verbal or physical abuse from pupils in the last year

- 86% had been sworn at

- 42% had been verbally threatened

- 29% had been hit, kicked, or punched

- 24% experienced physical violence from pupils at least once a week

Extreme behaviour doesn't appear out of nowhere. It develops in a culture where low-level disruption is given space, not only to exist, but to flourish because there are not any real consequences. In fact, the disruptor is admired by her peers for flouting the rules and so she now has a reputation to live up to. Unsurprisingly, this eventually gives rise to more extreme bad behaviour. Therefore, the first instances of poor behaviour in Year 7 need to be shut down, and fast.

When someone in my Year 7 class stepped out of line, I asked myself the following two questions:

If I let them continue in this way, what kind of person will they become?

(If it's something negative, I need to address it.)

Would I want to see this in my own children?

(If not, I need to address it.)

When Asher, a real cutie in 7 Jupiter, had not done his homework, I thought about him at the age of 16. I thought about him without GCSEs and job prospects. I remembered that his older cousin had just been arrested for mugging people at knifepoint. I made myself think about the very real risk that Asher could join a

---

1   NASUWT (2019), https://www.nasuwt.org.uk/article-listing/violence-against-teachers-weekly-occurrence.html.

gang and end up in prison. And I made myself give him a real telling-off because I wanted his success and cared about his future. He knew this.

This was hard.

At Michaela we often talk to the pupils about the weak choice (the easy option) and the strong choice (difficult, but the right thing to do). The easy choice would be to excuse Asher and not make a big deal about his incomplete homework. But this sets a dangerous precedent by allowing the first step in an increasingly negative spiral of behaviour.

It was not a fun conversation with Asher, but it was a necessary one. And if the relationships you have built are strong enough, that relationship will recover – and it will be even stronger because they know you have held them to account from a place of genuine love and care.

Seeing the Y11 pupils opening their GCSE results illustrated the above point for me. Simon, a Year 11 pupil, was often known to be naughty and lazy. He had been on the receiving end of plenty of reprimands and negative conversations in his time at the school. In another reality, he could quite easily have ended up in a gang. On results day, having done very well, Simon sought out all of his teachers and repeatedly thanked them for all they had done for him. It was one of the highlights of the day. He knew that his teachers had held him to high standards for the entirety of his school career, and he was incredibly grateful that they had.

That Year 11 pupil had succeeded because of the high standards we held him to, not in spite of them. If I am to set my own form on the path to success, it is vital that I maintain these standards. So whilst it may have been hard to discipline Asher in that moment, I knew it was best for him in the long run.

Harry: Trust and Honesty

'Knocking over your trust bucket' is an analogy we constantly refer to at Michaela. Everyone has a trust bucket: it's hard to fill and easy to spill. We praise kids when they have been trustworthy and admonish them when they haven't. This, I believe, is a key reason as to why our relationships with our pupils are so strong. Pupils need to be aware of the benefits of having a full trust bucket and understand the negative repercussions of having an empty one. For instance, if a child regularly fails to complete his homework, why should his teacher believe him on the one occasion when he genuinely left it on the bus by accident? Pupils need to learn the importance of trust and to avoid the classic 'boy who cried wolf' scenario.

We need to incentivise kids to tell the truth and discourage them from being dishonest. This is something I didn't fully understand until last year. The trust bucket narration is useful but in order to be most effective, there needs to be positive consequences for telling the truth. Children are rational beings – if the consequence (receiving a detention) is the same whether you tell the truth or not, there is clearly no incentive to be truthful. Therefore, where appropriate, if a child has broken the rules, **and has been given clear opportunities to be honest** but has not done so, the consequence ought to feel more negative than the original sanction would have been. The narration around this ought to feel drastically different.

The bold part above is incredibly important. As adults, we must guide children towards making the right choice. When they have done something wrong we need to make it very clear to them that the right choice in that moment is to tell the truth. Even when they have dug themselves into a hole by not being entirely honest from the outset, I always ensure that I give pupils an honest way out and multiple opportunities to come clean, where it is clear that I want them to be truthful and that I will have a lot more respect for them if they are.

Here is an example of how to use the 'trust bucket' analogy in a situation that all teachers have faced at some point: pupils not having the correct equipment.

When a pupil has been honest and has told you immediately, you might say: 'I'm really disappointed that you've forgotten your calculator. You know you need to be more organised. But you have at least told me the truth, so your trust bucket is still full.'

However if a pupil has been sneaky and has tried to avoid you noticing, despite being given opportunities to tell the truth, they need to know that they have let you down. I distinctly remember one boy who, during equipment checks, hadn't brought his pen to school. He didn't put his hand up to admit this, and I made sure to say to the whole class 'right team, now's the time to tell me if you're missing something – I'm going to have a lot more respect for you if you tell me the truth now than if I find out later'. He still didn't own up and then pretended to hold up a pen during that part of the equipment check.

This was my response: (in front of the class) 'Harry, I *cannot believe* what I have just seen. I have just watched you try to deceive me even after I've given you multiple chances to be honest. If you had put your hand up and told me you had forgotten your pen, I wouldn't have been angry – mistakes happen, and it would've just been a detention to help you remember your equipment next time. Now you've just emptied your trust bucket and made it really hard for me to believe you in future.'

Of course, my reaction in the second scenario is massively exaggerated. But it's worth making a big issue out of it because if you do it once, the rest of the class will see it and fall into line. Exaggeration and careful use of public reprimand is an important tool for teachers, particularly with younger year groups. This kind of scenario has occurred on only two or three occasions with 7 Jupiter because they have learnt early on that the best option is to always tell the truth.

Isaac: Bouncing Back and Great Relationships

> *I am the master of my fate, I am the captain of my soul.* – Invictus, William Ernest Henley

When schools have excellent behaviour systems, it is easy to think that relationships with pupils do not matter because pupils will behave for you anyway. Having good relationships is key in *all* schools. As well as instilling the importance of bouncing back and personal responsibility, relationships have been utterly transformative for all my pupils, including for one in particular: Isaac. Isaac was terribly behaved throughout primary school and his parents were at their wits' end. Now Isaac is polite, generally very well-behaved, and one of the most studious pupils in the class.

Both myself and the Head of Year 7 were constantly narrating to pupils the importance of taking responsibility for their behaviour and the need to bounce back from a bad lesson or a bad day. As teachers we all know a child like Isaac: a child who, upon receiving a demerit (a minor consequence carrying no sanction), would instantly sulk and whose behaviour would fast deteriorate, leading to detentions and removal from lessons. Isaac sulked because he didn't know how to react appropriately to demerits. Moreover, he saw demerits and detentions as sanctions that just *happened* to him, rather than things he had earned as a result of his own actions. In short, Isaac wouldn't take any responsibility for his behaviour.

As a side note, the way that detentions are expressed and communicated to children is incredibly important. We rarely say, 'I'm giving you a detention'. Instead we opt for, 'You've got yourself a detention now' or 'You've now put me in a position where I have to give you a detention'. This emphasis shifts the responsibility onto the pupil and makes the teacher seem like less of a bad guy who is choosing (or wanting) to dish out detentions.

Along with Isaac's Head of Year and his other teachers, I found opportunities to praise Isaac where possible, without lowering my expectations of him. Like most children, he adored attention, and giving him positive attention for his achievements (when he genuinely deserved it) made him far less likely to resort to wanting the negative kind. It was a positive cycle, whereby he'd work hard and gain merits, and then work hard in the following lesson. Mentioning the possibility of getting a postcard or a phone call home later that week, should the excellent work continue, also worked wonders for both his behaviour and my relationship with him.

I was a bloodhound, forever seeking Isaac out: before school, in detention – you name it, I was there. I would watch 7 Jupiter in lessons (often standing at the front to make my presence known). I would make sure I sat at Isaac's lunch table regularly. If he got himself removed from a lesson and I was free, I would ensure that I was the one that picked him up.

I would always ask how his day was going. If it was going well, I celebrated his success with him. If it was not going quite so well, I would be encouraging in a way that also held him to account: 'You've got music next, right? I'm going to message Mrs. Ting later to ask specifically how you were and how many merits you got'. If he had behaved terribly in other lessons, I made sure he knew the extent of my disappointment, so that he felt he had let me down as well as himself.

At Michaela, we are very lucky that we have many opportunities in the day to build relationships with pupils outside of lessons. I am also lucky enough to teach my form group, which makes the conversations mentioned here easier.

My relationship with Isaac is as good as it is because I have always made sure to narrate explicitly how much I/his teachers/his parents were doing for him; we were instilling in him a real sense of gratitude.

I would tell 7 Jupiter how I'd spent hours marking their quizzes or planning their lessons the night before. On an individual level, when I had to tell Isaac off, I told him I was doing it because I was on his side and I wanted to help him be better. When he *was* better, I would celebrate that with him, and take the time to phone his mum and tell her. I explicitly told him during our many catch-ups that I was deliberately taking time out of my day to find out how he was doing, even though I had a million things to do, because that's how much I wanted him to succeed.

I'd strategise with the Head of Year to play good cop/bad cop, and tell Isaac, 'Look, you almost didn't make the football team because the other teachers were not sure your behaviour was good enough. I fought for you and told them to give you a chance. I've stuck my neck out on the line for you, so you can't let me down.'

Over time, instilling this gratitude cemented my relationship with him. It became simply impossible for him to believe anything other than that I genuinely wanted the best for him. The emotions I shared with him thus became much more meaningful: he was pleased when he knew I was proud of him and ashamed when I was displeased or disappointed.

I remember a specific instance a few months into Year 7, where Isaac had been (unusually) poorly behaved in my Maths lesson. Afterwards I gave him a real telling off, telling him how disrespectful he had been to me, particularly given how hard I was working for him. His exterior completely crumbled – my words had struck a chord. I then dismissed him but before he left he said, looking deeply ashamed, 'Miss, I'm really sorry. I won't let you down again'. Whilst his behaviour hasn't always been perfect, true to his word, Isaac never again behaved like that in my lesson.

Establishing the right culture from day one of Year 7 gives children the best possible chance of future success. Every child goes on their own journey throughout secondary school – I hope that, through the stories of the three children above, I have illustrated some of the ways in which we have done this.

SYSTEMS AND STRUCTURES

Being PA to Katharine Birbalsingh

Gita Khatri

Who am I? Some may say I have one of the most difficult jobs being PA to Katharine Birbalsingh. After all, she has been given the title of Britain's strictest headmistress and is sometimes referred to as the Dragon Lady.

I am 44 years old and the mother of two teenage children. I often refer to myself as a tiger mother. I have spent 12 years working as a PA at other schools for other heads so I would say I know this job pretty well. But I don't think anything could have ever prepared me for how different this job as a PA would be. My other PA jobs to Heads followed a similar pattern. But being PA to Katharine is something totally different. It takes being a PA to a whole different level!

I remember the first time I entered Michaela, the rather confident and outspoken me did stop and think do I really want to be here? I had prepared for the interview by watching a video with Katharine in it and I had read some of her articles. I walked into Michaela for my interview thinking, it is so quiet and this isn't normal and so this is just a bit scary. It didn't feel like a normal school.

Before meeting Katharine, I got the feeling that she was a very confident and unapproachable person. I thought she would be one of those bosses who thinks, 'this is what Katharine thinks, I am the Head, and this is what has to be done'. So I was worried about whether I would be able to make a difference. I like having input in my job and I want to make an impact. I didn't want to be a 'yes person' who just does what they are told.

The brief I had received from the agency was that Katharine was very scary. I was told to maintain eye contact and shake hands firmly.

I did as the agency suggested. In talking with Katharine, I knew I wanted to work for her. Katharine doesn't do panel interviews. She insists on having 'chats' with candidates for jobs. That is what she did with me. When we spoke, I saw something in her that related to the person I am. She is someone who has a no-nonsense approach and who is upfront and straight talking. I liked that about her.

There had been a mistake with my application from the agency. In my letter, 'diary' had been spelled 'dairy' and Michaela had rejected my application because of this mistake. As Katharine explained to me at my interview, it is such a common word for a PA to use. If the application has it wrong, then that tells her that this person doesn't notice details. She only wants to hire people who notice details.

But I hadn't made the mistake. It was the agency and I told the agency to go back to Michaela to look at my application again. I explained all this to Katharine and I could see she was thinking, something was wrong with the system they had. I now know that Katharine changed the systems we have at Michaela thanks to that interview of mine. She trusted my feedback even though I was just a candidate for a job.

Since working at Michaela, I have seen her do this many times. She takes feedback and implements change all of the time. That feedback might be from anyone: staff, and that's not just teachers, kitchen staff, caretakers too. And then even visitors. It means that we feel listened to and we can all contribute.

I knew at the point of interview that this was the job I wanted because Katharine listens but also because I respected the fact that she really stands up for what she believes in. I wanted to be part of the bigger picture.

So now it's been 18 months and the journey has been nothing short of amazing. No two days are ever the same here and what I love about Katharine most is how her passion for bettering the lives of these inner London kids just never stops. She keeps going and there appears to be no off button.

It isn't easy. I need to be switched on all of the time. Katharine is always 10 steps ahead and I need to be 9.5 steps ahead in order to keep up with her. Katharine moves at a very quick pace and I don't want to slow her down. Her expectations of herself and of others are very high, so we try our best not to disappoint. It is as if I am helping to prop her up so that she is able to be that 10 steps ahead.

Before Michaela, I was used to the normal pace in schools. Katharine isn't normal. As an example, staff pop in to see Katharine all the time. She encourages them to do so. Someone will then make a suggestion or spark an idea. Next thing you know, Katharine is asking me to organise a meeting with the Heads of Department and she'll want to see them briefly that day, or the next day, always sooner rather than later. Katharine doesn't believe in meetings that are booked way in advance. She likes to move quickly on things. She'll see people in smaller groups if necessary, or even run around the school looking for staff to have a 'quick chat' and get a plan in motion. My job is about making sure she can do that easily.

The main thing that makes Katharine different to other heads I've worked for is that Katharine is always there. She is in school all of the time. She believes in being there for the staff and in having a hold of what is going on. So if a parent wants to see 'the headmistress'– here, they will see her in a couple of days. In all the schools I've known, you book the parent in for a meeting for 2 or even 3 weeks later. Everything is more formal elsewhere. Katharine instead wants to have 'chats' with staff, parents, with everyone! It is the same thing with the pupils. The children come to see her and they can see her immediately. Elsewhere this wouldn't happen.

Katharine is in school every single day. She goes to the occasional conference but they are rare. In other schools I have known, the senior leadership team are segregated from the rest of the school. They and especially the heads don't want meetings on the same day. Normally I would book meetings with staff for days in advance. Heads don't want to be on the back foot. They would never say to staff, 'just pop in'. They need to get ready for the meeting. I would never be allowed to book back to back meetings. I had to put in 30 mins between meetings to create a gap. People take time making decisions normally. Katharine doesn't. I always used to have to find out 'why does this person want to see the head'. But at Michaela, there is no investigating going on. The senior team seem to be at one with the staff and they know what's happening. Katharine trusts her staff so she doesn't have to prepare in advance of a meeting so that she can defend herself to them.

There is a constant stream of people walking in and out of Katharine's office every day. Acting as Katharine's guard dog is one of the biggest challenges of this role. I often think she doesn't want me to be a guard dog. But I like it.

At Michaela, you can feel like your head might spin off but then you just need to keep calm, refocus and you're back up again. I'm not saying it's easy. I have worked really hard to prove myself, but the mutual respect and trust goes a long way. It is very rewarding to be valued. I feel that I can make decisions and when I tell Katharine she trusts me.

I think Katharine gives huge levels of trust because she knows that we believe in what the school is doing. Any decisions we have taken have been well-processed and have the goal of the school at heart.

I was the one who came up with the idea of asking guests for donations. It is expensive to have the school open to over 600 visitors a year. When I first went to Katharine with the idea, she said "no, no, no" – she wouldn't do it. But she listens to me and doesn't think 'I'm the head and the decision lies with me'. She thought about it, went to senior team with the idea, and then they decided to make the change. Then, like with everything, it happened very quickly. Once a decision is made, we run with it.

The hardest bit is the press. They are always calling. I never know what might trigger it. One minute everything is fine and the next, Katharine has said something on Twitter and everyone is ringing. I have to be on top of it. That's why I feel like a guard dog. Sometimes I wish she would stop saying things, but that's who she is and that's what we are, so I enjoy the ride.

When I first started working as Katharine's PA, I got a number of phone calls from my old colleagues and various acquaintances, worried about my well-being. The conversations would often would go something like this:

'Are you ok Gita? How are you coping?'

'Yes, I'm fine.'

'NO, it's ok Gita, you can tell me, really you can talk to me....'

They would tell me I have so much experience, that I could have found a job somewhere else, that I shouldn't feel I have to be working here.

But I love it. There is a lot of work but I believe in what we are doing at the school. I am just as invested as any of the teachers are. I feel I have more of a purpose here. But my friends don't believe me. They would ask how I could be happy working for Katharine Birbalsingh!!

They thought Katharine must be some kind of witch. But the truth is, I think Katharine is too nice and it is a weakness of hers. I often tell her this. I can understand that you may be smiling as you're reading this, thinking "Katharine, too nice?!" but I can honestly say it is true.

This job is not for the faint-hearted. But it is this direct access and open approach that I love. I have already told Katharine: I hope we can stay working like this forever.

The School Office

Victoria Squire

The flutter of a butterfly can cause a typhoon halfway around the world. As my chapter describes it, the school office is just as influential as that in the success at Michaela. We office staff live and breathe the school's values and goals, just as much as any of our teachers.

When thinking about schools, people may assume that the staffroom or the classrooms are the important hubs of activity. Little do they know that the *real* engine room is the school office; a great melting pot of calls, emails, printing, parents, teachers, visitors, contractors, naughty pupils, good pupils, sick pupils. Juggling all these swift-moving parts can very easily lead to chaos, but when the office runs smoothly, so does the rest of the school.

When I first joined Michaela in December 2016, the office was just chaotic. There was a receptionist, an administrator (who'd joined a few weeks before) and a temp who'd joined a few weeks before that. The Head of Music would come down each morning to make the absence calls and a history teacher was managing lunch payments. While this was a brilliant example of the Michaela motto, 'row together', it certainly wasn't how the office could continue. As I began organising the office to be able to cope with the inevitable growing demands, I realised how important we office workers are. We are contributing to the school and the pupils' success in our own individual way, distinct from that of the teachers.

The office is the foundation of the school, it sustains everyone in the building. A systematic, well-organised office ensures that all other aspects of the school are equally as organised.

The Butterfly Effect posits that when a butterfly bats its wings on one side of the world, it can stimulate a typhoon on the other side. I take this to mean that small, seemingly insignificant events can lead to significant results over time. For example, if a letter fails to go out informing parents of a particular change to a club meeting the following afternoon, mayhem ensues: some pupils turn up when they shouldn't, others don't go and then wonder why their parents aren't outside to pick them up. With this, streams of pupils come to the office to call home, and after that, parents don't trust us to give them correct and reliable information. One small task left undone can have mighty repercussions for the entire school.

The relationship that office staff members have with pupils and parents can sometimes differ from their relationship with teachers. Often, school office staff are thought to be less authoritative, perhaps a little softer and more forgiving. This policy can be detrimental to the wider school. Take the pupil who tells a teacher that they're unwell, all to get out of a test in the next lesson. Down the pupil comes to the office hoping to be sent home. But here's where the office staff have a crucial role. They can dig deeper with the child to check if there could be another reason for that pupil wanting to leave. Communication and support between teachers and office staff on these incidents are extremely important. Our office must enforce the same expectations of pupils that teachers have. That the office aligns practically with the school's ethos is indispensable to the future success of Michaela pupils.

Being on the 'front line' is not easy, wherever you work. But I've found that at Michaela, the office staff know that the senior team will support them strongly when they're dealing with challenging parents. As staff, here, we are empowered. I used to work as a PA in a private school, where the parents were viewed as paying customers. Empowered was never a word I used to use to describe my feelings in that workplace.

Working in that kind of private school, you bend over backwards to accommodate parental demands. We would let children out of lessons or detentions for a wide range and number of appointments; we would send home reports six times a year, hold parents' evenings three times a year for every one of our pupils. It meant that staff were constantly exhausted and unable to give their best to the children. It also meant that parents were bombarded with too much unnecessary information.

I began as a receptionist at the private school. There was a pupil who was late every morning. A new rule was introduced: if you were late three or more times in one week, you'd get one early morning detention. This meant that the usual (and unusual) suspects realised they could turn up late twice a week with no consequences. The pupil who was late every day, did start arriving right on time a few days a week. Her mum would drop by weekly with coffee and muffins for me from Gail's Bakery. So what did I do when her daughter came late a third time? I'd mark her in as punctual! I would completely undermine the school, and all because I'd been bought off by a muffin. I felt sorry for mother and daughter, I thought I was doing them a favour. At the time, I didn't realise that my so-called kindness meant I was helping the school to fail that child.

At Michaela, the office staff are not viewed as an entity with separate values. The vision and reasoning behind the school is always fully explained to us. We can ask questions and challenge answers to gain more understanding of why we do things the way we do. All of us follow the same rules to the letter, because we understand the importance of 'holding the line'. We don't get up in the morning and look forward to issuing detentions for being late, we get up in the morning and recognise that our 'holding the line' is our forceful way of contributing to making our pupils better, stronger people. We believe absolutely in the school's vision to transform the lives of these inner-city children.

The same can also be said for our caretakers and cleaners. They're equally valued and respected members of staff. They are greeted by the pupils with 'good morning miss' or 'good morning sir'. It's a stark difference to my previous school where the day cleaner used to come to me crying every day. Every day. Taps were left on in the boys' toilets, flooding the floor. The pupils had no respect, and disorder was allowed to spread. Pupils were allowed to leave their bags and coats all over the floor without a challenge, wreaking havoc in the corridors at lunch time.

James Q. Wilson and George L. Kelling introduced the Broken Windows Theory in 1982. It's the idea that if one window in a house was left broken in an environment where people don't take pride in their surroundings and low level deviance is tolerated, more breakages inevitably follow. But if instead that window is fixed, then other windows will not get broken.

Graffiti is treated seriously at Michaela. Chewing gum is nowhere to be seen! All staff inform me of any vandalism, no matter how small, just as soon as it's noticed. Immediately it is dealt with by the caretakers. Details matter at Michaela. Both pupils and staff take pride in our building, which is why order there can be maintained.

Pace also matters at Michaela. We need to move quickly on everything. There is always a sense of urgency in the air, and poor behaviour is not something any of us are prepared to get used to. We all ask questions, all the time. Katharine holds a meeting with support staff once a half term, including office staff and caretakers. She meets with the kitchen staff once a term. Here, we talk about the school ethos and why Michaela selects the guidelines it follows. All of us are encouraged to ask questions so we understand what goals we as a team are aiming for.

Just like the impact of a flutter of a butterfly on the world, what we do in the Michaela office has a large impact on the wider school. My friends always encourage me to find a different job. One where I could start at 9am rather than 7:30am, or where input is 75% rather than 110%, every second of every day. They don't understand, is always my response. Yes, it's fast paced, yes, big decisions are made more quickly, more often than in any other workplace I know of and yes, it's not a place you can coast or have a day where you take it a bit easy – but that's what makes each day so exciting. Despite the pace, I've never experienced 'Sunday dread', thinking about what Monday will bring. I believe this is because we're all about the 'we' at Michaela and not the 'I'. Whatever the day throws at us, the team meets it with positivity, a can-do attitude and a willingness to find solutions together. We don't blindly follow – we challenge each other and respectfully listen. This challenge means that I learn every day. I've grown so much as a person working at Michaela. I can confidently say to my friends that being part of a greater project, one that changes children's lives, leaves no doubt in my mind that I'm in the right job for me. Feeling you have a purpose and you're making a difference, makes you strive to achieve each day. That drive and those achievements are fully recognised. The gratitude and respect for each and every person, from teachers to office staff to caretakers, makes the Michaela office a very special, very rewarding place to work.

Cutting the Crap

Alice Cresswell

As a new member of the team at Michaela, joining just after the success of its GCSE results, I arrived with sky high expectations of the pupils' abilities. Although this is important, what I underestimated was that these incredible results didn't happen because the pupils are exceptional – they're inner-city London kids after all – but because of the intricate details surrounding the running of the school and how the teachers who work here are working hard at the right things.

Like many other Teach First participants, in my first two years of teaching I came close to quitting multiple times. I was permanently drained, anxious and frustrated by the mental gymnastics that surround the job; specifically, everything involved in teaching that isn't the actual teaching. When asked what I did for a living, I responded, 'Currently, I teach'. Ironically, the reason I couldn't bring myself to say, 'I am a teacher' was because I felt as though I never really did much teaching. As well as trying to manage behaviour in chaotic classrooms, I spent too many hours a week planning, marking, chasing up issues, and entering (then re-entering) data.

When the first Michaela book, *Battle Hymn of the Tiger Teachers*, was written in 2014, the DfE published that 1 in 10 teachers left the state sector within their first year of teaching. According to their Schools Workforce Census, published June 2019, it is now the case that 'one in six teachers leave within a year of entering the classroom.'

A well-documented reason for low retention is that teachers are burning out. Early on in my training year I was told that the reason I found the job so difficult was because 'I cared so much'. I came to see how true this was – many of those who managed to successfully juggle each aspect of the job without crippling anxiety had managed to detach themselves from it, and had learned to accept a lower standard. That was their survival technique. I came to see that the school was filled with teachers of two kinds. The first – whose strong drive to inspire meant they were completely overworked and therefore physically and mentally unable to achieve their goal of inspiring. The second were those who had given up on their hopes of inspiration (or the reason they went into the profession in the first place) in order to stay sane – they had resigned to the fact that all they could ever do in teaching is have a small impact on the status quo.

But at Michaela, things are different because the expectations of each teacher is radically different. By removing all of the nonsense, Michaela has shown me that it is not necessary to separate emotions from the job, and you certainly do not need to lower your standards. It has shown me that it is possible to work in a school where the focus of everything done is whether or not it has a high return on the investment of time and effort. At Michaela, if something is not valuable to pupils, it is not done. No doubt these ideas surface in other schools. I can only talk about my own experience and Michaela has been a breath of fresh air.

So what specifically is different, on a day-to-day basis?

Planning / Resources: Since joining Michaela, although I still work hard throughout the week, I've got my weekends back. Previously, I spent Sundays trawling the internet for lessons. *TES* was my best friend. If I couldn't find anything compiled by someone else, then I'd spend hours putting together detailed slides that I would then either rely on too heavily, or completely ignore. I also received limited guidance on what my lessons should look like. I imagine levels of support will differ from school to school, but it is certainly the case that the expectation of high levels of autonomy is everywhere in teaching, even when training. Michaela rejects this. Michaela believes that teachers are stronger when working together.

As an alternative, we create resource booklets within our departments. They take a long time and great care to make. We all make them together and we all use them together. Each teacher does not have to create their own power points. In fact, we rarely use PowerPoint. We stick to the booklets, and once they're created, they're created. Everyone who teaches that module is provided with clear and consistent resources. We know at the beginning of the module where the pupils need to be by the end. Booklets are carefully designed to 'layer the learning'; we want students to acquire new knowledge and skills without losing what they have previously learned. On a day-to-day basis, this means we can focus on planning details such as questioning, and we can get on with purposeful teaching.

Booklets can bring some problems though and any school wanting to do this should be careful about the pitfalls. The booklet is not the lesson, but a resource like any other. You need really committed teachers using them, who will adapt them to ensure they're the ideal resource for the class they are teaching. We also rely on the fact that our teachers will bring personality and pace to the booklets; the lessons need to be interesting. If the teacher using the resources were not like this, then I can imagine some teachers might just rock up to their lessons without ever planning a thing.

Marking: Marking a class of books takes a long time, particularly in English. Your department might have a policy that requires you to highlight different aspects of each pupils' work or to write out every word each pupil has misspelled. It might require you to include two 'stars' for every piece of constructive feedback. In my – albeit limited – experience, marking simple classwork (assessments and extended writing are a separate matter) is always a waste of time. Pupils either ignore what you have written or fail to act on it. In my first two years of teaching, I even had a pupil who Tipp-exed out what I had written in her book. (She, and the teachers I told, simply laughed when I mentioned this). Marking classwork is not about improving pupils' learning, it's about making teaching visible. By this I mean that SLT (Senior Leadership Team) and parents want to see that you're engaging in the education of each pupil. They want 'proof'. But we all know that one can teach badly but mark work thoroughly. This is high input from the teacher, with little effect on the pupil. Michaela recognises this, and therefore we don't do it. Instead, we read classwork regularly, identify errors that the class are making, feed back to the group as a whole and allow our reading of their work to inform our teaching practice. We concentrate on making our teaching better instead of trying to prove that we are good teachers.

But again, you need teachers who are going to be motivated to do this. It is difficult if this is not part of the school culture; building the right culture in school is everything.

Termly reports: At Michaela, classroom teachers do not write lengthy reports on their pupils' behaviour or classwork. We recognise that, like marking pupils' books, such reports have a low return of investment. This used to be a task that would push me to my limits. I taught 280 pupils in my first year, and writing their reports meant working late into the night multiple times a year, for my comments only to be largely ignored. For many teachers, the only way to avoid insanity was to copy and paste comments. Michaela recognises what a waste of time these types of reports are and so we don't do them.

At Michaela, we are all feeding back to form tutors so regularly (through emails and online platforms) that they are aware exactly of how each pupil is doing and can report back to parents wherever necessary. All I have to worry about, as their English teacher, is teaching them.

Registers: The register is done at the beginning of the day. We don't need to do it again, because, thanks to our strict behaviour policy, we know where the pupils are at all times. As a result, we don't waste time taking it at the beginning of each lesson. We're not having to update it throughout the lesson as pupils wander in as they choose (something that doesn't happen here). We're not bothered by office staff ringing us up and confirming whether a pupil is or is not in the classroom. We are able to simply get on with teaching.

Feedback: We constantly observe each other at Michaela. In the long run this saves both time and stress in multiple ways: it happens so frequently that you get used to it; we learn to teach better, quicker; we are given actionable feedback which is followed up within a short space of time and no time is spent planning anything flashy – we simply get on with it. Often, feedback (such as 'sharpen the contrast between your warm and strict voice') will be followed up with a role play session offered to demonstrate, or a suggested observation. This massively contrasts with my previous experience. Observations were difficult to organise, happened so infrequently that it was impossible to implement a cycle of progress, and the observer was often far too busy to be fully invested. Feedback given often included phrases such as: 'Yeah it was fine', 'You need to think about how you have the attention of everyone in the room' (with no suggestion of how to) and the classic, 'If Ofsted are watching, make sure you do that differently'. This is not advice that helps to improve my teaching, nor does it improve my pupils' learning. I often felt before Michaela that people just didn't really know HOW to improve the teaching and learning. Certainly, if it was outside of their subject, they were at a loss. At Michaela however, we are all so clear about what makes for great learning and there is so much CPD (Continuing Professional Development) around this, that we can all help each other become better at our trade.

Homework: Cutting out these time-wasting elements means that we have more time to focus on the right things. For example, it's easy (and therefore common) to accept low return on homework and to accept low quality homework. At least they did it... right? At Michaela we expect 100% return of quality homework, 100% of the time. If it's not here, not well presented or minimal effort has been put into it, then our pupils will get a detention. As a result, failing to produce good homework is the exception, rather than the rule. Detention is a deterrent. So, the kids do their homework!

As a result, I have 30 pieces of homework to mark, from each class, every week. In English this would take hours to mark. Do we spend too much time on it? Of course not. We recognise that a vast range of varying factors (busy homelife, possibility of copying, no quiet workspace) make it impossible for homework to be an accurate measure of pupils' understanding. Therefore, our marking system is based on effort. I will spend 20 minutes on one class's homework; I sift through the pile, placing each piece into one of four piles: Fail, Pass, Good and Excellent. I will make a note of what pupils did to be in each category, with some extra feedback notes to present to the whole class. 'Excellent' is reserved for those who went above and beyond – the pupils must feel as though they really earned it in order to maintain mutual respect. I do not write individualised feedback on every single piece – echoing my comments on marking earlier, this would be high effort on my part with little effect on the pupils. Finally, I select the best and the worst pieces to show the class under the visualiser in our next lesson. Over the past half term, I have seen my year 7s' homework become neater and more detailed, as they adjust to Michaela's expectations. This has happened because I have appealed to their desire to be recognised as good, or excellent, rather than because I have spent hours giving them menial comments.

In English we also get pupils to do something magical with their homework. We get them to check their capital letters with their green pens before handing it in. If they haven't checked them, they get a detention. So, they check them. This transfers into their classwork as well; all of a sudden, every single one of my pupils uses capital letters and full stops correctly, and I've gained back hours of badgering children about the simplest thing to complete in writing – something that so many pupils just didn't bother about at my previous school.

Management of behaviour: Lastly, the routines of behaviour at Michaela mean that one of the biggest issues that I had found so far with teaching was removed: lesson anxiety. That creeping fear that every teacher has known, that can completely override your ability to think about the content of the lesson rather than its pupils. My previous school believed that giving pupils detentions could only be damaging, and as a result the behaviour was very difficult to manage. Not being able to give pupils a detention placed intense pressure on me, as a classroom teacher, to micromanage low level disruption for long periods at a time. This often became extremely stressful and unmanageable. Here, if a pupil behaves in a way that doesn't match our expectations, I give them a detention. Nine times out of ten, the result is that they don't behave that way again. Pupils then attend a same day, centralised detention, another efficient system within the school that results in effective punishment that doesn't place a burden on individual teachers. As a result, I am able to be a teacher. I can focus on the wonderful intricacies of teaching English, rather than worry about whether or not pupils are about to disrupt the lesson. If I ever think I've had a tough day, all it takes is a reply from a teacher friend, who teaches elsewhere, of 'oh yes me too, I cried in the book cupboard again' and I regain my sense of perspective. I don't spend hours dreading to see any of my classes. I definitely used to.

The above list of changes Michaela has made to state education is by no means comprehensive. Other teaching 'necessities' that Michaela has cut out include:

- Entering data regularly into multiple places

- Analysing sub grades of progress

- Parents' evening

- Detailed classroom displays

- Individually differentiated resources

- Teaching assistants

- Seating plans revolving around SEN / pupil ability data

- Split timetabling

- Starters and plenaries

To conclude, I would like to point out that at Michaela, we work hard. We work long hours during the week and are just as exhausted as other teachers around the country. However, the difference is that we're working hard at the right things. It's therefore easier to stay mentally balanced; there isn't a constant frustration that you have too many things to do that have absolutely no benefit other than box ticking. These days when people ask about my job, I tell them proudly that I'm a teacher and the hard work feels a hell of a lot more worth it.

Behaviour at Michaela is Misunderstood

Amelia Andrews

'No-excuses discipline is unfair and unkind.'

All our pupils at Michaela are expected to be on time, properly equipped, and polite at all times. We do not pay lip-service to these high standards, and pupils are taught from day one that they face demerits and detentions when these expectations are not met. To people both in and outside the education sector, the idea of no-excuses discipline can seem unfair and unkind: "They're just children", "We all make mistakes", "Life happens." My experience at Michaela has revealed the opposite – no-excuses discipline is both fairer and kinder than the alternative, a 'some excuses' system. In such a system, rules are not really rules, and not all pupils are held to the same standard.

While we maintain high standards, we do everything we can to enable our pupils to meet them. If pupils were repeatedly punished for not meeting unattainable standards, they would quickly lose faith in their teachers and school. A good example of this is our school stationery shop. From even before their first day at Michaela, we clearly lay out our expectation that pupils always have a full set of working equipment, including a ruler, a calculator and various coloured pens. Pupils will receive detentions if they do not have the expected equipment. Our school stationery shop is open every morning and pupils can buy any items they need, which are cheaper than in high street shops. If the stationery shop runs out of a particular item, we waive detentions for that item on that day. In summary, we make it eminently achievable for the pupils to meet our expectations regarding equipment.

One of the reasons a 'some excuses' system is inherently unfair is that pupils quickly find ways to work the system. If pupils see that an excuse is accepted, soon every pupil will be using it to avoid sanctions. This is just human nature! If some excuses are accepted, we are incentivising pupils to lie. This creates a situation in which only the most honest pupils, who are willing to admit their own culpability, get detentions. No-excuses discipline is fairer because it means that teachers do not have different standards for different pupils. We expect the same of all pupils regardless of their circumstances and we give children agency by holding them accountable for their decisions. We do not limit them to being pre-destined victims of their circumstances. What's more, we narrate the control that every child has over their situation: late because of the bus? Plan to get an earlier bus! Don't have all your equipment? Take five minutes before you go to bed at night to double check what's in your bag. The overwhelming majority of excuses can be addressed by just a small change.

In making pupils responsible for their choices, we avoid the toxic scenario of pupils blaming their teachers for sanctions they receive. When each teacher sets their own standards, pupils say things like, "Miss *gave me* a detention; Miss hates me so I hate Miss." Among pupils, this creates destructive resentment towards teachers. Among teachers, it instigates a race to the bottom to become the hero teacher who always lets pupils off. When rules are explicitly communicated and consistently upheld, the consequences of poor decisions are not "my teacher's fault"; the pupil knew the rule and chose to break it. The teacher was just following the system as every other teacher in the school would have done in the same situation. This clarity and predictability is beneficial for all pupils, but most of all for those who have unstable and chaotic home lives.

We believe at Michaela that no-excuses discipline is, in fact, kinder because it enables pupils to create good habits which will set them up for success when they leave school. If we constantly overlook, for example, a pupil forgetting their pen, or being late, we will not be insisting on them becoming more organised or punctual. Nor will we be preparing them for their adult lives. An insurance company, for example, won't pay out if you forgot to renew your house insurance, nor an airline delay a flight because your taxi broke down. In the moment, upholding the rule and implementing the sanction can feel difficult or unkind, but no-excuses discipline puts the child first. As adults, we have a duty to prioritise our pupils' long-term interests over our short-term impulse to avoid feeling unkind. When we let them off, we let them down.

Finally, I cannot help but wonder if the discomfort surrounding no-excuses discipline is rooted in its bringing into stark, uncomfortable clarity our tendencies to make excuses in our own lives. The philosophy of no-excuses discipline is one of *personal* responsibility and *individual* agency which, although empowering, can also be daunting. In unashamedly refusing to allow our pupils to use their circumstances as an excuse, we are indirectly challenging people to face up to the reality of their own agency. Since coming to Michaela, I have been challenged in my own life to spend less time fixating on things which are outside of my control, but easy to blame. This philosophy of personal responsibility asks us to account for the impact we have on our own lives and the lives of others. It is only by shouldering this weightier responsibility that we can find true meaning and fulfilment in our lives. It is only when we own our failures and our successes that we learn, change, and grow as individuals.

'Teachers at Michaela are detention-giving robots.'

It might be assumed that at a school like Michaela, with such effective and consistently applied behaviour systems, there is less need for teachers to form positive relationships with their pupils. Similarly, it is easy to imagine that teachers who implement an inflexible no-excuses discipline system must be robotic and unfeeling. The reality is that relationships are just as important, if not more, in a no-excuses school as in any other, and that rather than constraining them, tight systems and structures create a school environment in which relationships flourish.

Teachers at Michaela invest in relationships because we recognise that systems have limited power in making children work hard. The threat of detention might be effective in motivating an eleven-year-old to complete thirty minutes of homework but it is futile in motivating a fifteen-year-old to put in the hours of revision required to achieve top GCSE grades. It is not the systems at Michaela that inspire, motivate and encourage our pupils to work hard, it is the excellent relationships that teachers develop with pupils. Then, because we hold pupils to such high standards and are not afraid to give demerits and detentions, it is vital that we show our pupils that we do this because we care. Teachers at Michaela consistently follow up sanctions with narration and restorative conversations which remind pupils that we're on their side and that we want the best for them. You might hear a teacher say, "I'm giving you a demerit because I know how important this lesson is and I'd hate for you to fall behind". For Michaela's approach to discipline to be successful, there must be a collective pupil trust that their teachers are doing right by them, even when pupils might not like their teachers' decisions.

Michaela's systems and no-excuses discipline policy enable positive teacher-pupil relationships to flourish. The duties system, which has teachers doing multiple daily duties, provides regular opportunities for positive, relationship-building interactions with pupils throughout the school day. The good manners and sense of gratitude for their teachers that we instil in our pupils are the foundation for respectful and enjoyable conversations. In the classroom, our sky-high standards of behaviour enable teachers to share moments of laughter and light-heartedness with their pupils without fear of derailing their lesson. Michaela's highly-effective behaviour policy is not a substitute for positive teacher-pupil relationships, but these relationships are at the same time necessary because of, and enabled by, our no-excuses approach.

'Strict behaviour systems don't allow children to be children.'

Inevitably, there are as many ways to respond to this misgiving as there are ways to conceptualise what it means to be a child. Some argue that the essence of a child is to be curious, to make discoveries and to figure things out for oneself. This conceptualisation leads the conversation down the well-trodden 'discovery learning' versus direct instruction track which I will not rehearse again here. For others, the idea of childhood is closely connected with a particular idea of freedom. For them, the freedom of the child involves not having any real responsibilities; it is about being carefree. The fewer restrictions placed upon the child, the freer they are. Proponents of this view argue that the best thing schools can do for pupils is to place minimal restrictions on their behaviour and allow them to choose what to learn and how to learn it.

We don't do this at Michaela. Instead of negative freedom, we seek for our pupils a higher, positive freedom – their freedom to be the masters of their fate. In order to maximise the positive freedom our pupils will experience when they leave Michaela at 16 or 18, we restrict their negative freedom in the short term.

If we want to give our pupils maximum freedom to control their future, we must ensure that they acquire grades, knowledge and individual habits. GCSE and A Level grades act like keys which open doors in further education and the workplace. The better the grades, the more doors our pupils are free to open. The foundational knowledge they receive through a rigorous, traditional education will enable them to access further learning formally or informally as they so choose. They will also have the necessary cultural knowledge and confidence-imbuing familiarity to engage with and appreciate a wide-range of cultural activities. The habit of self-discipline and the ability to make sacrifices will be essential for their pursuit of personal and professional goals. All of the restrictions we place upon pupils' freedom in school are in the service of this greater freedom for their adult lives.

It is not only positive freedom in their adult lives that Michaela's no-excuses discipline system facilitates. Through the imposition of limits and boundaries, we seek to free our children from two of the greatest threats to their childhood, the use of technology (particularly social media) and bullying. This freedom that Michaela pupils have to enjoy their childhood is most visible when they are playing at lunchtime. They are chatting and laughing with their friends, skipping, playing table football, and all without the toxic invasion of camera phones, social media or the threat of unkindness from bullies. The consistent presence of adult authority means that children do not feel pressured to fill an authority vacuum by acting older than they are, and instead are given permission to enjoy being children.

You would be hard-pressed to find a school in the country which doesn't profess to practising 'zero tolerance' when it comes to bullying. Yet never before have I come across a school which has taken this commitment so seriously. At Michaela, we fill the spaces where bullying typically hides – the corridors during transitions, in the toilets, at the back of chaotic classrooms – with authoritative teacher presence, thereby dramatically reducing the possibility of bullying. This is a clear example of freedom arising as a result of limitations and boundaries. It is explicitly *because* they are not free to roam around the corridors without teacher presence that our children are free to enjoy their school life without worrying about being bullied. If teachers want to protect their pupils' childhoods in the present and give them the freedom to craft flourishing adult lives for themselves in the future, then it is teachers' duty to wisely choose and steadfastly enforce the right restraints and boundaries for their pupils.

Although I have only been teaching at Michaela for a few months, it is clear that its reputation for strictness is deserved. Rules and policies are in place and both staff and pupils are expected to respect them. But we do this in the belief that our pupils, rather than being constrained and squashed, are in fact being provided with a consistent and safe school environment. They are learning the self-discipline and responsibility which will equip them to succeed and find fulfilment in whatever path they follow after Michaela.

Being New at Michaela

Charlotte Perry

Although my two previous schools were very different from each other, they had at least one thing in common: the induction of new staff. From my experience, and from discussing this with other teacher friends, I have found that often the expectations of new staff can be very low. These low expectations do not come from a poor opinion of the new staff member or unkindness on the part of established staff. Rather, schools expect new staff to not know anything about the school and instead of showing them where things are or how things are done, they simply take tasks away from them. For example, at my previous school I was not expected to photocopy something on my first INSET day because I did not yet know where to find the reprographics room. At the time, as a new member of staff who was already battling with learning staff names, deciphering timetables and wrestling with room changes, I was extremely grateful to the colleague who took a job off my list. It was an act of kindness; of that I have no doubt. That said, taking jobs off my to-do list did not help me to establish myself as a member of staff at my previous schools. It hindered my ability to make progress and adapt to the routines of the school.

What strikes me about my induction at Michaela is that the high expectations of newbies are themselves an act of kindness. Asking new staff to learn the names of all established staff and pupils before the start of term empowers them, as they are able to make connections straight away. Knowing the names of the people that I was going to work with made it very easy for me to ask for help when I did not know where to go or what to do. Similarly, the established staff at Michaela are extremely supportive. From day one, they provide a wealth of knowledge that enables new teachers to start working through their to do lists. I have lost count of the number of emails sent by more senior staff, with instructions or advice on "what to do if...". Staff here are only too happy to pass on the information that new staff desperately need in order to make them a highly functioning member of the team; they challenge them by stretching them to complete the tasks that other schools may shy away from.

I think that this 'being thrown in the deep end' approach with maximum support is part of the reason all of us feel we learn far more on how to teach well in a few weeks at Michaela than we do over months or even years elsewhere. It is also why when you visit the school, it is hard to tell the difference between the well-established staff and those who have only just joined.

This difference in the approach to new staff is in many ways similar to the way schools can think of children. Not all schools want to challenge them. We want to look after them too much and so they miss out on really stretching themselves. Kindness is misunderstood; true kindness is pushing the teacher or the child to be the best version of themselves.

Another example of this type of thinking with regard to staff was at my first school where I remember the Head of Induction proudly telling new staff about her after-school training programme. She had devised a programme where all new starters would attend a weekly after-school session to learn the processes of the school. To my naïve, PGCE eyes, this seemed a logical and sensible approach. That was, however, until I realised that the programme lasted for the entire school year; unbelievably, it was expected to take a full year to teach me how to navigate the school's systems and policies. The most ludicrous of these sessions came the week before we broke up for the October half term holiday when a member of the IT department came to show us how to log onto the computers (that we had been using for six weeks) and how to take a register. To this day, I am still confused as to what they thought we had been doing for the six weeks prior to this training session. Although she was kind and trying to help us, I suppose it would have been better had it been done faster.

I can say in no uncertain terms that I have never been so exhausted at the end of a first half term as when I started here at Michaela. However, I have also never felt as prepared for a school year as when I started here at Michaela. Where my previous schools have had low expectations of new staff and have hoped I would learn as and when situations arose, the famously high standards at Michaela begin long before you take your position at the school. On being offered the post, you are handed a folder full of reading material that you are expected to consider and discuss one-to-one with Katharine. On my induction day, remarkably I was allocated an hour and a half to speak individually with Katharine to discuss my initial gut reaction to the material and challenge things that I either did not understand or did not feel comfortable with. Never had I been able to do this before. At my first school, I asked for a meeting with the Headteacher and was told that she did not have time to see me for three weeks; incidentally, I left shortly after this. But at Michaela, we can see Katharine whenever we want. She even gives us chocolate biscuits and encourages us to visit her as often as we wish! At Michaela, things are done differently. We are encouraged to seek out conversations with colleagues and to debate that which makes us uncomfortable or uncertain.

Newbies, as we are affectionately known, are also expected to learn the names of all staff and as many students as possible before starting at the school. We use apps such as Quizlet to test ourselves and are quizzed on this in school to ensure that we really know all of our children. We are taught and tested on the behaviour policy and are given comprehensive documents outlining what each duty entails. Further to this, we watch videos of good practice within classrooms and we discuss our weaknesses with line managers. Before starting at Michaela, new staff can also expect regular check-ins with their line managers who help to set targets and consider the school ethos long before arriving in September. While this can be overwhelming at times, it meant that on a practical level I knew where to go and what to do before arriving at the school. I knew what to do in different situations, I knew where to find things, I knew who to call and most importantly I knew why we do things the way that we do. I felt like a new member of the team, rather than just somebody who was new.

There's a reason that we use the term "being brought on board". This is how Michaela helps new staff to become a link in the chain. It is not the case that you are given a job at Michaela and left to your own devices to teach. The leadership team work incredibly hard to create the environment that makes Michaela such a special place to be; a place where children are free to be children, and where they are encouraged to feel pride in being kind. There is no way that new staff would be allowed to come in and undermine the ethos of the school with their own way of doing things. This would jeopardise the culture that the Michaela staff have worked so hard together to create.

At Michaela, new staff are brought on board through the constant and unapologetically honest feedback, the suggested readings, and the weekly meetings with the Headmistress in which we discuss the ethos of the school. We are taught and shaped into Michaela teachers, as new recruits would be trained in an army, so that the strategy is understood and there are no gaps in our armour. One thing I know to be true from working in different schools is that children are always looking to undermine teachers, especially new staff. Therefore, to allow new staff to enter your school without training them adequately is to invite your pupils to undermine them. The staff at Michaela work so hard to ensure that newbies are prepared, not only to make our lives easier but more importantly to ensure consistency throughout the school and that we are also singing from the same hymn sheet. Of course, as a newbie at Michaela I am nowhere near the finished article, but I feel I have been better prepared for my position at this school than I ever have been previously. I know that I can succeed here and can feel the support of established staff who are constantly challenging me to ensure that I do. I feel more a part of the team than I ever have and although the weight of expectation to maintain the high standards is undeniable, it is refreshing to be at a school where you are considered able to do so.

Update: Six months in

I definitely no longer feel like a new member of staff! In the beginning, I was exhausted due to the sheer volume of new information and the number of routines that I needed to make second nature. Now, happily in my fourth half term here, I sometimes do not recognise myself from even six months ago. The routines have become a part of my normal working day and the CPD has made me reflect on my previously loosely held opinions. I feel far more settled here than I have in previous schools because I am a member of the team, with a responsibility to maintain the ethos of the school. Although the induction process is highly demanding, when you challenge yourself to meet the expectations you become a much more valuable member of staff and far more confident in your own practice.

Silent Corridors

Jane Brierly
@janebrierly

'Il y a un moment où les mots s'usent. Et le silence commence à raconter.'

There comes a time when words tire. And silence starts to tell the story.

— Kahlil Gibran

I am Head of French at Michaela and my chapter is about our lovely, silent corridors. I am writing this chapter because for some reason the blissful, zen and organised corridors at Michaela still shock people, offend them even! When describing my school to friends, I don't need to finish the word 'corridors' before I can see that 'silent' has confounded and horrified them. I, like lots of my friends, was privately and red brick university educated. So, like many people who have had my education, before my first year teaching in a state school as part of my Teach First training, I had never seen what the corridors of a so-called 'normal' school looked like. The corridors were not much fun as a teacher and (judging by the damaged displays and queue for sickbay after lesson transitions) were not much fun for pupils either.

But we don't like it, do we? The idea of telling pupils to be silent and get to lessons quickly. The instinctive feeling is that silence suppresses their *personnalité, créativité* and *abilité* to form relationships. How cruel! Schoolchildren must hate all teachers who enforce silence. But do they? I remember being on a school placement during my teacher training. I was really struggling to manage the behaviour in a certain Year 9 class so I asked Ms Leonard, their Head of Year, to come in and offer me some feedback. Before long, the pupils were shouting across the room and out of their chairs. Ms Leonard immediately came to the front and glared at the misbehaving pupils. Within moments they were back in their chairs and I could have heard a pin drop. She said, 'For the remainder of this lesson, you will sit in ABSOLUTE SILENCE and copy out the content pages of your French textbook!' I looked out at the pupils, feeling awful for letting the situation escalate to this, expecting to see them looking back at me, angry or upset.

But I did not. The pupils actually looked relieved, happy even. I actually saw a small boy at the back literally fist pump at the moment Ms Leonard said 'silence' and a thought struck me: these kids want order. Now ideally, they want order *and* learning, but in the absence of any learning they at least want order. It makes them feel safe and relaxed to know an adult is in charge.

Last year, I read in disbelief as a mother removed her son from Ninestiles School in Birmingham following the announcement that the school would be adopting silence in corridors during lesson transitions. I want to stay open-minded on this *sujet polémique*, so I did some digging into why this well-intentioned mother might be so unsettled by the idea of silence in her son's school.

I came across article after article referring to Ninestiles and its decision to have silent corridors as 'prison-like' and 'the stuff of Matilda' – Miss Trunchbull! The supposed likeness between one headteacher who wants calm lesson transitions and another who hammer-throws children by their pigtails does seem a bit far-fetched, or is it just me? How are our viewpoints so different? How do some people think Michaela treats children like they are in prison, while we think we are setting them free?

I am a linguist and obsessed with words. I started looking into the word 'silent'. It makes so many professionals physically recoil. Why? In its essence, 'silence' simply means not speaking. On the one hand, the notion of silence can bring about connotations of unquestioning, by-standing, even oppression – none of which we want associated with a good education. On the other, we can also understand silence as peace, calm, and freedom from uproar. Much better. I am not personally offended by the word 'silence' and actually it is important that we keep it in our policies for the very reason that there are no grey areas. You are either silent or you are not. It's much easier for children to be silent than it is for them to be 'quiet' or 'less noisy'. Any teacher will know that children find it difficult to stay 'quiet' and that is because everyone's idea of quiet is different depending on so many factors. Ed Tech companies have invested thousands on apps that teachers can download and display on their boards to alert pupils when they go above a certain volume. That might work in classrooms if you are so opposed to working in silence, but in corridors? How are schools supposed to maintain an orderly volume? The truth is that they cannot, and with the escalation of volume, so too comes the escalation of chaos, shoving and bullying.

I want to shed some more light on why we keep the corridors silent for Michaela pupils and how that is really nothing to be worried by – rather unlike the alternative.

Logistics

The word 'corridor' actually comes from the Latin *currere* meaning 'to run'. Similarly, in French *couloir* deviates from the verb *couler*, 'to flow'. Both suggest a smooth or swift motion from A to B. Certainly, the movement of pupils around a building like Michaela's is something that requires a certain amount of logistical expertise. We have 600 pupils who need to shift between 40 classrooms, along twelve narrow corridors, up and down six floors, across two staircases – and all in approximately one minute (it can be done!). Our corridors are particularly narrow but even in schools with wider corridors, moving children around quickly is a real challenge. Crowd management is a very specific discipline.

The crucial ingredient to any *transition triomphante* is, of course, an absolute focus – and therefore silence – from all the pupils. It is a sight to behold from the top of the stairs as form groups enthusiastically jet off to their respective floors in single file like a scene from Fantasia. In any case, our corridors are only three-pupils-wide so we couldn't just have them arriving en masse. Some schools of course spend some 30 or 40 million pounds building a school with very wide corridors. We were not able to do that. So what we have done instead is demonstrate that transitions with narrow corridors *can* happen quickly, and without strife.

Shhh! They're Not Really Silent!

Sorry, not technically, no. In the same way pupils move with purpose during lesson transitions, so, too, do our teachers. Each stairwell and corridor is also occupied by at least one teacher using the transition as an opportunity to say 'Good morning!' to pupils, especially those they don't get to teach or see very often. This is a great time to help pupils practise their greetings and model how to be polite and look professional. We would not want to miss an opportunity for them to practise being sociable.

On the other hand, it is also a good time to bring a bit of fun and silliness into the school day (another essential part of life at Michaela). Our Head of Sixth Form, for example, uses the focused audience of pupils to polish up her hilarious regional accents (ask for her Scottish!) and on the humanities floor, you will often hear pupils projecting, 'Edward the Confessor!' 'The Battle of Agincourt!' as they pace their way along the corridor; the history teachers are firing questions at them again. Meanwhile, on the English floor the Head of Year 7 chants poetry with Year 8s as they enter his classroom (why waste a minute of learning?). Pupils are sometimes awarded merits for the best smiles, greetings, and projection, and there is an overwhelming feeling of warmth and community. Not oppressive or silencing.

They Actually Prefer It

Critics of Michaela worry that we are muzzling our pupils' rights to express themselves and develop relationships by expecting them to walk in silence to lessons, where pupils in most other schools are free to talk and act as they like. I'll reply to this with a few questions:

1. Who is worrying about the good, hard-working (usually small and/or shy) children who become victims of the inevitable bullies when they decide to 'express *themselves*'?

2. How much power do teachers have to intervene in misbehaviour in corridors when pupils have few or no rules to follow?

3. How much must go on that is unseen and unheard during lesson transitions in schools?

4. Do we realise that children have an hour at lunch to chat and play and a 15 minute break time in the morning, not to mention all the time after school?

5. How much meaningful, relationship-building chat do children actually do rushing to a lesson, anyway?

Gavin Williamson (Education Secretary) announced in 2020 that the government would be supporting headteachers to increase disciplinary measures in schools to create calmer and more nurturing environments for learning. A key motivation for him is that teachers deserve better. Too many wonderful teachers are leaving our profession, citing pupil behaviour as a main reason.

I have worked in schools where teachers hide in their classrooms during lesson transitions and I know from speaking to many teachers that this is not uncommon across the country. Why risk going out into the corridors and being undermined or even assaulted in front of hundreds of pupils? In most schools, pupils feel like *they* own the corridors. Meaning *bullies* own them. Do we want any part of our schools run by bullies? Even if the teachers feel safe in the corridors, the children do not. Fights break out, kids push and shove each other, they run, shouting and screaming, doors flying open and slamming against the walls. Of course there will be *some* schools for whom this is not the case and pupils are able to make their way between lessons safely and calmly. However, every single teacher at Michaela strongly advocates our silent corridors because of what they have personally witnessed at other schools. We are not making it up! We have all become teachers because we want the best for children.

Perhaps you are a teacher at a regular secondary school and you are reading this thinking 'we don't have silent corridors and the kids are fine!' But we have seen that silent corridors reduce the type of bad behaviour that can often flare up into even bigger things – the shoving that turns into bullying, the tardiness that turns into truancy.

And, yes, perhaps it is a shame that in order to avoid all that the pupils need to be silent. But only if you see silence as a bad thing. We see it as a clear thing. Something that pupils understand and know how to achieve. Something that shows them that the adult is in charge, they find peace in that. No teacher wants someone else to be in charge of *their* classroom. The corridors should not be any different because the unruly behaviour in the corridor does not end there; it has a spill-over effect into the classroom so that pupils often arrive late, hyperactive or just shell-shocked! Of course, it is not only what *teachers* deserve: also, *pupils* deserve the best chance at succeeding in their learning and arriving calmly and in silence means they can get straight on with the lesson, no fuss, just learning. Is that not what we should all be striving for in schools?

Don't the Children Eventually Rebel?

It's worth noting here that these transitions are only a teeny-tiny part of the children's school day and an even smaller part of their *journée complète*. They also get an hour at lunch to chat to their friends and teachers and, of course, plenty of time in lessons and extra-curricular activities to take part in discussions where they develop the social skills that our pupils are so renowned for.

As for the corridors, would all six hundred of Michaela's pupils really stay silent if they did not see the benefit in being so? An important part to all this is that the pupils, like us, know the alternative. They know about the bullying and other nastiness that went on in primary school and now goes on in their friends' secondary school corridors, where it is sadly the most vulnerable children who suffer. On the whole, our children stay silent even when a teacher is not around, because they are bought in to the system and culture that keeps them all safe.

Of course there is inevitably a tiny minority of pupils who use the corridors as a stage to 'rebel' against the system. Examples of this we have seen include an exaggerated cough, a whistle or a stomp here or there. This kind of behaviour is pretty normal and to be expected when working with teenagers. In fact, you might be surprised to hear that we are quite happy for pupils to rebel with a whistle! This means pupils are much less likely to rebel in other, more dangerous ways, like joining a gang or bringing a knife to school (not that abnormal if you work in an inner-city secondary school). This is the wonderful effect of our sweating the small stuff; we're much happier to give out detentions for occasional stomping in the corridors, than watch children spiral out of control and end up in danger. It is our job to show them the line and hold it. As our Senior Team often reminds us, the tighter the fence, the harder it is to get lost.

Pupil infractions in the corridors also provide teachers another opportunity to talk to pupils and remind them about their responsibility to uphold the lovely environment from which we all benefit. Along the corridors here at Michaela, there is a tremendous feeling of everyone rowing together (an expression we frequently use), and not against each other. Pupils feel purposeful and safe under the caring eye of their teachers. We are here for them, not for some kind of power trip. I say this because I think the idea of there being silence in school often gives critics the impression that children are being silenced in some larger way, but that is not the case here; it is more of a general understanding that this is the way we keep everyone happy and safe. Is that not what a school *should* be like?

If you are still not convinced, our doors (and corridors) are always open for visitors.

Tough Love

Jozef Butterfield
@JozefTeacher

Since its opening in 2014, Michaela Community School has been dubbed the nation's 'strictest school' by major media outlets. Its no-excuses ethos has achieved notoriety, and in early years saw threats and attempted break-ins from protestors. Now in its sixth year, Michaela has already left an indelible mark on the national education debate, and it continues to rewrite the established doctrines of UK secondary schools.

When I started here in January 2019, it was hard not to be intimidated by such a reputation. Would I spend my days screeching at pupils who forgot their pencils? Admonishing eleven-year olds for minor offences? Crushing all vestiges of individuality? No doubt, our critics would paint us as such.

The reality, however, is a stark contrast. Yes, we are strict – but that is only one side of the coin. What makes the school truly great is the climate we cultivate – one where poor behaviour is not only minimised, but where all staff are empowered to build transformative relationships with the pupils in our charge. I appreciated the idea of this when I started. Now, after more than a year in the English department, I understand the foundational importance of positive relationships alongside high behavioural standards.

This is what I know: if you call us Britain's strictest school, you must in the same breath say we are also its most loving school. For every punitive word there are many more celebrations of the great things our pupils achieve. You could, of course, see examples of this at almost any school. The difference is that at Michaela these relationships are consistently strong across all classes, because relationships are underpinned by a strict policy that creates a safe environment for pupils. There is no rowdiness in our silent corridors. Detentions are frequently set. Pupils are aware that their teacher can be light-hearted one moment and instantly authoritative the next ('warm/strict'). It is only by maintaining these high standards that we avoid the wanton chaos my colleagues and I have experienced at our previous schools.

Why are we so adamant about the need for a firm behaviour policy? Aside from personal experiences, we stand by the idea that all humans are inherently flawed, children even more so. Unguided and left to their own devices, children will inevitably rebel, rejecting generally agreed standards of how civilised people should behave. School, alongside good parenting, is the essential intervention that turns imperfect children into self-actualising citizens. It takes a great deal of persistence to achieve this, and we have a duty to speak harsh truths and punish when necessary. The mantle of authority must be donned for the sake of the child, or else we fail them.

But a strict behaviour policy alone is not enough. Indeed, some staff apply to our school on the basis that, with such a policy, they can just 'get on with teaching'. The implication is that this alone can provide a transformative education, when really it is only the beginning. For, without strong relationships, involving mutual respect, inside jokes and – indeed – occasional banter, you will never get the most out of your pupils. This might seem obvious, but understand that before joining Michaela I had come to see the term 'relationships' in the pejorative – the tool of a teacher who could not rely on their school to enforce a decent standard of behaviour. Up until then, I'd got by on a close adherence to my schools' behaviour policies and my own force of character. Still, there were pupils who remained unreachable to me, and this would have continued to be the case so long as I remained the teacher I was.

To appreciate my journey at Michaela, it's important first to understand my previous school. It was a 'good' school – both my colleagues and Ofsted agreed on this. It wasn't fraught with marking overload or the fear of a capricious senior management team that had made life at my training school miserable. There were, however, issues with behaviour. Detentions were meaningless, as attendance rested entirely on the whim of the pupil involved, with no functional means for staff to follow-up with non-attendees. Fixed-term exclusion became the only recourse, but this would be hampered by the high cost of provision for the growing tide of uncontrollable pupils. Lessons suffered, and by the time I left it seemed to me the school was accelerating towards disaster. In a short space of time, I had received verbal abuse, a physical threat from a pupil while separating a fight and, climactically, my car tyres were slashed.

Colleagues would say, 'Well you should see what happens at other schools – it's Bedlam there.' They were undoubtedly right; there are of course two grades below an Ofsted 'good', and schools with those grades no doubt made our school seem an Eden by comparison. But I simply refused to accept this as a reasonable justification for our own ever-declining standards.

I decided that, in my classroom at least, there would be order. I clung to the behaviour policy like a drowning man to a plank. I became 'the strict teacher'. The smallest details were sweated: pupils waited behind chairs, silence was insisted upon, consequences were quickly accelerated. And let me not be misunderstood – this wasn't wrong. It generally worked, particularly with the younger years. I could see the benefits soon enough: kids who had previously run riot were now calm and attentive. The same pupils that were, I was told, menaces elsewhere behaved fine for me. This of course raised the question – what on earth was going on in other classrooms such that eleven-year olds, *eleven-year olds*, were able to run around like animals?

Despite my successes with the younger years, issues arose further up. There were several disaffected pupils in my Year 9 form, enough to create a critical mass that made it difficult for me to isolate and attend to the main offenders. I'd inherited them from a teacher who, for a variety of reasons, had a more *laissez faire* approach, which the pupils were accustomed to. Through my own persistence and a myriad of interactions with parents, I brought most of the form to heel. But that was the extent of my success. They behaved – mostly, but there was no joy here, only a begrudging acceptance that they were less able to get away with their old tricks with *this* form tutor than their last. Each day was a battle. It was exhausting.

In my bottom-set Year 10 class there was a pupil, Ryan, who posed similar problems. Every teacher has encountered a Ryan – most have known several. While much of the class's attention stayed with me, Ryan, functionally illiterate and very weak academically, couldn't get through five minutes without some silly comment or absent-minded distraction that pushed the whole class off-course. The strict-teacher routine had taken me this far, so I doubled-down here – to no success. My daily removals of Ryan from lessons, usually within the first five minutes, continued to sour our relationship and built up into time-wasting clashes that impacted everyone else in the vicinity.

Behaviour is Not Binary

Evaluating my experience with both Ryan and my form, what lesson should I have gleaned? Before Michaela, I lacked the insight and the guidance to understand why my strategies were not working. The disaffection I felt towards the system drove me further to the extreme, and while my hardline approach was not the worst I could have adopted, I was clearly incapable of endearing myself to the most difficult pupils. I had assumed, falsely, that behaviour management was a simple binary action that moved between authoritative and affectionate as an either-or. If pupils could not be cowed by a blisteringly strict escalation of consequences, I effectively wrote them off.

This had to change, and it took the vital juncture of my employment at Michaela to affect this. After an initial period of getting used to new routines, resources, and timetables, I was settling into the day-to-day routine. My lessons were, in a word, functional. I imparted knowledge, gave out merits and demerits, expected pupils to give their full attention to the teacher, etc. The behaviour of my previous school was unimaginable here. And yet, despite such progress, a phantom lingered. The horse led to water cannot be made to drink, and the sum of my teaching ability could not inspire more than a begrudging acceptance from pupils. They went through the motions just to avoid my ire. With younger classes, such as Year 7, this was less catastrophic because of their boundless enthusiasm to please. But, as before, it was further up the school that the consequences were most keenly felt, as evidenced in the piddling number of raised hands and a general paucity of effort.

Somehow, I had to up my game, and Michaela facilitated this. In my first few weeks I received plentiful amounts of low-stakes feedback from my colleagues, providing more professional development in a fortnight than I'd received in the previous two years. The most common refrain was, 'Relationships need to improve', with specific actions on how to do this. Again and again, 'Relationships need to improve,' – I'd never had feedback like that before! At many schools, observers would be over the moon just to see that pupils weren't being disruptive and were all giving the teacher their attention. But, given that Michaela doesn't aim to be most schools, our expectations are considerably higher. Here, we maximise every moment of learning. To do that, teachers must endeavour to build relationships with their pupils, raised from the foundation of our behaviour policy.

'Warm/Strict'

How do we go about this? The answer lies in just how much time we invest – just how comprehensive we are – in building familiarity between the pupils and ourselves. Much of this is done with specific narration of praise – no revelation there. More unusual are our multiple duties throughout the week;

we optimise the amount of time we are around our pupils: conversing with them every lunchtime, every break, and on frequent stairwell duties. This is in addition to family lunch, where staff and pupils discuss the day's chosen topic. We ask them about their weekends, their thoughts, their hopes and dreams. We show genuine interest and care, which they then reciprocate in the classroom. This is central to creating the 'buy-in' from pupils they need to fully reach their potential.

In time, I came to know my pupils far better than any I'd taught before. This had huge implications on my teaching potential. I settled into a far more relaxed and jovial teaching persona. Pupils now know me more for my sarcastic sense of humour, and the random facts and jokes I inject into my explanations, than for my strictness. A particularly powerful strategy that I employ is my attempt to think of nicknames for every pupil I teach, and a few I don't. K-Dogg, Mustardman, Return-Of-The-Mak, Muminator, Big T, Gracie Grace, Petey McPeterson. Of course, these only come about after I've known a pupil for some time – well enough for the nickname to be both apt and mutually approved. Enjoyable as they are to think of and use, their utility is indispensable. They act as a shorthand for the relationship I've built up with that pupil, a subconscious reminder that I value them individually, that they are special. Equally, a switch back to normal names can be used as shorthand for disapproval, working alongside a shift in vocal tone to redress a pupil's actions. Or, as a colleague wrote in feedback, 'it allowed you to use a simple code-switch – using their real names – in order to add weight to your strict narration.' And therein lies the power of the 'warm/strict' approach: these strong relationships not only make pupils eager learners, but also supplement the no-excuses behaviour policy underpinning it.

This process was neither easy nor brief. It took months of receiving feedback, then observing colleagues who did something especially well, trying it and receiving feedback again, repeating and refining in the pursuit of perfection. I've also spent hundreds of hours talking to pupils outside of the classroom. The payoff is indisputable. There has been a seismic shift in the number of hands up, the level of effort, the desire to please and do well. All of this is because my pupils genuinely love and respect me, as I love and respect them, because I've been given the time and the direction to get to really know them. I've never enjoyed my job more.

And yet, a strange caricature of us persists online and in the media. I find myself marvelling at the descriptions of our school and our methods still bandied about by critics. Authoritarian, Dickensian — screaming teachers, quivering pupils — how shocked these critics are when they visit and find, instead, pupils who love their teachers and their school. Come visit us and see for yourself.

Digital Detox

Samuel Hurst

The common denominator of our woes

As a Head of Year at Michaela I meet our pupils' parents every day. On some occasions, these meetings are simply to have a quick catch up with a pupil's mum or dad, where I'll give them some information from their teachers on how their child is getting on. More often, the meetings are to discuss a behavioural or academic problem. Naturally, all meetings are different, because every pupil is different, and the details of what is holding them back vary. Yet, I will always ask one question:

"Does your son/daughter have a smartphone?"

The common denominator of almost all of the issues I deal with can be traced back to overuse or misuse of smartphones. Parents normally appreciate that the smartphone presents a problem, but they don't follow the chain of causality from smartphone misuse to problems at school. I find this is the case with most people, even my friends. Few understand just how destructive smartphones are to the peace, happiness and success of the kids I teach.

Here is a small sample of what parents have said to me over the last year:

"She's a good girl, and she does her homework really well. But she's just obsessed with messaging this boy all evening once her homework is done."

"I caught him the other day. He said he was doing his online maths on the phone. But I looked, and he was on a game."

"I did a check of her WhatsApp conversations, and found this... [swearing and abuse to and from another pupil]."

"Every night he does his homework, and it takes him a very long time. I wonder whether it is a good idea to let him have YouTube on his phone whilst he's doing it."

"I got her exams results through, and I really wasn't very happy. She works very hard at home from what I can see. Does she need tutoring? What more can I do?"

If I had a penny for every time I've heard a parent say a variant of one of the above, I would be taking early retirement. So the starting point for sorting out these issues is to be in charge of the pupil's smartphone usage. On average, Brits spend more than two hours a day on their phones. That adds up to approximately 14 hours a week, or 60 hours a month, or 30 full days a year! That is unfortunately the average smartphone usage. When a pupil is brave enough to show me the "Screen Time" function on their phone, I find it is normally around five hours per day. Some children will even be on their phones for eight hours a day. They are on their phones in the middle of the night. I am Head of Year 9. I know the Head of Year 11 has it much worse on the phone front. The older they get, the worse the habit takes hold of them.

Now I'm aware these issues are not unique to the smartphone generation. All adults, back when we were at school, had ways of timewasting without the help of YouTube make-up tutorials and Netflix binge-watching. And of course we all had our various methods for deceiving parents into thinking we were working. But smartphones are more dangerous than our old tricks, because:

a. They are addictive and seriously harm our pupils' brains.

b. Social media is extremely dangerous for our pupils' wellbeing and relationships

This is evidence I have gleaned from two years of being a Head of Year at Michaela, and five years in total as a maths teacher (three at Michaela, and two years outside of London). First, I want to make the point that smartphones are damaging the poorest pupils the most. Sadly, people who never meet our families just don't know the impact smartphones are having on their lives.

Putting the 'con' in Silicon Valley

Initially, when computers became affordable to have in schools, the worry was that the well-off pupils would reap the benefits, whilst lower-income pupils would be left out. Part of the 21st century skills drive was to have "computer-literate" pupils, who could code and program. Would this create a digital divide between rich and poor?

Ironically, the advantage that middle-class children now have is that their parents are on average more attuned to the dangers of technology. Equally, these parents are able to control the amount of time their child spends on their smartphone with the use of nannies and more adults surrounding the child. As with many things, the USA is ahead of the UK on this. It is the families of Silicon Valley tech companies that are eschewing smartphones the most. Famously, Steve Jobs would not allow his children access to iPads. The Gates family did not allow their children mobile phones until they turned 14, and regretted allowing them access even then (*Business Insider 2019*).

The families of Silicon Valley appreciate more than anyone else the dangers modern technology presents. It is the addictive nature of the smartphone, tablet and computer game that worries them. The kind of smartphones we have now are different from any technology that has gone before. Catherine Price, who has written *How to Break Up with your Phone*, quotes a former Google product manager: "Your telephone in the 1970s didn't have a thousand engineers on the other side of the telephone who were redesigning it … to be more and more persuasive." These companies, the makers of the phones, but also the makers of the apps like Snapchat, Instagram and WhatsApp are deliberately making their devices more and more addictive so that children simply *cannot* give them up. Companies gather huge amounts of data on group and individual preferences and then use them to manipulate people, including children.

There was a company, Dopamine Labs, who created computer code for app companies. The purpose is to keep us glued to apps. (It appears that Dopamine Labs no longer exists under this inauspicious name.) Tech companies can keep us scrolling by manipulating our levels of the pleasure hormone: dopamine. One example that shocked me from Price's book was that Instagram deliberately holds back on showing users "Likes", so that they can send notifications at the most effective moment possible to claw us back onto the app. Even the bright red colour used for notifications on the iPhone is clinically chosen as being most appealing to the human eye.

One of the founders of Dopamine Labs also created an app called Space, which caused a twelve-second delay every time a social media app is opened. This was supposed to give you time to change your mind about time wasting. The App Store did not initially allow Space to be sold from the store because it would encourage people to use their iPhones less. This reminds us that we are essentially just money and guinea pigs to the big tech companies. The more we click on their apps or websites, the more money they can make from advertising. And the more they understand our behaviour, which they are constantly tracking, the better they are at fixing our eyes to the screen.

Remember in "the old days" when you had scrolled to the bottom of a page on YouTube, Facebook, you name it, you would have to click "Next page"? Designers found that by creating "continuous scroll" we would spend far longer mindlessly trawling through our news feeds. So they changed it. Most of us have been there: you're scrolling through a news feed and you get down to the stories or posts you've already seen. But you keep going! We are naturally so lazy that we cannot even be bothered to turn away from our phone.

It is the middle class that are cottoning on to this the quickest. In the neighbourhoods of Silicon Valley workers, nannies are now being made to sign "no-phone" contracts that prohibit the use of a smartphone in front of children, apart from to take calls from the parents. The nannies are therefore spending the time with the children going to play parks and playing cards and board games. This all sounds fantastic, and I think most parents would prefer their children to go to the park than to be on a smartphone. This requires you to be either rich in spare time or rich enough to afford a nanny, which the vast majority of parents are not. Most parents are extremely stretched for time and money. A relative of mine even said his life "would not be worth living if the PlayStation did not exist" to give him some respite from his children.

Many families are still a long way from the realisation that technology is ever so damaging. You see this in a kind of race to the bottom of who can have the latest iPhone and spend the most money on the online PlayStation store. The kids I teach all say that they would much rather just have money for their birthday rather than presents. When I ask them what they would spend it on, they explain that they can purchase new style clothing for their avatars/characters on the PlayStation store. Parents understandably think the more they can spend on technology for children, the happier they will be. Unfortunately, it is quite the reverse.

Breaking your brain

The problem is affecting the disadvantaged the most. If you only have one parent at home, and they are stretched with childcare, then they will rely on phones more. If no one in the household has been to university, then they are less likely to be attuned to the current advice on technology.

But what are smartphones actually doing to our brains? The answer is alarming.

Let's start with by putting our brains to the test. Try solving this maths question:

Mohammed buys 6 cans of coke for 30p each.

He pays with a £5 note.

How much change does he get?

The amount of information your brain has to marshal in order to answer this question is actually surprisingly impressive. (The answer is £3.20.)

You need to find what 6 lots of 30 is somehow. Embedded in the answer of 180 is probably the knowledge that 6 x 3 = 18, which you've then scaled up by ten. You may have also switched it into pounds, getting £1.80, automatically using your knowledge that £1 = 100p. But then you would need to have also practised the fact that if £1 = 100p, then £1.80 = 180p, which is not obvious to everyone. Trust me, I'm a maths teacher. Then to get the change you need to realise that it is the difference between £1.80 and £5. You could then have used addition, or subtraction to work that out, and again your brain will be drawing on the links between your knowledge of money, conversions, subtraction, number bonds to 100, all sorts!

I hope you are still with me. If you're not, then that partly proves my point.

The connections our brains naturally make are detailed and complex. If you were able to do the question easily, then the connections in your brain have become pretty strong. You have absorbed primary school maths into your long-term memory (where you have information learnt and mastered, and stored indefinitely). Storing this knowledge in your long-term memory is not easy, however. Ask the millions of people who say "I'm just not very good at maths." To be able to answer a question like the one above takes a lot of repeated practice with the necessary procedures and mathematical concepts. In order to have these concepts in long-term memory, we need our short-term memory to have grappled with the concepts on several occasions (short-term memory being the active part of your brain that can hold a few things in it at one time).

The problem presented by smartphones is that short-term memory can be easily overloaded. We are not able to hold many ideas in our short-term memory at one time. When you add a smartphone into the equation, there is very little room left for you to strengthen the connections in your brain when you are learning. This is because the distractions presented by your smartphone take up space in your short-term memory (e.g. notifications, vibrations, or even the anticipation of a message). Moreover, to create long-term memories, you actually have to create new proteins (that means, creating *new* brain cells). So pupils really struggle to learn properly or do homework to any meaningful quality when their phone is taking up some of the mental capacity. For our pupils, they are always trying to do their homework with their phone next to them in case they get a message. This is a bad idea for a number of reasons.

Firstly, we all know that notifications on our smartphones these days occur constantly. This repeatedly interrupts their thought process, and does not allow their brain to strengthen or build connections. For children, this is even worse than for adults, because they have notifications raining down on them from many more apps. We all have those WhatsApp groups that never stop pinging. Of course, you can mute them, but a child is not going to do that. The defaults are all set for notifications to be on. The more messages they receive, the more popular they feel. Sadly, the more messages they receive, the less likely they are to be able to retain the knowledge for their quiz the next day.

I know full well that WhatsApp groups are damaging the quality of homework, and our pupils' concentration. For every class in our school, there is a group WhatsApp chat with several members. Again, the pupils who have shown me their Screen Time have revealed that they can spend 4 hours on Snapchat in the evening at the same time as studying. Please do not think this is something to celebrate because it seems like they are doing 4 hours of studying. That's what their parents think. But the reality is that 30 mins of studying without the phone would have far more impact than this does. Their supposed 4 hours of studying results in them failing their quizzes the next day.

This reminds me of the parent who says they are not happy with the exam results, because their child (let's call him 'Aahil') seems to be working really hard at home. Aahil's parents ask to come in and speak to me, because Aahil's grades are only *good*, rather than *very good* or *outstanding*. At first glance, the situation is slightly confusing: Aahil is a very polite boy, has next to zero homework detentions, and is passing all his weekly quizzes in his subjects.

It is also great that the parents are being so proactive. But I ask the common denominator question:

"Does Aahil have a smartphone?"

The parents reply, "Yes he does, but we are very strict that he *must* complete his homework before he goes on it."

This sounds good, but it isn't. It is possible that despite the supportive parents, Aahil is sneakily answering messages in between the questions he is completing in his homework. Thereby nothing is truly "sticking" or working its way into his long-term memory. If the parents have secured the phone, so that it is out of his room when he is working, there are still problems. Why would Aahil spend careful time on his homework, when he can whizz through it and have more time on the games? If the smartphone is on offer, everything else pales into insignificance. Life becomes a game of "Get through this, and then I'll be able to go on my phone."

The second problem is the fact that a phone in the same room as you, or even in your vicinity is in itself distracting. It does not even need to be ringing with WhatsApp messages; its presence alone will take up some of your mental capacity. We are always anticipating the next time our phone goes off. For children this is even worse, because they derive a lot of their self-worth by attention gained from others (many adults do this too). So our brains are half-thinking about when our phone will next go off. This is so critical that a study found that 83.5% of us have experienced the situation where we think our phone has gone off when it has not (Sauer et al. 2015). Known as the "Phantom phone sensation", we are so obsessed with contact from other people we start to dream it up. If that isn't distracting from concentrating on your work, I don't know what is.

Third, even if we are still able to learn, phones are nevertheless hindering the propensity for higher-order thought. To be able to add insight to a topic (or be creative), your long-term memory needs to have a very complex and nuanced structure. At Michaela, we want some of our Sixth Form pupils to be able to go to the best universities in the country. If they are to be able to go there and succeed, then staying away from phones will be vital for them. What I find sad is that many pupils who could be successful academically may be held back because of our societal misunderstanding of how smartphones are covertly weakening our brains.

On the one hand, smartphones are weakening the connections in our brain. In addition to this however, they are also making us more and more distractible, shortening our attention spans. You may have noticed yourself that since you have been spending more time on your smartphone, you find it harder to concentrate. I almost find it difficult to watch a feature-length film now without wanting a break at around the time a TV show would end.

There are good reasons for why we have become more distractible though: it makes us more valuable to web companies.

We all naturally prefer distraction to concentration, because concentration is difficult. When you are concentrating on something your brain is having to decide to stay focused on the task at hand. This is down to the part of the brain called the pre-frontal cortex. So concentrating is hard work, as our pre-frontal cortex has to block distractions. The job is made far harder for our brain if we are on a smartphone or the internet.

Catherine Price uses a great example for this. Compare reading a book to reading something on your smartphone. Distractions when you read a book are external to the page. A dog barking or your partner hoovering is not right there on the page. Consider when you read an article on your phone: links, ads, notifications are popping up literally left, right and centre. All of these distractions claw our attention away for a split-second. Consequently, our phones are teaching us terrible habits of essentially mindlessly doing tasks without ever fully focusing on them. After all, the more distractible you are, the more links you click on, and the more value you are to websites and advertisers.

Have you ever picked up your phone for one reason, seen a notification, been distracted by it, and then put your phone back down without having even started the task that caused you to pick it up in the first place? I know I have!

Ruining relationships

I should say that I realise there is no turning back now. Smartphones are here to stay. There are of course huge benefits to them, like the ease with which we can speak to (and see) loved ones who are in a different city or even a different continent. So I won't be arguing here for a complete technological reversal. What we do need is to understand how smartphones and technology are damaging human interactions, and to understand that children especially need to be shielded from this.

The concerns raised above relating to smartphones and our brains are only half of the problem. What I find equally worrying is the effect they are having on social interactions and how relationships are formed and maintained. Before talking about what we can do to take control of our technology usage, I will explain what I have encountered as a Head of Year in dealing with numerous disputes between our pupils.

I estimate that 90% of pastoral problems start on smartphones. I can be more specific than that. The majority of that 90% is due to WhatsApp and Snapchat. For those of you fortunate enough not to use these apps: WhatsApp is just a messaging platform; Snapchat is a messaging platform that also allows you to send additional photos or videos as well as your message which disappear after a set time limit (between 0 and 10 seconds, normally). Snapchat is a bully's medium of choice due to its ephemeral set up: send someone a nasty message, and unless they are savvy enough to screenshot it immediately, it then disappears without a trace moments later.

To compound the deceit of Snapchat, WhatsApp's "Group Chat" feature is the perfect medium for a disgruntled teenager to suck others into a downward spiral of negativity. Pupils have WhatsApp groups with more than 30 members. It only takes a ringleader who wants to sound off about how so-and-so gave them "dirty looks in the playground" before there is a hate campaign against one pupil. They can then turn a whole group of pupils against someone else.

Here I have to add a caveat, and then a further problem. The caveat is that a bit of complaining amongst secondary school pupils is not a problem. Nobody goes through secondary school getting on with absolutely everyone. But before smartphones, this complaining remained in the confines of the home, or between you and your friend with whom you walked home. Your life was not being shared with 20, 30, 40 or more other pupils in the same school on a private messaging platform.

My advice to any parent is immediately to delete WhatsApp, Snapchat and Instagram from their child's phone. This reminds me of a conversation with Aaban's mum, which I have also had with several other parents this year.

> "Mr Hurst, I agree with you that Aaban needs to stop playing Fortnite, but he says his classmates don't want to talk to him if he doesn't play the game."

I totally appreciate this concern because friendships at school are important. It may or may not be true that Aaban's classmates will not want to talk to him if he does not play Fortnite. In a lot of cases, this is an argument pupils use to tug on the heartstrings of their parents. It is a last ditch attempt to save themselves from losing their PlayStation. It is true, however, that pupils do spend a lot of time talking about the latest game. In fact, it's probably their favourite topic of conversation if there is no adult around. Aaban's mum can be reassured though, because there are plenty of pupils at Michaela who do not spend lots of time on Fortnite and social media. This number is increasing as we do more work on "digital detox". In any case, Aaban is a case where if he could shrug off his addiction to Fortnite then a Russell Group university will be a far more likely part of his future. Alternatively, he can stay in the group of boys who play Fortnite endlessly and thus struggle to get to university at all.

If children are still yearning for more contact with their friends, then invite them over. It sounds slightly strange saying "invite them over" these days, because so much communication is done online. What parents do not realise is that by their child having a smartphone, especially one with social media apps, they are effectively inviting all and sundry into their home anyway. My experiences at school tell me that any child who has social media and uses it in an unsupervised environment will have chatted to a person over the internet that they have never met in real life. This is a fundamental shift in the nature of the family home. Parents can no longer control, or even monitor, who their children are speaking to and the influence they may be having. Of course, children have forever been having secret rendezvous, but smartphones add an intensity and an ease to these interactions.

This is illustrated by the account of another Michaela Head of Year. A girl in Year 8 had been messaging someone through an internet chat room – someone older, someone unknown to the family. It turned out that the person was a man in his mid-twenties. This all stemmed from the daughter's use of her smartphone in her bedroom. If a child is allowed their smartphone in their room, then you have no idea of the kind of messages they are receiving or sending. In fact, if they are allowed their smartphone in broad daylight, as long as they have Snapchat or are quick at deleting WhatsApp messages, then there could be someone extremely undesirable winning their heart.

You could accuse me of being nostalgic, but the situation of the 90s, or even the 00s, created children better prepared for adulthood. I would much rather the quick landline call to my friend's house to ask if he wanted a kickabout in the garden, than three hours on FaceTime, followed by two hours of Fortnite.

In those days we also lived in relatively blissful ignorance of the lavish lifestyles that celebrities were living. For our children today, they are regularly seeing the unobtainable lifestyles of "Instagrammers" and "YouTubers". What makes it even more awful is that many of these social media celebrities come from very normal backgrounds and seem totally self-made. When I used to watch Tiger Woods winning every golf competition under the sun, the dream died pretty quickly because it was so obvious how much more skillful he was than I would ever be. For our pupils though, it feels possible that you might acquire the make-up skills of "Zoella" (who has over 12 million subscribers). The dream of fame seems real. This then makes the reality of homework seem laborious and an utter waste of time. Who cares about GCSEs when in minutes, just by being online all the time, you can become famous and rich?

One of the latest studies also had an interesting finding that smartphones are having a material effect on how families spend time together (Mullan and Chatzitheochari 2019). Over recent years, families are spending around 30 minutes more per day together. Yet, almost all of this extra time is spent on devices, meaning family members are effectively spending time alone, hence the slightly depressing term, "alone-together time".

We live in a difficult period to make the argument of how damaging this is, because we are yet to see the true results, and they are also tough to quantify. I often find myself in conversation with a parent when a phone buzzes, causing the thread to be lost, and for the parent to then stop listening. When raising children, we want them to be able to hold sustained conversations without getting distracted. No child addicted to their smartphone is going to fare well in life, have a meaningful relationship, cook a meal, read a book, when they cannot concentrate because they are forever wondering whether the phone in their pocket is full of messages and Instagram "likes".

Winning the battle, brick by brick

Since realising the problems technology was causing us, we have started a number of initiatives at Michaela to support pupils in decreasing their screen time and controlling their use of technology. We are honest with parents that when their child is 18, then they probably should have a phone, and possibly a smartphone. What we need to do for now is to educate our children without technology holding them back; especially since we are competing against middle-class families who either shun social media, or who have a head start in the first place.

The strategy for taking control is twofold: raising awareness and encouraging alternatives. It is not a battle that can be won easily, or indeed won at all. But our various initiatives around "Digital Detox" are having a huge net gain to the school and our pupils.

The first method for raising awareness is with Ms Birbalsingh's induction assemblies with Year 6 parents. Early intervention, before addiction sets in, is the most effective time to raise awareness. In the parent assemblies for pupils soon to join the school, Ms Birbalsingh gives a very clear message of "Do not give your child a smartphone". Our staff body all attend at least one of these meetings so that we can convey the same message in form time, and when we narrate how our pupils are supposed to complete their homework (i.e. a smartphone-free zone). When our current Year 7 cohort joined the school 56% of them had smartphones; hopefully this will be lower next year. Since joining, our Head of Year 7 has done a lot of work on helping pupils give up their smartphones, and now 30% of them remain with a smartphone. Our Year 11s last year and our current year 9s, 10s, 11s all have smartphones like any other school. We have noticed a huge reduction in Years 7 and 8 thanks to the work we have been doing with the families.

In many cases, pupils already have a smartphone by the time they join the school. For the older years, they are ubiquitous. The school hosts "Digital Detox" parent assemblies, where Ms Birbalsingh describes the problems I have outlined above in passionate terms to the parents. All of the heads of year sing from the same hymn sheet in our meetings with parents, and make sure we continue the dialogue set in motion by the parent assemblies.

We show a video conversation with a parent at our parent assemblies, Imran's dad. Imran was previously addicted to Fortnite, and would not want to do any family activities. He was forever longing to play Fortnite, and consequently was not doing well at school. Imran's dad made the very tough decision of totally taking away the games console. As he says, initially it was very tough, Imran would cry, and ask for it back. But eventually, when Imran realised it was not going to happen, he moved on. He came top of his class in the latest set of exams, hugely out-performing expectations in maths. Best of all though was what his dad said: "I've got my son back."

There are still problems, however. Many parents do not come to the parent assembly, either because they don't think it is important or they are busy. Moreover, when discussing with parents and pupils, giving up a smartphone is not viable. Going "cold turkey" is not always the best way to cure an addiction. This is where encouraging alternative options to smartphones becomes so important, of which more below.

A key reason for not giving up a smartphone is because, understandably, parents want to be able to ensure their child is safe. The best alternative is, therefore, to have a phone without the addiction potential. In the school shop we sell "brick" phones for £9.99. As Ms Birbalsingh says in her assemblies, we sell these phones at a slight loss (they cost the school £14), because we are so keen to encourage parents and pupils to take this option. The difference this has made to so many of our pupils is unmissable. Pupils who have given up smartphones in favour of a brick phone are, without exception, doing better academically and behaviourally at school.

Eshal in Year 8, for example, was a golden pupil in Year 7, but as social media started to take hold she was beginning to accrue a number of detentions each week. In a meeting with her father, I told him much of what is written above about the online stranger danger and the effect the apps were having on Eshal's brain. He and his wife took Eshal's smartphone away and gave it to a relative. I see her call her dad after school before she gets the bus now, but on her brick phone instead. She has barely had a single detention since, and when I spoke to her about missing out on group chats, she said it did not bother her. Seeing a pupil smile when they are released from the burden of tech addiction is what makes my job worth it.

In addition to the brick phone, three other alternatives that we offer are "Screen Time", "digital drop off" and "blocking distractions clinic".

Screen Time

The most effective measure I have found is to encourage pupils to put a screen time limit on their phone. I have had most experience with this on Apple iPhones, where you can set a screen time limit for each evening. The conversation normally goes as follows:

> "So David, it's two weeks till mid-year exams, do you think using your phone less would help you get a better grade?"

"Yes, sir, it probably would."

"Okay, well would you be tempted to give your phone up until end of exams?" I ask. It's always worth checking, in case they are brave enough!

"No, sir, I do still need it to call my parents for when I'm on the bus." Probably a lie, but the argument is going to be time-consuming, and a losing battle.

"Sure. Well how about we set it so that you have unlimited access to phone calls, but then about 45mins per night of extra time?"

"I think I can do that. Can it go back to normal after exams?"

This is overall a big win. Sometimes I offer less time, and then let them negotiate me upwards so it does not feel such a hit to their addiction. But the effect this strategy has had on exam periods has been excellent.

Digital Drop Off

We have also bought a school safe, which is manned each day after school by a member of the office team. This allows pupils to go and give their phone up for a set period of time. We often recommend Monday to Friday as a good half-way house towards giving it up. For our Year 11 facing exams, they commit to giving their smartphone up until their final exam. The reason the digital drop off is so important is because simply having the temptation of the smartphone at home can be too difficult to avoid. One of our Year 11 pupil's mums was willing to take the smartphone away for the Christmas holiday, but the pupil candidly said "Mum, I know I'll give in, and then you'll give in to my nagging. So I'm putting it in the safe." This kind of self-awareness and commitment only comes when the whole-school message is clear.

Blocking Distractions

Finally, we periodically run a "blocking distractions clinic" where parents can bring in the device in question, and a tech-savvy member of staff will help them put in the relevant blocks. These blocks may limit screen time, delete/block specific apps, or block distracting webpages. In many cases, the children have more technological know-how than their parents, and so the parents require our support to help them take control of how their child is using their devices. In praise of Apple, the "Screen Time" feature of the iPhone and iPad does allow close tracking of device usage and practical ways of limiting screen time on specific apps.

Meeting the parents at this event also provides a good opportunity to reassure them that they are doing the right thing. I met the parents of Rehan at the last clinic, who were describing how Rehan tries to manipulate them by saying they are making him depressed by not allowing him to play Fortnite, and deleting social media apps from the smartphone. I could see the pained expression on their faces. All the while, neither Rehan nor they were at all happy with his last exam results. Indeed, Rehan's attainment is far below the national average. I said to them that it would be tough, but that is because Rehan is addicted to these games. Once he gets over the addiction, his homework will improve, his grades will improve, and he will be much happier without the pressures social media puts on him.

After this conversation, Rehan's grades improved and his concentration at school was markedly better. Unfortunately, the parents gave in to his persistence after some time, and he has started using his PlayStation again. This kind of relapse is not uncommon. This just emphasizes why our pastoral model where the heads of year check in with particular pupils and parents consistently across the year is so important. In a similar way to the pupils, parents also need consistent messaging and encouragement to do the right thing.

But all is not lost. Sometimes I have said to Ms Birbalsingh that winning this battle feels almost impossible. In fact, sometimes I feel like I am undermining myself by talking about the dangers of tech so much, when the pupils continue to play as much PlayStation as ever. Part of our strategy though is one of building up a sense of guilt that they know they should not have a smartphone or PlayStation. Then when we get to Year 11, a blanket policy is that none of our pupils are allowed to have a smartphone. I am confident that my year group will be on board with the key messages, and know that if they don't give up their phone in Year 11 then they won't achieve what they want to. Time will tell, but if you speak to our first cohort of Sixth Formers, they are extremely attuned to the effect smartphones had on their GCSE grades. One recently said to me: "Mr Hurst we have to convince my [Year 9] sister to get off her phone now. I did it in Year 11, and I regret so much not doing it earlier. You just can't study properly if you have a smartphone."

The Do's and Dont's of Digital Detox

Do	Don't
Start your intervention and narration as early in the child's school career as possible (e.g. Year 6).	Expect people to give up technology without persistence on the school's part.
Discuss the dangers of technology at whole staff meetings to ensure alignment and that everyone understands how bad it is.	Believe pupils or parents when they say "I don't really use my technology that much, so I don't think giving it up would make much difference."
Create systems within school to support families and pupils to gradually wean themselves off the technology.	Give up. If you consistently raise awareness, then at some point the pupil will wake up to the reality of technology.

Michaela Family Lunch

Michael Taylor
@mike_taylor11

'One of the very nicest things about life is the way we must regularly stop whatever it is we are doing and devote our attention to eating.' – Luciano Pavarotti

Since time immemorial, humans have ritualised the process of eating food. The routine of eating used to be hugely symbolic. Tragically, it has become a functional activity with unfortunate consequences across all work places.

'Family Lunch' at Michaela is special. Every day, pupils and teachers eat together in a communal dining room, share conversation, serve each other and appreciate acts of kindness.

The role of good nutrition in boosting educational achievement has been well documented. Rather than outline why healthy eating is beneficial though, this chapter is intended to outline what makes our dining experience unique for both pupils and staff.

My first visit to Michaela was as a guest in 2015. During my introduction to the school, I was politely informed that I would be eating lunch with the pupils. After a tour of the school and some lesson observations, my young tour guides dutifully deposited me in the main dining hall, where the children were being addressed by a teacher. I was informed that I was to take a seat on a table with some pupils. Alarm bells started ringing in my head.

I was looking forward to my packed lunch, and chatting to staff to learn more about the school. Never mind, I thought. Slightly bemused, and with some trepidation, I sat down at a table of six pupils and awaited further instruction, whilst at the same time conducting a quick visual reconnaissance of ambush positions and suitable tactical escape routes.

'Roles one and two... GO!' I was jolted out of my Special Forces mind-set. The sudden movement gave me a shock. I made to duck, an image of meatballs in a rich Bolognese sauce on a ballistic trajectory flashed through my mind. However, I quickly managed to regain my composure. I needn't have worried.

The whole room was alive with activity. The food arrived at the table and the pupils began to serve portions to each other, starting with me. I immediately felt awkward. I could not put my finger on what was wrong. The penny dropped. The pupils seemed to have better table manners than I had.

The pupils readily engaged in conversation and I remember it vividly. One explained: 'Sir, every day we are given something to talk about whilst we are eating.' I enquired as to the conversation topic for that day. The pupils were to discuss the most inspirational person they had read about in history.

The pupil to my left kicked things off: 'In my opinion, the most inspirational person was Rosa Parks because she was the trigger for the civil rights movement in America.' A second pupil politely interjected: 'I really like Alexander Fleming. He invented penicillin.'

I pressed him further, to see if he knew any more. He continued: 'He invented penicillin in 1928 at Paddington Hospital. He really changed medicine and we all benefit from that today.' I continued to press the pupil, asking him why this was so significant. 'Well sir, I suppose we would all be living much shorter lives without him, so that's a really big thing.'

The first thing that struck me as a visitor was the level of knowledge that these twelve-year-old pupils were able to deploy. However, I was more impressed by the atmosphere of polite intellectual discourse that was so evidently a daily routine.

This is Family Lunch at Michaela.

Guests are astounded by the level of politeness and camaraderie that pervades the atmosphere. How is this achieved? Firstly, pupils are sat in a random seating plan to encourage them to mix with other children from their year who might not otherwise be in their immediate friendship circle. Within a short space of time, this has led to an incredible community ethic among the pupils. There are no groups who feel ostracised and no individual pupils who feel lonely. Lunch can be a difficult time for many children, particularly the younger or more vulnerable ones. Family Lunch ensures that they will always have a friendly, safe and convivial atmosphere in which to enjoy their food.

Each pupil has a role to play. One pupil serves the lunch, and another pours the water. The third pupil clears the plates and the fourth collects and serves the dessert. Finally, two pupils clear and clean the table. Practically speaking, this is an incredibly efficient way of doing things. Fundamentally, however, these pupils are learning how to help one another. They are learning how to serve each other, not just literally but in a figurative sense too. Family Lunch is designed so that the act of giving is given equal weight to the act of receiving.

Each table seats six pupils and one adult. We always eat with our pupils. This is the most valuable opportunity we have to teach the children good habits. Guests are always served first, and teachers are insistent that pupils use the correct table manners. Often, the children arrive at Michaela unable to correctly use a knife and fork. The food itself is always vegetarian, to enable all pupils from every ethnic, religious and cultural tradition to eat the same food together. Teachers lead pupils in a conversation topic, which is explained in the dining hall each day by the member of staff leading lunch.

Conversations are wide ranging and previous topics have included morals, culture, history, current affairs and the joys of reading. It provides us with an ideal opportunity to embed our values and to narrate the school's ethos every day. During important national events or anniversaries, the lunch topic will be about that particular day and on other days, the topic will be much more responsive, by giving the pupils a space to talk about current affairs and events in the wider world, or to help prepare them for something in the school calendar. On other days, we like to just have some fun! Riddles, imaginary scenarios, listing your favourite breakfast food or designing your perfect theme park are all examples of some of the light-hearted topics that are covered each week. One member of staff is tasked with setting the lunch topic each day, but all staff contribute with great ideas for conversation starters.

After the meal, we set aside five minutes in which the children are able to offer 'appreciations' to the rest of the cohort. They say a few words to thank somebody for an act of kindness. Two claps follow the address to appreciate the person in question.

Why do we do this? Think of your average school lunch hall. The noise would probably be the first thing you would think about. A clamouring of hands straining for food, surging and barging to get through. A din of loud conversations, if they can be called as such, accompanied by the not-so-dulcet tones of children shouting across the table and clanging cutlery on their plates. Younger pupils are pushed and shoved in the queue and more vulnerable children are left isolated. Dinner ladies shout frantically to restore order, and the children often respond in the same way they would treat a supply teacher.

The sense of dread that overcomes many teachers prior to their weekly lunch duty is a common theme. We all remember the cheers and jeers every time somebody dropped a tray of food. We remember the overworked and undervalued dinner ladies who would frantically clear up the mess, without any contribution from the offending pupil. We remember the fights that broke out and the surreptitious creation of edible projectile missiles that were flung across the room. Those who say this is a normal part of school life should evaluate what exactly this is teaching the children. More importantly, there will always be somebody who has to clear the mess up at the end. It is safe to assume that in many schools where this occurs, the children themselves are not those taking responsibility.

This is not the case in every dinner hall, but there is no denying the existence of one or many of these facts in most English secondary schools. Family Lunch avoids all of this, thus creating a happy, purposeful and caring environment in which to eat.

Instead of a canteen culture where pupils can leave their trays behind, expecting an anonymous cleaner to clean up after them, at Michaela, pupils not only clean up after themselves, they clean up after each other. They demonstrate kindness and a sense of responsibility. Family Lunch embodies the wider values of the school. We believe that in the same way we teach academic subjects, we must also explicitly teach soft skills and values such as empathy, responsibility, gratitude and kindness. Every single day we model these values at lunch, and provide opportunities for pupils to display the attributes which will enable them to live fulfilling lives.

> 'A good wine should always be accompanied by a good topic, and the topic should be pursued around the table with the wine.' – Roger Scruton

Substitute wine for a healthy and nutritious lunch, and this comes close to the underlying philosophy behind Family Lunch at Michaela. Many children do not have the chance to sit down at a dinner table at home. Through such a simple routine, we give the pupils this opportunity. Studies have shown that eating at a table with others increases children's confidence and boosts their concentration. According to Snow and Beals in *Mealtime Talk that Supports Literacy Development*, children who eat at a formal dinner table have also been shown to dramatically improve their vocabulary when compared to those that do not eat at a formal dinner table with an adult.

Ultimately, what we do every day builds the pupils' cultural literacy, enabling them to access the mannerisms and habits of some of their wealthier peers. It is perfectly reasonable to assume that many of our pupils will be able to achieve great things academically. There is also no doubt that many of our frontier cohort will attend prestigious Russell Group universities. What is less clear, however, is how well hard-working and academic high achievers will do in environments where their peers are from far wealthier backgrounds. It is true that many students who attend prestigious ancient universities from working-class backgrounds can often feel intimidated by their peers. By building their characters through Family Lunch, they are less likely to find it difficult to hold their own against classmates who have had a radically different upbringing. At Family Lunch, we teach pupils the soft skills of conversation. An eleven-year-old who is able to hold a conversation with an adult over dinner, whilst exhibiting exemplary manners, is just beginning that process which will enable them to survive and thrive in any environment.

Family Lunch is one of the many ways in which we aim to create well-rounded citizens, enabling them to engage with people from all walks of life. This manifests itself during the five minutes set aside for appreciations. Pupils are required to project to a room of over 150 pupils, teachers and visitors. They often thank their teachers, classmates and those who work behind the scenes to make their school experience so unique. The children are always looking out for opportunities to thank people. I remember, during my second visit to Michaela, being pleasantly surprised when a pupil stood up and thanked me for the lesson I had taught for my interview earlier that morning. Pupils are prompted by teachers to be grateful and kind to others and Family Lunch provides the perfect opportunity to model this. It is clear from the beaming smiles and words of thanks at the end of each lesson that gratitude has become a heart-warming characteristic of Michaela pupils.

In addition to embedding gratitude in their daily life, giving appreciations offers them a superb opportunity for public speaking. Family Lunch provides them with the confidence that is so often only the preserve of pupils at the best private schools.

We insist all pupils take part in Family Lunch. The ethos of Family Lunch is so central to the underlying philosophy of what we do; it is absolutely critical that every pupil partakes in this wonderful tradition. Crucially, it also means that no child is ever allowed to go hungry at Michaela. At too many schools, children may never get a healthy and nutritious meal at school. If a child's lunch money is stolen at another school, that pupil may not eat that day. If a child's parents do not give them lunch money, that child will go hungry. This would never happen at Michaela.

At Michaela, we believe in developing children's habits in addition to their knowledge.

Our mantra is 'work hard, be kind.' Lunch is the perfect time to teach our children how to be kind and helpful towards each other. We are teaching our pupils valuable lifelong lessons: the art of fine dining and conversation needs to be taught as explicitly as mathematics, history or science.

We hope that the prospect of a middle-class dinner party, or a formal meal at an Oxbridge college would never daunt a Michaela pupil who has experienced five years of Family Lunch.

What we do transforms our pupils' lives. The utter delight of enjoying a good meal, and discussing wonderful topics of great weight is something that is fast disappearing in today's 'grab and go' society. In the culturally impoverished and technologically saturated world of the contemporary teenager, Family Lunch at Michaela provides a beacon of civility.

TEACHING

Thinking Hard and Asking Questions: AFL at Michaela

Dani Quinn

I recently had interesting conversations with two of our weakest pupils: pupils who struggled academically in every lesson, who struggled with the basics of being organised and who generally seemed to be in a dream world.

Fadekah was such a pupil last year in Year 7. She was very sweet, but she never did her homework and, when chastised by her form tutor, she would giggle or put on a dopey expression, as if to say, "I'm cute and helpless and can't do anything". Everything seemed to pass her by. In my maths classes, she struggled with the simplest of abstract concepts and did not even know her times tables. She did not know what number comes before 1000, no matter how often I reminded her of that number. In lessons, she did little work, so I could not see how she could achieve a Grade 1, let alone a 4 or 5, in Y11. We teachers despaired over her, wondering how she would even be able to choose and microwave her own meals!

How would she complete routine tasks to earn a wage, let alone have meaningful and dignified employment and a fulfilling life?

Now, in Year 8, Fadekah is in my class again. On the first day of school, she was the star of the lesson. That night she did her homework .... and the next night, and the next ... She now frequently approaches me to ask questions about what was taught and takes copious notes, recording tips and explanations that I gave in lessons. She can explain her notes in her own words (even if simplistic or revealing an occasional misconception). Her quiz results are now typical of the class, even though she finds the material difficult to grasp and often feels challenged by the content. Her questions are insightful and thoughtful. She gets her homework in early, often doing more than was asked of her. She no longer needs to be corrected in lessons for not listening or not trying; in fact, she is often cited as a role model (which brings out a beaming grin from her every time).

At the end of September, I was compelled to ask Fadekah, "What happened? Why have you changed?"

Her answer: "I decided I wanted to do well, so I decided I would do my homework and do work in class".

THAT WAS IT!

She had nothing more to add. She just decided to do it…and she did it.

The other student with whom I recently spoke is Jana. Before this year, Jana had appalling results in maths and every other subject. She seemed to struggle to answer the most basic questions (i.e. How do you get home? 4 + 10 = ?). I assumed she must have a very low processing speed and a very limited working memory. Even an instruction like, "Pick up your whiteboard pens", seemed to be received on delay. Last November, I decided that my approach with her of being helpful and understanding was not the right one; she was only achieving marks of 10% in year group exams where the average exceeded 70%. So, I tried being tough with her. Thereafter in lessons, if I asked a simple question that she could not answer, I would tell her the answer, then ask her the question again. If she still could not answer the question (i.e. she had not listened), I would give her a demerit. Sometimes, she got two demerits which equal a detention. I worried that I was punishing a child who possibly had a fundamental problem. Yet, at lunchtime and in the yard, I could see Jana speaking in an animated and normal way with her friends, and there was no evidence in her file of any significant cognitive problems.

Amazingly, at the start of this year's September term, Jana was different, just like Fadekah. Though Jana does not learn quickly, her working now is always clear and leads to good quality solutions. Her errors make sense and are typical of any Year 8 student. As long as thinking time is provided, her hand is always up, she answers everything and asks good questions. She is earning lots of praise and her teachers admire her work ethic.

I was bewildered. I asked Jana, "What has changed with you?"

She said, "I realised that if I listen, I'll get it".

I admit to being torn between a sense of fury and delight, but the change in Jana is wonderful. She has stopped looking worried and lost in lessons, and seems to enjoy maths. She is proud of what she is producing, so I suspect she will not turn back.

One of my colleagues shared a similar story with me. When she asked Brendan about his transformation, his answer was simple: "I decided I should try working instead of daydreaming, and now, the work seems really easy".

These experiences underline for me how much of pupils' underachievement might have a simple explanation. More often than not, if a child cannot do what most other pupils in the same class are succeeding with, I think it is probably because:

- They are not listening properly

- They are not really thinking

- They hope they can fly under the radar with minimal effort

- They are not embarrassed to appear intellectually 'weak' (which is probably the hardest to empathise with, for a teacher!)

They may not be disruptive, but they are not learning. Instead, they are squandering their precious time at school, and their potential.

Normally, few pupils will get good results or have good life opportunities if they stay stuck in this rut. We teachers need to motivate and inspire these students by constantly stressing to them the need to listen carefully, think deeply and be accountable for their work, both on the page and in their heads.

Working with the rest of the maths department and Head of Science, we came up with some teaching strategies to address this.

Strategies for pushing more accountability onto the pupils

1. After an explanation or an example, pose questions that put the onus on the pupils to seek more help or clarification:

- "Who needs me to explain that more?"

- "Who would like to see another example?"

- "Who needs me to say it in a different way?"

- "Who needs me to ask them a question?"

- "Who would like to check a bit of that?"

Of course, it is essential that your voice and body language is neutral or encouraging, and not impatient. It should be that you expect that they would take responsibility for learning and understanding and that you want to see some of them asking for more instruction or support.

2. 'No Opt Out' (described in Doug Lemov's *'Teach Like a Champion'*). This comes into play when a pupil doesn't know an answer to a question (typically questions seeking an explanation, a definition or a description of a process). Lemov describes well the why and the how. In summary:

a. Pupil A doesn't know the answer

b. Tell Pupil A you will come back to him in a few seconds (eventually this can be dropped, provided you are consistent about (c) and (d))

c. The answer/explanation is supplied, either by you or by another pupil

d. Go back to Pupil A and ask the question again.

e. If correct: Say "Well done, you went from not knowing [thing] to being able to say it". (I know this is a shallow description of 'knowing'! It is the first of many steps...).

f. If incorrect: give a consequence for not listening / opting out. The consequence might simply be your disapproval or an admonishment; it may be a demerit or a 'warning.'

Levelling up: Pre-empt the risk of resentment (i.e. that the pupils might think that you are trying to 'catch' them, not help them). Narrate why it is important to listen carefully and be ready for the teacher to return to them. Encourage pupils to remind you to come back to them (by putting hands up politely), thanking them for reminding you and for taking responsibility for being held accountable. Praise it as behaviour that shows they really want to learn, that it is a sign of being 'grown up.'

3. If a pupil looks a little spaced out or disengaged, or often is a poor listener, say a variation of "I am about to ask three/five questions. You'll be picked for one of them." Make sure you pick them or you will lose credibility! Many teachers in our school have a post-it on their desk for each class of the 'most worrying' children (academically), to remind them to frequently check those pupils' focus and understanding in order to close the gap between them and the rest.

4. Everybody answers: before you accept answers to a question, every pupil writes their answer down. This gives more thinking time to the slower thinkers. It also holds them accountable, as it is visible if a pupil is writing or not. This is common in maths with the use of whiteboards (provided there is a good routine in place for pupils to write the work in a secretive fashion and show it simultaneously, so that pupils can't copy each other).

5. Describe – and enforce – the body language you expect to see when you ask a question. These are the ones I typically expect and insist upon:

   a. Looking at the question on the board or page, with an expression that shows 'thinking' (no vacant expressions). This is usually a focused or intense face. Some pupils' faces really screw up when they're thinking, some look quite calm. Some are clearly 'rehearsing' their answer in their head. This depends on you knowing your pupils, but the absence of focused thought is generally quite obvious.

   b. Doing working on the sheet / whiteboard. Typically, in maths there are jottings for a calculation, or other things to relieve the burden on working memory. For another subject they might jot down a keyword they intend to use in their answer.

   c. Hand up, waiting to answer, or otherwise showing readiness through their body language.

An important caveat is that you focus on the goal (learning), not on control (how they sit or move). This must be narrated with warmth and earnestness. With some classes, I've said "If you look at me once I've asked the question, instead of looking at the diagram, I will know you are wasting thinking time. That means we'll have to wait for you, and is stealing time from the people who started thinking straight away." I've moved to giving a small consequence if they persist in it after the warning. That might seem harsh, but the explanation of why I do it means the pupils seem to find it very fair (it's always palpable when pupils think something is unjust!). The quality and pace of responses has jumped up since I started this, making me wish that I'd moved to this sooner!

6. Give more thinking time for questions. We all think we do it. We all know we don't! A colleague pointed out that, for our many EAL pupils, they must hear the question, translate to their home language, think about it, decide an answer, translate back to English and THEN put their hand up. It also puts positive pressure on both teacher and pupils:

    a. If more and more hands are gradually creeping up, the coasting pupils think "Yikes! Better think of an answer" as their non-participation is becoming obvious. If you really want to keep them on their toes, you can ask the 1-2 without hands up to tell you what the question was. If they know, but can't answer, that's fine. If they don't know... make clear this means they are throwing away a chance to learn and to test themselves. Think beforehand about what consequence is appropriate: a disapproving eyebrow-raise, a demerit..?

    b. If the number of hands going up stops, you know the problem is probably you: you need to tell them again, and make it clearer. You also might need to improve the question, so it is clearer.

7. Pause before asking for hands up. Give them thinking time, then say 'hands up.' This means many more hands go up at once (giving the message "It is normal to participate in this classroom" "It is normal to be eager to answer") and slower pupils aren't dispirited by their neighbour who has an answer before the teacher has finished speaking. Additionally, you can't see pupils' faces and reactions as well once hands are up, so a delay allows you to better read the room.

8. Show most of the question, but leave out the final element. This means no one can put hands up until you are ready, but they can begin thinking. For example, you could give this simplification: $4a^3 \times 5b^?$ and leave the question mark blank for 5 seconds, allowing them to plan their answer for the rest of the question. This gives the slower thinkers time to catch up, and creates a slight element of drama when the number under the question mark is revealed.

For a different subject, you could give a broad theme before a specific question, such as "I am going to ask about how Shakespeare presents Iago's character...start thinking about how his character is presented..."

9. For recaps when pupils seem unsure, give letter clues:

"What is the name for a triangle with two equal lengths and two equal angles?"

[few hands]

"It begins with i....."

[many hands]

[take an answer]

Ask the question again

To be clear: the strategy above is <u>not</u> helping them connect 'isosceles triangle' to the definition. It is probably only helping them to remember the name of a triangle that begins with i. But, it can be a good way for pupils to see that they know more than they realise, and to build up their confidence. It also helps you see if the problem is remembering a word, or about connecting it to a definition. However, you must be honest with yourself about what you can reasonably infer from a correct answer in that case (i.e. not very much).

10. Reverse the question. If you've asked a question, like the isosceles one above, you can reverse it straight away: "Tell me two special features of an isosceles triangle." Assuming you made sure that everyone listened to the first answer, it is now not acceptable to not know the answer. This makes clear to pupils that they need to really listen to your questions, not just jump to answers. In an ideal world, every question would be answered in a full sentence, to better improve the connections between two or more ideas "A triangle with two equal lengths is called an isosceles triangle" is much more powerful than "isosceles."

11. Interleave questions. If pupils are struggling to match together a word or procedure and its definition or process, or to explain a concept, you need to ask it several times. However, repeatedly asking the same question means pupils quickly start to parrot back sounds, rather than strengthen the connection between words and ideas. Interleaving the important question with other low-stakes facts that they know forces them to listen more carefully and to do more recall (rather than repetition). For example, if the key question is how to find the sum of angles in a polygon, you might mix

it in with easier questions like "What does n stand for in the formula?" and "Which polygon has an angle sum of 180?" and "What is the formula for the area of a triangle?" This forces more thinking and practice of contrasting the new answer (the formula) with other shapes that seem similar.

Make them accountable for helping you to check their understanding

The main challenge with pupils who are struggling is that they can be adept at disguising it. Many options for 'whole-class AFL' are technology heavy, or fiddly in one way or another. We like the following:

1. Heads down, fingers up: if the groundwork is done, this can be a very quick way to check understanding. It works best for questions with two options (yes/no or true/false) but can also work for answers given in a succinct way (jealous/angry/sad or 30/60/90).

    a. Pose a question (typically focused on misconceptions)

    b. Tell them that option 1 is 'I don't know' (avoid false negatives and false positives).

    c. Give time to think and decide secretly on an answer BEFORE heads go down. Tell them the options before heads go down, too. This avoids extended time with heads down, as it can disorient them.

    d. "Heads down!" Pupils put their heads down in the crook of their arms (to avoid a 'thunk' and bruised forehead!) and one hand resting on top of their head.

    e. The teacher calls out each of the options and pupils raise their hand up a small amount (so the movement is imperceptible to their neighbours). It is important the teacher gives the same amount of time for each possible option, and uses a neutral tone, so as not to give away the answer. Counting to 4 in your head can help.

    f. "Heads UP!" ...give them a few seconds to readjust to the light... Having their heads in the crook of their arms means they don't get as zoned out as having it straight on the desk, which is also helpful!

2. Routines for whiteboards that keep answers secret from each other need to be embedded for younger classes (e.g. writing with their body turned away from their partner, or cradling it as they write, if feasible). You must narrate why it is not only important not to look at others' boards, but also why keeping one's own board secrets is essential. Narrate how it might seem kind to let someone see your answer, but it is, in fact, unkind, as it stops others from getting the help they need.

3. When answers are given on whiteboards, praise good-quality written explanation. For example, I will pick out and praise the clearest workings, showing them to the rest of the class and praising how those helped me understand what they were thinking. A colleague encourages his pupils by intoning, in a very funny way "…let me see your brains."

Levelling up: I have recently moved to giving pupils demerits if they show me the wrong answer with no working. This has made a huge difference in two ways: it means that children who are quick thinkers are forced to slow down, so the others aren't intimidated or disheartened when they need more time. It also means I don't waste time trying to guess where they went wrong. Full working allows me to quickly identify the point of error and give better feedback. Because this was narrated and 'trialled' for a lesson, the pupils who got demerits for this weren't upset when they got a consequence and, more importantly, have changed their ways.

4. If you are faced with the problem of a big split between how many get it and how many don't, and you feel badly for the ones 'waiting around' for the rest, you can try:

a. Writing up the exercise they will do once you judge they understand it

b. Posing a question to check competency/understanding, telling them to wipe their board quickly and start the exercise if you tell them they're correct.

c. As you see each correct answer, simply say "correct/well done/ correct" and let them get on with it.

d. Get a show of hands of who has not started the exercise, then tell those pupils they are going to see more examples and be asked more oral questions. I find that, once I start on the re-teaching, many pupils then say "Oh! I get it now" and then they join in the written exercise, quickly narrowing down how many I am trying to help.

Laying the ground for purposeful written work

Strategies that I've tried and seen others use to good effect are:

1. For short-form questions (i.e. those requiring only 1-2 steps), go through it first as an oral drill, cold-calling pupils. Then, use it as a written exercise. There are several benefits: every pupil has had a chance to ask for clarification on questions where they don't understand why that was the answer, or to note down hints to help them start it on their own; pupils can begin work quickly and in earnest, knowing that it is something they can do with more confidence; you get twice as much 'bang for your buck' with an exercise. This works best for things that are highly procedural, but I think it also works well for questions where the 'way in' must be found. If a good chunk of the exercise has been done orally, the written attempt will still require them to recall and decide how to begin.

2. Drill on step 1: If the exercise is focused on decision-making (e.g. an exercise mixing all fraction operations, where the main challenge is that pupils must work out different procedures for different questions), it can be done as an oral drill just for step 1.

For example, "For question a, what will you need to do? Find the LCD. Question b, Find the reciprocal and multiply." This can be a lower-stakes version of the exercise to allow you to check how ready they are before embarking on the more extended task of completing the calculations.

3. Before starting exercises, particularly more extended ones, or quite visual ones (e.g. an angle chase), give the pupils 30-60 seconds to scan for any that they might not know how to start. Then, give hints and tips for those (depending on the pupils, you might model a very similar one on the board for them to look at when they get to it). This prevents you from running around from pupil to pupil as they encounter the problem, and gives them confidence when they get to it...and no excuse for just sitting there waiting instead of attempting it!

4. If several pupils are struggling with the same thing, or asking the same question, or making the same mistake: STOP THE WORK! Make them all listen to the additional instruction, explanation or example. This prevents you from creating lots of low-level noise as you help others, and gives help straightaway to them all.

Culture of Thinking: do I understand this?

The ideal situation is that pupils themselves are thinking deeply about what is being taught. This usually can be observed when they ask question in the form:

Did _____ happen because _____?

Is _____ like this because _____ is like that?

If that is the case, does that mean that _____ is the case?

Is this similar to the way that _____?

I thought that because _____ we couldn't _____?

What happens if you try it with 0 / 1 / 2 / a negative number / a non-integer / a power?

I think there is a pattern in this. Is it _____?

Will the answer always be positive/negative/an integer/a multiple of __?

I have an idea to help remember it: _____.

Praise such contributions! Show your delight that their brains are in top gear. Narrate that this is the sort of thinking that makes someone good at your subject, and makes it stick as they are forming connections with other ideas. Their memories of the ideas will be richer and more powerful. You can also narrate how this is beneficial to the other pupils, and to you as a teacher, and express gratitude.

Culture of Thinking: What do I need if I want to succeed?

A good place to get to is if the pupils themselves identify what they need, and flag it up. This is usually seen with questions like "Could we try one first on whiteboards?" or "Could you show another example, please?" or "Could we do another question together before we begin writing?" This means they are really thinking about if they understand something (or, can complete a procedure) and aren't relying on teacher validation. Things that can help to bring this about:

Narrating why you show examples

Narrating what you want them to think about when you explain things, or show examples

Narrating what they should annotate and why

Narrating why you are asking questions

Narrating what should be happening in their minds when they think about something

As above, narrate how this is beneficial to the other pupils. You can even say "Who is glad that _____ asked that? Next time you can be the person who everyone else is thanking, by being alert and giving me helpful advice."

Miscellaneous suggestions

1. Choral response is nice to deploy to help practise new and difficult pronunciations (combustibility, hypotenuse, consecutive, and so on). It is utterly pointless otherwise, unless it is being used to make pupils think. Choral response is great for questions like,

1. $a^1 = ?$

2. $a^0 = ?$

3. $1^a = ?$

4. $0^a = ?$

...but is pointless if they are simply repeating sounds. It needs to help them put ideas together, or be a low-stakes way to practise recall of facts or saying tricky words.

2. Use as many memory aids and links as you can. The more ways that pupils can recall something and know that they are remembering correctly, the better. There is no use in a pupil correctly recalling the process to find the median if they doubt they have it correct. That is nearly as bad as not remembering at all, as it will feel futile to proceed. Even the weirdest memory aids can be valuable: my Y9s suggested remembering median with two prompts: (1) think of it as medIaN, because it is IN the middle, and (2) it sounds like 'medium', and medium is the middle size. These are not sophisticated, but it allows them to have two ways to recall the process, and two ways to feel they are on the right path. As always, don't muddle *aides memoires* with actual understanding.

3. Set a goal for the lesson. Our deputy head described this as being what a learning objective was meant to be (as opposed to exercise in the time-wasting that can be seen – and enforced – in many classrooms today). I sometimes start the lesson by silently modelling an example of the kind of question I hope they'll be able to do by the end, then putting a very similar question right by it. This will be on the left of the whiteboard. Then I use the remainder of the whiteboard during the lesson. Often I can be only 15 minutes into the lesson before (some) pupils' hands shoot up, thinking they know how to answer the 'goal question.' This puts positive pressure on the others, as it gives the message "We've been taught enough to be able to do this! You need to keep up!" and lets pupils feel smart, and feel intellectually rewarded, for paying careful attention.

4. Have a set of stock phrases to denote things that REALLY matter and make them feel motivated to push themselves mentally. Our head of science uses phrases such as

"I'll bet my bottom dollar this will be on your GCSEs"

"I'm already thinking, I bet Fadekah will do a really good job and lay this out really clearly..."

"I am already predicting that a lot of people in the back row will be so focused when we do this..."

"This is the sort of question that only pupils who get an A* can do"

"Pupils who master this always find A-level much easier"

I hope these strategies are useful to you. We are trying everything we can to get 100% of our pupils to do well in their GCSEs (and generally, to be smart and confident people). These strategies are, of course, in the context of a school culture that celebrates curiosity, a love of learning and the belief that hard work is the path to success. This chapter focused on some concrete behaviourist strategies, which are relatively easy to implement. They have their place within our broader aim of getting pupils to focus on big goals for the future and to become intrinsically motivated to be an educated and confident person.

The Culture of Feedback

Abi Smith
@abiasmith5

'Leave your ego at the door'

'Leave your ego at the door' is among the many pieces of advice Katharine gave me when I joined Michaela as a Maths Teacher in January 2017, after just over three years teaching in Derbyshire. Until recently, I had misunderstood this piece of advice completely: I had never before considered my 'ego' to be a problem as I associated ego with hubris and an overly-confident manner, far from my own natural manner. I now understand that ego is as much a problem for me as anybody else. It just manifests itself in a way I had not recognised: in trying to keep up appearances and cover up mistakes.

Why not keep up appearances? In many schools, teachers are faced with a couple of high-stakes observations each academic year. From this, teachers are expected to improve on a few teaching and learning targets which then contribute to performance-related pay. It is understandable that many teachers, knowingly or otherwise, cover up the day-to-day worries of 'perhaps I didn't explain that topic particularly well' or even, 'behaviour in my Year 9 class is so bad; I'm just altogether embarrassed'. It has taken me a while, but I now recognise that through trying to cover up my faults, my ego held me back from seeking the feedback that would have helped me to improve so much faster.

At Michaela, there is nowhere to hide: we have an open-door culture and so a colleague or visitor could wander into our classrooms at any moment throughout the day. And they do, pretty much every day. More importantly, though, there is no need to hide. Colleagues genuinely give feedback to help one another improve, not to tick boxes and not to undermine or catch anybody out. This is why, when a colleague or visitor arrives, there is no need to suddenly change course and put on a performance or to produce pages of paperwork such as seating plans or lesson plans. I used to feel so nervous at the thought of anybody being in my classroom and would feel obliged to spend several hours the night before planning the lesson. Now, I just continue teaching as normal. After all, it benefits the whole staff body to create a strong team of teachers, where pupils receive the same expectations and the same high quality teaching from classroom to classroom, every day, with no weak links in the chain.

In this chapter, I will discuss:

1. What feedback looks like – the practicalities of giving feedback.

2. Using feedback to train new staff – how we give feedback that focuses on teacher presence and routines.

3. Everyday feedback – how we give subject-specific and pupil-specific feedback.

4. Why it works – including the benefits of an open-door culture, how we learn to respond to feedback and how having shared values is the key to making these feedback methods successful.

What feedback looks like

In general, feedback at Michaela is regular and low-stakes. We have no proforma to follow. We simply go into the classroom and write out a feedback email on our phones while observing. We don't stick to a strict ratio of positives to negatives: instead, we give feedback as and when it is needed. Feedback is then sent in email form, comprising anywhere between one and ten bullet points. We copy in the Senior Leadership Team (SLT) and Heads of Departments (HoDs) to all our feedback emails, giving them a picture of what is happening around the school. Feedback is non-hierarchical: as well as giving and receiving feedback from newer staff, teachers are encouraged to give feedback to HoDs, Heads of Year (HoYs) and SLT.

Using feedback to train new staff

We believe in teachers having authority, a strong presence and great relationships with their classes. So when giving feedback, particularly at the beginning, these are the questions at the forefront of our thinking:

◆ Does the teacher's body language show to the pupils that they are the authority?

◆ Is the teacher using their face/voice effectively to give them presence?

♦ Is the teacher achieving a good balance of warm/strict?

I had never before considered in so much detail the way that I stand, the tone of my voice and the use of my facial expressions which can really make the difference between being a good teacher and being an inspirational teacher who really drives their class forward.

During the first two weeks of September, our Year 7s have 'Bootcamp'. This is not just a bootcamp for our new pupils, it is also a bootcamp for our new staff. For the first two days, new staff are given the chance to observe experienced Michaela staff teach in the Michaela style. For the rest of Bootcamp, all new staff are observed for all of their lessons as a chance to refine the Michaela routines, without needing to focus on subject content. This means receiving very direct feedback. For example: stand still instead of pacing, use a more authoritative voice when doing a countdown, or cut out 'umm' and 'errr' to come across as more assertive.

Once term starts for the rest of the school, new staff will continue to observe established staff, often two or three times a day, popping into their classrooms for around ten minutes at a time and writing feedback based on what they have seen, some examples being 'you open up your eyes really widely to highlight important parts and to keep them on their toes' or 'I like how you lean in over your visualiser when you are giving them a challenge. It draws the pupils in!' Observing others also helps to build up a bank of familiar phrases which helps to establish an individual teacher's authority at Michaela: several times a day, pupils will hear 'strong spines!', 'tracking me', 'strong hands!' and 'great projection!'

What may be striking is that nothing I have mentioned so far is revolutionary. Ask anybody, 'to come across as confident, should you pace about or stand still?' and the answer is obvious. Yet the beauty of feedback at Michaela is that we can discuss candidly 'how you come across': this allows for honest reflection and a chance to refine body language and tone of voice. We tackle habits such as saying 'okay' a lot, having a tone of voice that comes across as too high or too low, or coming across as nervous or uncertain by talking too fast. These are habits that the pupils themselves will pick up on in an instant but can sometimes go unnoticed by the teacher themselves. Feedback is not restricted to the classroom alone: it is given on corridor presence, duties and one-to-one conversations with pupils. For example, 'stand here when on duty in the stairwell to give yourself more presence and a better view of the pupils' or 'make sure to remind the pupil to maintain eye contact when you are speaking to them'.

For new staff, feedback can feel very overwhelming at the start: teachers might receive three or four emails a day with various points of feedback, as well as trying to take in everything they have seen. It is like completing teacher training all over again and at first, it is exhausting! Our philosophy is this: the faster new staff can adjust and assert themselves, the faster they can feel confident and adapt Michaela-isms to their own teaching personality. Although it is incredibly hard work at the time, it makes life so much easier once routines are embedded.

Everyday feedback

As staff become more accustomed to the Michaela routines, feedback takes a natural shift towards more subject-specific feedback and pupil-specific feedback, fine-tuning the pedagogy within the department as well as focusing on getting the most out of every individual in the class.

Subject-specific feedback

Before Michaela, my experience of feedback was far more black and white. Every term, my teaching skills were compartmentalised into 'strengths' or 'working on', based on just one lesson observation. With observations few and far between, and performance management cycles to adhere to, it is easy to see why many schools fall into this pattern. However, one huge disadvantage of such a system is that it encourages teachers to neglect the big pedagogical picture in the name of gimmicks and ticking boxes: just because 'planning' was a strength for me for Year 10 Set 2 on Thursday morning, it does not mean that 'planning' is a strength for me forevermore; just because Assessment for Learning (AfL) is my target this term, it doesn't mean that for every lesson, this should be prioritised over other aspects of teaching, for example, behaviour management or delivering clear explanations. In reality, strengths and weaknesses are fluid and impacted by a variety of factors, such as class, topic or time of the day.

At Michaela, we have a sustained focus on developing subject knowledge and pedagogy so that we can deliver strong explanations and effectively challenge our pupils' thinking. It follows that the most frequent visitor to my classroom is the Head of Maths. Instead of feedback consisting of generalised targets that are designed to last a term, the Head of Maths will visit my classroom several times a term and will analyse particular moments in the lesson, offering very specific advice each time. Sometimes, the feedback will be standalone and it is down to the individual teacher to make sure they implement the feedback given. Often, the feedback feeds into a bigger focus. As an example, I received this piece of feedback from my HoD:

When you asked "How do I generate the first term [of a sequence]?" don't just accept answers for the specific sequence – push them for a generalised answer, for example 'I want to know how to find the first term of any sequence, using the word "substitute"'.

Following this, we then had many conversations within department meetings about pushing our pupils for generalised answers to help them articulate and remember mathematical processes better. Using my HoD's suggested phrasing, I was able to incorporate this concept in my following lesson and now this is a technique I use regularly.

Here are a few examples of subject-specific feedback that has been given from other subjects:

Science:

 ♦ "What directly causes movement?" I think this question was unclear. But you picked up on this when two pupils gave unclear answers. You re-explained and asked pupils to repeat what you said. I think it would be useful to pay attention to the command word here and plan your question accordingly e.g. 'Describe how the forces acting on the rectangular coil cause it to rotate?' Perhaps it would also be useful to get pupils to use the term 'the motor effect'?

 ♦ You used two calculations to illustrate what a more efficient car would be like; their values for useful output were different despite having that same inputs. This could have been much better achieved with diagrams: it reduces the cognitive demand of the comparison. I've attached an example I used with my class. This segment could have benefited from lots of pairwise comparisons. E.g. here are two diagrams of light bulbs: show the same input and different outputs. Ask, which is more efficient? Why?

- Consider the level of challenge minute by minute in your lesson. I think you could have structured the lesson to add more challenge. For example, you took a few minutes to explain and practise what an anomaly is. Could you have shown them quickly and prepared some challenging questions to spot tables/graphs where there both were and were not anomalies? In this instance, the practice in spotting them is more important than reciting the definition.

- You constantly use concrete examples as we've discussed in department meetings to ensure pupils are following more generalised scientific ideas. For example, 'standards of living' came up and you immediately described how even 50 years ago far more people used to live in one house with shared bathroom facilities at the back of the garden, compared to today.

English:

- I absolutely loved the way you introduced the story of the poem. You used your voice so powerfully to create lots of drama and your pauses were really effective in keeping them with you.

- I think you could spend a bit more time using the images and linking them to key quotations to help them to really visualise the story/ empathise with the speaker before they dive into the poem. Let's run through some examples of this after school.

- They asked if Wordsworth was scared by the mountain and you replied 'Yes', but without explaining more. They accepted that was correct, but I'm not sure they fully *got* it. I think that it's worth spending some time helping them to relate to the emotions/thoughts of the speaker, otherwise they will struggle to articulate the experience. Essentially, they will find it a bit strange and silly that Wordsworth was scared by a mountain (understandable!). You could liken it to experiences that they can relate to, for example the feeling you might experience when looking down from a very tall building or an aeroplane, or looking up at the enormous sky. Again, images might be helpful here. Then if they can 'feel' that emotion a little bit more it helps them to empathise with the speaker and really *get* what he wants us to understand about the human experience.

- Quite a few were uncertain about the True/False questions. You felt it but got them to carry on. If you feel they're boggled, it's fine to stop them and instead go through the ideas with TTYP (Turn To Your Partner), or re-teaching them if they're really stuck. That's the purpose of that check for understanding – it's fine if they haven't quite got it so long as you then adapt accordingly.

French:

- When you say "which is the verb 'to go'?" but the answer is 'va' it's a bit confusing. Maybe just ask them for 'is going'.

- Have a listen to pronunciation of appareils on WordReference. You were wavering between two each time you said it.

- Did you link it back to the knowledge grid at the end of the lesson? It will be a great feeling for them to be able to read it more fluently now that you've broken all the sounds down.

Humanities:

- Anna gave a wish-washy answer to the provenance section. Later, Farhiya also gave an answer not using facts. The way you improved it was good: you got them to go back and start with some knowledge about Cromwell/the Pilgrimage of Grace, then say what the authors wanted, then say what was exaggerated – this made their answers much better. I think the way to teach it is to tell them that this is what they need to do for the provenance: 1) give a fact about author, audience, or period; 2) purpose, i.e what did the author want the audience to do?; 3) ask, what is exaggerated or left out? They are getting to good answers, and should be fine in the exam. Embedding the steps above, and drilling kids on them at KS3 will get them to clearly know what makes a good answer, and be able to produce one for any source.

- Fewer re-cap questions in more depth is better, as you cover a much broader range of content more quickly. Also, how much mixed practice are you doing on the Anglo-Saxons? It strikes me that some of that re-cap time needs to be much more focused on the last unit.

◆ Keep going back to why these terms would have angered Germans. The war guilt clause in particular needs to be laboured and you need to hone your storytelling here. Be more visceral in describing the palpable anger felt in Germany in 1919. You used a few adjectives to describe how Germany was feeling. Be much more vivid when describing why things were so bad.

◆ You pointed out how Izzie had used the word 'Protestant' and why this was important. This was on the examiner's report this year 'Too many pupils are using "some Christians"'. I need to make sure I correct pupils more frequently.

◆ When covering European countries and capitals, make sure you pre-empt the spelling of difficult ones. Pre-empt classic mistakes before the lesson and refer to them constantly. Madrid is a common one that they get wrong – I saw a few at the back spelling it as 'Midrid' (because that's how they hear it). I used to always say 'I'd be really MAD if you spelt this wrong' to help them remember.

Maths:

◆ When describing what profit is, use a tangible example: instead of saying 'I buy something for £3 then sell it for £5', say 'If I buy *this pen* for £3 then I sell it *to Mohamed* for £5...'

◆ Kurtis said "angles on a triangle sum to 180" and you rounded up to say "yes, angles in a triangle sum to 180". A lot of the pupils mis-draw angles (e.g. to be outside a shape, to be at the midpoint of a line instead of at a vertex). Be REALLY tight about prepositions for these things, especially given that the values 'on' the shape are its lengths, and those 'in' the shape are its angles (i.e. a core matter for this topic!)

◆ For the ratio calculation with 45%, I think there is a clearer 'catch-all' model you can use. It made a difference for 11X when they were in Y10, and you can use it for shape, etc, too. Write the word sentence, and the number sentence below it:

reading + not reading = total time

45% + ? = 100%

They then solve using balancing, which they are good at, and they can expand that method for lots of scenarios. I would also spend a bit of time with them on 'the rest' (always underline it when there is a 'the rest' situation and write in the amount) and on the difference between

- if we know the percentage for 'brown', we can find the percentage for 'not brown'

- if we know the percentage for 'brown', we can't necessarily find the percentage for 'blonde'

♦ I wonder if you could make this sort of investigation less structured? A key value in this kind of topic is that it allows them to form conjecture and trial methods and reflect on dead ends. At the moment it is being presented more as 'this is a good way to tackle this question' with snippets of 'how might you deal with this?' Given that the thinking is more important than the method for something like this (and for several parts of the Y7 curriculum from 7.1's perspective), this is a good chance for you to push yourself away from feeling you must always structure and scaffold (which is right for weaker and less confident groups, and which you do very well). I know we have touched on it before, and this isn't something you feel confident about, so let's plan to discuss it more and think about how you can trial it more with them as they will be very receptive, I expect!

♦ A few of them attempted to solve $64 + x^2 = 4x^2$ as $8 + x = 2x$. I showed Dan how $3 + 4 \neq 5$ and he seemed satisfied, but then happier when I showed it wasn't solving properly with the (inverse) order of operations. Maybe worth clarifying for them all?

Music:

♦ I was pleasantly surprised at the volume with 9H – I'll need some tips from you to get 9F to sing louder. I could see that you were doing your best to encourage participation and your enthusiasm came across well and genuine. Your counting in was very clear.

♦ I think they really need some ear/pitch training. So for example at the very start, after your warm up, do some pitch exercises – e.g. you sing a note (or a short phrase like do-re-do) and they need to sing it back, give them feedback e.g. row by row, and tweak/drill it until say 70% of the class is at/near your pitch. Get them to do the hand elevator thing so they know they are singing up and down with you.

♦ As this was the first lesson, I know a big part of today was gauging what kind of singing class they are going to be. But next lesson, once you start the song, don't be satisfied with the majority being so out of tune. Marie and Abdul are quite in tune so encourage people to listen out for their voices. Harry is very loud, but not in tune in the slightest – so if you hear him improve then you know you're going in the right direction. You could try massively slowing down the song and get them to match pitch (70%) phrase by phrase.

Pupil-specific feedback

Two sets of eyes are certainly better than one: teachers at Michaela will often feed back to the teacher on individual pupils so that the teacher can pick up on behaviours they might not have previously noticed before. This could be, for example, 'Beth is not really putting her hand up'. This allows us to identify the pupils who are falling behind or not putting in maximum effort and to hold them to higher standards. Recently, a colleague noticed that a particular pupil was taking much longer than everybody else in the class to start working. I now know to pay closer attention to this pupil at the start of the exercise and remind them to start their work quickly. Form tutors often observe their forms in different lessons to help build up a strong picture of how their tutees are performing in lessons.

The benefits of an open-door culture

Feedback is part of a normal working week at Michaela and this means that we are able to constantly develop our teaching through a combination of observing and being observed (though we usually avoid the word 'observing' altogether, using 'giving/receiving feedback' instead).

One of the greatest benefits of having an open-door culture is being able to take action immediately. Naturally, observations arranged in advance do not always give a true representation of a normal day-to-day lesson – it is far too tempting for teachers to want to show only their best. Here, there is no need to pre-arrange an observation in a week's time. Whenever I feel as though my teaching is becoming a little stale, I can walk down the corridor and watch another lesson to give me a fresh perspective. Open-doors give teachers a true sense of what is happening around the school on a daily basis and opens up far more opportunities for development, for both the observer and the observed.

Another huge benefit of open-doors is creating a sense of omnipresence. What better way to make your presence felt with a new class or to build relationships with a class than to go and observe them in their other lessons? Let's say my Year 10 class were a bit flat during Period 1 – I'd go and watch them in Science, Period 4. If my Year 7 tutees received a lot of detentions in Humanities today, I'd pop into their Humanities lesson tomorrow. This has allowed me to forge much stronger relationships with my pupils than ever before. It is so heart-warming to see a pupil's face light up when they hear 'you were on fire in French today – well done!'

There are plenty of motivated professionals across the country who are looking to observe and learn from their colleagues, as well as bravely inviting others into their classroom to observe their worst classes: for these teachers, I have the highest respect. Unfortunately, some teachers are not this brave. I used to be one of these teachers. There can be an observation culture in some schools where teachers cannot leave their egos at the door and feel safer powering on behind closed doors for fear of judgement if they should do otherwise. What makes the culture at Michaela different from other schools is that honest feedback is seen as a priority by all and we are free to observe anybody at any time. Above all, I would encourage any school to adopt an open-door policy to encourage a healthier culture of feedback and development.

How to respond to feedback

Undoubtedly, feedback can be hard to swallow at times. I remember some of my own feedback emails saying 'you looked nervous' or 'your explanation of question 2 was a bit of a fudge – I got muddled'. In this situation, it is very tempting to start to justify your decisions by replying with 'this happened because...' or 'I did that because...' When I first joined Michaela, I had this temptation almost all the time. But I have learnt that part of 'leaving your ego at the door' is fighting the temptation to justify your decisions. In fact, it is actively discouraged. I realised that I had likely wasted a lot of energy in the past by dwelling on the negatives and trying to justify them, to myself or to others, however small they might have been. Our shared attitude towards such feedback is to remember that our colleagues will always appreciate that there may have been rationale behind your decision to do X and not Y in that moment in the lesson. By giving you feedback, they are simply identifying that it was the wrong decision this time, or it did not achieve the desired effect. This is nothing personal, just an aspect of your practice to be improved upon or considered more deeply. This does not mean that we simply follow feedback blindly, either. If there is something in the feedback that indicates that the person watching has misunderstood, we may just ignore that bit of the feedback and use the rest. In other cases, the feedback may provoke further discussion. What is important is to use the feedback wisely to reflect and take action, rather than to waste time by being defensive or justifying decisions.

Now, I would feel far more embarrassed to continue to make mistakes every day than to hear it once in a feedback email and to move on. By avoiding the temptation to justify every piece of negative feedback, I have been able to accept responsibility for my weaknesses, reflect instead on what I could be doing differently, and not take it to heart.

Why our feedback culture works

We're able to give and receive feedback in this manner because we have an agreed vision of what good teaching looks like. Before joining, we read articles and blogs that help us to understand why we teach didactically, why we hold pupils to such high standards of behaviour and why it is important for the teacher to be the authority in the classroom. Much time is spent discussing our ethos which means that when it comes to giving each other feedback, we are unified in our aims.

Secondly, we do not have Performance-Related Pay. Katharine's blog 'Targets don't work' explains thoroughly her reasons for not having PRP at Michaela. It destroys trust, wastes time and diverts focus. She says, "In any given day, teachers are making thousands of judgement calls that make a massive difference to the school. Why not set targets for those too? Because of course that would be impossible. Set them 3 targets a year and you move your teacher's attention to the wrong thing." By eradicating performance management targets, Michaela teachers are free to work more flexibly on their professional development.

Katharine reassures staff at the very beginning that we are trusted to do a great job and there is no need to worry about feedback – if there were real concerns, we'd be told. My default mind-set is now 'the school trusts and values me'. I can now get on with my teaching and, instead of feeling ashamed of my weaknesses, I can take immediate action and have true ownership over my areas for development. It is so refreshing.

Hi _____,

Thanks for having me in with Year 10. They were loving working on the area questions, really focused.

1) When they were working, you gave a correction "Some people are doing.... in question 2. Make sure you....."

Always stop and get them to track you when you're saying this, rather than talking whilst they're working. They're not all catching everything you say as they are so focused on the question they are on! (Naomi put her hand up and asked you to repeat it afterwards.)

It can be super swift so won't waste time e.g 'Tracking me. Now look at your question 2: Did you remember to do......? If yes, great. If no, correct it now, go!'

2) Nice relationship moment: "Amit has had an absolutely cracking day! He's asked really good questions and...."

3) "We'll have four, no, three and a half minutes on this" – do you need to say this?

If you're saying it to get pupils to improve their pace I think it's more effective to say 'Look at which question you're on. Who is on Question 1? Question 2?... 'Or if you find it helpful, use a timer under the visualiser? Just the beeping of the timer will make them realise you're setting a time limit for them, without you saying anything at all.

4) You did a 'merit challenge' for reading answers to the exercises – loads of hands up. I don't do this enough with my Year 9s! Great to see.

5) You said "I need to remind you to say the units don't I? Merit to Cameron" (with a big smile). This is such a lovely phrase and avoided you coming across as 'embarrassed' for not noticing that the pupil had missed out their units. Instead, it felt really 'teamly': they clearly love that you routinely hold them to high expectations for their answers and they want to do the same for each other but also didn't seem frustrated/annoyed that you'd forgotten this time.

6) Nisha and Joe are sneakily using their calculator while you're talking!

Thanks again,

Abi

Knowledge Organisers: Proceed with Caution

Katie Ashford

@Katie_s_ashford

The knowledge-skills debate sits at the heart of educational philosophy in the UK. In recent years, a move towards knowledge curriculums has inspired many teachers to alter the way they teach, prioritising the dissemination and memorisation of important facts.

Whilst for some the idea of a knowledge curriculum conjures images of gowned schoolmasters, slate boards and endless lists of facts to learn by rote, at Michaela we believe that prioritising knowledge is vital. To make a knowledge curriculum work, teachers must ensure that their pupils can remember all the knowledge they've been taught so they might later apply it in different contexts. The science of learning shows that memorisation of key concepts requires frequent recall and testing. We believe that what some may term 'drilling' is an essential part of good teaching. If we want pupils to remember the things they have been taught, we must ensure they practise recalling these pieces of information over and over again until it has been committed securely to memory.

To this end, we devised a simple tool for aiding pupil memorisation. We called it the 'Knowledge Organiser': a single A4 sheet of paper containing all the important facts we expect a pupil to know off by heart. We combined this with quizzing homework (which we called 'self-quizzing') and daily recap quizzes. The results were astonishing. Pupils were able to remember vast quantities of information and dazzled teachers, parents and guests with their seemingly endless knowledge of history, geography, literature, science, maths and languages.

Visitors were impressed by the knowledge organiser initiative, and began taking the idea back to their schools. We wrote blogs and articles about knowledge organisers and their application in the classroom, and within months, they gained widespread popularity, and were discussed and shared at length on social media.

We do, however, have a worry. Whilst we believe drilling and committing knowledge to memory is essential, we worry that some teachers and school leaders have been too easily seduced by the simplicity of the knowledge organiser approach. Many people tend to believe that knowledge organisers can reduce teacher workload dramatically, and form the basis of a whole school approach to teaching and learning. We ourselves find this to be a misconception. Whilst knowledge organisers do have a place in the curriculum, they cannot and should not be applied too aggressively. A heavy dependence on knowledge organisers, particularly when combined with self-quizzing, can in fact *prevent* pupils from gaining a deeper understanding of the things we teach.

I'm therefore writing this chapter because we are concerned that too many schools have attempted to copy what we do, but may not be aware of some of the potential drawbacks. I hope here to outline some of the *limitations* of knowledge organisers. I also want to clarify ways of using them to support, rather than undermine, deeper understanding.

Since knowledge organisers first became popular, people have debated how best to use them in their classrooms. Two camps appear to have emerged. On the one hand the most enthusiastic advocates of knowledge organisers use them frequently: in lessons and for homework. These devotees test pupils on their memory of the knowledge organiser content in frequent, low-stakes quizzes.

At the other end of the spectrum, there are the people who believe that teaching knowledge is unnecessary and leads to a 'drill and kill' approach. They are very wary of directly specifying knowledge because they believe it might be too limiting.

At Michaela, we are somewhere in the middle of these two extremes. We don't believe that knowledge organisers should form the basis of the curriculum, but nor do we believe that imparting specific knowledge is a waste of time. Happily, there is a middle way, which I aim to set out clearly in this chapter for all teachers and school leaders who might be considering introducing them in their schools.

What is a Knowledge Organiser?

Knowledge organisers are grids made on one sheet of A4 paper. They contain sequenced, categorised lists of the facts you might want your pupils to retain from studying a unit of work.

Knowledge organisers can be used in any unit, across almost every subject. In History, a typical knowledge organiser includes lists of dates, names of important people and information about historical events. In Religion, a knowledge organiser includes quotations from religious texts, as well as relevant names, places, concepts and stories. In Science, a knowledge organiser might contain names and definitions of scientific processes, as well as labelled diagrams.

In order to provide stretch for the most able pupils, some parts of the knowledge organiser can be shaded in grey. These items of knowledge are not essential, but are a nice way to stretch those who are hungry for more.

Designed by the subject experts, knowledge organisers provide *both* teachers and pupils with unprecedented clarity. Teachers know exactly what to teach and recap, and pupils know exactly what to revise for success. At Michaela, every child carries a folder containing a printed copy of every knowledge organiser they have ever been given.

Knowledge organisers appeal because they resolve what is perhaps one of the biggest issues for teachers: that pupils frequently forget what they've been taught. During a lesson, an English teacher might spend a long time telling the myth of Sisyphus, for example. The teacher might explain what the story is about, read the text aloud with the pupils, pausing to reflect and ask questions, and then set some questions to test understanding at the end of the lesson. The teacher wants her pupils to understand the story in depth, and after marking a series of correct responses to the questions, might feel that the class have learned the story and understand it well. But the following week, with a return to the myth of Sisyphus, the teacher discovers her pupils have forgotten the story entirely.

Enter the knowledge organiser. Now, rather than moving from lesson to lesson without retaining what they learned previously, pupils have a sheet containing the knowledge they need to know. To ensure pupils can recall facts about the myth of Sisyphus weeks, months or even years later, the teacher can now provide each of her pupils with a copy of the knowledge organiser and ask them to go away and learn it. This puts an end to the dispiriting nightmare of pupils forgetting everything between lessons.

How are Knowledge Organisers Used?

At age 11, children are not yet equipped with the tools required to go away and learn every fact from every knowledge organiser in their folder. Knowing this, we therefore introduced self-quizzing as a way to support our pupils in memorising knowledge effectively.

In order to learn the content, pupils used a 'look, cover, write, check' method. They would look at the section of the knowledge organiser – for example, the line from *Julius Caesar*: 'The fault, dear Brutus, is not in our stars/ But in ourselves, that we are underlings'. They repeat this process until they have learned the relevant, necessary parts of the knowledge organiser.

The teacher does, however, need to check to make sure the pupil has committed this to memory. There are different ways of doing this. The most devoted knowledge organiser loyalists might test pupils' memory of the organiser content by simply having them write out important sections from the grid from memory. To adapt this specifically for the least able pupils, teachers might provide pupils with letter cues, or turn the quiz into a simple gap-fill activity.

Over the course of the term, the teacher might begin to add in questions from previous quizzes to ensure that information is retained from week to week. Perhaps in an end of year assessment, pupils might be asked to recall a sample of everything they had been quizzed on up until that point, ensuring that knowledge has been solidly retained for months, even years.

There are many benefits to this approach. Short weekly quizzes highlight the pupils who go above and beyond to remember what has been taught. Achieving 100% in a memory quiz is no mean feat: for many pupils, this takes serious commitment, self-discipline and time each evening, and it is all down to effort, not raw ability. This method can be immensely effective in helping the least able pupils to remember reams of poetry by heart, and to quote Shakespeare from memory. Self-quizzing shows pupils that educational success comes down to effort. It encourages them to work extremely hard and teaches them self-esteem.

What are the Problems with Knowledge Organisers and Self-quizzing?

We use knowledge organisers and self-quizzing at Michaela, but not in the way described above. For instance, we provide our pupils with knowledge organisers containing the poems we want them to learn by heart. They quickly learn the poems and are able to chant them in unison, and it is a wonderful sight to behold.

Furthermore, we use knowledge organisers when we want pupils to memorise quotations in English and Religion, and learn dates of important events in History. In Science, self-quizzing the names and descriptions of scientific concepts and processes is a vital part of what we do. In French, pupils use knowledge organisers to memorise translations of key phrases and structures. In Maths, knowledge organisers are less useful, but are still utilised when teachers want pupils to learn some of the most basic mathematical facts, such as the number of degrees in a triangle.

Crucially, however, knowledge organisers are only useful if they're used in a way that promotes flexible understanding of the facts, not just the facts themselves. The simple approach to quizzing described above has some drawbacks because we've found it to be too rigid. Teachers must make sure they test pupils' memory in a way that promotes understanding, not just rote repetition. Unless the teacher skilfully crafts quizzes that can successfully test understanding in multiple ways, those pupils relying on knowledge organisers might struggle to transfer their learned facts into flexible knowledge that can be used in different contexts. We have come to these important conclusions through repeated trial and error.

Inflexible Knowledge and Rote Learning

Cognitive scientist Daniel T. Willingham explains an important distinction between rote and inflexible learning[1]. The two concepts are often used interchangeably, but Willingham argues that there is a distinct difference.

Rote learning is learning devoid of meaning and understanding. For instance, if a teacher tells a pupil that Romeo was a Capulet, and asks the pupil to commit this fact to memory without understanding who Romeo is or what a Capulet is, that's an example of rote learning. It is relatively useless knowledge because it doesn't build on, or connect to, any prior learning – nor does it set pupils up to understand bigger ideas. Teachers who are very wary of knowledge curriculums tend to believe that knowledge organisers only lead to this sort of rote learning, out of context and without meaning. As I have explained above, there is a grain of truth in this belief: if used too rigidly, they can indeed lead to meaningless rote learning. However, this does not

---

1 Willingham, D.T. (2002) *Inflexible knowledge: the first step towards expertise*: Ask the Cognitive Scientist. Retrieved from URL: https://www.researchgate.net/publication/234665275_Ask_the_Cognitive_Scientist_Inflexible_Knowledge_The_First_Step_to_Expertise

mean that we should dispense with them or with knowledge curriculums completely. On the contrary, their moderate use sets pupils on a path that enables them to apply their knowledge in different contexts.

Inflexible knowledge, as opposed to rote learning, is a natural part of the learning process. It's quite normal to first grasp concepts in an inflexible way, and later be able to manipulate and apply them to different contexts. For example, when learning *An Inspector Calls* it is really helpful for pupils to know that the Titanic sank in 1912, shortly after the events of the play. At the early stages of learning, simply knowing these dates in a very inflexible fashion is helpful towards developing a deeper understanding. Later in the learning process, once the pupils grow to know more about the play's plot and themes, their knowing this date comes in very handy. Pupils are quickly able to make a connection and pour out interesting comments about Priestley's intentions in writing the play.

The crucial difference between the two kinds of knowledge lies in the emphasis on understanding. Rote knowledge is learned in its own abstract void, so that pupils struggle to be able to apply it to any new contexts. In strict contrast, inflexible knowledge is learned *within* a context that the pupils understand. If the teacher starts by explaining what *An Inspector Calls* is about, and gives some background information about the Edwardian era, pupils are far more likely to understand, to gain insight into the writer's intentions. That means that they'll be able to make interesting connections later, as they move further forward in the learning process.

It is wrong to conflate rote learning with inflexible knowledge. Knowledge organisers and self-quizzing should be carefully used to give pupils essential pieces of inflexible knowledge that will be useful to their later learning and lead to higher level analysis. If, however, there's an overdependence on knowledge organisers to form the curriculum, then teachers risk limiting their pupils to the kind of learning by rote that makes it almost impossible for them to transfer their knowledge into different contexts.

Knowledge Organisers Can Lead to Rote Learning, Rather Than Inflexible Knowledge

In short, a rigid use can prevent pupils from really thinking about the knowledge they're given to learn.

Imagine we ask pupils to learn the following information from a knowledge organiser by rote:

Shakespeare is widely recognised as the greatest writer of all time, and was a great dramatist.

Knowing this is useful, as long as we then make pupils apply this knowledge to different contexts. Learning any piece of information can lead to practical misconceptions. For example, if the pupil does not know what the word 'recognised' means, they might not be able to state this information in their own words. And if pupils only recite directly from the organiser without being able to rephrase it in their own words, or without having to apply it to other contexts, they are *not* being asked to think. This makes it much harder later on for pupils to be able to apply a fact to other contexts, and thus, to access higher order thinking.

Vocabulary

We see the negative impact of rote learning particularly clearly when a rigid, rote application of the knowledge organiser method is applied to vocabulary. Beware: many knowledge organisers feature 'vocabulary' sections, but teachers must be wary of depending on this too heavily. Learning words out of context, or through one-worded definitions, pupils find it much harder to use the words in their own original sentences. For example, rather than expressing good wishes 'from the bottom of [her] heart', a child who has learned new words out of context might instead send wishes 'from the nadir of [her] heart'.

They're very endearing, these errors, but they reveal a huge problem: particularly, the dangers of applying them to the acquisition of vocabulary. Many educationalists have written about vocabulary acquisition and teaching in schools, notably Isabel Beck and colleagues in the important book, *Bringing Words to Life* (2013). Beck makes it absolutely clear that one word definitions should *never* be used when teaching vocabulary. It's perhaps the clearest example of how rote learning can go wrong. True understanding of the meaning of a new word requires several examples, given in context, to tease out any potential misconceptions and support the child to be able to use the word correctly. If we rely too heavily on knowledge organisers and self-quizzing, then we overlook the importance of teaching new words in context.

Knowledge Organisers Have Gone Too Far

In the examples given above, the common theme is an over-reliance on knowledge organisers. Here are the main misconceptions that we were blind to, and that we fear other schools may not be aware of.

A knowledge organiser can comprehensively summarise a unit of work.

This is absolutely untrue. A knowledge organiser can only point to *some* of the key ideas you want pupils to take away from the unit. It's *not* the sum of what they learn in the unit. If teachers aren't careful, and if they hold knowledge organisers up to be a panacea, then there is a danger that *the knowledge organiser itself becomes the curriculum*.

Knowledge organisers are mere lists of important facts that fit on one sheet of A4 paper. If teachers teach only the content supplied on the knowledge organiser, they have unnecessarily *narrowed* the focus of the unit. Whilst it is very helpful to specify key learning points and takeaways, we shouldn't forget that this is merely an overview of the highlights of a unit, not the unit in its many-dimensioned totality.

Knowing a fact by heart is the same as understanding it.

As I've described above, rote knowledge is not the same as inflexible knowledge. If a piece of knowledge is learned out of context, pupils will neither understand it, nor be able to apply it.

Instead, we must aim to move our pupils along the spectrum from inflexible to flexible knowledge. Flexible knowledge is the ultimate aim: we want pupils to take what they know, manipulate it, see it from different angles, effectively apply it in new ways and connect it to other knowledge. That's flexible knowledge. It begins as inflexible knowledge. We teachers must then make pupils see links between pieces of knowledge, to use them in different ways.

If they can recite it back to me, they know it.

This point hasn't been an explicit argument in favour of knowledge organisers, but it *has* been implicit in its implementation. The danger of depending too heavily on knowledge organisers is that teachers are satisfied when pupils can merely repeat the definition given on the organiser. But as we know, this is not an indicator of true understanding. Teachers should constantly probe pupils' understanding of concepts, to determine if they're merely parroting facts. We must always be on the lookout for any pupils who are finding it a struggle to translate their knowledge into flexible insight.

For instance, if a teacher asks, 'Who was Shakespeare?' and pupils can only chant, '*Shakespeare is widely recognised as the greatest writer of all time, and was a great dramatist*', pedagogical alarm bells should ring. Teachers should instead test pupils' understanding from a range of different angles, and in different ways, to determine whether or not they truly understand.

The Middle Way: More Examples, More Practice

Whilst knowledge organisers have drawbacks, this does not mean that they aren't useful. As explained above, we do use knowledge organisers and self-quizzing at Michaela, but we do not use them too rigidly, which would promote rote knowledge. Typically they're used to give pupils inflexible knowledge that will later be transferred to flexible knowledge. Learning poetry, quotations, key phrase structures in foreign languages, dates, definitions of key terms, and so on: these are all useful ways to employ knowledge organisers.

However, when pupils learn more complex concepts, we would not use knowledge organisers for that. For example, in English, we wouldn't put the names and definitions of poetic techniques on a knowledge organiser. If we were to give pupils a definition of a metaphor as 'a comparison using is or was', pupils may still struggle to correctly identify metaphors. If they were given the phrase 'She is cold' or 'His hair is a deep brown colour', how would the knowledge organiser help pupils to understand that this is *not* a metaphor? Metaphor is a huge concept that takes detailed explanation. Pupils need to understand that metaphors are split into three parts: the thing that is being compared (the tenor), what it's being compared to (the vehicle) and what they have in common (the ground). In order to understand this huge concept, pupils need to see lots of different examples and non-examples so that they are better equipped to distinguish a metaphor from a statement. Pupils need lots of practice at this, as learning key concepts takes time and effort in order to commit them to memory. And of course, pupils need to learn how to apply the new concept to previously learned knowledge, and then to other new pieces of knowledge. A knowledge organiser definition simply is not enough: at worst, it prevents pupils from thinking and therefore hinders understanding.

Even when using knowledge organisers to learn dates, quotations, and so on, we would still ensure that pupils are given plenty of practice opportunity to use these facts in different contexts, and then we would rigorously assess that they know the fact's significance. Learning the line, 'Is this a dagger which I see before me?' from *Macbeth* quickly becomes useless, unless one knows when this line is spoken, by whom, or its significance.

In order to support pupils in transferring inflexible knowledge to flexible knowledge, knowledge organisers must be supplemented with more examples and more practice.

More Examples

We could teach pupils a simple definition of the term 'verb' as a 'doing word'.

Alone, this definition would not be sufficient for understanding the concept of 'verb'. The word 'are' does not *seem* to imply 'doing', yet it is a verb. Pupils might ask why 'quickly' isn't a verb, as it implies that someone is 'doing' something. The definition alone is not enough to understand this idea.

To understand the concept of 'verb', pupils need to be shown several examples contrasted with non-examples. Siegfried Engelmann, an educationalist and thinker in the field of the direct instruction teaching method, explains that contrasting examples and non-examples helps people understand the concept concretely. This process requires well-sequenced sets of examples that progressively reveal the underlying structure of the concept.

His observation applies when we teach any concepts so that pupils gain a well-rounded, fully accurate picture of the defining features of what the concept actually means. Prioritising thorough meaning and understanding is crucial.

More Practice

In order to embed their understanding, pupils need frequent, repeated practice. We know that giving pupils the opportunity to recall knowledge is important for ensuring memory in the long term. But quizzes are only helpful if they ensure that pupils do not recall knowledge in a 'rote' way. Quizzes shouldn't simply ask pupils to state the knowledge as written on the organiser, as this tactic doesn't force pupils to think.

So whilst a teacher might want to give pupils a definition on a knowledge organiser at first, she must ensure that practice opportunities do force the pupils to *think* about the knowledge being used. This method means varying question types and asking pupils to apply what they've learned in different ways.

Our pupils sit one quiz per subject every week, but the questions we ask pupils force them to think about, apply and manipulate their knowledge. Typically, these are short answer questions (where the pupil needs to give one or two sentences in response) or multiple choice questions. In some quizzes for older year groups, we might ask them to write out an essay plan for a given question. Only when pupils' knowledge and understanding is secure would we then set them a longer piece of writing, a paragraph or an essay.

In English, pupils use knowledge organisers to learn quotations, but we ensure that they understand the *meaning* of a quotation before asking them to commit it to memory. In weekly quizzes, pupils are asked to recall quotations, but are then asked to respond to a variety of questions about the quotation. We think of this as 'seeing it from different angles'. Pupils are asked to practise going over and over the same content, but in lots of different ways to ensure they have a thorough understanding and are forced to think about the meaning.

In a typical English quiz, pupils are asked to recall quotations, and are then asked to apply their understanding in a variety of ways, prompting deeper thinking:

1. *Which quotation shows that the witches disrupt the natural order?*

2. *Which of the following is the most precise interpretation of the line 'look like the innocent flower, but be the serpent under't'?*

   a. *Lady Macbeth tells Macbeth to go against nature.*

   b. *Lady Macbeth forces Macbeth to hide his true feelings.*

   c. *Lady Macbeth teaches Macbeth how to be deceptive.*

   d. *Lady Macbeth warns Macbeth of the dangers of intervening in nature.*

3. In the line 'Stars hide your fires, let not light see my black and deep desires', explain the significance of the word 'black'.

4. In act 1 scene 7, Macbeth says 'False face must hide what the false heart doth know'. Where else in the play has a character suggested that true feelings must be hidden?

In later quizzes in subsequent weeks, the teacher might want to go back to some of these questions, but would perhaps choose to phrase them differently. For instance, in week 1 the teacher might ask the question: 'Which quotation shows that the witches disrupt the natural order?' But in week 4 when the teacher goes back to this point, she might phrase the question instead as 'Which quotation shows that the witches bring chaos and disorder into Macbeth's world?' By varying the wording of the question, the teacher can assess the pupils' understanding from yet another angle, helping them to determine how flexible their pupils' knowledge and understanding of the play has become.

These questions require much deeper thinking than the knowledge recall quiz described above. Pupils are given the opportunity to practise *thinking* about their knowledge rather than simply recalling a rote fact. Pupils need more practice, but that practice must prioritise thinking about knowledge and applying it to different contexts.

Conclusion

Knowledge is essential for learning. It underpins all higher order skills. If we want our pupils to be able to analyse and evaluate, we must first ensure they know and understand what they are analysing or evaluating. We must not be afraid to teach knowledge. Building a reservoir of knowledge in our pupils' minds is the effective thing to do, and we should not see learning knowledge as 'mindless' or a waste of time.

But we do need to be careful when we implement a knowledge curriculum. Knowledge organisers are a nice, helpful tool to supplement good teaching and rigorous assessment. They are *not* a panacea. They are not the entire curriculum. They cannot replace good teaching or carefully designed questions.

Used thoughtlessly or too rigidly, knowledge organisers can prevent pupils from thinking deeply, and make it difficult for pupils to be able to transfer their knowledge into new contexts.

Pupils need to learn to *think*. Knowledge gives them something to think about, but they need to be able to apply it, manipulate it and use it to make links between ideas in their minds. To do this, we ensure that teachers check rigorously for understanding using carefully crafted quizzes that prompt pupils to think deeply about what they know.

Knowledge organisers have become hugely popular on social media in recent years. Whilst we are pleased that people find them useful, we hope that other teachers have not taken them too far, that they appreciate the importance of promoting thinking and flexible knowledge. These organisers are to be used to supplement learning but they should not underpin the entire curriculum, and this means teachers must ensure that pupils learn through frequent examples and practice.

Teach knowledge. Teach loads of it. Teach it all the time, in every lesson. But don't go too far, and remember that there is a middle way. If you are going to use knowledge organisers, make sure pupils are still having to *think* about the knowledge you teach them. So go ahead, make your very useful knowledge organisers and share them with colleagues – but proceed with caution.

Art at Michaela

Elizabeth Stiles

Art at Michaela is taught explicitly like all of our subjects. Here is an explanation of the methods that we have found effective for developing pupils' technical skills, confidence and knowledgeable enjoyment.

1. Visualiser/videos

A complete game changer. No need to ever have pupils out of their chairs huddled around one table while the teacher demonstrates. They really help with managing behaviour which means that every pupil can see what the teacher is doing clearly on the board. They allow you to break down the task into as many chunks as you like without the disruption of anyone moving.

2. It is all in the detail

A Michaela art teacher will really think about how best to guide their pupils through each piece of work. Describing not only the tone, but also, where to hold the pencil, in which direction and what kind of mark to make. Our pupils are never left to just guess and have a go.

This picture shows a before and after by the same pupil. The left one is the pupil's response when they are told all the steps in one go, with little detail about the proportion, shape and position of the features. The right picture is their response when given a number of smaller steps by the teacher using the visualiser. Instructions have been chunked up and they have been provided with more detail, including drawing their attention to all common misconceptions. The pupil was not left guessing but was instead guided from the very first step to the final step. Clarity of instructions results in increased quality of outcomes.

3. Mastering a select media

Our pupils concentrate on mastering a limited number of media rather than 'trying' a bit of everything. This allows them to frequently revisit each medium and truly master it, resulting in confident artists.

Here are a couple of Year 7 pupil pencil studies. Because they have had time to really refine their drawing skills, they are able to draw shapes accurately, use a range of tone and show graduation. If they had explored more media over the year they would not have had as much opportunity to refine their pencil skills. The pencil skills they develop in Year 7 are foundational and will be of value in all the other media they explore.

4. Time – quality over quantity

At KS4/5 pupils are graded on their technical ability. At Michaela they are given time to really develop their skills and produce high quality work without the pressure to rush through schemes of work and stick to termly deadlines. Sometimes art teachers teach standalone art lessons because they mean to try to manage pupil behaviour by 'entertaining' them with something new each lesson. But this effectively sets them up to fail at GCSE where a pupil is required to spend ten hours on their final response. At Michaela we believe our pupils are capable of working on one piece of work for a sustained period of time. We find pupils love seeing their progress over time and will always rise to the challenge.

Year 8 spent four hours on this colouring pencil study of a fish. This may seem quite excessive; however, in order for them to be able to blend the colours effectively, they needed this much time. This protracted experience was educationally powerful as the pupils learnt to persevere and realise the effort needed to achieve something so wonderful. Some teachers might worry this would leave pupils feeling bored or stunt their creativity but in fact it results in the opposite. Pupils love seeing their progress and feel so proud of their achievement. When pupils create something that they never, ever thought they'd be capable of, it supports their self-esteem and gives them an experience that helps their achievement in other subjects.

5. Mastery comes first, creativity second

Controversial I know, but do hear me out! Pupils first need to be able to draw and paint well before they can articulate their own ideas well. There is no point in 'expressing' yourself if you don't yet know how to work in this medium well. Because our pupils become confident artists first, who really do know their stuff, they later become so much more 'creative' because of it.

Here the pupil was able to express their ideas so much more skilfully because they were given the time to really master the media and perfect their skill and techniques.

6. Creativity doesn't have to mean chaos

Frequently you will see the standards and expectations of behaviour lowered in the creative subjects. There may be more talk, pupils moving around a lot, accidents, bullying etc. Pupils need to really focus like in any other subject. Allowing pupils to talk unnecessarily in your art lesson means you are expecting less from them and undermining yourself and the value of your subject. Yes there is a time for the sharing of ideas but it is naive to believe that all conversations happening throughout the lesson are about their work. Most likely they are discussing what level they are on in Fortnite or what dress they're hoping to get for prom. Instead, their talk needs to be structured and remain purposeful.

7. Really teach them how to 'see' using secondary sources…at first

Teaching pupils how to draw from observation can be tricky, it is hard to describe reference points and detail when each pupil is seeing the object from a different viewpoint to the teacher. So, first they need to learn how to really see; then, to understand how to describe the shape, to know how best to break down the image, where to start, how to work out its length against its width, etc. Teaching from the same picture allows teachers to show how and why they are using those reference points, to really help pupils see, so they can then use those skills later on for primary sources.

By teaching pupils how to really see, they are then able to draw independently with confidence and are able to apply detail and texture with accuracy by themselves in Year 9. Because they have been taught to really see and how to use reference points, they were able to draw these pictures completely independently during an exam.

8. Expect more = get pupils to expect more of themselves

Pupils are constantly challenged and encouraged to continue to develop as artists. We strive to get the absolute best from our pupils and this really helps build up their self-esteem and genuine love for art.

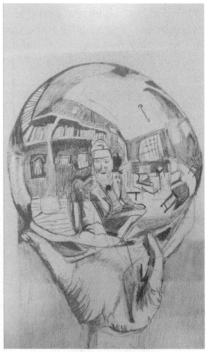

Here above is the same pupil's response of M. C. Escher's *Hand with Reflective Sphere*. The first attempt was completed in Year 8 and the second in Year 9. This is a very challenging picture to recreate – however, because they have learnt how to really 'see', they can rise to the challenge of refining their work. They now believe in themselves as they can see that they've developed as an artist.

Here are two self-portraits, drawn six weeks apart. By pushing the pupil on their graduation of tone, blending, and texture, they have been able to create a more refined portrait. There is something lovely about the first, how they have captured themselves with expressive mark-making, but there is something vivid about the second, more polished self-portrait. Whichever you prefer, the important point here is that by pushing them on, they have made progress as an artist and are able to understand their own style a bit better. This is the difference between settling for a grade 4, or instead pushing them to strive for those higher grades. The first no doubt demonstrates skill but the second definitely shows finesse.

9. Knowing your pupils' strengths

Sometimes there can be pressure on pupils to each produce a specific type of final response; a large painting for a final piece, or a large ceramic vessel. But what if painting isn't their thing, and in fact they are the absolute boss of chalk and charcoal? After exploring a range of media, by the end of year 10 our pupils know which medium they work best in. Each media has its evident aesthetic value and we let them run with this.

Some pupils flourish in one certain medium. If a pupil is most confident in chalk and charcoal, we let them fully explore this rather than pressure them to paint, just because that's what the final response 'should' be.

10. The choreography of setting up and packing away

It takes a class of 32 pupils 12 seconds to pass sketchbooks along and only 4 minutes to pack away after painting. It's true!

There is no chaos or madness. Successful applicants are appointed the role of 'Art Assistant'. They are the only pupils permitted to leave their chairs and collect work, wash up at the sink etc. The rest of the class has been briefed on what to do (pass equipment along, pass water pots towards the back row etc) whilst the teacher simply monitors all movement from the front.

11. Assessment and feedback in the lesson rather than commenting on every page in a sketchbook

It is still common in schools for teachers to have to comment on EVERY page in a pupil's sketchbook. In some schools, it is still common practice to write the typical 'WWW and EBI'. Then, the following lesson pupils write a comment stating how they intend to improve their work, and another concluding comment once they have made the improvement. This is to 'evidence' that feedback has occurred and a teacher pupil dialogue has taken place. This process eats up so much valuable time in the lesson, and means hours worth of marking during evenings, weekends and holidays. Just to survive you tend to need a statement bank of 'go to' comments.

At Michaela we give verbal feedback during the lesson so the pupil can act on it immediately. We can give whole class feedback in a couple of minutes. Pupils hold their work up (they are ideally seated in rows), the teacher will then tell relevant pupils what they need to do to improve. It would sound something like "Malik, beautiful graduation, now add more tone 5 to core shadow of sphere. Abdi fantastic form. Sally use rubber to lighten highlight of cone. Ismail work on your graduation between tones 2 and 3". I don't need to then write these comments after the lesson to evidence this has happened, the outcomes already show that assessment and feedback have taken place.

This system is of course only possible because the pupils are able to sit silently and behave whilst all this is going on.

12. Organisation of materials

'A tidy room is a tidy mind'. The nightmare stories I have heard from art teacher friends, of departments full of work some 10-20 years old, having no decent brushes to use, the work of past pupils piled in a mountain, just absolute disorder. I don't know about you but I can't think straight or start my work unless I am surrounded by an orderly space, or maybe that's just me!

I am by no means declaring this is the only way to help inspire young people to really love art and develop into confident artists, it is simply how we do things at Michaela. If you would like to come and witness our wonderful teachers and pupils at work, please do visit.

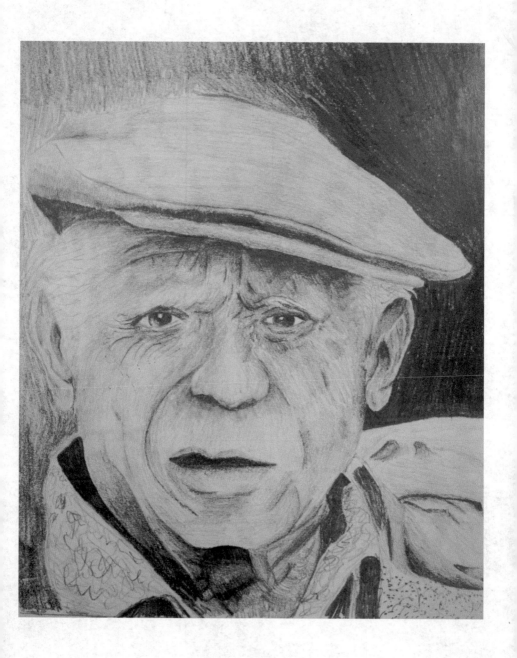